A SHORT HISTORY OF RUSSIA

University of Pittsburgh Bradford

The T. Edward and Tullah Hanley Library

This Book Presented By

Tom Spencer

A SHORT HISTORY OF RUSSIA

B. H. SUMNER

A Harvest Book
Harcourt, Brace & World, Inc.
New York

Copyright 1943, 1949 by
Harcourt, Brace & World, Inc.

All rights reserved. No part of this book may be reproduced in any form or by any mechanical means, including mimeograph and tape recorder, without permission in writing from the publisher.

Printed in the United States of America

CONTENTS

I. THE FRONTIER
1. TYPES OF FRONTIER 1
2. FOREST AND STEPPE 11
    (i) The Zone of Mixed Forests 13
    (ii) The Zone of Conifer Forests 18
    (iii) The Steppes 26
3. TYPES OF COLONIZATION 39

II. THE STATE
1. THE OCTOBER REVOLUTION: PARTY AND SOVIET . 48
2. THE 1905 REVOLUTION AND THE DOWNFALL OF TSARISM 59
3. REPRESENTATIVE INSTITUTIONS 67
4. THE ROMANOV DYNASTY 73
5. BYZANTINE AND TATAR ORIGINS OF TSARISM . . 78
6. THE GROWTH AND FUNCTIONING OF TSARISM . . 84

III. THE LAND
1. THE SOVIET REVOLUTION IN AGRICULTURE . . . 114
2. THE 1905 REVOLUTION AND THE EMANCIPATION OF THE SERFS 121
3. SERFS AND SERF-OWNERS 131
4. ORIGINS OF SERFDOM AND THE COMMUNE . . . 139
5. PEASANT REVOLTS 152

IV. THE CHURCH
1. THE REVOLUTION AND RELIGION 161
2. BYZANTINE CHRISTIANITY AND RUSSIA 164
3. MONGOLS AND MONKS 171
4. THE MUSCOVITE CHURCH 175
5. THE SCHISM AND ITS CONSEQUENCES 180

V. THE SLAVS
1. RUSSIA AND POLAND 186
2. PARTITION AND AFTER 198
3. THE UKRAINIAN QUESTION 211
4. PANSLAVISM 225

VI. THE SEA
   1. THE BALTIC 238
   2. THE BLACK SEA AND THE STRAITS 261
   3. THE BLACK SEA AND THE CASPIAN 279
   4. THE PACIFIC 287

VII. THE WEST
   1. RUSSIA AND EUROPE 303
   2. EUROPE AND RUSSIA 315
   3. ECONOMIC WESTERNIZATION 341
   4. THE SOVIET REVOLUTION IN INDUSTRY 361
   5. RUSSIA AND THE GREAT POWERS 379

CHRONOLOGICAL TABLE 435

NOTE ON BOOKS 447

INDEX 455

MAPS

1. The U.S.S.R. (Western Portion) 4
2. Soviet Asia 6
3. Forest and Steppe 14
4. The Steppe Lands 26a
5. The Western Lands and the Baltic 190

CHAPTER I

THE FRONTIER

1. *Types of Frontier*

THE SOVIET UNION—four times the size of Europe, but with less than half its population; as large both in extent and numbers as the whole of the North American continent—is the outcome of revolution on an immense scale and in all spheres of life. Despite the break with the past and just because of the very extent of its success, the Soviet Union has inherited from the Russian empire two of its most pervasive features: it continues to be a land of many peoples and to be a land of colonization. Throughout Russian history one dominating theme has been the frontier; the theme of the struggle for the mastering of the natural resources of an untamed country, expanded into a continent by the ever-shifting movement of the Russian people and their conquest of and intermingling with other peoples.

For many centuries the frontier played the same part in the history of western Europe, but owing to its diminutive size internal colonization for the most part ceased to be a dominating theme after the later Middle Ages; overseas colonization took its place, and the peoples of Europe struggled with new frontier conditions in new worlds. In contrast, Russian expansion has always been into contiguous lands and, owing to vast size and the material level of the people, internal colonization, even west of the Urals, has remained right down to the present day an outstanding element in Russian life.

The political frontier is the consequence of the Bolshevik triumph after three years of the most bitter, swaying civil war (1918-20), at the end of which the new Soviet state had gained almost exactly the same frontiers, except on the west, as those of the Romanov empire before its disruption through the First World War. On the west the Bolsheviks failed to restore the old boundaries. The emergence of Finland and the three Baltic states (Estonia, Latvia, and Lithuania) for the first time as independent states and the restoration after over a hundred years of an independent Poland barred the Soviet Union from the West, except for the icebound loophole of Leningrad, much as Russia was barred in the seventeenth century. To the south Bessarabia, under Russian rule since 1812, remained in the hands of the Roumanians and barred access to the Danube. The Second World War gave Moscow its chance to win Bessarabia, eastern Poland, the Baltic states, and a small portion of Finland (1939-40). Save for the rest of Finland, which had been in Russian hands from 1809, and the central Polish regions, which first came to Russia in 1815, Soviet Russia thereby regained all that Peter the Great, Catherine the Great, and Alexander I had acquired on the west (1700-1812), and in addition, for the first time, she extended to the Carpathians in eastern Galicia.

Apart from these western lands, the inheritance of the Romanov empire meant the inheritance of three centuries and more of Russian expansion (see maps 1 and 2):—Central Asia, now the Soviet republics of Kazakhstan, Turkmenistan, Uzbekistan, Kirghizia, and Tadzhikistan, the last four conquered latest of all, between 1864 and 1885, the first engulfed during the previous hundred years; Transcaucasia, now the Soviet republics of Georgia, Armenia, and Azerbaidzhan, conquered, in part ceded, between 1801 and 1828; the Ukraine, colonized, conquered, or seized between 1650 and 1793; White Russia, seized in 1772 and 1793. Last, and first, there remains the hugest of the Soviet republics, stretching from Leningrad to Vladivostok and the Caucasus to the Arctic Ocean, embracing three-quarters of the area and two-thirds of the population of the Union, the Russian Soviet Federated Socialist Republic, the heir of Muscovy and the Muscovite empire, that expanded since Peter the Great into the Russian empire.

The lands that are included in the Russian S.F.S.R. are made up of the core of Muscovy, stretching from the Oka to the northern Dvina, welded into a state by about 1500, and of the Muscovite empire, the far-flung conquests made roughly between 1550 and 1650. (There are important later additions, such as St. Petersburg (1703), the North Caucasus steppes and the Caucasus mountains (1760-1860), the Amur region and Vladivostok in the Far East (1860), but they are relatively small.) Muscovy in the century following 1550 had expanded gigantically to the east and southeast before the great advance westwards at the expense of Poland and Sweden, most of which was the work of Peter the Great and his successors. The Muscovite empire, the heir of Tatar khanates, was, to a large extent, an Asiatic state before its transformation into the Russian empire, turned towards the West. Thus, Smolensk, only two hundred miles west of Moscow, and Kiev were not finally won until 1667, by which time Kazan and Astrakhan had been Muscovite for over a century, and for some twenty years there had been a Muscovite post four thousand miles away on the Pacific.

The frontier in the European, political sense of a line marking the acknowledged limit of action of a regularly effective government did not take slow shape (except on the west) until the nineteenth century. As far as there had been a political frontier it had been, in general, a tribute or nomad frontier, the fluctuating limits of nomad migration and of peoples paying some form of tribute, at first none too regularly, to Moscow or St. Petersburg. The molding influences that largely shaped Russian development were due to other frontiers: linguistic, national, or religious; the frontier of soil and vegetation or of the hunter, the trader, the farmer, or the miner. Here again the usual conception of a frontier as a clear boundary line is out of place and has to yield to one of overlapping zones, oases, wedges, or routes of penetration.

Consider first the linguistic or national frontiers, which have now been crystallized in the Soviet administrative boundaries marking off the different constituent republics and autonomous national areas, and which show only too clearly the Soviet inheritance of the multi-national Russian and Muscovite empires (see maps 1 and 2). In summary outline, it is the fringes that are compactly non-Russian: the

Map 1

U.S.S.R. (Western Portion)

·—·—·— Western boundary of U.S.S.R., August 1939.
× × × × Boundaries of U.S.S.R., June 1941.
· · · · · · · Boundaries of constituent republics of U.S.S.R., June 1941.

    K.-F. = KARELIAN-FINNISH SOVIET SOCIALIST REPUBLIC.
    Es. = ESTONIAN S.S.R.
    La. = LATVIAN S.S.R.
    Li. = LITHUANIAN S.S.R.
    W.R. = WHITE RUSSIAN S.S.R.
    Ukr. = UKRAINIAN S.S.R.
    Mo. = MOLDAVIAN S.S.R.
    Ge. = GEORGIAN S.S.R.
    Ar. = ARMENIAN S.S.R.
    Az. = AZERBAIDZHAN S.S.R.

Principal national autonomous republics within the Russian Soviet Federated Socialist Republic:—

    Ba. = Bashkirs.
    Ud. = Udmurty.
    K.T. = Kazan Tatars.
    Ma. = Mari.
    Ch. = Chuvash.
    Mo. = Mordva.
    V.G. = Volga Germans.
    Ka. = Kalmuks.
    C.M.P. = Caucasian mountaineer peoples.
    Cr. = Crimean Tatars.

    D.B. = Donets Basin.

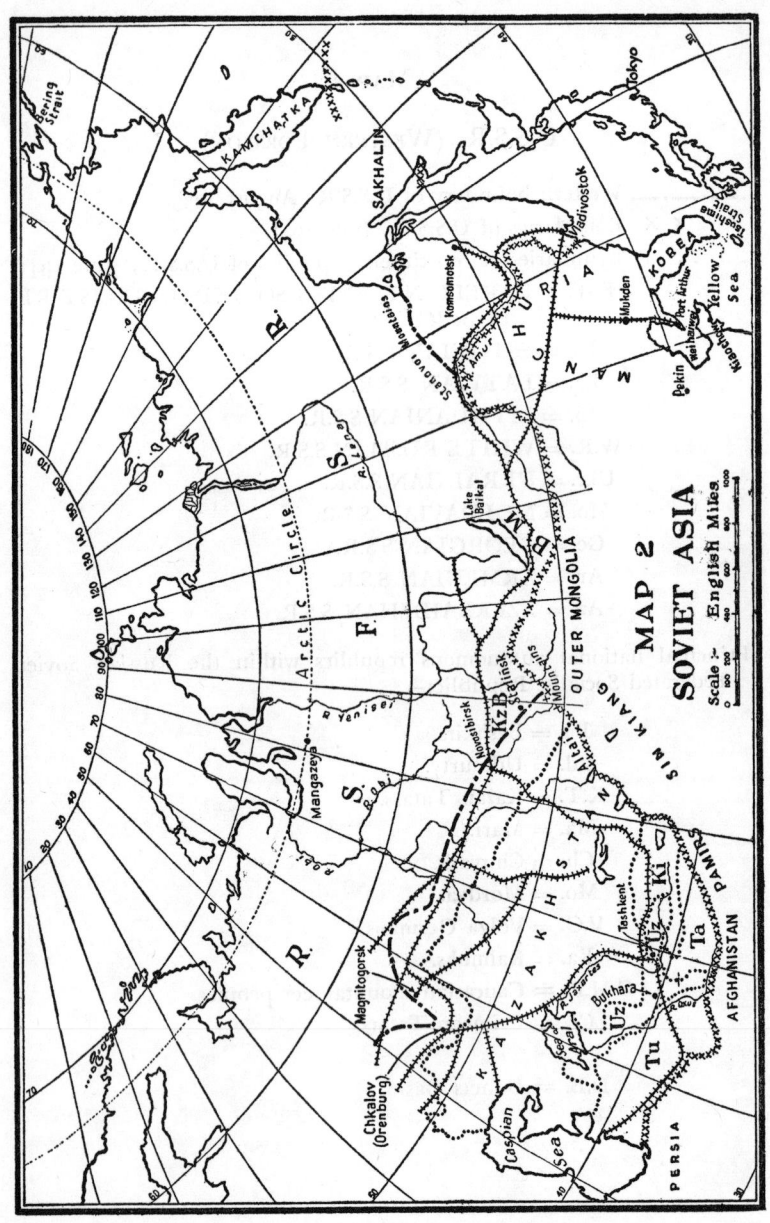

Map 2

SOVIET ASIA

++++++++++++ Principal Railways.
—··—··— Approximate southern line of zone of conifer forests.
———— Approximate northern line is shown by the Arctic Circle.
× × × × International boundary of U.S.S.R.
·········· Boundaries of constituent republics of U.S.S.R.

R.S.F.S.R. = Russian Soviet Federated Socialist Republic.
Tu. = Turkoman S.S.R.
Uz. = Uzbek S.S.R.
Ki. = Kirghiz S.S.R.
Ta. = Tadzhik S.S.R.
B.M. = Buryat Mongols.
Kz.B. = Kuznetsk Basin.

Central Asian republics (except Kazakhstan, now half-Russian), the Transcaucasian republics (except the oil center of Baku), and the new Baltic and Moldavian republics. White Russia, which is and always has been overwhelmingly White Russian, and the Ukraine, which is in majority Ukrainian, are different in that the two peoples are very closely allied to the Great Russians, with whom they form the eastern branch of the Slavs (see pp. 211-212). Elsewhere, the numerous non-Russian peoples, mostly of Finnish or Tatar origins, in the course of the centuries have become absorbed or increasingly outnumbered, as the unresting sea of Russians has seeped in and around or flooded over them.

The linguistic map of the Russian S.F.S.R., outside its central core of the old Muscovy, is a mosaic, but one color, the Russian, vastly predominates. The non-Russians, where they are compact, form islands or, for the most part, islets, and it is only in the Caucasus mountain regions and in the mixed forest and wooded steppe lands of the middle Volga-Kama-Urals that they are both numerous and contiguous to each other. Hence it took the Russians the first sixty years of the nineteenth century to reduce the Caucasian mountaineers --the equivalent of the Northwest Frontier in India; and the great stretches of the middle Volga-Kama-Urals were the scene of two to three centuries of intermittent struggle between the Russian conquerors and colonists and Finnish-Tatar peoples, that was not closed until the last of the large-scale Bashkir risings in the revolt of Pugachov (1773-75).

The increasing and finally overwhelming numerical superiority of the Russians, which was also in most cases a qualitative superiority, made the problem of nationalities in the last hundred years radically different from that, for instance, in Austria-Hungary; additionally so since in the Russian empire hardly any of the non-Russian peoples had independent states of their compatriots across the political frontier and only the Poles had a living tradition of national independent statehood. The Russian empire, like the Soviet Union, was a multi-national compound, but by 1900, even including the compactly non-Russian fringes, two-thirds of its subjects were Russians, a proportion that was increased after the Revolution and the loss of the western fringes.

Consider now the social frontiers; the Russian frontier in the sense of nuclei of shifting occupancy, following the rivers and the portages, gradually with the increase of agriculture and much later of mining and industry becoming solid zones of settlement, marking the slowly growing mastery of the Russians over their natural surroundings and non-Russian neighbors.

As with American so with Russian expansion, in the greater part of the north and Siberia the outer edge of the advancing wave was "the meeting point of savagery and civilization,"[1] though this does not hold true to the same extent of the advance to the south. Russian like American development exhibits "not merely an advance along a single line, but a return to primitive conditions on a continually advancing frontier . . . social development has been continually beginning over again on the frontier." In both, the advance of the settlers' frontier was uneven, with tongues of settlement pushed forward and indentations in the wilderness, due to varieties of soil and forest, the course and character of rivers and lakes, the lie of portages and routes and very latterly railways, the presence of salt or minerals, the location of army posts or defense lines, and the varying powers of resistance of non-Russians or Indians. Above all, both the Russian and the American advance has been that of the agriculturist against the forest nomad and the plains nomad; the conquest of the grasslands for the first time by the plow, in North America during the last century at a ruinously rapid rate of soil exploitation, with erosion now a national problem of the first order, in Russia at a serious but less ruinous rate owing to the much slower tempo of her development and the comparatively small use of machinery on the land until the last dozen years.

[1] This and the following quotation are from F. J. Turner, *The Frontier in American History*. Subsequent quotations, unless otherwise stated, are from sources contemporaneous with that to which they refer.

Far away back, before the Russian agriculturist came the Russian hunter-fisherman-beeman. Fur, game, fish, honey, and wax provided essentials for clothing, food, and light, as well as the wherewithal for tax payments, rarities for the rich and the staples of early Russian exports. Hunter and trader were apt to be one and the same, and often enough merged into river pirates or mounted buccaneers. Of necessity the hunting grounds of the little companies of trappers were fluctuating and indeterminate, in a vast land with so few inhabitants, in dependence on wild life migrations and tales of what lay untapped farther afield. The hard struggle to make a living, cupidity, adventure, pride in skill with trap, net, and bow, with canoe and axe, later the organized plans of Novgorod merchant-adventurers and Volga princelings—all combined to push the frontier ever onward to the east and north. To the south it was different. There the Tatar peoples of the steppes were strong, and the Russian frontiersman, as we shall see, was for long thrown back on to the defensive; but there eventually, in the sixteenth century, the most famous type of Russian hunter frontiersman was thrown up, the Cossacks.

The lumberman, specialized as such on any scale only within the last three centuries, fashioned a pioneer frontier of his own type. The miners' frontier is still more recent, hardly dating on a telling scale from before 1700, when Peter the Great created a largely new iron and copper industry, mainly in the Urals, and thrust out in more determined search for gold and silver in Siberia. The lure of gold produced its own variety of mining frontier with its own special history, but gold, even though Soviet development has made the Union the second largest producer in the world after South Africa, has played a less important rôle than the non-precious metals. From Peter onwards the state, directly or indirectly, planted mining colonies of serfs or deportees, who made Russia in the eighteenth century the largest European producer of iron ore, and who at one and the same time tamed the forest both to charcoal and to agriculture and drove another wedge into the life of the Bashkirs and Siberian tribes.

Iron in conjunction with coal produced an even greater colonizing effect when in the later nineteenth century the large-scale working of the Donets coal basin and the Krivoi Rog iron-ore region (see map 1) caused the influx of Ukrainian and Great Russian peasants into new mining villages and new industrial centers, the uprush of the great South Russian coal and heavy industry which has been so immensely extended during the last twenty years. Similarly elsewhere during the last seventy years workers of coal, iron, copper, lead, oil, and under the Soviet régime of much else, have repeated under new forms mining frontier conditions and have transformed the colonization map. The unrelenting pace of Soviet industrialization, above all in the Far North, the Urals, Kazakhstan and the Kuznetsk basin of central Siberia, has revolutionized the miners' frontier, which together with its dependent industrial giants has become the great melting-pot of the Soviet peoples.[1]

2. *Forest and Steppe*

Much the greater part of Russian history has been played out in five great zones (see maps 3 and 4), stretching from the southwest to the northeast, similar in their prevailing low elevation and, in certain respects, in climate, but differing widely in humidity, soil, and geological structure. Usually the zones overlap and shade into each other without clearly marked limits. Except for the first, they are not European and Asiatic zones, but both together; hence the recent term Eurasia as a geographical expression for the unity of the bulk of the Russian Empire or the Soviet Union, a conception harnessed and adapted by some contemporary historians.

(i) The zone of mixed forests, deciduous and conifer, spruce and Scots fir, larch, birch and aspen, oak and lime, ash and elm, but (in Russia proper) no beech or yew or holly;

---

[1] Admirable illustrations of the Soviet mining frontier are provided by J. D. Littlepage and D. Bess, *In Search of Soviet Gold* (1939), the unvarnished account of the ten years' experience of an American mining engineer in Soviet Asia; and of the Soviet industrial frontier by John Scott, *Behind the Urals* (1942), an excellent first-hand account of the early years of Magnitogorsk.

for the most part composed of the so-called podzol soils, gray sands and clays with a very low humus content, with much bog and lake; a zone roughly forming a great triangle, Lake Ladoga-Kazan-south of the Pripet marshes. This became the core of Muscovy.

(ii) The zone of conifer forests stretching to the north of (i) to the tundra, the Arctic version of the steppes, and to the east hundred mile after hundred mile, more than one-third the way round the globe to the Pacific Ocean.

(iii) The wooded steppe or meadow-grass steppe zone, to the south of (i) and (ii), to the south of the line of the spruce; the debatable, savannah-like stretches between forest and true steppe, mostly with a variety of rich black-earth soils; until the eighteenth century far more wooded than now; the favorite setting of Turgenev's novels.[1]

(iv) The feather-grass steppe zone, waving ostrich-gray-plumed grasslands before the coming of the plow a hundred years ago; to the south of Kiev-Kharkov-Kuibyshev (Samara)—the Trans-Siberian; again composed of black-earth soils; treeless save in the valleys or deep-cut ravines; the land of the tall "embrace . . . of a green-yellow ocean, besprinkled with millions of spring flowers" (Gogol, *Taras Bulba*, 1834); like "the green, ocean-like expanse of prairie, stretching swell beyond swell to the horizon" (Parkman, *The Oregon Trail*, 1846-47).

(v) The wormwood steppe zone, narrow along the Black Sea, shading off eastwards into saline steppe and eventually sand or stone desert in Central Asia; the arid ranches and pampas of the chestnut and yellow-gray soils, which are still in the main what they have always been, the preserves of the pastoral nomad.

Within the past thousand years man, with ax and fire and plow, has mastered the mixed forest, though hardly yet the bog. He has deeply dented the conifer forest. He has mastered for the plow the wooded steppe since the seventeenth cen-

---

[1] For instance his unmatched *A Sportsman's Sketches* (1852; translated by Constance Garnett, New York, 1906), one of the classic pictures of the Russian land and the Russian peasant.

tury, the feather-grass steppe only during the last century. He is but now, with the aid of science, at the beginning of the mastery of the arid and semi-desert steppes. These masteries, still far from complete, slow in comparison with the Australian, Canadian, or American onrush, have been up till now the great historical achievement of the Russian people, until the last fifty years pitifully equipped materially, but superbly equipped in spirit, a people of whom it has been written with just pride (1942): " 'You could make nails of them, and never would nails be stronger.' . . . 'Yes, of these people you can make everything—nails, tanks, poetry, victory.' "

(i) *The Zone of Mixed Forests*

The western part of the great triangle of mixed forest lands, which lead on to the west beyond the Pripet marshes to the Vistula basin and to the southwest to the Carpathians, was the center of the eastern Slavs, when at least fifteen hundred years ago they were centered along the upper courses of the Dniester, Dnieper, Niemen, Dvina, and Volga and were pushing through the Novgorod lake region (see map 3). They had succeeded in combining stock-breeding and agriculture with a forest way of life, instead of becoming enchained by the forest at the level of semi-nomadic hunter-fisher folk. Most of the land was poor and difficult, the climate severe, and their implements, cropping, and stock-raising were on an elementary level, dominated by forest, scrub, and marsh. Hence the great eastward colonizing movement of the eastern Slavs was much slower in conquering the wilderness than the somewhat similar advance eastwards of the Germans from the Elbe and the Main, which began rather later, at the expense of the western Slavs, in the tenth century. The extensive character of the economy of the Slav tribes and the comparative rarity of suitable sites and natural clearings led them to push on, mainly along the rivers, in scattered, strung-out settlements. Apart from the movement of game and fur-bearing animals, the shifting nature of cultivation encouraged movement, and the long per-

sistence of extensive methods of raising a living stamped upon the Russians love of land, but not so strongly of this or that plot of land.

From the rough line Kiev-Smolensk-Novgorod the Russians pushed out far into the wooded steppe, eastwards still in the zone of mixed forests into the lands lying between the Oka and the Volga, and northwards until their canoes were paddling through the solid pine forests beyond lakes Ladoga and Onega. Since about 1000 political conditions, and to some extent the Christian church which had just been imported from Byzantium, added to the tempo of colonization.

Between 1000 and the Mongol conquest in the thirteenth century the most vital event in the history of the Russians, apart from their conversion to Christianity, was their settling of the lands between the Oka and the Volga, later to become the center of Muscovy. This was achieved at the expense of Finnish tribes in occupation of them, who were gradually conquered and assimilated or driven farther afield, leaving the map still thickly studded with their river and other place names. It was accompanied also by continued struggle on the east with the Finnish Mordva and with the strongly organized Moslem Bulgars, centered around the junction of the Volga and the Kama. The southern advance into the steppe, as will be shown later, failed to be maintained against the nomad peoples, and the Mongol invasion of 1237-40 set the seal on the victory of the steppe. For the next two centuries the Russians, broadly speaking, were confined to the forest.

The settlements tended to be concentrated in moraine regions, on the better-drained slopes, by portages, on lakes or streams that were rich in fish, and on the natural clearings which, especially in the south-west and again between the Oka and the Volga, contained some good soils and more favorable conditions for agriculture. This remained, however, always closely bound up with the forest—wild bees, fur and game, tar and wood-working. Scattered homesteads, with the big undivided family, and small hamlets were the general rule, not compact villages. Towns, such as Kiev, Smolensk, Polotsk, and Novgorod, grew up out of trading, tribute, or stockaded refuge posts by the main river routes and portages from the Black Sea and the upper Volga to the Baltic, along which trade from eastern lands had long flowed.

In the ninth century, while the Norsemen were raiding and conquering in western Europe and the British Isles, their Swedish Viking kinsmen, the Varangians, penetrated the Baltic-Black Sea river routes and set themselves at the head of Kiev Russia, a loose bundle of the Russian districts, whose tribal organization was by then much decayed. Commerce, which grew and flourished until about 1200, contributed much to the rapid cultural and political rise of Kiev Russia. Apart from the long-distance transit trade, the Russians supplied furs and wax and honey, hides and tallow, and slaves; they received luxury goods and weapons, affecting directly only the top layer of society. The external contacts of Kiev Russia, particularly with the Byzantine empire, bringing Christianity, writing, and the arts, ultimately had the greatest consequences, but the flourishing trade and the brilliance of a few centers like Kiev did not alter the main basis of the great bulk of the population, agriculture and forest life.

The prevailing method of cultivation had been temporary cropping on the ash of burnt-over forest or scrub or on the more open spaces of wild grassland. The clearings, after a few years of continuous cropping, were either abandoned to revert to waste or kept as rough pasture until their productivity might be restored. Gradually the socketed axe replaced its less effective forebears. Gradually the plow-stick was superseded by the horse-drawn wooden "hook" plow, which by about 1000 had become usual. It was eventually developed, by the sixteenth century, into the light wheel-less wooden plow, with coulter, mold-board, and iron share, which with various modifications remained until this century the prevailing type of plow used by the peasantry throughout Russia outside the black-earth zone.

By the sixteenth century the scattered plots and rudimentary technique had given way on the estates of the big landowners to relatively more intensive cultivation on a two- or three-field basis, with some dunging and with nucleated villages; and after the Time of Troubles (1604-13; see pp. 73-75, 142-143) development was rapid into the open, three-field communal system, with scattered individual strips, typical of medieval western Europe and henceforward of Russia right down to the Revolution. Rye was the staple crop; barley, oats, and some wheat were grown; but the grain supply of the mixed forest zone was uncertain. The north-west was always dependent on imports and, as the population grew, the whole of this zone, together with the northern pine forests, has been classed as the "consuming provinces" for the last two hundred years.

Around Novgorod and in the upper Volga region flax and hemp were grown from very early times and became, together with the handicrafts based on them, increasingly important. From the eighteenth century they formed one of the chief items of Russian exports and developed into a large-scale modern industry. Stock-raising, for draught animals, hides, and tallow, was originally of more importance than in the recent centuries when Muscovy could draw on the steppes to the south.

The forest, much diminished though it was by the sixteenth century, especially in its fur value, continued to be the close concomitant of agriculture that it had always been; supplying the wherewithal for implements and transport, as well as fuel, building material, tar, and a whole range of other industries, many of which later became specialized in particular villages still of much renown and prosperity only half a century ago.

Thus from early times the Russia of the mixed forest zone was built upon a diversified economy, long before the rapid growth of the Moscow cotton industry, dating from the Napoleonic wars, and of St. Petersburg as a manufacturing center. For the serfs of this region seasonal or permanent labor in industries, in the forests, later in factories, was a regular subsidiary or alternative to work on the land, and hence labor services due to the serf owners very largely took various forms of rent rather than of work on the owners' fields.

Politically, the mixed forest zone was split asunder by the Mongol conquest of 1237-40. This completed the decomposition of Kiev Russia which had been at work for nearly a hundred years previously. The Kiev region itself, much ravaged, fell into long decline and became incorporated in Lithuania, as did the other principalities west of the Dnieper in the course of the next century (see pp. 192-193). To the north the oligarchic merchant republic of Novgorod, though paying tribute to the Golden Horde, extended her commercial empire far to the north-east, and in close connection with the Hanseatic League attained her zenith in the early fifteenth century (see pp. 246-248). The principalities to the east, between the Oka and the Volga, were subjected to the khan and for long moiled in internecine rivalry.

Here Moscow, first mentioned in 1147 as an outpost manor, tortuously grew in power from 1325 onwards, and under grand-prince Ivan the Great (reigned 1462-1505) definitely established her control both over the other Oka-Volga principalities and over Novgorod with her octopus-like fur and fish dominion of the great pine forests of the north.

(ii) *The Zone of Conifer Forests*

Into the zone of the solid conifer forests, much sparser in any open land, poorer in soil, and yet more rigorous in climate, Russian colonization, ever since the eleventh century, thanks to the wealth of waterways thrust out long tentacles, developing from trading-tribute forays and reaching out to the White Sea, the northern Dvina and even the Urals. The thinly settled Finnish and Lap tribes offered what resistance they could, and in some cases it was stubborn, but, just as to the south, there was much assimilation, and it was only between the Volga and the upper Kama that some of these peoples lived on un-russified, in dwindling numbers. There was no marked dividing line between the northern forests and lakes and the more southerly region, but climatic and other natural conditions made agriculture entirely subsidiary, save along the upper courses of the Dvina rivers. The lure that beckoned the adventurer groups and then the Novgorod bands, organized by rich merchant-landowners and led by tough, experienced boatmen-pioneers, was above all fur—sable, marten, fox, better and more numerous the farther north and east the "companies" pressed; beaver (still common right down to the seventeenth century all over Russia, north of the true steppes), squirrel, otter, of much less monetary worth, but invaluable for ordinary use. Fishing, sealing, and whaling in "the blue sea-ocean" drew men to stud the coast with little settlements, sending back to far-away Novgorod walrus ivory, blubber oil, and seal skins (admirable for the strongest ropes and thongs). These and, above all, fur, tar, pitch, and potash formed the staples of Novgorod's exports through the Hanse merchants to the western lands.

Along the White Sea shores and elsewhere salt made a new frontier. From the fifteenth century the industry expanded greatly, and there was a large export to the south. Thanks largely to salt two famous rival monasteries, Solovetsky (founded 1436) and Byelozero (founded 1397; see map 3), developed into semi-governmental centers of industry and of defense against the Swedes, while in the north-east towards the Urals the Stroganov family emerged as the chief salt monopolists two generations and more before their "conquest of Siberia" (1581).

These economic characteristics of the frontier in the North explain why so large a part of its colonization was due to the wealthy Novgorod landowners and merchants, and later to the larger monasteries, who alone could supply the outlay and organization required. But there were other trickles of colonization into the Vologda and Vyatka regions, in part due to free migration, in part to settlements made by appanage princes from the Volga, in part to the constant monastic outflow to the North in the fourteenth and fifteenth centuries (see pp. 172-183). Here Novgorod and the rising power of Moscow clashed, and here there developed semi-independent communities which were prepared on occasion to defy both alike. Ivan the Great after his final subjection of Novgorod in 1478 inherited her rough colonial empire, reduced to subjection the lands of Vyatka and the upper Kama, in part Russian, in greater part Finno-Ugrian, and multiplied trading and tribute expeditions into the Obi basin in Siberia.

For the next two hundred years the North, from the Volga and Lake Ladoga to the White Sea, grew greatly in prosperity and importance and developed differently from the rest of Muscovy. The English discovery of the White Sea route to Muscovy, dating from Richard Chancellor's voyage in 1553, and the failure of Ivan the Terrible in the next twenty-five years to batter his way to the Baltic in the face of the Poles and the Swedes transformed the northern Dvina into the gateway of Muscovy.[1] English and Dutch merchants vied for the Muscovy and Persian trade, and the great route up the Dvina from Arkhangel (founded 1585) to Vologda and thence to Moscow became a main artery.

The customs books of the seventeenth century and the efflorescence of architecture in the northern towns bear vivid witness to their prosperity. For instance, the wealthy burghers of Yaroslavl, where the route to Moscow crossed the Volga, raised the most remarkable group of churches of the century in the Russian style; unique in their size, their elaborate brick and colored-tile decoration and the copiousness of their frescoes, which owed much to Dutch illustrations of the Bible and other Western influences.[2] It was not until Peter the Great succeeded where Ivan the Terrible had failed that the North declined: then St. Petersburg and Riga promptly killed Arkhangel and the North sank into neglect.

The North did not to any large extent experience the shackles of serfdom, which at this same time were being clamped down upon the Center. The bulk of the population were relatively free peasants, earning a very varied livelihood,

[1] The English discovery of Russia (not only of the North) and relations with her are vividly portrayed in the accounts of mariners and agents of the Muscovy Company, printed in the Everyman edition of Hakluyt's *Voyages*, vols. 1 and 2 (especially Willoughby, Chancellor, Burrough, Jenkinson, Horsey, and Fletcher).

[2] There are excellent photographs of the mid- and late-seventeenth century churches of Yaroslavl and other northern centers in D. R. Buxton, *Russian Medieval Architecture* (Cambridge, England: 1934).

with distinctive communal institutions that preserved a certain measure of local autonomy. Later they became organized in the class of state peasants under conditions considerably easier than those imposed upon the serfs of the landowners. The North contributed much to the re-establishment of Muscovy in the final crisis (1611-12) of the Time of Troubles, and from the North came the conquest and early settling of Siberia.

When the Western nations were thrusting afield in the Americas and the Indies, the Russians spanned the continent of Asia with a rapidity—some fifty years—to rival even the Spaniards a century earlier; ever pressing on, "to the east of the sun, to the passage of the great Tsar Alexander, to the most high mountain Karkaraur, where dwell the one-footed, one-armed folk." The conquest of Siberia was the continuation of the Russian penetration of the unending northern forests east of the Urals, which are no dividing barrier; and until the eighteenth century the Russians remained almost confined to the forest and tundra zones, except in the extreme west of Siberia where the black-earth wooded steppe thrusts up its most northerly wedge (see map 2).

Here lay the main center of the loose khanate of the Siberian Tatars, which for a century before 1581 had alternately challenged the steady expansion of Muscovy from the Kama and paid irregular tribute to her. The last khan, Kuchum, a son of the emir of Bokhara and an active proselytizer of Islam, passed to the offensive against the Stroganov family, who had been confirmed by Ivan the Terrible as merchant-marcher lords on the Urals frontier. As a countermeasure they took into their service a Cossack soldier of fortune, Yermak—famous hero of Russian folk-poetry—and in 1581 equipped him with an expedition to forage eastwards for booty and tribute, "with fighting and without fighting."

Such was the origin of Yermak's "conquest of Siberia." He was a born leader of men and immediately won resounding successes; but he was besieged and drowned in 1585, and it soon proved to be beyond the Stroganovs' resources to consolidate his initial gains. The Muscovite government, somewhat reluctantly at first, took command, and in a series of carefully planned expeditions assured the routes through the Urals, smashed the Siberian Tatars, and conquered western Siberia. Kuchum, blind and deserted, fled south (1598), to die in the steppe. For another seventy years his descendants were a thorn in the flesh of the Russians, stirring the Tatars, Bashkirs, and others to revolt and restore their old khanate, but the main powers which denied to the Russians the Siberian steppes were the Kazakhs and the Kalmuks.

In any case it was the forest not the steppe that the Russians wanted. Fur still was the magnet: the sable led them on and on, by the great river routes closely linked by portages (see map 2)—to Mangazeya (the Siberian variant of Potosí of 1600), to the Yenisei (1607), to the Lena (1632), to the extreme north-east and the Pacific itself (about 1640), where the reindeer and dog tribes as yet knew not the use of bronze or iron. The Russians met strong resistance only around Lake Baikal from the Buddhist Mongolian Buryats, and a definitive counterstop only in the Amur basin. There for the first time they came up against the organized solidity of civilized power, the Chinese empire under the new Manchu Ch'ing dynasty, and for the first time encountered rival firearms. In the Amur region there were twenty-five years of intrepid exploration and colonization by runaways and of intermittent ferocity and battling with Chinese forces. Then in 1689 the first treaty between Russia and China was concluded. The Amur was kept by China and the savagely inhospitable Stanovoi mountains remained the frontier for a hundred and seventy years. The boundary posts that were set up were to be inscribed in five languages, Chinese, Russian, Manchu, Mongol, and Latin: with the Chinese negotiators there had been a Jesuit Father. China not only halted Russia; she also gave her what is now a national drink; fifty years earlier (1638) the first tea had reached Russia, via Siberia.

This astonishingly rapid conquest of the Asiatic forest lands was due to six main reasons:

(1) The Russians did not have to adapt themselves to any considerable extent to new physical or climatic conditions. Their own Russian North was substantially similar, and for

centuries they had been adept at using water routes. (2) Their expeditions were only a few hundred strong, but they had greatly superior weapons and implements, particularly firearms, clumsy though they were. Various types of Cossacks, however unruly they often were, furnished an admirable spearhead of frontiersmen. (3) The peoples of northern Asia were few in numbers, for the most part dispersed in primitive, mutually hostile hunting tribes, and prepared to some extent to serve with the Russians against each other. (4) The inexhaustible demand for furs in Muscovy and in Europe put a premium on rapid expansion farther and farther eastwards in search of better skins and more plentiful supplies. (5) The Russian equivalents of the *coureurs des bois* of French Canada were possessed of indomitable hardihood, energy, and courage: love of gain was mated with spirit of adventure, endurance and resource with rapacity and cruelty. (6) Behind, and frequently at odds with, the independent frontier pioneers the Muscovite government plodded laboriously. Expansion east of the Yenisei was mainly a result of local initiative, but there followed eventually the armed support of the far-away central authority, the methodical securing of stockaded posts on the river routes, the planting down of an administration.

Administrative and judicial powers were concentrated in the same hands, though not control of the customs, which meant primarily the fur trade. The upper officials in the seventeenth century were appointed for very short terms and were both venal and brutal. Central control was exercised by the Siberian department in Moscow, which worked as far as possible on the same bureaucratic principles as the other departments. After 1711 there was a governor-general for Western Siberia and another for Eastern Siberia, but previously there were a number of administrative districts, each subordinate directly to Moscow. This control from the far-away capital was inevitably very slow-moving and it was in many respects ineffective, but the Siberian department did what it could to maintain a hold on local officials and it did not spare itself in pouring out floods of regulations. There was all too much local tyrannizing and the different officials, often set to act as checks on each other, were equally often hand in glove in evading their instructions, to their own personal profit. The wonder is that the Muscovite government in the first century of conquest and occupation succeeded in keeping as strong a hand as it did. Moscow did at least ensure the basis of governmental organization, and eventually of economic and scientific development. Exploration, fostered or directly undertaken by the state, developed on scientific lines after the early eighteenth century, and the very striking achievements of Soviet Arctic exploration have behind them two hundred years and more of intrepid and often elaborately planned Russian expeditions.

To an even greater extent than in French Canada the fur trade dominated Siberia in the seventeenth century. Fur was an indispensable source of revenue and export for the Muscovite government. Hence its policy aimed at controlling tightly the trade through the fur tribute imposed upon non-Russians and through strict limitation of private trade. The regulations were intricate and constantly varying. Evasion of them was equally constant. The natives hunted mainly with bows and arrows, the Russians with traps and nets. The effect of the Russian impact on the backward northern tribes was as disastrous as the American impact on Red Indian life. On the one hand Moscow was prolific in instructions "not to drive them out of the Tsar's favor"; on the other hand there was a flood of other instructions, the gist of which was "to take the fur tribute, according to the number of the people and their occupations, as much as possible." There could be no shadow of doubt which profited most the authorities on the spot. One particular effect of the fur tribute system was that, since converts did not pay it, missionary activities by the Orthodox church were for long discountenanced in Siberia. The Orthodox church was for the Russians.[1]

Much the greater part of the state fur revenue came from

[1] The conditions of Russian missionary work in north-east Siberia in the nineteenth century are inimitably described in Lyeskov's deeply imaginative story *On the Edge of the World* (1876), translated (New York, 1923) in *The Sentry and Other Stories.*

the annual tribute in furs from the natives, the *yasak*, a combination of Russian and previous Siberian practice. In addition the state levied a tax of a tenth on all furs acquired by Russian hunters or traders, and it exercised rights of preemption. There was no state monopoly of the fur trade, as there was for instance of silk and caviare, until about 1700 attempts were made to make fur exports to China and other Asiatic countries a state monopoly. In the middle of the seventeenth century, when the fur trade was at its height, the private trade was nearly three times as large as the state fur revenue. This private trade in Siberia was wholly in the hands of the Russians; foreigners were rigidly debarred. Nevertheless, the regulations governing the *yasak*, the tax of a tenth, and pre-emption were all designed to secure to the state first pick of the best furs, especially sables, and despite much corruption and smuggling the contribution of furs to the Muscovite revenue was very important, in the best years perhaps over ten per cent of the total revenue. This fur revenue, apart from other revenues from Siberia, seems from the scanty figures available to have brought in a large profit over and above the expense of administration. Probably about four-fifths of the Siberian furs were exported (in Europe mainly to Holland and the German lands from Arkhangel and Novgorod).

Already by 1700 both the absolute and the relative value of the fur trade had much declined, and the principal state fur interest became concentrated on the Chinese market. In Europe the competition of North American furs was telling heavily, and the heyday of Siberia as a fur El Dorado was past. Thus in the eighteenth century the fur trade lost its dominant position. West of the Yenisei the fur frontier had by then yielded place to that of the peasant settler and the miner. In 1700 there were probably considerably over 330,000 Russians in Siberia (compared with 250,000-300,000 Americans in the thirteen colonies). Half a century earlier an official estimate (1662), for what it is worth, had put them at 70,000. From the time of Peter the Great the state concentrated more on mining development, and organized exploration and exploitation of gold and silver were pushed ahead, though the Siberian gold rushes did not occur until the nineteenth century.

In 1767 private trade with the non-Russians was allowed without restrictions. Thereafter for the first time trading companies developed on western models, which concentrated on a new Pacific expansion of the fur and sealing frontier. Under a group of remarkable merchant-adventurers and sea-captains, the Russian-American Company, somewhat similar to the East India Company, spread a new brand of Russian imperialism across the Bering Strait into Alaska and down the North American coast. By 1820, with a Russian outpost almost as far south as San Francisco and with the Russians active in the Hawaii islands, it seemed almost possible that the North Pacific might become a Russian lake and North America be divided between the United States, Great Britain, and Russia. In the face of American and British pressure, however, the Russian government withdrew to Alaska, found this too costly, and eventually succeeded in selling it to the United States in 1867.

The Russians were too few on their icebound Pacific, and too far from it. Their true line of expansion lay in the rich and varied Amur basin, where they had been halted ever since 1689. Thanks to a masterful pro-consul, Muravyov-Amursky, and to the weakness of the Chinese government during "the Taiping Rebellion," Russia acquired in 1860 all the northern bank of the Amur and the coastline down to Vladivostok, a vast new frontier for the Cossack and peasant pioneer, the miner and the lumberman (see pp. 289-291, 301-302). Meanwhile Siberia proper had changed character. Her life no longer centered in the great northern forests, but was intertwined with the black-earth steppe lands to the south (see pp. 45-48).

(iii) *The Steppes*

It has already been explained (p. 12) that the steppes vary much and fall into three main zones, but their history is so

MAP 4.
THE STEPPE LANDS.

Scale:— English Miles.
0 50 100 200 300 400 500

Dates of foundation or re-foundation are given in brackets.
Dates of conquest or cession are given without brackets.

———·——— Approximate lines of division between mixed forest, wooded steppe, and open steppe zones.
xxxxxxxxxx Main defence lines, with approximate dates of construction.

SLOB. UKR. = SLOBODSKAYA UKRAINE.
KT. = KAZAN TARTARS.
CH = CHUVASH.
V.G. = VOLGA GERMANS.

closely interlinked that it is better to treat them together (see map 4).

The early history of the steppes and of the forebears of the Eastern Slavs cannot be treated here, but it must be emphasized that the emergence of Kiev Russia as an important state in the ninth to the twelfth centuries was the outcome not merely of Varangian war leaders, but of a long previous development of the Antes and the Eastern Slavs, especially in the middle Dnieper lands.

The western corner of the immemorial corridor of grazing and hunting grounds stretching across south Russia, on the edge of the Greek world, had for some two thousand years been dominated by Iranian, Turanian, or other nomad peoples, not all of them savage and barbarous like the Huns of Attila. In the four centuries before 800 Slav tribes increased their hold in the western portion of the wooded steppe lands and penetrated farther east. From the ninth century the rising power of Kiev Russia, at the head of which stood the rapidly slavized Varangian princes and their war bands, fought and traded in the Black Sea above all with Byzantium, and challenged the two organized steppe powers of the time, the Khazars and the Volga Bulgars.

The Khazars, cultivated, tolerant of Christianity, Islam, and Judaism alike, and in close trading relations with Byzantium and the East, were based on the lower Volga and Don. At the height of their power (seventh and eighth centuries) they controlled all the southern steppe lands and were the overlords of the southernmost Slav tribes. The Bulgars were kinsmen of the present-day Chuvash (at least perhaps linguistically; map 4) and of the Bulgars of the Danube who had moved there in the late seventh century. They had their main center near the junction of the Volga and the Kama. They were, like the Khazars, in part settled, in part pastoral nomads, and were becoming Moslem from the tenth century. They made their living off the Volga trade-route and tribute from the Finnish-Tatar peoples of the mixed forest and steppe region between the Oka, the middle Volga, and the Urals. The Khazar dominion collapsed during the tenth century under the ravages of a new wave of savage nomads, the Pechenegs, and of their former Russian tributaries. But the Bulgar khanate was not seriously damaged by Russian incursions and maintained itself successfully until the Mongol conquest of the thirteenth century.

The Russian challenge to the steppes, radiating out from Kiev, itself on the frontier of the mixed forest and the wooded steppe, was epitomized in the grand-prince Svyatoslav (died 972), "stepping like a pard," warring from the Danube and Constantinople to the Caspian and the middle Volga, scheming a Slav variant of a Dnieper-Black Sea-Danube steppe dominion. For another century Russian expeditions sallied out from Kiev, usually with success, to clear the river route to Byzantium or eastward into the steppe. Thereafter

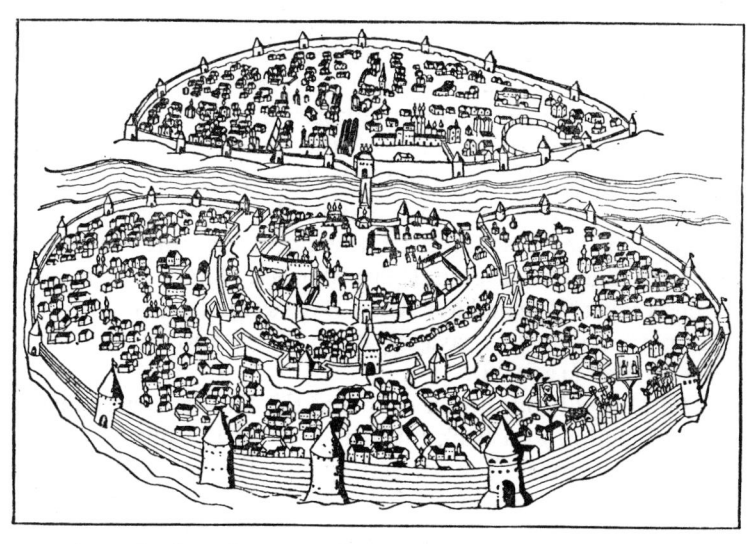

An early view of Novgorod showing the division of the city by the Volkhov River. One of Kiev's chief rivals during the medieval period, Novgorod, and other towns such as Chernigov, expanded and jeopardized the position of Kiev as the center of Russian commerce.

they proved less and less successful against the latest Turkish newcomers in the Black Sea steppes, the Polovtsy.

Sustained conquest was never achieved by the Russians and settled colonization, with a few exceptions, fluctuated within a hundred and fifty miles or so east and south of Kiev. Relations with the Polovtsy and other nomads were frequently peaceable as well as hostile: there was some intermarriage, the taking in of broken nomad tribes as frontier guards, and much trade: as the Russians pushed on in the steppe, similar conditions bred something of a similar way of life. In the end, in face of the Mongol peril Russians and Polovtsy attempted combined resistance.

After 1125 the Russians were continually on the defensive: the great trade-route to Byzantium had become very dangerous and the result of the first crusade (1095-99) was to divert Byzantine commercial interest from the North. There were too few Russians on the steppe frontier; those to the north combined less and less with the exposed southern outposts. It is possible that at any rate the steppes west of the Dnieper might have been permanently mastered by the Russians but for the internal dissensions of the Russian principalities. The sacking of Kiev in 1169 by Andrew Bogolyubsky, prince of Vladimir, far to the north-east in the Oka-Volga Mesopotamia, in a sense symbolized the declining interest of the northern Slavs in the southern steppes. There was a grim nemesis seventy years later when Batu's war host reduced the Mesopotamia no less savagely than Kiev, and in fact three years earlier (1237-38).

The Mongol conquest meant that the Russians were forced into subjection and back into the zone of the mixed forests. For two centuries frontier settlement did not edge farther south than the hazardous fringes of the woodland steppe between the Oka and the headwaters of the Don.

The Golden Horde was based on the military power and organized rule of a pastoral aristocracy mainly composed of Polovtsy and other Turkish nomads, headed by "the golden family," the descendants of Genghis Khan (died 1227). It became Moslem in the late thirteenth century (see later, p. 171), but remained tolerant in religion. It employed settled agriculturists and skilled handicraftsmen, fostered long-distance trade (notably through the Genoese via the Sea of Azov), and extracted tribute from a circle of vassal peoples, of whom the Russians were but one. The center of the khan's power lay along the lower Volga and his direct sway covered the whole of the Eurasian nomad steppes from the Dniester to the Aral Sea and from the Urals to the Caucasus. In addition he controlled, through tribute, raids, and the subjection of the Russian and other princes, the eastern half of the zone of the mixed forest.

The actual Mongol element in the Golden Horde was very small and the contacts with the far-distant original center of Genghis Khan's empire, Mongolia, soon became tenuous; but they were continuous and very close—economically, culturally, and militarily—with the two neighboring offshoots of that empire, Persia and Central Asia. Thus the Horde was to some extent for the Russians the intermediary of Eastern customs and civilization. In this respect, however, it was but continuing in the footsteps of its predecessors in the southern steppes. Certain Eastern influences on Russian life, *e.g.* in military equipment, customs, ornament, and decoration, long antedated the Mongol conquest. The specific Russian borrowings from the Horde seem to be mainly confined to various material objects and processes, though there was also Tatar influence on military and state organization (see p. 82). In thought, literature, or folk-tale little if anything was apparently transmitted from Isfahan or Baghdad during the Mongol period, and as intermediaries of Moslem culture the Tatars bear no comparison with the Moors in Spain.

For all its achievements, the Golden Horde did not for any considerable stretch of time bring a *pax mongolica,* as some have maintained, either to the Russian principalities or to the steppe lands. The habitual attitude of the nomad was that the sedentary townsman or peasant was an inferior being, lifelong slave of his nomad ruler, toiling for his advantage alone. Internal struggles for power and external struggles, especially with Persia, were constant. After 1359, when there were fourteen khans within twenty years, disputes as to the succession fatally weakened the Horde. For the upper class life largely revolved round prowess in fighting and hunting, and hunting included above all slave-raiding. When the central power was weak, as was frequently the case, it was impossible to prevent the outlying Tatars ravaging at will.

The Tatar yoke was a yoke, even though its results were not purely destructive or negative. In the memory of the Russian people the Tatars remained as the personification of all their foes throughout the long centuries; and their conqueror was no prince Vladimir but the freelance peasant hero Ilya Muromets, who "swoops upon the Tatar host . . . tramples down the Tatar with his horse, pierces the heathen with his spear."

The main burden was taxation, tribute elaborately organized in the first generation by Tatar officials, then farmed out to Moslem merchants, then collected through the grand-prince, ultimately of Moscow, assisted by Tatar emissaries. The grand-prince owed his title to the khan, to whom he journeyed to secure investiture, and his rivals in their principalities similarly revolved in the orbit of the khan, and frequently served on his campaigns. Revolts or recalcitrance from the princes brought major raids far into Muscovy; at least ten during a hundred and fifty years (1259-1408), with the Tatars "cutting down all the Christians like grass," with some of the Russian princes aiding or abetting.

Twice this was not so. In 1378 for the first time a major raid was beaten off before the Tatars could cross the Oka. Two years later Dmitri Donskoy, grand-prince of Moscow, defeated Mamai at Kulikovo, well to the south of the Oka, in a pitched battle ever famous in Russian tradition (see map 4). The defeat was decisive for Mamai, not for the Tatars. In 1382 under his successful rival Tokhtamysh they swept north again, laid waste the greater part of the principality of Moscow, captured the city itself, despite its new stone fortress, and reimposed tribute. Not Dmitri Donskoy, but Timur the Lame, Tamerlane, the greatest conqueror since Genghis Khan, shattered the power of the Golden Horde (1395). Unlike the Ottomans, temporarily stricken by Timur (1402), the Tatars of the Golden Horde never fully recovered.

By about 1450, when the Ottomans were capturing Constantinople, the Horde had split up into the three rival khanates of Astrakhan, Kazan, and the Crimea, and a little later the Nogai horde, paramount in the open steppes east of the Volga, and the khanate of the Siberian Tatars to the east of the Urals. The accompanying dissensions enabled Ivan the Great to rid himself of tribute and any formality of dependency (1480). The stage was being set for the great Muscovite advance from the forest against the steppe, but the breakdown of the Golden Horde marked no diminution, on the contrary an increase, in the frequency of Tatar raids, especially from the side of Kazan.

The advance began down the Volga, not the Don, against the Kazan Tatars, who were relatively near and at the time a greater danger than the Crimean Tatars, far away to the south and difficult to strike at. Kazan itself was not finally captured until 1552 by Ivan the Terrible, when the khanate was annexed, after nearly a century of Muscovite efforts to reduce it, in part by war, in part by establishing Tatar adherents as khans. The same intermixture of Russian and Tatar is exemplified in the policy begun in the mid-fifteenth century of granting lands to renegade Tatar princes and taking them into frontier service, a policy of assimilation which continued to be a main feature of Russian relations with Tatars and other Eastern peoples.

The conquest of Kazan had been a long and costly undertaking, but it was followed by a rapid sweep right down the Volga to its mouth and the easy seizure of Astrakhan (1556). Henceforward the rich ribbon of the Volga trade-route was in Muscovite hands, a winding waterway through the steppes, but not in itself the master-key of the steppes. A challenge from the Ottoman Empire, with its vassals the Crimean Tatars, for a moment (1569) endangered the new-won conquest and opened the vista of the Volga as another Danube. The challenge was not pressed; the Tatars and the Ottomans were at odds; Lepanto followed (1571), and the Crimean

Tatars, though they raided and burnt Moscow in that same year, disputed the Don steppes rather than the Volga lands.

Muscovy set about holding the great trade-route by fortified frontier posts on its banks between Nizhni-Novgorod (Gorki) and Astrakhan, such as Samara (Kuibyshev), Saratov, and Tsaritsyn (Stalingrad). The Volga never bred an organized Cossack "host" like that of the Don, but it remained until as late as 1800 a happy hunting ground and refuge for Cossack bands, river pirates, and a medley of vagrants from up river, combustible material that broke into raging flames in the revolts of Stenka Razin and Pugachov (see pp. 152-161). Settled colonization was still more retarded by the habitual raids of the Nogai Tatars, a very loosely organized horde, of the much more tightly organized Buddhist Mongolian Kalmuks (nomad incomers of the early seventeenth century), and of the Moslem nomad Bashkirs of the middle Urals, who struggled against Russian subjection right down to the end of the eighteenth century. The lands of the khanate of the Kazan Tatars, the heirs of the Volga Bulgars, were equally composite; including various Tatar-Finnish peoples in the mixed forest and border steppes of the middle Volga. They also took long to subject fully or to assimilate, and their main river valleys were not solidly occupied by Russian colonists until about 1650.

Even a hundred and fifty years after the conquest the Russian stockaded defense lines that marked the limits of secure colonization had not pushed much farther south than about the latitude of Samara (Kuibyshev), and not so far south to the east of the Volga; roughly the southern limits of the wooded steppe (see map 4). Beyond still lay "the wild grounds." Then from the second quarter of the eighteenth century there was adopted a sustained policy of reducing to "hereditary fear" the Bashkirs (themselves by now in part succumbing to settled life) and of developing new mines and metal works in the Urals and new defense lines which separated the Bashkirs from the Kazakhs and the Central Asian steppes. The disaster of the revolt of Pugachov (1773-75), which set alight the Urals and all the Volga below Nizhni-

Novgorod (Gorki), proved only temporary. From the end of the century the rich black-earth steppes between the Volga and the Urals became opened for good to the agriculturist, in the shape of the serf-owning landowner.[1]

Farther to the south, below Saratov, in the arid chestnut-soil steppe merging into the saline and semi-desert stretches of the lower Volga, agricultural colonization could make little headway without developed dry farming or irrigation. The most successful settlers here were German peasants, first tempted with special privileges by Catherine the Great; a solid block of over 400,000 at their maximum in 1914, who remained distinctively German though with few connections (at any rate until the last twenty years) either with Germany or with the leading German group in Russia, the Baltic German landowners. The First World War threatened them with wholesale expulsion to the East. The Second World War has seen the threat actually put into operation and the end of the Soviet autonomous republic of the Volga Germans a year before the great battle for Stalingrad close by.

To the west of the Volga, in the Don and lower Dnieper basins, there was the same dominant feature, the struggle against the way of life of the nomads, in this case primarily the Crimean Tatars. But here, in contrast, Muscovy was in competition with a Western organized state, Poland, and with the power of the Ottoman empire, of which the Crimea was from 1475 a tributary dependency. Here again in contrast there was no rich trade-route like the Volga to be seized at a leap by the Muscovite government. Leap there was, but it was due to the free Cossacks speeding down the Don and establishing their center about 1600 along its lower reaches in semi-independence of Moscow (see p. 41). At the same time social conditions in Poland fomented a similar outflow of Ukrainian hunting pioneers into "the wild grounds," who formed themselves into the Zaporozhian ("beyond the cataracts") Cossack "host" on the lower Dnieper, very similar to

---

[1] A vivid picture of colonization in this region is given in Sergius Aksakov's *A Russian Gentleman* (1856; admirably translated by J. D. Duff in the World's Classics series), one of the classics of Russian prose.

that of the Don Cossacks, and an even pricklier thorn in the flesh of all who came in their path (see pp. 214-218).

The Crimean khanate was a well-organized state of pastoral Tatars, based on the very mixed Crimea, where there was agriculture and handicrafts and much commerce. Their numbers have been much exaggerated, and it is improbable that in the seventeenth century at any rate the khan could put into the field more than 30,000 horsemen at the utmost, a number that was later much reduced. The Tatars made up for their lack of numbers by their mobility and tactics, in which they were at a great advantage in that they aimed not at the defeat of the enemy (they evaded battle if they could), but at the capture of booty—slaves and stock.

Four times within seventy years (1521-91), riding up their three main trails crouched "like monkeys on gray-hounds," they raided north of the Oka into the heart of Muscovy and in 1571 they burned Moscow itself. After 1591 they never succeeded in crossing the Oka, and gradually their raids penetrated less and less far northwards. The big musters headed by the khan in person became rare. The habitual danger was the swoop of small bands a few hundred strong, "running about the list of the border as wild geese flie, invading and retiring where they see advantage." As late as 1676-79 the constable of Orel received one hundred and seven messages as to such "short and sudden rodes." Still, under Peter the Great, there were raids into the Kharkov region almost every year between 1710 and 1718, one of which years was reported to yield the Tatars over 14,000 prisoners, a suspiciously high figure.

The reasons why the Crimean Tatars for some three centuries proved such difficult foes for Russians and Poles alike were their military specialization, distance, the fact that behind them lay the power of the Turks, and the fact that they acted now in conjunction with the Russians, now with the Poles, now with the Zaporozhian Cossacks against the other. The Russian military equipment only became superior to that of the Tatars as their firearms increased in quantity and improved in quality, and even so this superiority was usually of avail only in the timbered country or in holding forts and redoubts, not in the open treeless steppe; just as the American cattle-ranchers in the Great Plains had little advantage over the horse Indians until the coming of the six-shooter.

The Crimea itself was six hundred and fifty miles direct from the Oka, and far more in actual riding miles. The last three hundred were across the feather-grass and wormwood steppes, in which water and provisioning were acute difficulties. The Poles never attempted to strike at the heart. The Russians in the mid-sixteenth century were inclined to follow up their capture of Kazan and Astrakhan by a mortal blow at the Crimea, but Ivan the Terrible decided that the distances were too great and turned to the Baltic.

The Russians did not pass from the defensive to the offensive until the frontier was far down on the edge of the wooded steppe. Even then (1687, 1689) they signally failed to cope with the supply problem in the great stretches of open steppe between the Donets and the Crimea. Fifty years later (1736-38) they were successful in reaching the stronghold of the Tatars, who could put up little resistance beyond "scorched earth" tactics and suffered fatal damage, even though the Russian commander lost half his army through sickness. The successes in Catherine the Great's first Turkish war (1768-74) sealed the fate of the khanate. It was a prey to internal dissension and in 1783 the Crimea yielded itself to Russian rule.

The advance to the Black Sea, unlike that to the Caspian, had been slow, but it was sure, for it was based on a continual process of settled colonization at the expense of the seasonal rhythm of pastoral nomadism. From about 1500 the northern fringes of the wooded steppe belt were a debatable ground between Tatar bands and Russian frontiersmen pushing southwards, followed slowly by the plow, into the virgin black-earth lands that were acting as a magnet to the peasants of central Muscovy, more and more hard pressed by landowners and the state. But, unless they went Cossack, they could not escape from the state and they needed its protection.

In the course of the sixteenth century the Muscovite government built up an elaborate, fourfold defense system, initially intended to prevent the Tatars crossing the Oka, but additionally providing security for colonization (see map 4). The system included the founding of fortified garrison centers settled by the government with military colonists, and in the last twenty years of the century there was rapid progress in consolidating the frontier. The advance of settlements was along the tributaries of the Don or Oka, then navigable for small boats, in the wooded valleys, which provided the essential timber and better means of defense than the swelling open country. During the next twenty years (1600-20), owing to the Time of Troubles, the frontier "went Cossack" and there was chaos. It was only after 1633 that the defense system was thoroughly reorganized and the planned advance resumed, marked by the founding of more garrison centers and the construction of the Byelgorod defense line roughly along the northern limits of the present Ukraine and thence northeastwards to Voronezh, Tambov, and the Volga at Simbirsk.

The state did its utmost to control and plan the frontier, which was for long predominantly military in character: arms and horse ready saddled were as essential as plow and ax. The settlers, in part voluntary, in part conscripted, were mostly various types of the "men of service." The siting and building of the garrison centers, which developed later into big towns such as Kursk, Orel, or Voronezh, were minutely planned on almost identical lines by the central authorities. They multiplied instructions on the construction and maintenance of defense lines (abattis in the woodlands, earth and wooden stockades in the open country studded with redoubts and forts); on the patrol system; on how to act during Tatar raids; on the privileges and obligations of new settlers. Much of this was mere waste paper, disregarded or nullified in practice: the demands made sometimes reveal fantastic ignorance or miscalculation: continual levies for labor service, often from far afield, and for military duties, whether temporary or permanent, were very heavy. Yet, despite evasion, flight, or rioting, the relentless perseverance of the Moscow bureaucrats and their local officials, in combination with the stamina and resource of the peasants trekking south, bore rich fruit. The woodland steppe was won.

Into the Muscovite frontier a new element swelled to a great scale after 1650 when the Ukrainians rose against the Poles and turned to Moscow (see p. 216). The bulk of the original Ukrainian immigrants formed five regiments, which took up land in the middle Donets region, founded and garrisoned Kharkov and other towns with a new defense line in advance. They enjoyed special privileges, including the much-prized right of free brewing and distilling, and until far into the eighteenth century were allowed comparative autonomy in their Slobodskaya Ukraina, free Ukraine, joining on to the west with their compatriots in the Little Russian provinces, the so-called Left-bank Ukraine (*i.e.* on the left bank of the Dnieper), which the Poles were forced to admit as part of Muscovy in 1667. Behind the soldier-settlers came other non-military farmers, traders, and artisans, mostly families of some means. Ukrainian colonization was much less dependent on the state than Great Russian. To the northward of Kharkov Ukrainians and Great Russians for long kept apart, but from the late eighteenth century they merged together. To the south it was different; the solid Ukrainian colonization maintained itself and spread over the open steppe; Great Russian penetration on a large scale took place only with the industrial and mining development of the last sixty years.

The Ukrainian line of the seventeen-thirties, from the Donets to the Dnieper on the borderland of the wooded and the feather-grass steppes, was the last of the big fortified lines. By then Slobodskaya Ukraina had not far short of 400,000 inhabitants: its military character as a frontier region was less all-pervading. To the north frontier conditions were largely a relic of the past; the lesser "men of service" had become state peasants and were being swamped by the gentry moving south with their serfs and the three-course open fields in strips. Forty years later (1774) the Russians were down to the Black Sea and controlled the mouths of the Dnieper, the

Don, and the Kuban. The Zaporozhian Cossacks were broken up and transplanted (1775), the Crimea passed into Russian hands (1783), and the Turks for the third time within fifty years were soundly beaten (1787-92) and yielded the coastal steppes between the Dnieper and the Dniester.

The frontier was now the open Black Sea steppes, New Russia. Behind, the fertile zone of the black-earth wooded steppe, with its woods by then much depleted, developed into the land *par excellence* of serfdom and grain cultivation, where Great Russian landowners acquired vast estates, Ukrainian officers followed their example and transformed themselves into serf-owning gentry, and Polish landlords retained their position and their serfs when the Right-bank Ukraine (*i.e.* on the right bank of the Dnieper) came under Russia by the second partition of Poland (1793).

New Russia developed rapidly under Catherine the Great's favorite Potemkin and a succession of other energetic governors-general. It was a land of latifundia, at first given over predominantly to sheep, later to wheat, interspersed with independent farmers and state peasants, with comparatively little serfdom and from an early date much hired, and seasonal, labor. The modern Odessa, founded in 1794 and settled in the first place mainly by Greeks, Italians, and other southerners, under the direction of the Duc de Richelieu and a group of French *émigrés* grew apace, thanks to a free port régime, to be the main commercial center of New Russia, followed by other wheat-exporting ports.

A polyglot character was also given to these Black Sea steppes by the constant settling on the land of foreign colonists, Germans, Greeks, Bulgars, and others, besides Moldavians. The government had begun as early as the third quarter of the eighteenth century with ill-thought-out and ill-executed attempts to settle Austrian Slavs and Germans on the then frontier, but its later colonizing policy was successful in helping to develop the country and diversify its economy, notably in southern Bessarabia, conquered from the Turks in 1812. The Germans, Lutherans or Mennonites, in particular built up solid, prosperous colonies, but, as on the Volga, they remained aloof, neither influenced by nor, save to a slight extent in farming methods, influencing the sea of Ukrainian peasants which surrounded their islands.

By the middle of the nineteenth century New Russia had grown to 2,250,000, by 1900 to well over 6,000,000 (if Bessarabia and the Don are included, the numbers would be nearly doubled). Wheat-growing had largely replaced stock-raising, based on a variegated extensive system of cultivation, not on the three-field system. The density of the rural population was still sparse, two to three times less than the crowded black-earth lands of the old Ukraine, but already in 1900 it was fifty per cent greater than the density of the whole of Iowa, cities included, in 1920; and Iowa is comparable in many respects in climate and soil conditions. By 1900 half the land was held in individual ownership, mostly by the gentry in great estates, and only forty per cent in communes. By then, too, the coal of the Donets basin and the iron ore of Krivoi Rog had begun industrialization, and wheat was somewhat less dominant. Thus New Russia, the land of the open steppes, differed considerably from the wooded steppe zone to the north, almost solely given over to agriculture, serfdom, and the commune, solidly Great Russian or Ukrainian.

3. *Types of Colonization*

During the past ten centuries of Russian expansion there has been a constant tug or struggle between the compulsory and the voluntary elements, between the authorities—at times damming back, at times forcing forward—and the individual and the family—at times determinedly on the move, at times reluctantly conscribed. For long a certain degree of mobility, as has been noticed earlier (p. 14), was encouraged or necessitated by the nature of forest economy and by the prevailing agricultural technique. In the early centuries the evidence is insufficient to decide whether compulsion by the princes and their chief retainers and by merchant-adventurers or the voluntary co-operation of freemen played the bigger rôle in colonization; but it is undoubted that the special advantages, economic and military, that the former offered were essential factors in the settling of what became the core of Muscovy.

For the two centuries after 1350 the monasteries played an important part as centers of new settlement, especially to the north of the Volga (see p. 173), but thereafter they were not, except in the middle Volga, conspicuous. Missionary activity in advance of occupation or conquest was a rare exception, and later there was nothing corresponding to the colonizing work of the churches for instance in New Zealand.

From the sixteenth century onwards the despotic character of tsarism became a decisive and ubiquitous force. From the seventeenth the landowners acted as the other most powerful agency in internal colonization, until the emancipation of the serfs in 1861; for, as the Russian word for serfs signified, they were bondmen, bound to do their master's will wherever he might move them. Grants of land by the tsar, without or more usually with serfs, and of exploiting rights (mines or factories) swelled the labor army of the landowners, who used it to people the new lands that fell to them in the rear of the advancing frontier. The most advanced frontier regions were the hunting ground of the individual pioneer, followed by the state with military colonists working the land but bound to service as garrison or field troops, the lesser "men of service" who in course of time developed for the most part into various categories of fairly independent state peasants.

Against the twin forces of tsarism and serfdom there was perpetual and intense reaction, and for long the most prevailing expression of individual initiative in colonization was simple flight. Escape from the religious authority of the Orthodox church was added to the attempt to escape from secular authority, when in the later seventeenth century the Schism in the church occurred, which resulted in the multiplication of persecuted sectarians and their making off to the frontier (*cf.* pp. 180 ff.). "Vagrants" was the official term for all those who ran away from that station in life allotted to them by the powers that be: there was a continual effort to round them up, bring them back, ascribe them to service, or by some means tie them up to the needs of the state. Many of the "vagrants" were ne'er-do-wells who contributed much to brigandage and jacqueries and little or nothing to settlement, but many were also pioneer frontiersmen who led the way to permanent Russian advance.

The most striking type of free colonization, dependent on a combination of individual initiative and group spirit, was the Cossacks, whose history, in particular that of the Don Cossacks, supplies an admirable sample of the Russian conquest of the steppe and of the gradual extension of state power at the expense of local autonomy in accordance with the transformation of the structure of frontier society.

The original Cossack was a "vagrant" whether from Muscovy or the Polish Ukraine, a steppe frontiersman; bee hunter, beaver hunter, game hunter, fisherman, pastoralist; half going Tatar; pushing farther and farther afield in the sixteenth century. He might develop into a rancher; he might take service as scout and light horseman (the original meaning of the Tatar word *kazak*); he might turn bandit-freebooter: usually he combined by turns all these occupations. The Cossacks were a liberty-loving and equalitarian but unruly and marauding element, and they played an anarchic and destructive rôle in the Time of Troubles (1604-13). In 1600, in complete contrast with 1900, they represented to some extent the challenge of social revolution by the underdog and the untamed.

On the frontier, however, as freebooter rivals to the nomads they might be a great asset, as Muscovy, though not Poland, found. By 1600 the boldest spirits had gone down river far away south into the feather-grass steppe and had organized themselves in three separate Cossack "hosts," on the middle and lower Don, the middle Ural river, and the lower Dnieper where the Zaporozhian ("beyond the cataracts") Cossacks played a somewhat similar rôle for the Ukrainians under Poland as the other Cossacks did for the Great Russians under Muscovy.[1] All three "hosts" were stoutly

---

[1] Gogol's prose epic *Taras Bulba* (1834; translated in Everyman edition) on the Zaporozhian Cossacks in the seventeenth century, for all its romantic idealization, gives the feel of the steppe and the fighting spirit of the Cossacks with compelling power.

Orthodox, a fact of special importance in the struggle of the Ukrainian Cossacks against Poland (see pp. 214 ff.).

Apart from these three spontaneous, independent "hosts," Cossacks were used by the government for courier and other military services, and in the eighteenth century the state formed, more or less on the model of the original "hosts," Cossack defense forces to guard and settle the frontier, in the North Caucasus, the southern Urals, Siberia, and latest of all in the Far East. They enjoyed special privileges, but unlike the Don, Ural, and Zaporozhian Cossacks they were founded and always controlled by the ministry of war.

The Don Cossacks, recruited mainly from Great Russians, maintained themselves for a hundred years, until 1671, in semi-independence of Moscow as a "host," organized on a military basis, but democratically governed by an assembly and elected officers, with full control of admission into their ranks. For this first hundred years they were very nominal subjects of "the White Tsar." They paid no taxes and had free trading rights. "We fight," they declared, "for the House of the Immaculate Virgin and the Miracle Workers of Moscow and for thee . . . Sovereign Tsar and Grand Prince of Great and Little and White Russia, Autocrat and Sovereign and Possessor of many Hordes." In fact, like any other of his hordes they fought, pillaged, and negotiated when and as they pleased, particularly with the Crimean Tatars and the Turks holding the Don delta with their stone fortress of Azov. They then mustered probably about 10,000 fighting Cossacks; equally formidable as river or sea corsairs and as land buccaneers. For long they despised the plow as the badge of bondage. Boasting "we serve for grass and water, not for land and estates," they lived by fishing, stock-breeding, trading, and hunting, above all for slaves and booty, raiding far afield in "the wild grounds," along the paynim shores of the Black Sea, or, as they sang, "like young falcons . . . on Mother Volga . . . on the blue sea, the blue sea, on the Caspian."

But they depended as well on the annual grant made by Moscow, flour, munitions, and cloth. This was their Achilles' heel. The distribution of the grant was made by the Cossacks themselves, but the amount was fixed by Moscow, and it paid the "host" to keep itself small. Yet they were too few to oust the Turks from Azov, save for a brief spell, and they needed the succor of Muscovy. A democratic oligarchy began to harden; then an inner ring of the senior officers grew well-off; outside, the floating, unprivileged semi-Cossack fringe increased as more and more runaways from the North trekked down; for the Don clung to its tradition of being an asylum for all and sundry.

The divorce between the richer, old-established Cossack families of the lower Don and the needy newcomers showed itself to be acute when the former stood against the two leaders of revolt, Stenka Razin and Bulavin (1670-71 and 1707-78; see p. 152). Moscow suppressed the risings with some assistance from the Cossack oligarchy. Henceforward (1671) the Don Cossacks were bound to the tsar by oath of allegiance. The right of asylum was more and more effectively challenged by the government. The southward surge of colonization from Muscovy made it possible to deprive the "host" of its middle Don lands (1708), and Peter the Great went a long step further in state control by abolishing the free election of the commander (ataman) of the "host" and directly appointing him himself (1723).

Henceforward the atamans, holding office for long periods but failing to become hereditary, worked in closer and closer accord with St. Petersburg, and so did the senior officers, themselves after 1754 no longer elected but appointed by the war ministry. Together they formed a governing oligarchy and the old assembly of the "host" counted for little. The privileges and more especially the duties of the Cossacks became more closely defined: they figured regularly in the Russian campaigns of the eighteenth century and began to be used as an internal police force. Agriculture had spread now that there was a plentiful supply of non-Cossack labor. By the end of the century the officer class had become large landowners and they succeeded in securing admission into the "estate" of the gentry, with the consequent legal right to own serfs. The frontier by now had moved south to the Kuban and the North Caucasus steppes.[1]

For the next hundred years the Don Territory formed "a province governed by special institutions," but in law and administration more and more assimilated to the rest of Russia. It grew greatly in population and wealth. By 1914 the Don Cossacks supplied nearly 150,000 cavalrymen, but as a whole they formed by then well under half the total population of about 4,000,000, though they owned three-fifths of the land. Divided amongst themselves, they stood over against the great mass of incomers, ex-serfs, independent farmers, laborers, and coal miners. Rostov, founded in 1761, which was non-Cossack, had grown to be a city of over a hundred thousand and the greatest center of the southeast.

Thus two centuries of colonization had transformed the frontier and radically changed the structure of Cossack society. The Cossacks had always differentiated sharply between themselves and Russians: while continuing to cherish the forms of their traditional customs and privileges, they developed a new tradition of loyalty to the tsar, not only as against his enemies abroad, but as well against his enemies at home. The watchwords of one of their songs in the 1905 Revolution summed up the attitude of the Cossack right wing: "We don't need a constitution. We don't want a republic. We won't betray Russia. We will defend the Tsar's throne." And so they did. But many of the poorer Cossacks and the non-Cossack people on the Don swung to the left. Divisions were deep, and in 1918 when it came to civil war the Don did not prove a reliable bastion for the White armies.[2] Death, emigration, and deportation thinned the Cossack ranks; the victory of the Bolsheviks, and later collectivization, spelled disaster for many of them. Then in 1936 the Kremlin

---

[1] Life on this frontier a generation later is brilliantly illustrated in parts of Lermontov's classic *A Hero of Our Times* (1840) and graphically described in Tolstoy's equally autobiographical novel of the Terek line *The Cossacks* (1862) (various translations of both, including the World's Classics series).

[2] Sholokhov in his well-known novel *Quiet Flows the Don* (1929; New York, 1934) has painted on an immense canvas the Don during the 1914 War and the first years of the Revolution.

altered course, formed special Cossack contingents in the Red Army, and harnessed the old fighting traditions of the Cossacks to the new Soviet patriotism, with results that the German army has only too bloody reason to know.

There remains to consider one last sample of colonization and of the interplay of the compulsory and the voluntary, of the state and the individual or independent group, as seen in the modern development of Siberia.

It has already been emphasized that Russian Siberia until the eighteenth century was almost entirely a fur colony of the great conifer forest zone. Thereafter it changed character as mining, agriculture, and lumbering developed and as the Russians settled the black-earth wooded steppe strip and expanded into Siberia of the steppes merging into the dry grasslands of Kazakhstan, up to the last generation the immemorial preserve of the nomad pastoralist (see map 2). The rate of development, however, was much slower than in the steppe lands of Russia until the great colonizing wave that began in the eighteen-eighties.

Peter the Great, in search of minerals and trade routes to Central Asia, had pushed out the frontier and established new chains of Cossack posts to check nomad pillaging. His successors continued his work, particularly in the extreme west of Siberia, well-watered and with good black-earth soils, but settlement was for long slow and sparse, a mixture of serfs ascribed to mines, Cossacks, "men of service" settled by the state, particularly for transport duties, and independent peasants and runaways, many of them sectarians fleeing from religious persecution. Siberia never knew the gentry and bonded serfdom to any extent, but the commune, passing from cooperative clearing of the land through various stages of development, was general. Legally the land was in the first place state or imperial land: in fact most of the settlers simply worked as much land as they needed with nothing but first occupancy as their title, until with increasing pressure on the natural resources the commune gradually evolved various types of periodical redistribution and other forms of economic control over the freedom of action of individual families. Right down to the end of the nineteenth century surveyed land grants remained the exception.

Almost throughout that century the official policy was to discourage or prevent movement into Siberia, except for one period of enlightened state-aided migration of state peasants. Ascription to the mines continued to be a regular feature, and a series of gold rushes, very nominally controlled by the government, brought new developments. For the first time now deportation bulked large in Siberia. Between 1823 and 1881 nearly 700,000 persons were exiled or deported across the Urals, to hard labor mostly in mines or on construction work, to prison camps, disciplinary battalions, or mere police supervision.[1] Apart from the criminal element, the very numerous political exiles, such as the Decembrists (see pp. 77-78) and the Poles, contributed innovations in agriculture and industry, as well as to science and education. The share of the deportees in the making of Siberia has, however, usually been exaggerated. It was considerable only east of the Yenisei, and on the whole the importance of deportation was probably less than in the early history of Australia. A very large number returned to Russia after serving their time, and those that stayed were generally looked askance at by the born Siberians.

What really made modern Siberia was the unappeasable land hunger of the Russian peasantry and the coming of the railway. The flow of settlers, largely in defiance of government regulations, at times dwindled to a trickle, but in the eighteen-eighties it swelled mightily and the old methods of attempting governmental restriction were palpably breaking down. The great famine of 1891 and the building of the Trans-Siberian, begun in that same year, caused a gigantic outpouring. The railway, like the Canadian Pacific built a decade earlier, turned a stream into a torrent. Despite ebbs and flows, despite the Russo-Japanese war, the population of

[1] Dostoevsky has written unforgettable descriptions of his Siberian prison life in *The House of the Dead* (1857; New York, 1915). *The Letters of Lenin* (translated and edited by E. Hill and D. Mudie, London, 1937) give a good picture of what in fact exile to a village in eastern Siberia (not imprisonment) meant.

Siberia and the Far East doubled within twenty years. In 1800 there had been rather over a million people; the 1897 census gave five and three-quarter millions; by 1914 there were over ten millions, nearly half as many again as in Canada, and Siberian co-operatives were competing successfully on the English butter market. This very rapid expansion was mainly confined to Siberia proper, *i.e.* between Lake Baikal and the Urals. Eastwards of Lake Baikal the stream of colonists—whether by land or by sea half round the globe from the Black Sea ports—ran much lower, despite the inducements of the government. Meanwhile, here in the Far East, Chinese migration on a scale even larger than that into Siberia was transforming Manchuria, the battleground of Russian and Japanese imperialism (*cf.* pp. 290 ff.).

The Trans-Siberian and the mass movement east forced the government to change its policy. A special colonization department was set up (1896) which attempted to organize migration and settlement. Regulations were poured forth on surveying, cheap transport rates, tax and other exemptions, grants in money and kind and loans. Nevertheless perhaps half of the incomers came on their own, weary or suspicious of the delays and complexities of bureaucracy. They came mostly from the overcrowded northern and central black-earth lands; usually in large groups, not too badly off; preceded by "locators" to discover suitable sites. Some settled in the old Siberian villages; most in new. By 1914 the best and most accessible land was taken up, and the Russian peasant-farmer was already pressing ominously on the grazing grounds of the Kazakhs, since transformed by their 1916 rebellion and the effects of the Soviet Revolution.

This new Siberia—sprawling, vigorous, rough, wasteful, erratic; too varied and too rapidly developing to have bred any one "Siberian type"—emerged bloodstained and for the moment spent from the First World War (in which Siberian troops covered themselves with glory), the Revolution and the Civil War (in which the Trans-Siberian was the key-thread alike for the Czech Anabasis, Admiral Kolchak, and the Red Army; see pp. 296 ff.). Within a few years the pulsing energy of Siberia was revived with the ruthless drive and the far-flung vision of the Communist party.

Soviet Siberia, unlike the new Siberia of 1890-1917, has grown above all through the new or vastly expanded mining and industrial frontiers born of the five-year plans. The uprush of towns on an ultra-American scale has been the dominant feature, both in Siberia proper and in the Far East. Magnitogorsk, Novosibirsk, Stalinsk, Komsomolsk, previously non-existent or diminutive, are known now the world over (see map 2). Agricultural development has been far less striking, save recently in the open steppe. Even more than before 1914 Siberia is mixed in composition, though as before predominantly Russian. Deportations on a very large scale and the insatiable demand for hands have dragged and drawn men and women from all parts of the Union. Soviet Siberia —still sprawling, wasteful and erratic, brutal and unsparing— has attracted as never before the energies and imagination of Soviet youth.

CHAPTER II
THE STATE

1. *The October Revolution: Party and Soviet*

IN 1917 tsarism collapsed and the October Revolution proclaimed a wholly new basis and form of society and government. Four years of revolutionary upheaval and civil war and then the second, Stalinist revolution of planned industrialization and collectivization have made a new Russia—the Union of Soviet Socialist Republics. The contrast between the new and the old, both in spirit and institutions, could not be greater. And yet there are certain very general features which are common to the soviet and the tsarist régimes: great centralization of power, enormous range of state action, massive bureaucracy, extreme emphasis on the army, drastic use of force and the secret police, semi-deification of the leader or sovereign.

The resemblances are to be explained by four main reasons: the problem of governing an immense area and a multitude of peoples with relatively low material and cultural standards; the problem of defense; the impossibility of a complete break with past customs, attitudes of mind and feeling, and ways of doing things; and, fourthly, the communist view of the state.

The Soviet Union is a socialist state, made possible by the seizure of power by "a Government of the armed workers" and the establishment of the dictatorship of the proletariat. With socialism two principles are realized, "from each according to his ability, to each according to his work," and "he who does not work neither shall he eat." The transition to a communist society remains to be achieved, and with it the principle of "from each according to his ability, to each according to his needs." This can only be realized "when people have become accustomed to observe the fundamental principles of social life, and their labor is so productive, that they will voluntarily work *according to their abilities*": until then the state will not "wither away," but on the contrary it is necessary that there should be "the *strictest* control, *by Society and the State,* of the quantity of labor and the quantity of consumption." This doctrine of Lenin has been greatly reinforced by the practice of total planning and by the emphasis placed by Stalin on the urgency of strong state power "in the present international situation . . . of capitalistic encirclement with its consequential dangers for the land of socialism" (1934).

The Leninist doctrine of communism gave to Russia at one and the same time a revolutionary ideal—the goal of communism and the vision of man new made—and a revolutionary method—the dictatorship of the vanguard of the proletariat organized through the Communist party and linked up with the masses through the soviets. The idea both of party and of soviets was new to Russia in 1917, but they are the two institutional bases upon which the revolutionary régime has been built up.

Party was the creation of Lenin, in opposition to Western

social-democratic ideas of it as a parliamentary group. It was to be the trained nucleus of the class-conscious element in the proletariat (and consequently small in actual numbers), steeled in the doctrines of Marx as expounded by Lenin, welded together as a fighting body by one central organization for the whole of Russia so as to receive one directing will, and working in close conjunction with the peasantry. Only such a party would be capable of guiding the revolutionary movement, of eventually smashing the existing form of government, and of establishing the dictatorship of the proletariat which was the necessary preliminary to and concomitant of the building up of socialism, eventually to be transformed into communism.

This was a conception of method that was alien to the revolutionary movements in Russia which hitherto had shied away from rigid organization and strong centralized control. They had varied between the loose federation of groups dear to anarchism, small secret societies of terrorists or believers in a Blanquist *coup d'état,* populists or social-revolutionaries inspired by the idea of the great mass of the peasantry in their communes as the key to revolution, and, lastly, social-democrats or marxists of various brands.

Lenin's Bolshevik party emerged from this last trend, which in 1898 took shape in the Russian Social-Democratic Workers' Party. For the next twenty years it made comparatively little headway, partly because most of its work was illegal and therefore underground, partly because of internal divisions, particularly as to organization. These gave rise to the formation of the Bolshevik group under Lenin in 1903, and in 1912 to its complete separation from its main social-democratic rivals, the Mensheviks. The Bolsheviks were far too few to play a large part in the 1905 Revolution, though they were in the forefront of the Moscow rising. Despite their name, meaning majority men, they had fewer adherents than the Mensheviks, the minority men, while both were inferior in number of supporters to the Social-Revolutionary party, whose appeal was above all to the peasantry. The Bolsheviks, however, though a tiny handful, alone had a real organization; they were devoted to their cause; they were formidable underground fighters; and they had in Lenin a leader of genius.

A month after the outbreak of the revolution in March 1917 Lenin, then aged forty-seven, returned to Petrograd after eleven years of exile abroad. Nobody was less of a refugee than Lenin (or of the middle-class intellectual which he was by birth and early education), and nobody combined more ardently grasp both of the international and the national. A Russian from the middle Volga, he had a wide knowledge and a deep understanding of Russia, and he had never lost touch with her. He was the undisputed leader of the Bolshevik party, then a catalytic drop of 80,000 organized workers in the swelling ocean of revolution. He was also from the start a revolutionary hero for Petrograd, and he rapidly showed himself to be not only the ablest theoretician and the most trenchant pamphleteer—as which he was already well known—but the most incisive and compelling speaker, the hardest worker, the ablest man of action, and the most iron-willed of all the workers' leaders.

With the Bolshevik *coup d'état* in November 1917 (according to the old Russian calendar then in use October; hence the name by which it lives in history, the October Revolution), Lenin became the head of the new revolutionary government, the Soviet (Council) of People's Commissars, with Trotsky as commissar for foreign affairs, later war, and Stalin for nationalities, later in various war posts. For some months the Bolsheviks governed, in so far as any government at all was possible, with the uneasy collaboration of the left wing of the Social-Revolutionaries. Thereafter all the commissars and the overwhelming majority of the Congress of Soviets were Bolsheviks. Thus almost from the start the new régime was founded substantially upon a one-party basis, in fact a corollary of Lenin's conception of party.

The party, over 600,000 strong by 1920, was the general staff and fighting kernel of the bloody, tumultuous period of "war communism," the Civil War and Allied intervention. By 1921 it was triumphant—and the country utterly exhausted; and yet further prostrated by the great famine of that year, far the worst for thirty years. Lenin turned to a temporary accommodation with the peasantry in the shape of the New Economic Policy (see pp. 119-120) and to an all-round reorganization of the party and the country.

The chaos of 1918-21 was immensely increased by the fact that the Bolsheviks swept away the old army, the old local government bodies, the old judicial system, and (very largely) the old civil service. On the other hand, this was one of the main reasons for the final triumph of the Revolution. Having destroyed they succeeded in creating the indispensable essential, a *new* army and secret police,[1] and more slowly *new* courts and a *new* civil service, in all of which they controlled the key-posts. In local administration they worked, however, chaotically, through the *new* soviets.

The N.E.P. interlude, 1921-28, was the period of the making of the Union, the consolidation of the new administration under the party, and the extension of its control over the trade unions and co-operatives. After Lenin's death in 1924 it was also the period of open struggle within the party, above all between Stalin and Trotsky, radically opposed to one another in temperament, abilities, and policy, and each with bitter scores from the past. Stalin (Djugashvili; b. 1879), a Georgian, had well earned his pseudonym "man of steel" in twenty years of underground revolutionary struggle as a Bolshevik with frequent arrests and deportations—but always in Russia, never in exile abroad. He had played a conspicuous part in the Civil War, often in conflict with Trotsky, especially in the defense of Tsaritsyn, renamed in his honor Stalingrad. Trotsky (Bronstein; 1879-1940), a Jew, was similar only in being a professional revolutionary. From 1902 to 1917 he was almost continuously out of Russia in exile, and

---

[1] These were new, not in the sense that the entire personnel was new, but in the sense that the old army and police were disbanded and new revolutionary organizations were set up—the Red Guards, the Red Army, and the Cheka (the predecessor of the G.P.U.)—staffed at the top by Bolsheviks or revolutionaries working with them, but otherwise largely composed of re-enlisted men.

he had been guilty of various deviations from the Leninist line. He rose to fame during the Brest-Litovsk peace debates with the Germans, and then with dramatic energy set about creating the Red Army. Brilliant both as a speaker and a writer, he represented above all the intellectual internationalist for whom Russia was essentially the springboard for world revolution.

Stalin, who had been entrenched at the center as general secretary of the party since 1922, won the day for "socialism in one country" as against "permanent revolution." Trotsky and certain other leaders were expelled from the party, and in 1929 he was deported. A year previously Stalin launched the second revolution, rapid large-scale industrialization and collectivization of agriculture, *i.e.* total planning over the whole range of economics and finance.

From 1930 onwards, three years before Hitler, eight years after Mussolini, Stalin was acclaimed as "the leader" (the Russian word has the corresponding root and the same literal meaning as *führer* or *duce*). Unlike Lenin, he did not head the government, the Council of People's Commissars (until May 1941); nor was he even a member of it after 1923. He remained officially only general secretary of the party and member (as he had always been) of the Politbureau, *i.e.* the Political Bureau of the Central Committee of the Party. But this was the inmost citadel of power, the real center of government (nominally elected by the Central Committee, in fact it seems usually co-opted), not the Council of People's Commissars, which, though entirely composed of party men, was officially the servant of the Congress of Soviets.

From 1928 onwards the party, working through an increasingly elaborate series of committees, both central and local, became more and more a general staff for organizing and enforcing the carrying out of collectivization and the five-year plans and of all-round defense measures. Its controlling position was to some extent officially recognized for the first time in the 1936 constitution, which described it as "the directing nucleus of all organizations, both social and state, of the workers," but the parallelism of two governments—the Politbureau and the Party, the Council of Commissars and the Supreme Council of Soviets—remained unacknowledged.

While the party has thus been more than ever the driving center of the state apparatus, it has at the same time during the last ten years almost entirely changed its composition, as a result of the mass purges and the trials (and for the first time execution) of most of the Old Bolsheviks and the higher army officers. For the first time since the early twenties the party declined heavily in numbers. Then in the two years 1939 and 1940 a special recruiting campaign produced a million new members, drawn from "people of a new formation," "non-party activists," Stakhanovites, works foremen, collective-farm brigadiers, technical experts, the new Soviet intelligentsia. This was an immense increase, amounting to forty per cent of the membership of the party (February 1941, 2,515,481 members; in addition, 1,361,404 "candidates," *i.e.* probationers); and of the remainder far the greater part were also men and women of the Stalin generation who had come in during the last decade. At the top, in control of all this new and largely young blood, there remain Stalin and his small band of seasoned henchmen.

The second main basis of the revolutionary power, the soviets, was likewise new; but, unlike the party, the soviets did not originate in any Marxist theory and were not modeled on any preconceived plan. Soviets, or councils, of workmen and others sprang up spontaneously in the 1905 Revolution in a number of places, particularly St. Petersburg and Moscow, mainly as strike committees, though not merely of trade unionists. They were incoherent in their aims, had practically no interconnections, and quickly dissolved or were suppressed. The St. Petersburg Soviet, which was mainly a Menshevik body and included Trotsky, with Lenin in the background, after six weeks' existence accepted disbandment by the government; but the Moscow Soviet literally stuck to its guns, and it took a desperate week of street fighting before guard battalions, summoned from the capital, overpowered the Moscow workers (December 1905). This was the culminating point of the 1905 Revolution. Henceforward the soviets had the aureole of blood and martyrdom, as Sinn Fein after the Dublin Easter Rebellion.

Lenin had preached the necessity of self-constituted committees of the peasantry taking the law into their own hands and settling the land question for themselves (as happened in 1917 and 1918), but he had not formulated soviets. Now, with his unerring feel for popular initiative and for what was Russian, he seized on the soviets as spontaneous fighting organizations in which lay the germs of a revolutionary government, as the indispensable form for a radically new kind of democracy, not that of a national parliamentary republic, but one to be combined with party dictatorship.

When the March Revolution broke out, soviets of every description sprang up everywhere, in the army and navy included. After a few months they linked up with each other on a national scale in the Congress of Soviets of Soldiers', Workers', and Peasants' Delegates, under the leadership of the Petrograd Soviet. This body acted as a rival to the Provisional Government, headed first by the moderate liberal Duma leaders (see p. 65), then by the vaguely socialist radical Kerensky. Lenin proclaimed as his watchword "all power to the Soviets," which summed up the only two things which the immense majority of the country wanted, an end to the war, the land for the peasants immediately. By the end of October 1917 both the Petrograd and the Moscow soviets had Bolshevik majorities. The moment had come for the Bolshevik seizure of power.

It coincided with the second All-Russian Congress of Soviets, which immediately declared that it had taken "power into its own hands," adopted decrees offering peace and handing over the land forthwith to the peasants, accepted as its own the revolutionary government formed by Lenin, and rendered itself permanent through its central executive committee. This committee and the congress counted for much in the early period of the Bolshevik Revolution. Though the Bolsheviks had a majority, and after July 1918 an overwhelming one, it was not a packed body. Lenin had to exert himself to the utmost, for instance, to secure acceptance of the German terms imposed at Brest-Litovsk, and even then 261 voted against the treaty and 115 abstained. Later it subsided relatively into the background, but it always remained the central national revolutionary institution, linking the party and the people at large, and it was according to the constitution the supreme authority in the Union.

The local soviets were of even more importance. Elected originally largely on an occupational basis, they too were formed on a class but not on a party basis; *i.e.* all those who were branded as bourgeois or in any way counter-revolutionary were excluded. After the successful fight for the seizure and maintenance of power, the network of soviets reaching up from the village at the bottom to the Congress of Soviets at the top was gradually hammered into shape, and the soviets became the indispensable apparatus, especially in the large cities, for the local social services and the organization of distribution and production; all the more indispensable if the Communist party was to be preserved as a permeating *élite*, in 1925 only a million in all, in 1941 under 4,000,000 in a sea of 170,000,000.[1]

The revolutionary régime was thus built up on the alliance of the party with a body which, like the Red Army and the new bureaucracy, was both nation-wide and non-party, and this alliance has remained the cornerstone of the U.S.S.R., the *Soviet* Union. As in 1918, so now, constitutionally "all power in the U.S.S.R. is vested in the workers of town and village in the shape of soviets of deputies of the workers" and "the highest organ of state . . . is the Supreme Soviet"— until 1936 the Congress of Soviets.

The new constitution of that year restored the soviets to the center of the picture as the fountain-head of power and as an essential means for the transition from socialism to communism. All over eighteen were made voters and eligible for election, irrespective of their past or parentage: secret voting was introduced: more important, all elections were

---

[1] A vivid picture of the interworkings of party, soviets, and factory committees is given in Gladkov's novel of the North Caucasus, *Cement* (New York, 1929).

made direct, whereas hitherto almost all had been indirect, and the previous preponderance at the center of the towns over the countryside was abolished. On the other hand, since in fact only one candidate is allowed for each constituency and every candidate belongs to the official "bloc of communists and non-party men," soviet elections continue to be completely different from those in the West. Nominations are confined to the party and certain other approved organizations. The task, however, of organizing the nomination of 1,300,000 deputies and a ninety-eight per cent poll of an electorate of 94,000,000 is a very elaborate and a major undertaking of internal policy, in which the alliance of the party with sufficient active non-party men is essential, particularly in the village soviets (the old communes reborn as it were) which always have been overwhelmingly composed of non-party deputies. At the same time, the 1936 constitution (in which the words democracy or democratic do not appear) was certainly intended to maintain in force, in Stalin's words, "the régime of the dictatorship of the working class as well as the present directing position of the Communist party."

Economic planning and the overriding needs of defense have led to greater and greater control by the center, not only through the party and the Supreme Soviet, but through the Union Commissariats (by 1940 swollen to over forty in number) and the Red Army high command. The range of state action, always totalitarian in principle, has become so in fact. Federalism was very marked for the first ten years, notably in the Ukraine, "where the remnants of distrust of the Great Russians had not yet disappeared, and centrifugal forces still continued to operate" (Stalin) *(cf.* p. 106); but it has since been whittled away substantially into restricted local self-government, again working through the party and the soviets. Although the right of secession for the constituent republics of the Union still figures on paper in the constitution and one chamber of the Supreme Soviet is formed on federal lines, in fact the Soviet state has become a multi-national union rather than a federation of many nations. In glaring contrast with tsarism, the local languages, arts, and history of the Soviet peoples have been continuously encouraged by every means; but for the last dozen years strictly within the limits of the Stalinist slogan "nationalist in form, socialist in content." This means very close control and extreme penalties for anything which might be interpreted as political nationalism.

For some years past the policy of socialist nationalism has been combined with the intensive inculcation of Soviet patriotism. Russia, "the prison house of peoples," has been succeeded by the Union, "the friendship of the peoples of the U.S.S.R.," a rival formula as it were to the British Commonwealth of Nations. "For Soviet patriots homeland and communism are fused into one inseparable whole" (Molotov). Military service is obligatory for all, Moslems included, unlike the tsarist conscription which in general excluded them. The 1936 constitution declared that "the defense of the fatherland is the sacred duty of every citizen of the U.S.S.R.," and the present tremendous struggle on the Eastern Front shows with what heroism and implacable resolution the Red Army and the Soviet peoples interpret this duty.

While every emphasis is put upon the equality of Soviet peoples—which as regards opportunity to serve the Soviet fatherland is largely a reality—the inescapable fact remains that of all the Soviet peoples the Russians bulk far the largest, in numbers, in achievements, and in experience. More and more stress has been laid on the Soviet régime as the heir of all that is best in the Russian heritage. Peter the Great and Suvorov have been restored to their pedestals; Pushkin and Lermontov to Parnassus; Alexander Nevsky, victor over the German knights seven centuries ago, and Kutuzov, victor of 1812, give their names to the new medals; Ivan the Terrible and Catherine the Great are once again household names. "We Bolsheviks have come from the bowels of the people," said Molotov, a Russian through and through, "and we prize and love the glorious deeds in the history of our people."

2. *The 1905 Revolution and the Downfall of Tsarism*

How was it possible for the Soviet régime, founded on two such new bases as party and soviets, to stand in the place of tsarism and eventually wield such immense power?

For the last four centuries one persistent feature in Russian history has been the strength in fact and in idea of untrammeled central state power personified in one man and unshackled by defined constitutional norms. "The rulers ot Russia," Ivan the Terrible wrote in the middle of the sixteenth century, "have not been accountable to any one, but have been free to reward or to chastise their subjects. . . . The Russian autocracy . . . ," which he was specifically contrasting with the contractual nature of the monarchy in Poland, "has been ruled in all things by sovereigns, not by notables and magnates." As late as 1906 Nicholas II, even when forced to grant what was in effect an embryonic constitution, laid it down in the fundamental laws that "the Supreme, Autocratic power belongs to the All-Russian Emperor," and repeated the ancient formula: "Obedience to his authority, not only for wrath but also for conscience sake, is ordained by God Himself."

Tsarism operated through the landowning class, the army and police, the bureaucracy, and the church. The landowning class, which in the eighteenth century became substantially an "estate" of the nobility and gentry somewhat similar to that in the German countries, despite divisions within itself dominated, directly or indirectly, in the army and the bureaucracy until the latter half of the nineteenth century. By then it was rapidly losing ground in face of the great development of Western economic and industrial influences.

Half a century after the emancipation of the serfs (1861) the old fabric sustaining the autocracy was revealed in the Russo-Japanese war (1904-5) and the 1905 Revolution as so undermined that the tsar, confronted with the alternative of military "dictatorship or entry onto the path of a constitution," was reluctantly compelled to choose the latter course and issue the October Manifesto (30th October 1905), equivalent to a constitutional charter. The five liberties of person, conscience, speech, meeting and association, which had been clamorously demanded in a general civilian strike, were conceded, though only in very general terms. An All-Russian representative assembly, the Duma, was to share some legislative power with the tsar. But at least he had forestalled a constituent assembly; he had himself prescribed the powers of the Duma and had laid down the fundamental laws; what he had granted he might withdraw or modify. Witte, the prime minister and author of the October Manifesto, congratulated himself that there was "a constitution, but a conservative constitution and without parliamentarism." Nicholas, like his father and grandfather, shared the opinion of Pobedonostsev, the arch-conservative mentor of tsars, that "it is terrible to think of our condition if destiny had sent us the fatal gift—an All-Russian Parliament."

In certain respects the 1905 Revolution was the Russian counterpart to the 1848 revolutions in Austria and Prussia. The constitutional outcome was similar to that in Prussia, whose 1851 constitution (which lasted on substantially unchanged until 1918) was one of the models for the Russian fundamental laws of 1906. There was no ministerial responsibility to the Duma, and the council of ministers was a committee without cohesion. The Duma was at first elected on a very wide male franchise, with very wide provisions as to eligibility, and with secret voting. On the other hand the elections were indirect, except in the largest towns, and were based on a complicated grouping of the electors in separate colleges, borrowed from Prussian and Austrian practice. The intention was to secure the dominance of the conservative forces among which were reckoned the peasants, still regarded in the main as faithful children of "the Little Father." Bitter experience of jacqueries and the first two Dumas brought final disillusionment, and in 1907 Stolypin, the prime minister, in violation of the fundamental laws, drastically transformed the electoral laws to the disadvantage of the peasantry, as well as of the workers and the non-Russians. Thereby he secured a solidly conservative, upper-class Duma, which unlike its two predecessors did not require to be promptly dissolved but lived out its legal term of five years.

The tsar retained an absolute veto on legislation, full control of the army and foreign affairs, and very wide powers of legislation without the Duma when it was not sitting. Its financial control was very limited, though it was difficult for the government to embark upon large new schemes, such as military reorganization, without some arrangement with the Duma. Yet another brake upon the Duma was provided by an upper chamber with concurrent powers, the Council of State, already existent for a century as a nominated administrative and drafting body, now refashioned with half its members elected.

In contrast with the westernization of Japan and the constitution granted by the Mikado in 1889, the Russian autocracy attempted to cope with the impact of the nineteenth-century Western world only after defeat in two wars, the Crimean and the Russo-Japanese, and under the direct challenge of revolution at home. 1905 was spoken of as a dress rehearsal. It had profoundly shaken and greatly alarmed tsarism. Henceforward there was a new climate of political activity in Russia. The Duma, however weak and conservative after 1907, marked the beginning of a transition to some kind of constitutional régime, and the forces of reaction, though they regained ascendancy, failed to sweep it away. A later chapter will show that at last the problem of the peasantry was seriously tackled in the ten years before 1917 (see pp. 124-125). The other fundamental problem, illiteracy, was tackled also, though with less effect (see p. 328). The bureaucracy, it is true, remained the real government, but under the shadow of loss of prestige and restrained to some extent (except in its treatment of Jews and other non-Russians) by the fundamental laws of 1906, to a far greater extent by fear of a repetition of 1905. There was no lack of prophecies of such a repetition, and despite great economic revival industrial unrest was acute. When the President of the French Republic paid his state visit to the Emperor of All the Russias in the late July of 1914, barricades were beginning to go up in the workers' quarters of St. Petersburg. Ten days later immense crowds were kneeling in front of the Winter Palace to sing the national anthem, then surging to sack the German embassy.

Tsarism would not have collapsed as it did but for the War. Traditional patriotism carried Russia through two and a half years of war on the all-inclusive modern scale. By 1917 the old emotional loyalties had been used up or worn thin. Without them, for the great bulk of the army and country, there was nothing left to fight with. Russia lacked both the organization and the sustained moral purpose to withstand further the effects of such defeats and such strain as she had undergone.

Her casualties can be only approximately computed: over two million killed, two to two and a half million prisoners; something like forty per cent of the Allied dead were Russian dead. The valor and marvelous endurance of her soldiery, badly led and worse armed, saved, though they could not decide, the Allied cause. It is doubtful whether any other people, except the Chinese, could have stood such a war and such misgovernment for so long. Economically Russia was not exhausted by 1917, but her virtual isolation from the West through the closing of the Baltic and the Black Sea had crippling effects, economic, military, and psychological; the transport system was in chaos; and the extreme inefficiency of distribution added acutely to the hardships of the rear.

The Revolution began when it did, in March 1917, because the government had failed so disastrously in the war that the old traditional binding ties to authority were sapped or snapped, with the result that strikes and bread riots in the capital, where there was an enormous undisciplined garrison, could lead to mutinies and precipitate the avalanche. In the army men were saying: "The government want us all killed so that our wives and children may be starved by the landowners." "We have had many Allies, but it is all no good. The Germans are people like ourselves, we want liberty." In the villages the police reported: "All are waiting and impatiently demanding: when will this cursed war end. Political resolutions are being talked about everywhere and resolutions adopted against the landlords and merchants."

It has already been said that tsarism had operated through the landowning class, the army and police, the bureaucracy, and the church. By the time of the war the last was but a hollow prop (see pp. 184-185), the first was as such a spent force. The army was not the old army, but the peasantry mobilized; having suffered great defeats; at the front already much demoralized, in the swollen rear quite unreliable, with a great weakness in officers, without any leader who had the halo of victories or the personal magnetism to galvanize the mass. And now for the first time millions of illiterate peasants and workers had arms in their hands. Actual revolutionary propaganda was not important at the front before 1917, but it had an ideal field for action, and in the six months after March it reduced the bulk of the army to a mob intent only on getting back to their villages and sharing in the land.

The bureaucracy meant the government and, as personified by the tsar, the principle of authority. Of all the factors which help to account for the course of the Revolution the most fundamental is that feature which for the last two centuries has been the major problem in Russian history, the chasm between the small minority of the educated and the vast mass of peasants and working men living in a different world of thought, speech, and emotion. The educated minority were the rulers and civilizers of modern Russia. Effective government depended on sufficient cohesion being maintained between the bureaucracy and the remainder of the educated minority. By 1917 there was no question of cohesion; there was almost complete divorce (*cf.* pp. 311-315, 359).

The bureaucracy in Russia, which began to take its modern shape as a result of administrative reforms under Alexander I (1801-25), was the stock butt of Russian literature,[1]

[1] For instance in many of the ever popular fables of Krylov (1768-1844); admirably translated by Sir Bernard Pares in the Penguin series (London, 1942, with Russian text; also a fuller selection, without Russian text, London, 1926).

anathema to revolutionaries, and for half a century before 1917 the despair of progressives. Many of the diatribes against it were all too justified; nevertheless Russia owed far more to it than is generally allowed. It included a long series of able, sincere, and hard-working administrators; but always there were too few of such, and at the time of the War, so it proved, all too few. Its greatest weakness was that it could very rarely produce or absorb statesmen or leaders. It required as its coping-stone the traditional belief of the masses in the authority of the tsar. If this belief faded, and if the army were unreliable, the bureaucracy could not govern by itself. It was in some ways alien to Russia and, though it inspired a certain prestige of fear, it never enjoyed prestige such as the German civil service. It developed a strong *esprit de corps* and in so doing became more and more divorced from the liberal section of the educated minority outside it, *e.g.* in the Duma, the provincial councils, the municipal bodies, the professional classes, the co-operative societies.

During the war the government machine signally failed to meet its immense tasks and to co-operate with the various voluntary organizations run by the progressives. The bureaucracy, not the progressives, supplied the ministers, who were the appointees of the tsar. They were nonentities or worse. Public accusations of treachery were made. There was no leadership from above, no concerted policy; nothing but drifting incompetence and senseless routine like a horse on a disconnected treadmill. In the last year of tsarism there were four different prime ministers, four different ministers of interior, three different war ministers, and three different foreign ministers.

Nicholas II, pitiable had he not been tsar, was responsible for this final divorce of the government from the country. Ruled by his wife, he proved incapable even of reigning. He was possessed of many amiable qualities as a private individual, but the Rasputin scandals (see p. 186) and his refusal to listen to any sane advice or to choose any ministers who might inspire some confidence, and give at least a semblance of unified leadership, had produced a situation so electric that even members of the imperial family were talking of a palace revolution, such as Russia had known so often in the eighteenth century. As the last hour of tsarism began to strike, the tsar for his part was writing to commiserate with the empress on the children having caught measles and to complain: "I greatly miss my half-hourly game of patience every evening. I shall take up dominoes again in my spare time" (8th March 1917).

On that day disorders broke out in Petrograd. Within a week it was Revolution. So completely was Nicholas estranged from all sections of society that there was nothing for him to do but to abdicate immediately. He did so, for himself and his young son, in favor of his brother the Grand Duke Michael. The Grand Duke declined to assume the crown until it was offered to him by a constituent assembly. That was the end of the Romanov dynasty, and with it the end of any unquestioned authority for many a long year of travail.

The war had brought tsarism to its downfall. With the army in decomposition, there was nothing to hold on to which had the spell of prestige and the cement of custom. The new Provisional Government had neither; "driftwood floating on the waves," as its head described himself and his colleagues. They represented the very heterogeneous "progressive bloc" of the best elements in the Duma, the provincial councils and the municipal bodies, that second section of the educated minority which had become so fatally divorced from the bureaucracy. It had come to the front during the war and for the moment it was the one political center for the country as a whole, but it was too new and too conservative to command wide prestige, and it was immediately challenged by the soviets, as new indeed but vibrant with the pulsating energies of a new world.

The Provisional Government, which in July was reconstituted under Kerensky with a pink complexion, was positive in one respect—continuation of the war side by side with the Allies, negative in almost every other—deferment of the land settlement and of the whole question of the new régime until the meeting of a constituent assembly. The soviets soon became positive on two things—peace and land *now*. And the soviets were armed; they had behind them the great bulk of the army in the rear and more and more of the army at the front. A military dictatorship in the name of the forces of order proved impossible. A constituent assembly was elected by universal suffrage under chaotic conditions late in 1917. By that time the Bolsheviks had overthrown the Provisional Government, and the constituent assembly, in which the Bolsheviks were a small minority, was suppressed in favor of the rival Congress of Soviets (January 1918; *cf.* pp. 361-362).

>"The merry wind, malicious, gay, . . .
>Tears and pounds and buffets the great streamer,
>'All Power to the Constituent Assembly' . . .
>March to the revolution's pace,
>The tireless foe hides not his face.
>Comrade, don't funk; take aim.
>Let's fire a shot at Holy Russia—
>Russia of the peasant huts,
>Solid as wood,
>Broad of bottom.
>Without a cross,
>Without a cross.
>Our boys have gone to serve,
>In the Red Guard to serve,
>In the Red Guard to serve, . . .
>We will set the world aflame,
>Bitter woe to all bourzhooy,
>With blood will set the world aflame—
>Good Lord, give us thy blessing . . .
>March to the revolution's pace,
>We've a tireless foe to face.
>Forward, forward, the thundering beat
>Of the marching workers' feet.
>And the twelve,
>Unblessed,
>March ever onward,
>Ready for all,
>Pity for none . . .
>So they march with mighty tread,
>The twelve.

Behind, the hungry mongrel.
In front, with bloody banner,
Unseen in snow storm,
Unharmed by shot,
With gentle gait above the storm,
In the pearl quicksand snow,
With aureole of roses white—
In front—Jesus Christ." [1]

3. *Representative Institutions*

The main reason for the failure of the liberal section of the educated minority and its type of representative government was that tsarism had thwarted it so consistently that it only got its chance in the most desperate circumstances imaginable, a maelstrom swirling downwards towards anarchy. It could make little appeal to the past, and in appeal to the future was completely outdistanced by the soviets. The basis of the Provisional Government was the national representative parliament, the Duma, and the local representative bodies, the provincial and municipal councils. But the great majority of the Duma had been extremely conservative, and the councils were narrow in their composition. The principle and practice of elective institutions had a history in Russia, but it was thin, disconnected, and almost wholly subordinate to the history of the central power. Consider first the history of local self-government, then that of national representation.

Local government, right down to the great reforms of the eighteen-sixties, had been overwhelmingly controlled by the central authority. Efforts had been made from time to time, *e.g.* by Ivan the Terrible (1549-50, 1555) and Catherine the Great (1775, 1785), to combat the gross abuses of tax-farming and render government and justice more effective by some reliance on locally elected officials and bodies, or to infuse into the towns some element of autonomy. But the response

[1] Alexander Blok, *The Twelve* (January 1918), the most famous poem of the Revolution. There is an English translation in *Russian Poetry: An Anthology*, by A. Yarmolinsky and Babette Deutsch (1923; New York, 1937) from which I have borrowed some of the lines quoted: also one by C. M. Bowra in *Horizon*, July 1944.

had been feeble: responsibility was a charge to be evaded if possible, and the state having to impose service virtually killed organized local initiative or self-dependence, except to some extent in the peasant communes. Justice and administration for the most part remained undivided in the same hands. In so far as local affairs were not caught up into the central mesh, the general tendency was to leave matters to the separate classes of landowners, clergy, merchant-traders, and some sections of the peasantry, organized on a local not a national basis and acting in isolation from each other. Catherine the Great especially, by her charter to the landowners (1785), gave a new basis to their provincial and district assemblies and created substantially an "estate" of the nobility and gentry. Yet these assemblies did not develop into vital institutions, and the separation of classes, always encouraged for fiscal purposes by the state in its perpetual effort to regiment its subjects into accessible pigeonholes, had the fatal effect of still further sundering from each other the various elements that went to make up Russian society.

The great reforms (1861-70) under Alexander II were primarily the achievement of the progressive section in the bureaucracy, working under the stimulus of a press then for a time comparatively free and in conjunction with committees, sometimes elected, sometimes appointed, of the serf-owners or the professional classes. The direct share of the non-bureaucrats was of great importance in some of the reforms, but broadly speaking these were the handiwork of the bureaucracy, and they were not linked up with any national body, not even with a national representation of the serf-owners.

The greatest of the reforms was the emancipation of the serfs (1861), which will be discussed in the following chapter: with it went a reorganization of the commune as an organ of peasant self-government (see pp. 126 ff.). The others were largely inspired by the ideas of separation of administrative from judicial powers, of decentralization and of self-government. This last caused a prolonged struggle in which the conservative forces won the day. The new (1864) provincial and district councils (*zemstva*) were indeed based on the joint participation of all classes in a given area, but elections were on a three-class basis, analogous to that of the Prussian provincial assemblies, with indirect election for the peasants through heads of households. Predominant influence was given inevitably to the gentry, the progressive among whom for some years set the pace.

These new bodies, which were established in most of European Russia but not elsewhere, were additional to the existing local government machinery; there was no clear delimitation of their competence; their financial powers were very confined; and they were subject to the close control of the provincial governors and the ministry of the interior. After an initial period of hopeful activity reaction set in, and under Alexander III (1881-94) the dead hand of the central authorities paralyzed most of their activities. In 1890 they were reorganized; election by the peasantry was virtually suppressed, and a large absolute majority given to the gentry. At the same time (1889) the justices of the peace, who had previously been elected by the district councils, were replaced by reactionary appointees of the ministry of the interior, who again combined judicial and administrative functions and together with the police were the main rulers of the peasantry, until a law of 1912 modified their position. A like fate (1892) befell the elected municipal councils which had been set up in 1870 on similar lines to the *zemstva*. A very high franchise qualification was now imposed, with a three-class system, and the municipal councils were even more tightly controlled from the center than before.

Despite the opposition of the bureaucracy, however, the practice of local self-government and activities of voluntary associations had made headway in the half-century before 1917. The work accomplished by the *zemstva* and many municipal councils had been remarkable, particularly in education, public health, and agriculture. Immediately before and during the 1905 Revolution they emerged as a prominent political force on the side of liberalism through the new device of All-Russian congresses, and after 1914 they played the outstanding part in struggling with the war organization of the rear. They had great popularity among the liberals and the professional classes in general, but little appeal outside of them. They were the indispensable element in the process, but just begun after 1905, of transforming tsarism into some kind of modern monarchy, but in 1917, without any tsar or any reliable army, they proved powerless to act with the Duma as the corner-stones of a new régime.

If local self-government had thin roots, national representation had only memories. Russians had to hark back to the seventeenth century for any parallel to the Duma as an elected, representative body on a national scale limiting the power of autocracy.

Alexander II on the very eve of his assassination (1881) had secretly agreed to new consultative commissions, with a small elected element from the *zemstva*, which might perhaps have been a fruitful seed of development. His murder immediately caused his son, Alexander III, to renounce any such dangerous idea and to proclaim that it was God's command that he should govern "in faith in the strength and truth of the autocratic power, which We are called to fortify and preserve for the national good from any inclinations against it." Alexander I had three times dallied with projects for a constitution with a species of elected parliament, but Speransky, the most thorough and consequential of his reformer friends, was sacrificed (1812) and only a portion of his far-reaching plans was put into operation (see pp. 99-101).

Catherine the Great had actually convoked a Legislative Commission (1767-68), elected from all parts and peoples of the empire and all classes, except the clergy and the most numerous, the serfs.[1] Its task was to supply information with a view to a codification of the laws. Unlike the small elected committees of landowners and merchants only, which five

---

[1] Her *Instructions* to the deputies, which were widely circulated in Russia and excellently illustrate Catherine as an enlightened despot under the influence of Montesquieu and Beccaria, are printed in W. F. Reddaway, *Documents of Catherine the Great* (Cambridge, 1931), together with selections from her correspondence with Voltaire, both in French.

times within the previous forty years had been summoned to cope with the same immense problem, the Legislative Commission was a very large body and was given great publicity. It supplied Catherine with a mass of opinion and material used by her in subsequent legislation, but it did nothing to further the task of codification, eventually to be the great achievement of Nicholas I's reign (1833), thanks mainly to Speransky, and it was an experiment that Catherine did not repeat. Nor was there any demand that it should be repeated. The dominant class of landowners were still content to secure their own interests piecemeal by themselves and had no ambition to fortify their political position by a national institution which might act as an organized counterpoise to tsarism.

At the beginning of the seventeenth century the situation had been different. Then Muscovy was submerged in social strife, civil war, and Polish and Swedish intervention, culminating in the occupation of Moscow and Novgorod and the instalment of a Polish tsar. This was the Time of Troubles (1604-13). One result of the Time of Troubles, when there was no one effective tsar, was the growth of the idea of the indivisible Muscovite state as opposed to the hitherto prevailing conception of Muscovy as the patrimony of the tsar, a great collection of his manors that included among its assets all classes of the inhabitants. Another result was that, as the government had broken down and the state was in chaos, local bodies acted for themselves, elected their own councils, and joined together in concerted resistance to the Polish invaders. The idea grew that the reconstitution of Muscovy required the collaboration and sanction of "the whole land." Hence there developed a new national institution, the elected assembly of the land, analogous to the estates-general of western Europe. For half a century this played an important rôle and for ten years (1613-22), when it was in almost annual session, shared in the reconstruction of the country.

The assembly of the land had originated at least as early as 1566, when Ivan the Terrible added to the old combined assembly of the council of magnates and the council of the upper clergy selected members from the backbone of his army and officials, the middling landowners, "the men of service" *par excellence,* somewhat corresponding to the medieval English knights of the shire. It took on a new form when provincial members of this class predominated in it and election, which was at that time in wide use for various local government purposes, replaced selection. It included as well elected representatives of the merchants and burgesses and occasionally of some classes of free peasants and certain other categories.

The evidence as to its exact composition, competence, and procedure is limited, but it is clear that they did not become firmly fixed, and that the assemblies of the land varied in accordance with the different purposes for which they were summoned. We find them being consulted upon war or peace, additions to the code of laws, the Ukrainian question, taxation, the reconstruction of government after 1613, and, most striking of all, upon the succession to the throne. The representatives were elected in varying numbers by the different classes separately in the shires and towns; "from all ranks, from the best, the middling and the lesser, good and discreet men"; with the Russian equivalents of the sheriffs apparently playing much the same part as in later medieval England. Collective, as well as individual, petitions figured more and more prominently as its meetings after 1622 became more occasional and power, with all its abuses, slid back into the hands of the council of magnates, the leading officials in Moscow and local governors appointed from the center.

Control of government is a burdensome task, especially when representatives are very inadequately paid, and joint co-operation to that end the most difficult of duties, above all in an enormous country with poor communications and much diversity. The lesser landowners won their principal object in 1649 when the new code of laws substantially gave legal sanction to the binding of the serfs to their masters. At that same time an alarming outbreak of uprisings in Moscow and a whole number of other towns reinforced the need for strong government. The upper clergy and the upper officials disliked the assemblies of the land. After 1653 the tsar summoned no more full assemblies. His consultations, apart from the old council of magnates and from church councils, became limited to representatives, some elected, some selected, of this or that particular class for issues specially affecting them. The full assembly of the land died, thirty-nine years after the estates-general in France, at the very time when its equivalent in Poland was entering upon its final century of subjugation of the monarchical power and of development of the *liberum veto*.

4. *The Romanov Dynasty*

The most remarkable of the actions of the assembly of the land was the settlement of the succession to the throne. In contrast with the Byzantine empire, but somewhat like the Golden Horde in which the khan had to trace his descent from Genghis Khan, Russia had always clung to the idea of one family, that of the Varangian Rurik, as the sole provider of grand-princes, first of Kiev, then of other principalities, finally of Moscow alone. Ever since the early fourteenth century Moscow had been disposed of by each grand-prince to his eldest son or, failing sons, to his next brother (with one temporary exception).

In 1598 tsar Feodor, Ivan the Terrible's only surviving son, died, without living issue or any male blood relatives, "entrusting the sceptre" after him to his wife. Although no woman had ever before occupied the throne, she was accepted, but immediately resigned and took the veil, directing the Patriarch of Moscow to arrange as to her successor. This delicate and entirely novel task he successfully accomplished by summoning an assembly of the land, which elected as tsar his ally and her brother, Boris Godunov,[1] who had been the real (and an efficient and enlightened) ruler of the land during the reign of the failing tsar Feodor. The election was

[1] He is the subject of two of the great creations of Russian art, Pushkin's tragedy (1825) and Musorgsky's opera (1873) based on it. There is a translation in *The Works of Alexander Pushkin;* ed. by A. Yarmolinsky (New York, 1936).

concerted by the partisans of Boris; yet the sanction of the assembly of the land was not a formality, but considered by Boris to be essential for his position. The election was not accompanied by the imposition of any conditions. Significantly, this new but necessary departure from family succession to the throne was officially buttressed by copious citation of Byzantine parallels.

But it was fifteen years before Muscovy could find what proved to be a dynasty. Boris's little son did not succeed him. Two pretenders (each claiming to be a son of Ivan the Terrible), one magnate (Shuisky), one Pole (Vladislav, the son and heir of king Sigismund III), succeeded or disputed each other as tsars. At last, after the recapture of Moscow from the Poles, the assembly of the land elected (1613), not a foreigner and not a magnate, but Michael Romanov, of middle noble rank, who linked up with the old dynasty through being a relative of Ivan the Terrible's very popular first wife.

Shuisky had had to swear conditions, at least to the magnates, if not to the whole land. Vladislav, a foreigner and a Catholic, had had to accept conditions from what claimed to be an assembly of the whole land. Michael, on the contrary, was elected (almost certainly) without any formal limitations by a patriot assembly which represented above all the middle ranks of the territorial levies and the freer northern townsmen and peasants, to whom the intrigues of the magnates, Polish ideas of *pacta conventa* and the license of the "robber" Cossacks were equally abhorrent, and who thought in terms of ancient custom applied to their own present needs. Michael, who was only sixteen, would certainly have to meet those needs.

Thus at this crisis in her history Russia did not follow the example of her conqueror Poland, still almost at the height of her power, but within a century to pay only too dearly for the binding limitations imposed by the nobles and country gentry upon their elected kings. "Unite with us"—said the Poles—"and you will then have freedom." "Your way is freedom for you"—said the Russians—"but for us it is unfreedom. You do not have freedom, but license . . . if the Tsar himself acts unjustly, it is his will: it is easier to suffer injury from the Tsar than from one's brother; for he is our common ruler."

Few long-lasting dynasties have started under more unpromising auspices and been later beset by such succession difficulties as the house of Romanov. It began with four minorities. There were two *coups d'état* (1682, 1689), largely decided by the attitude of the permanent Moscow garrison, the *streltsy,* and one woman as regent (1682-89), a portent for the future in a country which, with the momentary exception already mentioned of tsar Feodor's wife, had never known a woman on the throne and only one, long ago, as regent. But the succession was at least a family struggle: there was no question of going outside the Romanov family. Some play was made with the precedents of election by a national assembly (1682), but it was not more than a gathering of those in Moscow. Then in 1694 Peter the Great, who had been since 1682 nominal joint tsar with his incapable halfbrother Ivan V, at the age of twenty-two took power to himself.

Peter pondered for years over his successor; decided negatively and had his eldest son publicly condemned and then killed, as being the rallying point for opposition to his policy (1718). Finally he issued a mockery of a succession law (1722), whereby the tsar was declared to be invested with arbitrary powers to appoint whomsoever he willed. It was still more of a mockery in that he failed to nominate his own successor, though it is true that a year before his death, when he had no sons living, he had his second wife crowned as empress, who did in fact succeed him. At the very end, as he lay dying (1725), unable to speak he scrawled "Leave all to . . .," but his fingers were too weak and the name was illegible. That was the true will of Peter the Great, not the alarming schemes of foreign expansion elaborated by a French adventurer a generation later and given to the world by Napoleon as part of his propaganda for 1812.

The lack of any fixed succession and the fact that there was no direct male heir of age but a number of competing women resulted in the throne becoming the catspaw of rival groups and of Peter's new guard regiments, in which the bulk of the rank and file, as well as the officers, were drawn from the landed class. Between 1725 and 1762 four women became empresses; one boy, one baby in arms and one toper emperors. Three out of these seven sovereigns were Germans; one was a country wench from Livonia. Nothing could seem more unpromising for tsarism or more promising for a Russian version of the Polish or Swedish oligarchic constitutions.

Oligarchy there was—and for ten years (1730-40) a mainly German oligarchy—but the formal basis of the Russian empire remained "autocracy such as Your glorious and renowned predecessors had." This was the formula which won the day in the struggle over the accession of the empress Anna in 1730.

The small knot of old aristocratic families, influenced directly by the Swedish oligarchic shackling of royal power in 1720, required of Anna the acceptance of written conditions designed to perpetuate their rule. Anna, a daughter of Ivan V, had no qualms as to signing conditions, for she was by marriage duchess of Courland and accustomed to being constitutionally controlled by her Baltic German nobility. In opposition to the blood aristocracy, the service aristocracy of the generals and higher officials, a very heterogeneous group thanks to Peter's new "table of ranks" (see p. 97), suspected them of aiming at the position of the German electoral princes who "have so strengthened themselves that the Emperor now has no power, while they have become the masters." They made play with ideas of natural law and social contract and demanded the creation of a legislative body, in which they would entrench themselves.

There remained the decisive voice of the two thousand officer-gentry present in Moscow. One section of them sponsored proposals somewhat on the lines of the Polish Diet, but the great bulk, and especially the guards' officers, clung to old ways against new-fangled devices and came out for the formula already quoted, "autocracy such as Your glorious and renowned predecessors had." "God grant," a country squire wrote, "that we don't get instead of one autocratic sovereign ten powerful and despotic families." He was satisfied. The conditions originally signed by Anna were solemnly torn up.

The victorious gentry naturally required their particular grievances to be met and their privileges to be extended, and they gained all that they wanted in the course of the next generation (see pp. 133 ff.); but they were too lacking in corporate feeling and political development to appreciate the need for any kind of constitutional framework to alter the basis of government. When Catherine the Great issued her charter (1785) establishing the nobility and gentry as an "estate," it had no effect upon the political structure of the state or the legal plenitude of her power.

After 1730 nearly a century elapsed before any further specific attempt was made by the upper classes to challenge the principle of autocracy, as distinct from the person of the autocrat. (Three tsars were deposed by palace revolutions, and murdered.) The challenge, when it came, was revolutionary (December, 1825). The Decembrist rising in St. Petersburg and certain regiments in the south took the form of an eighteenth-century *coup d'état,* but it was entirely different in idea. It was led by groups of discontented guards and army officers, but they were educated through the Napoleonic wars in Western, primarily French, ideas, and they looked forward not backward; they were the first examples of that "conscience-stricken" nobility which played so notable a part in the cultural and social development of nineteenth-century Russia. The Decembrists planned a radical reconstruction of government and society; some of them on liberal and (borrowing from the American constitution) federal lines, with a strictly limited monarchy, abolition of serfdom and the guarantee of the rights of the individual; others of them on democratic republican lines but with a strong, centralized, revolutionary dictatorship. Thus they were not united in their aims. Nor did they have any backing in the country at large. They were easily, though bloodily, suppressed by the army, the great bulk of which proved loyal to Nicholas I (*cf.* p. 339).

The struggle of 1730 had settled that autocracy should not formally be limited, but there had been no attempt to define the succession to the throne. This continued to be all too uncertain until tsar Paul in 1797 issued a "fundamental law," the first appearance of the term in Russian law. It was an adaptation of the rules governing German princely families (Paul's wife was a Württemberg princess) and its essential was that the crown should pass in the direct male line. Thus at long last an orderly basis of succession was laid down, and one that was followed. Yet destiny ironically decreed that Paul himself, like his father Peter III, should be deposed, with the assent of his son Alexander I, and murdered; that his second son should renounce his right to succeed his childless brother Alexander; that his grandson, Alexander II, should be assassinated; and that his great-great-grandson, Nicholas II, should be forced to abdicate and be butchered.

So the Romanov dynasty ended; or more strictly that of Holstein-Gottorp. Since 1762 all the rulers of Russia had been descended from Catherine the Great, German on both sides, and her husband Peter III, duke of Holstein-Gottorp, German by his father, Russian by his mother (a daughter of Peter the Great). And all these rulers of Russia, save one, had married German princesses. These German connexions, which had begun with Peter the Great, helped to bring much that was valuable to Russia, but they reinforced the divorce of St. Petersburg from Moscow and the core of Russia, and imported into foreign policy interests that often made it dynastic rather than national (*cf.* pp. 385, 387-388, and 410).

5. *The Byzantine and Tatar Origins of Tsarism*

Tsarism took shape under Ivan the Great, Vasily III, and Ivan the Terrible (1462-1584), at about the same time as the concentration of power in the national monarchies of the West. The word tsar, an adaptation of the word Cæsar, was the Russian title for the Byzantine emperor and later for the khan of the Golden Horde, though it was also used unofficially of other rulers or princes. Ivan the Terrible was the first reigning tsar to be crowned as such (1547), in a coronation service based on the Byzantine model. Thereafter tsar was the invariable official title until Peter the Great substituted for it the imperial dignity (1721).

In addition, the Byzantine two-headed eagle was adopted and a fictitious but very popular Byzantine origin given to the crown jewels. Already in 1498 Ivan the Great had styled himself "Tsar-Autocrat chosen by God." Just as the Byzantine title *autokrator* was in origin the Greek equivalent of *imperator*, the leader of the army, and symbolized the fundamentally military character of New Rome, so Moscow, "the third New Rome," which was even more of a military state, very fittingly took it over, together with its additional Byzantine meaning of divinely instituted, independent supreme ruler. This latter conception was reinforced by the further title "Sovereign of All Russia," first formally adopted again by Ivan the Great after his repudiation of any subservience to the Tatars. His marriage, in 1472, to Zoe Palæologus, niece of the last Byzantine emperor, was primarily of importance for Muscovite relations with Renaissance Italy, but it also gave new forms to Ivan's court and new trappings to his sovereign power.

The Byzantine inheritance is more deeply illustrated by the prevailing teaching of the church in Russia as to the position of the lay power, from the introduction of Christianity at the very end of the tenth century. Here a word of warning must be given. Both the theory and the practice of the lay and spiritual powers in the Byzantine empire varied much in the course of its thousand years' existence. After the capture of Constantinople by the fourth crusade and the Latin empire (1204-61), the restored Byzantine empire of the Palæologi was the merest shadow of its former self. Russian acquaintance with Byzantine law and literature was not more than fairly extensive even in the fifteenth century. From one and the same passage Russians could and did draw conflicting conclusions. They never received from Constantinople a compact, thoroughly worked-out doctrine of the supremacy of the imperial power.

The idea of the prince as divinely ordained runs throughout early Russian teaching and literature. Even the tyrant, or weak prince who yields to evil counsellors, is instituted by God and must be obeyed. All the woes of the land, especially at the hands of the Tatars, are attributed to the anger of God at the sins of His people and particularly at the quarrels of the princes. Repentance, not revolt, is the task of the Christian. The idea of non-resistance to the ruler was applied also to the khan of the Golden Horde, as being ordained by God as a punishment for backsliding.

The authority of the prince in temporal matters is limited only by divine law: he is responsible only to God. In temporal matters the church has no direct part: in spiritual matters the prince is at least the guardian and protector, sometimes more: equipoise between the two powers is the ideal regularly, though not invariably, preached. The Byzantine law books known in Russia, and notably the version of Justinian's *Novellae,* enjoined Christian law as limiting the powers of the prince, but the idea of law as a norm to which the prince himself was subject was expressed in terms so general as to allow of varied interpretations and to be of little practical import.

From the fourteenth century, when the power of the new grand-princes of Moscow was being extended by any and every means, increased emphasis was given to the regular quotations from the Epistle to the Romans xiii and the first Epistle of St. Peter ii as to the paramount duty of obedience to the powers that be. From the middle of the fifteenth century the dominant elements in the church, in extolling the grand-princes of Moscow as the Tsars of All Russia, magnified and exhorted them as successors to the divinely instituted Byzantine autocracy, as requiring all honor and obedience and as wielding authority not only in all temporal matters but, with reservations, in religious matters. The grand-prince was now "the Sovereign and Autocrat of All Russia, the new

Tsar Constantine for the new city of Constantinople—Moscow. . . ."

The formula of Moscow as "the third Rome," first set out early in the sixteenth century, perhaps in part suggested by southern Slav models, was popularized for the next hundred and fifty years in a variety of forms as one of the constituents of the new nationalistic, Orthodox tsarism: "All Christian tsardoms have come to an end and have been gathered together into one tsardom of our sovereign, according to the book of the prophets, that is to say the Russian tsardom: for two Romes have fallen, but the third stands, and a fourth there will not be."

The ground for this magniloquent conception was the double collapse of the Byzantine empire, its religious betrayal of Orthodoxy at the council of Florence (1439) when the eastern and western churches were nominally reunited, and its material extinction by the capture of Constantinople by the Turks (1453). The effect of the former event will be explained in a subsequent chapter (see pp. 164 ff.). The latter was represented in Moscow not only as a punishment for acceptance of "the Latin heresy," but also as a consequence of the lack of rule in the last years of the Palæologi, when power was usurped by a council of magnates and an overmighty clergy. Ivan the Terrible himself used this closing period of the Byzantine empire as an awful warning of the necessity for unfettered autocracy. It is to be noticed that, when pressing genealogy into his service, Ivan made no use of his grandmother, Zoe Palæologus, but harked back either to his Kiev inheritance and the connexions of St. Vladimir and Vladimir Monomakh with the empire in the days of its strength, or for preference to a mythical Prus, own brother to Cæsar Augustus himself. Any stigma of subservience to Byzantium was similarly avoided by the new prominence at this time given to the old legend of St. Andrew as the apostle of the Russians.

While for Ivan the Terrible the Byzantine empire in its final stage of collapse served as a warning, the triumphant Ottoman empire could serve as an example. One of his supporters against the magnates, an experienced military man, eulogized both the justice and the severity of sultan Mohammed, the capturer of Constantinople, precisely because his rule was autocratic: "as a horse under a tsar without a curb, so is a tsardom without terror." He went on to suggest the adoption of that sultan's reforms and above all the reconstruction of the army, with particular praise for the janissaries: tsarism should be based on a good army and the masses, not on a privileged aristocracy and serfdom. Such praise of the Turks was exceptional among Russians, who as yet had little direct knowledge of them, but they had known only too well at first-hand another arbitrary and cruel, but organized and at times efficient, military despotism. In the make-up of tsarism the ideas and ritual traceable to Byzantine influence were fused with the hard fact and practice of the Tatar khans.

The degree of Tatar influence during the period of subjection to the Golden Horde has been variously judged by Russian historians, though almost all agree in ascribing to it brutalizing and degrading effects. While most give chief weight to local causes and Byzantine tradition in the growth of the power of the grand-princes of Moscow into tsarism, other writers ascribe the autocracy of the tsars to imitation, conscious or unconscious, of the Tatar despotism.

There is no doubt that the emergence of the grand princes of Moscow in the fourteenth century was closely linked up with their privileged relations with the Golden Horde, especially as the khan's tax-gatherers; and there is also no doubt as to the constant comings and goings (sometimes long sojourns) of the Russian princes to the khan's capital of Sarai on the lower Volga, where there was a Russian colony. There was intermarriage with Tatar princesses, though it seems to have been rare, much rarer than with the Polovtsy before the Mongol conquest, and except in two cases only minor princes were concerned. Certain general features of the rule of the Horde and of Tatar influence have been sketched above (pp. 28-29), where it was pointed out that it is often difficult to determine whether particular instances of borrowing by or influence on the Russians came during or before the Mongol period. The Russian Slavs had been in contact with the steppe peoples for centuries and the Mongols themselves formed only a very thin top layer in the Golden Horde. But it was under them that a governmental and a new military system was created with which the Russians had all too good cause to become acquainted, in contrast with far-away Byzantine administration.

The inscribing of the taxable population, the system of taxation by households, a new coinage and the organization of customs dues and of transport and courier services were distinctive features of the first century of Mongol rule (1240-1340). They appear in kindred forms in the Muscovy of Ivan the Great. What requires further investigation is whether, in this outlying fringe of the far-flung dominions of the Mongols, their governmental methods were made to fit somewhat similar existent Russian practice, and exactly to what extent later Muscovite practice directly inherited or adapted them. In military matters there was certainly some direct borrowing; and the state monopoly of drink, later a cornerstone of the state budget, was likewise taken from Tatar practice. Whether the khan's central administrative departments, the *divans*, were to some extent the prototypes for the Muscovite departments, the *prikazi*, or whether these developed solely from the manorial administration of the princes and court offices, is not known. Nor is it known whether the frequent Muscovite fusion of civil and military powers in the same hands, so unlike the general Byzantine practice, was a legacy from the Tatars, with whom it was regular.

In the Golden Horde the despotism of the khan depended upon his personal qualities, above all as a military leader. It was normally limited by the existence of a council of his blood relatives and leading retainers (in the khanate of Kazan also by the upper clergy), and in addition in fact by the economic and military power of the semi-independent, hereditry, big stock- and land-owners. Yet in the Golden Horde and most of the khanates that succeeded it the personal power of a khan was overriding and ubiquitous so long as he was feared, and, whether he were strong or not, most of his subjects were only too well accustomed to arbitrary caprice and despotic subjection. For one half of Ivan the Terrible's mixed forest-steppe empire, after the capture of Kazan and Astrakhan, "the White Tsar" figured as the heir of the Tatar Khan. To the European envoys penetrating sixteenth-century Muscovy it appeared as a country governed by an autocrat similar to an Asiatic despot or the Turkish sultan. "He uses his authority as much over ecclesiastics as laymen, and holds unlimited control over the lives and property of all his subjects. . . . It is a matter of doubt whether the brutality of the people has made the prince a tyrant, or whether the people themselves have become thus brutal and cruel through the tyranny of their prince." [1]

6. *The Growth and Functioning of Tsarism*

The arbitrary ruthlessness of the tsar and the servility of his subjects which so much impressed European envoys to Muscovy in the sixteenth century continued to be striking features of tsarism, but they were combined with other characteristics that were more important in the building up and functioning of tsarism as it developed in the four centuries between 1500 and 1900.

The main characteristics of tsarism may be summed up under six headings:

(i) The semi-sacrosanct personification of authority in a supreme ruler, whose power, though closely circumscribed by the weight of custom and dependence on the landed and military classes, never became explicitly limited by clearly formulated or regularly operative checks of a legal or institutional kind, and frequently was of decisive consequence.

(ii) The conception of service to the state to be enforced in some form or other, first from all land, later from

---

[1] There is a translation of Herberstein's *Notes upon Russia*, from which the above quotation is taken, by R. H. Major in Hakluyt Society Works, first series, vols. 10 and 12 (1851-52). The account of Herberstein, who went twice to Moscow on diplomatic missions, was first published in 1549.

all groups of subjects, a conception that was never fully realized in practice, though it was more and more effectively applied until the middle of the eighteenth century.

(iii) The application of this conception of service to the landed class in such a way that not only must no land go out of service, but all land must be in service, with the result that all land came to be regarded in the last resort as under some control of the tsar.

(iv) The linking up of the idea of service with that of the omnicompetence of the state, of its unlimited range of action (except, prior to Peter the Great, in regard to the church), of the state as the creator and not merely the regulator of all associations within it, other than the church.

(v) The lack of differentiation between legislative, administrative, and judicial functions and the development of a centralized bureaucracy on an exceptionally large scale, corresponding to the exceptionally wide range of state control and extent of the empire.

(vi) The paramountcy of the military needs of the state, which made the army, directly and indirectly the first concern of tsarism and intensified the use of force and arbitrary police action in government.

These six characteristics inevitably took on various hues in the course of four hundred years, and in the nineteenth century a seventh appeared—the attempt to impose uniformity in the greater part of the vast and polyglot Romanov empire. They may best be illustrated by an outline of the growth and functioning of tsarism through the central institutions of government and in its relations to the landowners.

"In our state of Muscovy the serving men of every grade serve . . . by service from land, and the peasants plow the tenth plowlands [a particular form of service on one kind of state land] and pay dues, and no one owns land for nothing." In these words an edict of the late seventeenth century summed up the great change which had been effected by the growth of the centralized Muscovite state during the preceding two hundred years. The compulsory-service state had taken the place of the congeries of competing appanage principalities which had made up northern Russia during the period of Mongol rule or overlordship (1240-1480): the military allies of the suzerain grand-prince of Moscow had become converted into the serving subjects of the All-Russian Tsar. The next chapter will show (pp. 139 ff.) how during the same period (1480-1700) serfdom was extended and transformed in such a way that it became the dominating fact in the structure of society, much as it had become in most of western Europe between 1100 and 1300. In Muscovy, however, this development of serfdom was not paralleled by a corresponding growth of political feudalism.

On the contrary, political feudalism, if it may be so called, was disrupted and finally destroyed by Ivan the Great, Vasily III, and Ivan the Terrible (1462-1584). The preceding period of subjection to the Golden Horde used to be termed by nearly all Russian historians the period of appanage Russia. It was distinguished by what may be called political feudalism, although further comparative investigation is needed before a final answer can be given to the disputed question as to how far feudalism in appanage Russia can be substantially identified with feudalism in Europe, itself varying greatly in different regions and at different times.

Appanage Russia had the equivalents of fiefs and vassalage, of commendation, homage, and fealty, of immunities and franchises; but the close tie of fief and vassalage seems to have been lacking. No feudal law books or treatises are known to have existed in Russia. Above all, the personal tie of lord and man was weakly developed as compared to the West, while the "right of departure" of a vassal from his lord was recognized to a degree and in forms which in the West seem to have been exceptional or confined to disputed or border regions.

Immunities and franchises, both judicial and fiscal, both lay and ecclesiastical, in the fourteenth and early fifteenth centuries had increased the parceling out of power and the weakness of the grand-princes, in title and by descent the shadowy heirs of the pre-Mongol grand-princes of Kiev, the descendants of Rurik and his Varangians (*cf.* p. 16). If customary practice and usurpation had been the breeding ground of the jurisdiction and rule of the minor princes and lay landowners, immunities and franchises came to be sanctioned and granted by charters from the grand-princes, and the khans of the Golden Horde as regards the church (see p. 172); and in the fifteenth century more limitations were imposed and the exclusion of the major criminal offenses from seigneurial jurisdiction became regular.

Ivan the Great (b. 1440; grand-prince 1462-1505) went a long way towards breaking down the semi-independence of the princes and other hereditary landowners and towards gathering Muscovy and northern Russia under one hand; by his reduction of Tver (Kalinin) and other principalities, in part through force, in part through negotiation, by his subjection of Novgorod and her northern colonial empire, by his military successes against Lithuania and the Kazan Tatars, and by his ending (1480) of any form of subjection to the Golden Horde.

Ivan was a man who did not take risks or challenge custom unwarily, but when he struck he struck hard, as the men of Novgorod, amongst others, had good cause to know. When they asked for terms (1477) he replied; "Our grand-princely dominion is of this wise: there is to be no assembly and no bell in our own land Novgorod, and no lieutenant; our rule is to be exercised by ourselves." And so it was. When the landowners and merchants of Novgorod conspired against him, he dispossessed four-fifths of the landowners and resorted to wholesale arrests and "removal" to central Muscovy; and he applied the same policy of forced "removal" elsewhere.

This method of dealing with dangerous elements, of whatever classes, became a regular feature of tsarism. As practiced by Ivan the Terrible with peculiar savagery on the Muscovites themselves and not merely on conquered lands, during seven years of deliberate terror (1565-72), it contributed to a major crisis. Compulsory "removal" involved confiscation of property but was usually accompanied by the new grant of lands or trading rights in whatever places those who had been expelled were resettled. Thus it was not the same as the later practice of deportation, *e.g.* to Siberia, with loss of civic rights and frequently with hard labor. It was of much importance both as a means of breaking down local resistance and of intermingling the heterogeneous elements of the rapidly expanding Muscovite empire.

In close connection with compulsory "removals" another practice became regular from about the time of Ivan the Great, that of "selection," *i.e.* voluntary or nominally voluntary recruitment of so many persons or families for all sorts of purposes or forms of service, some temporary, some permanent. In addition, compulsory levies became more and more frequent for temporary labor or defense duties, reaching their highest pitch perhaps with Peter the Great's building of his new capital and his other gigantic demands on labor.

"Selection" might involve a northern commune producing so many men or families for temporary or permanent enrollment as carpenters or transport men on "the great Siberian way." It might involve a commune producing so many men or families for enrollment on garrison duty in the expanding frontier in the wooded steppe, or for hereditary service as musketeers or Cossacks. It might involve so many craftsmen of this or that kind being moved away to one of the new Volga towns or one of the state foundries. It might involve the settlement of some hundreds of White Russian gentry, who had come over from Poland, hundreds of miles away on the Volga-Kama defense line (though in fact most of them preferred the relative comforts of Kazan to the rigors of the frontier). Illustrations could be multiplied. "Selection," though nominally voluntary, was frequently indistinguishable from compulsion. Frequently, on the other hand, neither "selection" nor force could produce what was wanted: evasion, passive resistance, and open refusal were regular. None the less, the Muscovite state persisted in trying to meet its needs, especially its military and colonizing needs, by "selection" in one form or another, coupled with various tax exemptions and advances.

The methods and general lines of Ivan the Great's policy were followed by his son Vasily III (1505-33), and his grandson Ivan the Terrible (1533-84), whose personality and reign brought the struggle against political feudalism as represented by the landed aristocracy to its final crisis.

The lay landed aristocracy in the fifteenth century had consisted of appanage princes (the lesser descendants of the lines of Rurik and of the founder of the grand-duchy of Lithuania) and of some non-titled territorial magnates. They exercised wide governmental powers within their hereditary estates, often very large in extent but worked as a number of small, separate manors. They owed service to the grand-princes of Moscow or other princes either as a result of land grants from them or on terms of personal contract. In the latter case they did not consider themselves "servants" and exercised the "right of departure" without losing their hereditary estates. As a result of Ivan the Great's consolidation of power the "right of departure" gradually became extinguished, largely because after about 1500 the only alternative to service under the grand-prince of Moscow was service under his great rival the grand-duke of Lithuania, who was also the king of Poland, and this in the sixteenth century became regarded as treason and involved confiscation of all lands.

By the middle of that century it was impossible to be a hereditary landowner without owing service to Moscow, and it was impossible to leave service without losing one's hereditary estates. The nature and amount of service, however, had been very fluctuating and uncertain until in 1556 Ivan the Terrible systematized the military service due from the aristocracy in dependence on the amount of their land.

This measure, which was only one of a great series of reforms undertaken between 1549 and 1556 in state and church alike, was bound up with Ivan's reorganization of the army and the new class of middling and lesser landowners, "men of service" paid by temporary grants of land so long as they were in service. This class had been growing up during the previous hundred years, mainly owing to the expansion of Muscovy against Lithuania and the Tatars, which heavily increased the military as well as other requirements of the state and rendered largely obsolete the undisciplined, ill-armed levies of the old aristocracy.

Ivan the Terrible developed the new kind of service fief on a large scale, both to meet his military needs and his economic and colonizing needs, though the two objects were not easily compatible. He concentrated, for instance, a picked body of the new officer fief-holders around Moscow and issued detailed regulations as to their obligations and their rights—somewhat analogous to knight service in medieval England. The service fiefs, though at first they were very shifting and changed hands frequently, became gradually regarded as hereditary and virtually the full property of their holders. The process of their assimilation to allodial lands, *i.e.* those in full private ownership, went on throughout the seventeenth century, until it was completed by an edict of Peter the Great (1714) making the two kinds of land identical in law.

Owing to the differences in wealth, social status, and traditions among the middling and lesser landowners holding service fiefs and between them and the aristocratic magnates, the landed class in Muscovy was deeply divided within itself, and its different groupings did not succeed, as in Poland or medieval Aragon, in consolidating any institutional bulwarks against the principle of autocracy. There were three possible such bulwarks, the council of magnates, the assembly of the land, and the code of precedence.

The code of precedence was an elaborate, officially recognized code, whereby appointments to the higher commands and offices were controlled by the relative positions of the holders to each other as calculated by genealogical tables and service precedents in the past. It applied only to the old princely families and certain others, and it was the creation of custom and tradition, not of public law, so that the state only regulated, as far as it could, its application. It caused great difficulties, especially in military affairs (on occasion it had to be circumvented or even suspended), and it was not until 1682 that it was solemnly abolished; but it was an ineffectual check on the power of the tsar because its primary purpose was to protect the position of each great family against the rival great families rather than to protect their combined position against the tsar.

The second possible check, the assembly of the land, failed to develop into a permanent institution, as has been seen earlier (see pp. 71 ff.). The third check, the council of magnates, had a far longer history and was of greater consequence.

The council of magnates, accustomed to regard themselves and be accepted as the hereditary ruling families, had been from of old the traditional body of counsellors of the grand-princes. By the sixteenth century it was almost entirely composed of the princes, now subject to Moscow alone, and of certain other great landed families. Ivan the Terrible, after bitter experience in his minority (1533-47), saw the most serious obstacle to his own power in this aristocracy, which remained a powerful force even though its earlier semi-independence had been broken down during the two previous reigns. The underlying constitutional issue in the struggle that followed was whether the council of magnates could transform itself from a body based on long practiced but indefinite custom into a crystallized institution expressly limiting the freedom of action of the tsar. The struggle left its mark in the most famous memorial of Russian sixteenth-century literature, the polemic between Ivan and prince Kurbsky,[1] and reached its climax in seven years of monomaniac suspicion and revolting excesses on the part of Ivan (1565-72).

Ivan the Terrible (b. 1530, reigned from 1533, ruled 1547-84, seven times married) is, with one exception, the most debated figure among the twenty-three sovereigns of Russia. All recognize his reign to be of the greatest conse-

---

[1] There is a German, but no English, translation by K. Stählin (Leipzig; 1921).

quence, both externally and internally, and the latter half of it to be bloodily seared by his personality; but there agreement ends. The divergence of opinion on him is largely due to insufficient evidence. "Sharp of wits," an eager controversialist with "an especial bitterness in remembrance of Holy Writ," ungovernable in temper (he killed his eldest son with his own hand), in his later years more cruel even than his cruel contemporaries, Ivan appeared to possess a dual personality, belying the first ten years of his rule (1547-58) when the resounding conquest of Kazan and Astrakhan and the all-round reform of state and church seemed to stamp him with the seal of greatness.

Thereafter, in the words of one contemporary chronicler, "there did sweep upon the Tsar as it were a terrible tempest, which set him beside himself and disturbed the peace of his goodly heart. In some manner which I wot not it turned his mind, with all its plenitude of wisdom, into the nature of a wild beast, and he made sedition in his own state." These last words reflect the attitude of his opponents, the magnates, at whom he struck so savagely. Much misery there was indeed among all his subjects up and down divided and harried Muscovy, but the lesser folk could scarcely have looked upon the tsar with the eyes of the magnates. It is symptomatic that one of the king of Poland's secretaries, closely connected with the last years of the Livonian war, should express his surprise that "for all such cruelty of his there could exist a singular and incredible love of the people towards him, which is the faith of the same toward their princes . . . and they showed unbelievable steadfastness in the defense of fortresses." It is symptomatic again that for the next century Ivan lived in the memory of his countrymen far less as the Terrible than as the Conqueror, the subjugator of Kazan, the epitome of the deep, popular resurgence against the Tatars. This glorification of Ivan was not dimmed by his failure to win his way to the Baltic as he had to the Caspian: the Livonian war left no such deep mark on the Russian people, for whom the touchstone was the Volga and the steppe, Asia not Europe.

Although "Bloudinesse is a slippery foundation of Greatnesse," Ivan's reign of terror, known as the period of the *oprichnina,* was not solely the eruption of personal vindictiveness and aberration, but was in part a definite administrative and political policy; and it had great social and economic consequences. He did succeed to a large extent in smashing the power of the old aristocrats, mainly by severing them from their historic local roots in this and that region and by impoverishing them. One result was the greater dispersal and the rapid changing of hands of the estates of the aristocracy, and in particular the great subdivision of the land round Moscow itself. Unlike the magnates in Lithuania and Poland, hardly any of their equivalents in Muscovy henceforward held their lands in such solid blocks as might form compact centers of resistance or develop into new principalities.

In the century following Ivan the Terrible a new aristocracy grew up, merging with the remnants of the old, but it never regained such dominance as before and it comprised only about sixty families. The magnates continued to be much divided by family rivalries, and they failed to unite and show themselves the indispensable leaders of national unity during the prolonged crisis of the Time of Troubles.

Similarly, the council of magnates did indeed exercise decisive weight in government during much of the seventeenth century; it became more systematized in its working, particularly through the creation of a standing committee, and its members were recognized in some legislative formulæ as collaborators with the tsar in the exercise of supreme power. Yet the council did not perpetuate itself as a constitutional check upon him. Its members came to be drawn no longer so predominantly from the magnates. New men were appearing in it and wielding more and more influence; families personally connected with the tsar, provincial gentry entering the bureaucracy, who in the last half of the century supplied a handful of men of a new stamp and of great ability, with a marked westernizing tendency. The increasing complexity of the mechanism of government and military needs favored the power of the working heads of the main departments and led to the creation from the tsar's chancellery of the department of secret affairs (1655), which went far to undermine the practical importance of the council of magnates. By the late seventeenth century lineage and blood were no longer decisive; office was by then almost separated from rank and genealogical computations; as has been mentioned above, the old code of precedence was officially discarded in 1682. The council of magnates dwindled away into an indeterminate species of ministerial council. The way was open for Peter the Great, "the Tsar-Reformer" (b. 1672, reigned from 1682, ruled 1694-1725).

The impact of Peter the Great upon Muscovy was like that of a peasant hitting his horse with his fist. Muscovy bore many of the marks permanently, and henceforward she became known as Russia. Yet his reforms, for all their importance, did not create a new form of state: they were to a large extent the very rapid and energetic extension of ideas and practices already to be found in the generation before him. The old and the new continued to live on, in part conflicting, in part coalescing. Tsarism in his lifetime received a new stamp owing to his wholly exceptional character and abilities, but its functioning remained as before dependent upon different sections of the landed class and the machinery of government. Peter did not introduce the idea of the service state; he pushed it to extremes, enforced compulsory service in the army, navy, and government on the landowners, and himself set the example as the first servant of the state. He wrote of himself with full justification: "I have not spared and I do not spare my life for my fatherland and people."

Peter was repellent in his brutality, coarseness, and utter disregard of human life; but he was mightily propellent, through his ever-flaming energy and will-power, his insatiable curiosity and love of experiment, his refusal to accept any defeat and his capacity to launch, however crudely and overhastily at first, great schemes on an immense, however wasteful, scale. From earliest childhood his overriding personal interest was the art of war, by sea as well as land; but he understood it in the widest sense as involving the full utilization of the human and material resources of his country. He was at war for twenty-eight consecutive years, from 1695. He began when he was twenty-four; when he finally had peace he was fifty-two and had little more than a year to live.

Almost all Peter's reforms were born of military and naval requirements. Russia must be westernized in order to ensure the "two necessary things in government, namely order and defense." His task was, again as he himself put it, to convert his subjects from "beasts into human beings," from "children into adults." His strongest modern critics allow that he was inspired by devotion to Russia not by personal ambition, and that he aimed at inculcating by example and precept rational ideas of citizenship in terms of efficient, and therefore educated, service to the state, in contrast with blind service to a sacrosanct ruler throned far away on high in the hallowed veneration of Muscovite ceremonial.

His reforms until about 1715 were effected piecemeal, chaotically and (as he himself admitted) far too hastily, in dependence on the urgent pressure of the moment. He was constantly scrapping or remodeling this or that portion of his own handiwork in frantic search for more recruits, more labor, more revenue, more munitions. In his last dozen years, when war was less onerous and his contacts with the West were closer, the peremptory edicts, often conflicting with each other, often none too clear for all their laconic bluntness, gave way to systematic, carefully elaborated legislation that remolded state and church alike. His brutal violence, the enormous demands that he exacted and his external flouting of national ways and prejudices supplied fertile ground for opposition. He had to crush in blood four serious risings, and he condemned to death his son and heir, Alexis, on the ground of his being the ringleader of reaction (1718). In actuality Alexis was a passive creature who was only hoping for his father's death in terrified fear of his own. The opposition was leaderless; and as well it was too heterogeneous; almost all interests in Russia were divided between supporters and opponents of Peter.

He aimed at transforming tsarism into a European kind

of absolute monarchy, and to a considerable extent he succeeded. Russia was never the same again, even though the pace was too hot and there was regress after his death. He declared himself to be "an absolute monarch who does not have to answer for any of his actions to anyone in the world; but he has power and authority for the purpose of governing his states and lands according to his will and wise decision, as a Christian sovereign." This version of enlightened despotism, typically enough, appeared in Peter's new code for the army (1716). The creation of a national standing army on Western models was one of the most fundamental of his legacies, and the links of tsarism with military power and the military spirit were henceforth knitted even more closely than before. One external sign is significant. Peter himself almost always appeared as a soldier or sailor (when not dressed as a mechanic), and all succeeding emperors did likewise: his predecessors (when not hunting) had usually appeared in hieratic pomp, half tsar, half high-priest.

No tsar has made such a lasting impression on Russia as Peter, whether in his works or in his personality. He was an unheard-of tsar—for some no tsar at all, but Antichrist (see pp. 181-182). He brought the tsar to earth and entwined himself in the hopes and fears and groans and memories of his subjects as a dark and terrible force, rooting up the past, putting to rout the Swedes; as a ruler such as they had never conceived before, to be seen throughout the length and breadth of the land, immense in stature, with his tireless stride that was more of a run and his huge calloused hands of which he was so proud; a ruler who went into battle as a bombardier, who wielded an ax as well as any of his subjects, who could kill a man with a single blow of his fist—and on occasion did. The Russian people have never forgotten him. "That was a Tsar— what a Tsar! He didn't eat his grub for nothing: he worked harder than one of us." Such was the tribute of a peasant who had been with Peter and shared his sweat. He gave all his powerful mind and powerful body to Russia: he bestrode her implacably and spurred her too fast; but it was to high purpose. He made Russia conscious of great destiny, and ever since Europe and Asia have had to reckon with her.

> "Ah, lord of doom
> And potentate, 'twas thus, appearing
> Above the void, and in thy hold
> A curb of iron, thou sat'st of old
> O'er Russia, on her haunches rearing." [1]

During the half-century following Peter's death (1725) the landed class reacted strongly and successfully against his conscription of them, and against his extremely unpopular edict (1714) substituting for division of estates by will bequeathal to one son or heir only (abolished 1731). What most of the landed class wanted was not direct political control of government, but full power in their estates over their serfs and a privileged position for themselves: under Catherine the Great they secured their full desires in her charter of 1785, establishing them as an "estate" (see pp. 77 and 133 ff.).

On the other hand, they could not undo the lasting effects of Peter's "table of ranks" (1722). By this long-pondered edict, carefully worked out on foreign (chiefly Danish and Prussian) models, status and, in effect, new landed wealth were made dependent on a man's position in the ladder of state service which was divided into fourteen military and naval rungs and fourteen parallel civilian rungs. Money salaries were fixed for each rung. Just as Peter himself chose many of his most trusted advisers or executants from "ill-born persons"— many of them foreigners—on the ground of their capacities and personal loyalty to him, so personal capacity, not family connections or wealth, was to be the touchstone for advancement in the service of the state, and all were to start their careers from the bottom rung. Inevitably in fact, blood, money, and favoritism continued to be very powerful influences, but the door had been opened and was never thereafter fully closed to the admission of persons of middling or

---

[1] Pushkin, *The Bronze Horseman* (1833; translated by Professor Oliver Elton in his *Verse from Pushkin*, London, 1935), in part inspired by Falconet's imperious equestrian statue of Peter (1775).

humble position to the officer class in the army, navy, and civil service, and thereby to their admission to the privileged, hereditary class of serf-owners.

The "table of ranks" and Peter's new "colleges" transformed the old Muscovite bureaucracy, which had been haphazardly growing into an indispensable instrument in the working of tsarism. Already by the mid-seventeenth century there were thirty-six departments of one kind and another, headed by about eighty "secretaries," variously recruited but mainly from the middling "men of service," Moscow and provincial landowners. Pay was partly by land grants, partly by fees; corruption was already a byword. The departments, enmeshed in formulæ and tradition, ground very slowly, and their functions were not delimited on any one principle: some dealt with certain territorial areas, some with certain classes of persons, others with certain categories of subject (*e.g.* particular kinds of military service, foreign affairs).

Simplification and concentration were taking place before Peter, but it was he who transformed this jungle by converting the more important of the old departments into eight "colleges" and adding two new ones (marine and mines and manufactures). The "colleges," adapted from Western models, were intended by Peter to rationalize the division of labor, above all as regards finance and the army, and to sweep away the caprice and delays of the old departments by placing at the head of each a small board which was responsible, by majority vote, for all decisions. In fact the "colleges," though they did represent an improvement, failed to realize the impossibly high hopes placed on them by Peter. In the course of the eighteenth century they underwent numerous transformations; the "colleges" of war, navy, and foreign affairs developed into more or less independent powers; under Catherine the Great the collegiate principle became increasingly abandoned, and it was finally discarded in Alexander I's great reorganization of the central administration.

The third major reform in government effected by Peter the Great was his creation of the senate (1711). Originally composed of nine senators and entrusted with virtually full governmental powers during Peter's frequent absences in the field or abroad, it was later shaped by him to act as a kind of "ministry of ministries," controlling and directing the administration (especially in finance), the judiciary, and the provincial governors. Its members, always appointed by the sovereign, increased in numbers and it developed a very large secretariat. Like the new standing army, the fleet, the "table of ranks," the "colleges," the synod (see p. 184), the poll tax and internal passports (see pp. 130 and 144-145), the senate was a legacy of Peter which succeeding generations modified or developed, but did not destroy. It lasted indeed to the very end, till 1917: supplanted by Peter's immediate successors; restored as the main center of government by his daughter, the empress Elizabeth (1741-61); reconstituted with reduced powers by Catherine the Great; then reorganized by Alexander I (1803, 1811) on lines which it retained in general throughout its second century as the final judicial and administrative authority for the empire.

The recasting of the senate by Alexander I (b. 1777; reigned 1801-25) was part of his general reorganization of the central government, which included as well the setting up of the council of state (1810) and the replacement of the "colleges" by ministries (1802, 1811). To the council of state he entrusted the task of preparing legislation, a task undertaken in the previous hundred years in part by the senate, in part by the "colleges," in part by special commissions. The council of state had no representative element in it, but was simply another cog in the bureaucratic machine, being composed of the emperor's nominees, varying from thirty-five to sixty persons, with a large subordinate staff. It did not have the right of initiating legislative proposals; its recommendations were purely advisory; and the emperors had no qualms either about acting upon the minority opinion or about promulgating decrees without consultation with it. Nevertheless the council did much necessary and efficient work, and it continued in existence until the 1905 Revolution, when it was transformed into the second chamber of the new parliament (see p. 60).

Alexander's third great reform involved the definitive conversion of the "colleges" into ministerial departments, each headed by one minister, appointed by and solely responsible to the tsar, with the key-right of personal report to him. The organization and procedure of each department were governed by revised and thorough regulations. At the same time a committee of ministers was instituted to secure co-ordination. This committee, however, was to function on the Napoleonic rather than on the English model, which had earlier found favor in Alexander's inner circle of advisers. The ministers did not form a ministry: they were not collectively responsible, and they often had widely divergent or even radically opposed views. Thus the committee of ministers was a very weak means of co-ordinating policy, and in this respect was usually of secondary importance. After the creation of the Duma, in 1906, the committee, reconstituted as the council, of ministers was of far more consequence, and Stolypin as its president (1906-11) wielded something like the powers of a prime minister, thanks to his forceful personality. Yet it remained to the end in essence a collection of individual heads of departments, each responsible separately to the tsar, not to the Duma, before which they could appear but of which they were not members.

Questions of high policy were decided in the nineteenth century in fundamentally the same way as in the eighteenth, after the death of Peter the Great—that is to say, not by any regularized procedure or definite body, but by shifting procedures and by the interplay of various bodies and various favorites or outstanding persons revolving round a formally supreme sovereign, whose sanction, whether nominal or not, had to be obtained by means that varied with the personal characteristics of this or that sovereign.

Thus, in the eighteenth century, directing power for the most part ebbed and flowed between the inmost council (whether it went under the name of the supreme secret council, the imperial cabinet, the conference of ministers, or the state council), the senate headed by the procurator-general (in the end a combination of minister of justice, finance, and interior), and the colleges of war, navy, and foreign affairs. In the nineteenth century directing power was disputed between the chief ministries (especially army, interior, and finance), the imperial chancellery *ad hoc* imperial councils, and the viceregal governors-general (nearly always military men) in Poland, New Russia, Transcaucasia, and Asia. Even at the end of the nineteenth century it could be said without much exaggeration that "autocracy" or "tsarism" was "an irresponsible federation of independent departments, whose relations with each other were not always friendly, or even neutral, and sometimes partaking of the character of almost open hostility."

Partly in order to control the regular bureaucracy, partly in order to provide flexibility in place of its rigidity and narrowness, partly as the result of personal idiosyncrasies, most of the sovereigns from Peter the Great onwards made frequent use of specially constituted committees for this or that particular purpose or of trusted individuals (under Alexander I and Nicholas I particularly their generals-adjutant), armed with special powers, whether only of report or negotiation or of decision and executive action. This practice, employed for foreign as well as internal affairs, of going outside the ordinary machinery of government, had its advantages and was to some extent inevitable, but it often added yet another element of confusion and arbitrariness.

The Russian bureaucracy, large in the eighteenth century and growing ever larger in the nineteenth, was recruited mainly but by no means solely from Russians (*cf.* pp. 330-331). It played an indispensable part in holding together the vast, multi-national empire in its cumbrous tentacular net (*cf.* p. 62), even though both at the center and in the provinces there was much red tape and corruption, combined with much inefficiency, secrecy, arbitrariness, and too often brutality. But the reforms effected by Catherine the Great in provincial government and by Alexander I at the center bore some fruit, especially in the better standard of education required of the upper officials. Again, the reforms of Alexander II in the eighteen-sixties, particularly the introduction of the new provincial councils (see p. 69) and law courts, brought real improvement. It remained true, however, that the ministry of the interior and the provincial governors continued to be dominating influences, and that over-centralization and bureaucratic control of local and unofficial bodies were essential evils in Russian life right down to the 1917 Revolution.

The reorganization of the central administration (1802-11) effected under Alexander I had been mainly due to Speransky (b. 1772, d. 1839), the most methodical and constructive of Russian reformers, like the great scientist Pavlov one of the most outstanding Russian laymen to be the son of a country priest. Only a small part, however, of his comprehensive scheme of constitutional, financial, and administrative reform was put into effect. In particular his project for representative central and local elected assemblies was pigeonholed, and his efforts to delimit the legislative, administrative, and judicial functions of the various organs of government were successful only to a very limited degree.

Speransky was right in laying special emphasis on the necessity for some such separation of powers. In all countries the line between legislative, administrative, and judicial functions is difficult enough to draw, but in no country has the failure to draw such a line been responsible for more confusion, tyranny, and irresponsibility than in Russia. The overriding claims of the state as against the individual had always obstructed or ridden roughshod over civil, let alone political, liberties, and officials had always been to a greater or lesser extent privileged persons. Despite the attempts of Peter the Great, Catherine the Great, and Speransky the courts continued to be confounded with or subservient to the bureaucracy until the great legal reforms of 1864. Both courts and procedure, "the mere recollection of which makes one's hair stand on end and one's blood freeze," had been based on antiquated European models. They were characterized by extreme complexity, endless references to higher courts, great venality and great delays, secrecy and inquisitorial methods, reliance solely on written depositions, and almost total lack of adequate redress against officials.

The reforms of 1864, elaborately and admirably prepared, swept away the old system and replaced it by an original combination of French and English practice. A simple and effective series of new courts was set up; judges were made virtually irremovable; elected justices of the peace, somewhat on the English model, were set up in the country districts. Oral evidence and trial by jury for criminal and certain other cases (including even for a time political trials) were introduced. Above all, administrative and judicial functions, with certain exceptions, were no longer to be performed by one and the same body of persons, and all proceedings were to be held in public. These judicial reforms were a very remarkable achievement and had very beneficial consequences, and they resulted in the rapid growth of an exceptionally capable legal profession.

On the other hand, like the other reforms of the sixties, they soon suffered from the general effect of political reaction (*cf.* p. 69). Any cases "the public pleading of which might excite public opinion" were to be held *in camera,* should the authorities so decide (1881), while the jurisdiction of the courts in anything of a political nature was almost nullified by the powers of the police to take independent and secret action. Further, during the last fifty years of tsarism, large parts of the empire were frequently being governed under special régimes of security, which meant the partial or complete supplanting of the ordinary courts and authorities by the provincial governors armed with special powers, by the police, and in the last resort by military tribunals.

The rule of the police in the functioning of tsarism had become even more far-reaching under Nicholas I (b. 1796; reigned 1825-55) than previously, important though it had been ever since the mid-seventeenth century. Nicholas, who was faced on his accession by the Decembrist rising (see pp. 76-77), reconstituted and greatly extended the secret police under what soon became so notorious as the third section of the imperial chancellery. Russian autocracy for contemporaries of the second quarter of the nineteenth century, both at home and abroad, was "the police state" *par excellence.* Nicholas was not only "the gendarme of Europe," but much more the gendarme of his own empire. He ruled it as a colonel his regiment and a paternalistic landowner his estates, yet toiling at mountains of reports, with the same kind of assiduity as Philip II of Spain, whether they dealt with great questions of state or individual personal details. From his time onwards the police and the gendarmerie, though subsequently undergoing various changes in composition and powers, remained the chief arm of tsarism in its efforts to stamp out, curb, or canalize anything that was regarded as politically dangerous, and one of the chief means of supplying the tsar with information as to the state of opinion in the country and in addition, particularly under Nicholas I, as to the malpractices of his own servants.

Both the third section itself and the rest of the imperial chancellery, as reconstructed by Nicholas, were designed in part to control the regular bureaucracy and to prevent the power of the autocrat from being helplessly dissipated through the multitudinous routine channels of the ordinary mechanism of government. His corps of gendarmes were instructed that one of their principal tasks was to break through the official wall shutting off the tsar from the mass of his subjects and to encourage the idea that through the police "the voice of each citizen can reach the throne of the tsar." Nicholas, who himself looked every inch a tsar, could appear in the rôle of "father of his people" to great effect, but his conception of the rôle of the police had the fatal consequence of increasing both the rivalry between it and other organs of government and the use of denunciation and espionage. The employment of agents-provocateurs by the police among the revolutionary groups, and in a different form among the trade unions, went to its furthest lengths under Nicholas II; as shown most notoriously in the public (and in part official) revelations made in 1909 as to the career of Azev, at one and the same time secret service agent and terrorist conspirator, who, apart from other assassinations, was deeply involved in the murders of two ministers and the governor-general of Moscow, the tsar's uncle.[1]

The great development of organized police rule in the last hundred years was paralleled by a new characteristic of tsarism, the policy of uniformity. The enormous extension of the empire in the century preceding 1815 involved in large part a new kind of acquisition, namely that of long-settled lands previously belonging to European states, Sweden and Poland, with very different customs and methods of government from those of Russia, with a different religion (Lutheran or Catholic), with a more advanced upper-class culture, and for the most part with a non-Russian population (the Baltic provinces, 1721; the partitioned Polish lands, 1772, 1793, 1795; Finland, 1721, 1743, 1809; "Congress Poland," 1815). This raised the great question whether the new acquisitions should be governed on the Russian model or in accordance with their local institutions, laws, and customs.

Catherine the Great acted on a new policy which she described as being directed "as imperceptibly as possible towards russification," but this was not followed by Paul and Alexander, despite the acuteness of the Polish question (see pp. 202-203), either on the west or to the south in Bessarabia (1812) and Georgia (1801). Local autonomies were, in general, respected or restored. In the Baltic provinces the German nobility and burghers of the towns succeeded in securing the reconfirmation of nearly all their old privileges granted by Peter the Great and his immediate successors. Thereby they kept their own institutions, laws, language, and religion and in effect controlled the government of the provinces. Finland, when it was conquered from Sweden in 1809, was made into a separate grand-duchy almost entirely distinct from the rest of the empire and was governed under its own constitution, laws, and tariff. The same held true at first

[1] Azev appears as Doctor Berg in *What Never Happened* (1912; English translation, 1919), the semi-autobiographical novel by the terrorist and social-revolutionary leader Boris Savinkov, writing under the name of V. Ropshin. This and his still more powerful earlier novel *The Pale Horse* (1909; English translation, 1917) are very remarkable both as works of literature and as studies of terrorism and the 1905 Revolution.

of Alexander's Polish kingdom, the "Congress Poland" of 1815.

A century later, by the time of the 1905 Revolution, the situation was entirely different. Local rights or privileges and customs had been canceled, effaced, or attacked; uniformity and russification were the watchwords; the Russian language was being made compulsory. The reversal had begun under Nicholas I, with his anti-Polish policy in "the western lands" and "Congress Poland," intensified after the 1830 revolt, when an end was made of the Polish constitution, and again after the 1863 revolt (see pp. 207-209). A campaign followed against the Uniat Church and the Ukrainian national cultural movement (see pp. 208, 220). Under Alexander III (b. 1845, reigned 1881-94) the policy of extending Russian law, administration, police methods, and Orthodoxy came into its own. The position of the Germans in the Baltic provinces was directly challenged, and in 1899 Nicholas II opened an attack upon the exceptional position of Finland and her diet, an attack that was only temporarily suspended by the 1905 Revolution. The chief result of this drive towards centralizing uniformity was that in 1905, and still more in 1917, russianization was added to the other counts against tsarism by all the non-Russians of the empire and by Russian liberal and revolutionary opinion. "Great Russian chauvinism" was not, however, merely a creation of the tsarist government that could disappear at a stroke in 1917: it had popular, if unsavory or distorted roots, and for many years after the Revolution its legacy was one of the main obstacles in the rebuilding of the Soviet peoples in the Union (*cf.* pp. 57 and 223).

The last of the characteristics of tsarism that have been singled out in this section is the range of state action, the idea of the omnicompetence of the state and of the derivative character of all other associations, save the church. Even the church was from the sixteenth century onwards so closely identified with the tsar that it could be recast by Peter the Great without any violent struggle in such a way that there after it became to a large extent yet another arm of the lay power (see pp. 182 ff.).

During the two centuries before Peter the growth of the compulsory service state had involved a growth in the effectiveness and range of state intervention, even though the rule of custom remained a very strong rival and even though, as will be seen in the next chapter, the largest single class in the country, the bonded serfs of the landowners, was becoming in effect handed over to the rule of their masters with less and less control from the state. In the seventeenth century the main functions of government comprised not only defense, foreign affairs, justice, internal order, and currency, but colonization, communications, ransom of prisoners, foreign trade and important sections of internal trade, in addition to a medley of lesser functions. Increasing, though spasmodic, attention was also being given to the development by the state of new sources of production, especially in connection with the army. Tsar Alexis (b. 1629; reigned 1645-76), with his enormous properties, was himself in his later years the largest single producer and trader in his realm. The confusion of the tsar's private and public character aided the growth of the conception of the state as the director of the economic life of the country, which was reinforced by the fact that the expanses of Siberia and the Far North were almost entirely state lands. In the same century the numerous government monopolies (*e.g.* of furs, salt, alcohol, potash), whether they were directly operated by the government or were farmed out, further accustomed men to state control of production and trade.

Under Peter the Great state economic control was vastly extended, partly in continuation of previous practice, partly as a direct result of his acquaintance with Western mercantilism. It was almost solely concentrated on the development of production to meet the needs of his reconstituted and much larger army and his entirely new fleet. The very title of his new "college of mines and manufactures" indicates clearly enough the extended scope of state action. Most of his new state factories and mines were soon handed over to private companies or individuals (at any rate for some time), but they and the other large-scale undertakings that now developed in Russia were dependent on treasury grants, government control, and the vagaries of the empresses and their favorites. It is typical of Peter that he pumped capital into industry, in his own words, "not by offers only, but by compulsion," looking upon it as a form of state service, and that he organized new forms of compulsory serf labor for the munitioning of his armies and fleets. The close connections of the state and heavy industry were never lost. It is true that under Catherine the Great (b. 1729; reigned 1762-96) there was a reaction against state monopolies and direct state action in the economic field, chiefly owing to the growing interest of the landed gentry in local industries and trade, but throughout the nineteenth century most of the more important branches of industry continued to be, directly or indirectly, closely tied to the state.

Under Peter the Great communications and public works were developed by the state on a wholly new scale, for instance canals and the building of St. Petersburg, with a corresponding increase of forced labor; and for the first time lay education was directly undertaken by the state. It was on a very small scale, severely utilitarian, and crudely carried out, but it was not originally on a class basis and it was of great importance that lay education, hitherto scarcely at all developed and unrecognized as a national task, substantially owed its origin to the sovereign. Similarly, in an allied sphere, the newspaper in Russia owed its origin to the direct action of Peter, and the development of the periodical to that of Catherine. The impress was never lost; thereafter education was very closely controlled by the state, usually acting in combination with the church.

If we compare the Russia of Alexander I with that of Peter the Great there is no fundamental change in the functions of the state, but they are being carried out on a larger scale and by different means, and for instance in education in a quite different spirit. In one field, however, the state has virtually abdicated direct control: the landowners' serfs have been for most purposes handed over to the rule of their masters (see pp. 132-137, 143-144). In another field, that of the censorship, state control has changed in kind.

Printing had been introduced into Muscovy in the mid-sixteenth century from eastern Poland, but it remained little developed and almost completely a preserve of the church until Peter the Great. Even then only 918 books, apart from church service books, were published in Russia in the first half of the eighteenth century. In the second half the number leapt up to 8595, and at the same time the importation of foreign books enormously increased. Previously, the question of censorship in any modern form did not arise; it had been a matter of prohibitions and confiscations, usually enforced by the ecclesiastical authorities. The outbreak of the French Revolution, coupled with the new scale of book production and import, brought an immediate change. Henceforward the state, in conjunction with the church, devoted itself to the control of all reading matter.

After a dozen years of wholesale, erratic suppression under Catherine the Great and Paul, Alexander I instituted (1804) a regularly organized preventive censorship, *i.e.* all publications, both Russian and foreign, had to pass the censors before being put on sale. His system was at first worked in a liberal spirit but was succeeded by much more severe and very harshly administered regulations under Nicholas I, which culminated after the 1848 revolutions in an almost complete gag. The effect on Russian social and political thought and activities and on literature was profound, even though the reign of Nicholas (1825-55) saw the publication of the greatest works of Pushkin and Lermontov and all of Gogol.

The decade of the great reforms (1856-67) under Alexander II brought first a fluctuating relaxation in the censorship, then in 1865 the supersession of the preventive by the "punitive" censorship for Russian books and the press in St. Petersburg and Moscow, *i.e.* fines, suspension, confiscation and other measures taken after publication. These new regulations, soon amended to the detriment of the press, governed the censorship down to the 1905 Revolution, when for a time it became quite impossible to enforce any regulations at all, though afterwards they were revived in a much modified form.

Freedom of the press in some form had been demanded more vociferously than anything else in the earlier years of Alexander II, yet none of his reforms gave so little satisfaction, however great the contrast remained with "the plague zone" of Nicholas I. During the forty years following 1865, while the publication of books and literary and learned periodicals was indeed relatively free, foreign books were subject to the most capricious exclusion (*e.g.* Marx's *Capital* was allowed, but not translations of Hobbes's *Leviathan* or Spinoza); the press in the two capitals was closely confined and that in the provinces completely muzzled; and it was impossible for any cheap political press to grow up legally.

On the other hand, despite the arbitrariness and narrowness of the censorship, Russia did now have at any rate something of a political press, whereas prior to Alexander II she had not; and in questions of foreign affairs, for various reasons, considerable latitude was in fact allowed. In 1863 Russia for the first time had experience of a press campaign, led by the redoubtable journalist Katkov, against the Polish revolt and threats of intervention by France and England. Similar nationalist press outbursts could not be prevented during the Balkan crisis of 1876-78 and the Bulgarian crisis of 1886-87, when Katkov, thanks to his privileged relations with Alexander III, reached the summit of his, then anti-Austrian and anti-German, influence.

One reason for such precarious freedom of expression as there was lay in the conflicts between different ministries and the various censorship authorities. This division of views at the top had a further important result. While the state was thus hampered in preventing or canalizing the expression of opinion, it also failed to pursue any consistent positive policy of propaganda. Tsarist control of opinion was essentially negative, aiming through the censorship at prevention; it was very weak in positive means of propagating opinion, though as a result of the 1905 Revolution increased efforts were made in this direction, chiefly along such noxiously reactionary lines as "the black hundreds" or anti-Semitism.

If we compare the Russia of Nicholas II (b. 1868; reigned 1894-1917) with that of Alexander I, there is again no fundamental change in the functions of the state, but again their scope has been greatly increased and they are being carried out by much more elaborate means. Apart from the field of education, this is seen most notably in the results of the emancipation of the serfs (1861) and the industrial and financial revolution of the same period.

As a consequence of emancipation, the ex-serfs were brought into the same direct relations with the state as other citizens, whereas previously they had been left for the most part to the rule of their masters except as regards direct taxation and recruiting for the army. The whole problem of the peasantry in all its vastness, including famine relief, colonization, and the improvement of agriculture, took on a new form and became one of the major tasks of the administration, both central and local.

The economic revolution that was transforming so much of Russia between 1860 and 1914 (see pp. 361-379) could not fail at the same time to be transforming both the scale and machinery of government and the bases of tsarist power. There was a great expansion in the activities of the central government in communications, industry, finance, and trade, and to a lesser degree in its regulation of labor conditions.

The development of railways (1000 miles in 1860; 44,000 in 1914, and 8000 building), telegraphs (since 1851), and telephones (since 1881) involved a vast extension of the direct control that the state had always exercised over communications. The great bulk of the railway and telegraph system was state owned and operated, after an early period of leasing to private companies, and even when the state was not the actual constructor and operator it was deeply involved financially. State action was yet further extended by the conquest of the new colonial empire in Central Asia (1864-85) and the great expansion in Siberia bound up with the Trans-Siberian railway (begun in 1891) and leading to the new imperialism in the Far East and the war with Japan (1904-5). All the railways and other communications in Asia were state lines and planned as part of state policy, and Russian economic expansion in Manchuria and Persia alike was mainly dependent on the government, especially the ministry of finance which created and directed the Russo-Chinese Bank and its equivalent in Persia.

Industry continued to look to St. Petersburg for subsidies (direct or indirect), concessions, and tariff protection, and it was, in many of its most important and expanding branches, very closely tied to the state as being the largest consumer (*e.g.* army, navy, railways, inland waterways, building construction). The linking together of capital, technique, raw material, and transport was effected to a large degree by governmental means. It is significant that at the end of the nineteenth century the minister of finance, the energetic and capable Witte (1849-1915), who had risen from a junior post on a provincial railway, was at the same time minister of transport, commerce, industry and, to a considerable extent, labor.

The advance in Russian economic development was very striking, but it was, as it had always been, swaddled with bureaucratic strait-lacing. The whole atmosphere stunted the growth of a strong, independent industrial and mercantile class. That class did in fact owe much to the state, but it was mainly conscious of all the shortcomings of bureaucracy and tsarism, linked as it still was to a large extent with its historic but now rapidly declining partner, the landowners, and imbued with a military spirit of a kind that did not work in harness with modern capitalism. As one of the leading industrial papers put it (1901): "It is time to realize that European industry cannot grow in a climate of almost universal illiteracy and ignorance and almost complete absence of economic independence. It is time to realize that the complex and delicate mechanism of industrial development cannot be administered from one single center" [St. Petersburg].

If conservative opinion was thus critical of government and

administration, liberal and socialist opinion was violently antagonistic. The 1905 Revolution challenged not only the working of tsarism but its essential bases. Russia was indeed one of the great states of the world, great in the capacities of her peoples and the magnitude of her resources. These capacities and these resources had been given far too little scope or been far too little utilized. The Russian state as it had developed during the course of four centuries, despite great achievements, was still terribly weakened by corruption, arbitrariness, and inefficiency, and the element of force—however necessary an ingredient in any state—stood out only too nakedly. The conditions of the twentieth-century world demanded a radical transformation of government, if not a radical diminution of state power. In such an empire of such a size any profound and rapid transformation could not fail to be of terrifying complexity and acuteness, if not inevitably a full-scale revolution without the impact of the First World War. The words attributed to Witte at the time of the 1905 Revolution should not be forgotten (though they are not an adequate defense of tsarism):

"The world should be surprised that we have any Government in Russia, not that we have an imperfect Government. With many nationalities, many languages and a nation largely illiterate, the marvel is that the country can be held together even by autocracy. Remember one thing: if the Tsar's Government falls, you will see absolute chaos in Russia, and it will be many a long year before you will see another Government able to control the mixture that makes up the Russian nation."

CHAPTER III
THE LAND

1. *The Soviet Revolution in Agriculture*

THE SOVIET UNION, like Russia throughout her history, was overwhelmingly a land of peasants until the last decade. Through the centuries the land not the town dominated: hence the relative "backwardness" of Russia. In the latter part of the nineteenth century economic development was rapid and resulted in the concentration in a few centers of up-to-date large-scale industry and of an urban proletariat with an *élite* of skilled workers. The divorce between town and country was, in many respects, very pronounced. By 1914 a qualitative change of balance had occurred whereby the world market and Western science and ideas, represented by the big towns and large industrial and financial concerns, set the pace despite the immense retarding weight of the "dark" and "deaf" countryside, where (1897) hardly a fifth of those over nine years of age were literate. But it was not dumb. The "red cocks" of the 1905 Revolution, the burning country houses and barns, were eloquent. The peasants were still the major problem for any Russian government, and the first act of the Bolsheviks in November 1917 was to give them free rein.

In 1914 something like four-fifths of the population lived on the land: a dozen years later the proportion was still much the same, despite the October Revolution. During the next dozen years (1926-38) the Second (Stalinist) Revolution took place. During that period the countryside lost perhaps twenty-four million people to the towns: for the first time there was an absolute decline in the rural population: by 1939 almost one in every three Soviet citizens was classed as urban, mainly in towns of over one hundred thousand: by then over three-quarters of those over nine in the countryside were literate: almost all the peasantry were collective farmers, and they constituted slightly under one-half of the total population. These staggering changes, on a scale and at a tempo unknown in the modern history of any people, were the fruit of the five-year plans and collectivization of agriculture.

The Soviet revolution in agriculture was an entirely new approach to the problem of the peasantry, originally shot through with the idea of solving the divorce between town and country by the transformation of the peasants into something like factory workers on the land. The results of the revolution were that in 1940 almost all the agricultural production in the Union came from the 240,000 consolidated collective farms that had taken the place of the 25,000,000 separate peasant holdings that had existed in 1928, still in many cases in scattered strips in the open fields. On the collective farms, very variable in size but averaging perhaps seventy to eighty households and 1200 acres under crops, 75,000,000 individuals lived, mostly in compact villages. An administrative and technical staff of well over a million toiled with the task of organizing the planned work, with accountancy, plant biology, soil science, veterinary and other expert assistance. Another million served in the machine-tractor stations, the key to mechanization, which, after the consolidation of small holdings into large farms, was the second most essential feature of collectivization.

In 1914 the use of machines was the exception, though it had been increasing: half the plows in Russia were still of a primitive wooden type, most of the sowing was done by hand, and, except on large estates and in the south and Siberia, the scythe, sickle, and flail were still the rule. By 1938 nearly three-quarters of the land was plowed by tractors, and perhaps something like half the sowing and reaping of grain and almost all the threshing were done by machines. This was indeed a revolution such as the Russian village had never known, and it made most of the collective farms vitally dependent on the machine-tractor stations, which were organized quite apart from them, and in turn were entirely dependent on petrol supplies. They were also of decisive political importance through the "political sections" attached to them, composed of picked party men.

This large-scale mechanization, although its application (to agriculture, as opposed to forestry) in many of the northern provinces may be of limited value and although it may lead to more rapid soil exhaustion, had three overwhelming advantages: it made for quicker working, especially for instance in quicker completion of sowing in the very difficult conditions of the arid or semi-arid steppes; it enabled a much larger area to be cultivated and was essential for the Soviet colonization of new steppe land in the east; thirdly, it set labor free from agriculture for the insatiable maw of the construction and industrial works of the five-year plans.

The collective farm was to a certain extent modeled on the native Russian co-operative association known as the *artel,* which abounded in various local industries, fishing and building, though not in actual farming. *Artel* is indeed the official name for the association of members working a collective farm. It also has links with the village commune, or *mir,* again a native Russian institution, and one with as long or an even longer past (see pp. 146-148). Consolidation of holdings or of farms in place of scattered strips in the open fields had been going on pretty rapidly since 1907, as will be seen shortly, but the pace was revolutionized by collectivization and the size of farms gigantically increased.

The other distinctive features of a collective farm, including the use of machines on a large scale, are quite new. It is a "collective, *i.e.* socialist farm," which cannot be either sold or let or diminished in size, though it may be increased. It is national state property, but leased permanently to the *artel* by precious title deeds. Cottages, a very limited number of animals (except draught animals), small implements, gardens and allotments are owned individually. Everything else forms part of the capital of the *artel.* Substantially no hired labor can be employed.

What is to be produced is decided in accordance with the state plan and state-fixed prices as worked out for different regions and applied in detail through local committees and in the last resort by the collective farm itself, under the management of its chairman, whose election is usually in effect controlled by the Communist party. What is produced is subject first to state taxation, mainly in the form of compulsory deliveries of produce at a specially low price. These deliveries are fixed at an absolute figure, not as a percentage for instance of the crop harvested, and are now calculated, for the main crops and most animal produce, according to the cultivable amount of land and not as previously according to the area planned to be sown and the actual number of livestock. What is produced is subject, secondly, to payment to the machine-tractor stations and to seed, insurance, and various social and other funds.

The remaining produce is a dividend available for consumption and sale, either by contract to the state or on cooperative or other "open" markets at much higher prices than those paid for the compulsory deliveries. This dividend is divided among the members of the *artel* according to the amount of labor-days worked, *i.e.* on a piece-work basis, with every inducement latterly to apply Stakhanovite methods, in the shape of bonuses to workers who get through more work than planned, with the aim both of increasing national production and of realizing the officially avowed object of a collective farm, namely to make it "a Bolshevik one and all members . . . well-to-do people."

Collective farms of various types had been started since the early days of the Revolution, but they did not make much headway; and the state farms, on which originally special emphasis was laid as combining the panaceas of large-scale management, socialization of the means of production, and organization of farm workers on the lines of a factory, proved in most cases a failure owing to their colossal size and their refusal to allow for the needs of human individuals and the psychology of the peasant. Their subsequent transformation substantially into research, experimental and training farms, or into stud farms, has, in contrast, proved generally successful.

The policy of wholesale collectivization was not adopted

until 1928, but it was then pushed through in the course of the next six years, untiringly and mercilessly.[1] It involved at one and the same time a technical, an administrative, and a psychological revolution. Inevitably none of them, especially the last, could be regarded as completed by 1941, but decisive results had been attained.

Collectivization met with determined and desperate resistance from the better-off peasants, since it deliberately involved "the liquidation of the kulaks as a class," and for some time with very widespread hostility from the middling and some of the poor peasantry. The pace of collectivization was so violent and led to such reactions that Stalin himself (1930) had to rebuke the party extremists as suffering from "giddyness from success," *i.e.* compulsory and indiscriminate conversion of the peasants into collective farmers without any individual property of their own. Resistance and counter-repression were particularly severe in parts of the Ukraine and the North Caucasus, and punitive expeditions and deportations took place on a large scale. The chaos inevitable in such a revolution was much increased by the fact that collectivization had been planned primarily in terms of grain needs, and its application to most other crops and to stock-raising had not been closely thought out.

As a result, in combination with severe famine in 1932-33 (though far less widespread than that of 1921-22), the peasants and the nomads, for instance the Kazakhs, took to wholesale slaughtering of their stock. These losses were on such a catastrophic scale that even by 1938 there were only half as many horses and two-thirds as many sheep as ten years earlier. Stock-raising was always a weak side of Russian agriculture and the recent Soviet campaign to make up the lost ground had an immense task to cope with. On the other hand, Soviet efforts have been very successful in diversifying agriculture by irrigation and by the extended cultivation or the intro-

---

[1] The mixture of tragedy, cruelty, and idealism in the struggle for collectivization is admirably expressed, from very different angles and in regard to different parts of Russia, in Sholokhov's novel *Virgin Soil Upturned* (1932; New York, 1935) and Maurice Hindus's study *Red Bread* (New York, 1931).

duction of a wide variety of industrial crops and sown grasses, even though cereals still remain the standard crop of at least three-quarters of Russia.

The years of the Second Revolution, 1928-34, when food-rationing had to be reintroduced and when the new industrial plans were being forced through at the same time as the revolution on the land, were indeed "Russia's Iron Age." By 1935 comparative order was achieved through the reassurance given to the peasants in the collective farms that they could keep most of their animals in individual ownership and could have considerable opportunities for private production on their own small holdings, apart from work on the collective farms; concessions which were strictly limited in 1939 when a general tightening up of collectivization began.

The reasons for the Second Revolution were partly economic, partly political. When revolution come in 1917 the peasants in their communes took for themselves what was left of the gentry's lands, and there was a welter of parceling out and redistribution of holdings, and much of the previously consolidated holdings was reincorporated in the communes. Ten years later, by 1928, there were approximately twenty-five million holdings where before there had been perhaps sixteen million. Some were compact, others still in scattered strips in the open fields, as they had been for centuries. But if the peasants at long last had the land, they had also to undergo the agonies of the civil war which pressed upon them with hardly less grimness than upon the townsmen. It ended with the great famine and wave of disease of 1921-22, which was so widespread and so serious that international relief from Western countries was necessary, as had happened privately on a very small scale in certain pre-1914 famines.

Important concessions were made to the peasants, beginning with the abandonment of "war communism," which had meant forced requisitions, and the substitution of an organized grain tax, at first in kind, then in money (*cf.* pp. 363-364). Under the New Economic Policy, adopted by Lenin in 1921— a policy of "state capitalism," "a mixed system" combining large-scale state industry and transport with small-scale private industry, private trade, and small-scale peasant agriculture—considerable progress was made in the sense that by 1927 the pre-1914 level was said to have been nearly reached in most branches of agricultural production, and in some to have been surpassed. But at the same time the divorce between town and country had become acute. The hopes of 1924-25 had been falsified that socialism could be built up in the villages on the basis of the alliance of the middle and poor peasantry through co-operatives; "by gradually permeating agriculture with the principles of collectivism—at first for the sale of agricultural produce, and in due course for agricultural production" (Stalin).

While on the one hand large-scale socialized industry was forging ahead, on the other hand an increasing number of peasants, taking advantage of legislation allowing the renting of land and the employment of hired labor, were extending their holdings into farms of some size. These were the so-called rich peasantry (however poor by Western standards); the kulaks, or "fists," known as such fifty years or so before the Revolution. Whatever their energy and skill, they had enemies enough and to spare among the village proletariat. They had been the class which had been specially encouraged by the agrarian reforms of 1906, to be described in the next section, and against them the Bolsheviks from the summer of 1918 had conducted their campaign of class war in the villages through soviets of poor peasants. In 1921 the attack was called off and the N.E.P. substituted. Then, in 1928, the attack was renewed with final intensity in the collectivization campaign. In the struggle the dividing line between kulak, middle peasant, and poor peasant, in any case wavering and indeterminate, only too frequently disappeared altogether and the category of kulak came to be a question of revolutionary politics or personal feuds.

Owing to the acute lack and bad quality of consumers' goods and the gap between industrial and agricultural prices ("the scissors") the country was refusing to feed the towns: the political and economic divorce between the two had reached most dangerous proportions, all the more serious in view of the extreme numerical weakness of the Communist party in the villages. In 1927, according to the official history of the party, the amount of grain coming on to the market to feed the towns was only 37 per cent of the pre-1914 level, even though total grain production had reached 91 per cent of that level. The blame for this catastrophic situation was laid on the shoulders of the kulaks as the largest grain producers. It was certainly imperative by some means or other to increase very largely net agricultural production and control its distribution.

It was decided that no compromise should be made with the idea of a Russia based on small-scale peasant agriculture, somewhat as in France, imbued with "a petty-bourgeois ideology" and anchored in the habit of "buy in the cheapest, sell in the dearest market." It was held that any such capitulation to the peasantry would involve the bankruptcy of the Communist party and the collapse of the dictatorship of the proletariat, and would render impossible totalitarian planning and the gigantic program of capital construction which was designed to meet the needs of defense and industry and to supply agriculture with the machines that were necessary both to raise enormously its production and at the same time to set free more labor from the land for industry.

Such was the immediate, ten years' background to the Second (Stalinist) Revolution. Behind that lay the 1905 Revolution and the agrarian reforms that were its outcome, the emancipation of the serfs (1861), and centuries of peasant struggling with and for the land, peasant ways of thought and feeling, prejudices and superstitions; centuries of the commune and serfdom when, as the proverb ran, "The body belongs to the Tsar, the soul to God, and the back to the squire."

2. *The 1905 Revolution and the Emancipation of the Serfs*

In the fifty years before 1917 the Russian peasants, still with their perennial land hunger, were slowly and confusedly developing towards independent small holders or farmers. The immense change-over from serfdom was bound to be slow and complex. The general trend of economic and social life was towards a system of relations entirely ruled by a money economy, mobility of labor, and freedom of contract in contrast with the long rule of status; but this transformation by the beginning of the present century had not proceeded very far in the 120,000 communes that still sprawled over the face of European Russia, and even after 1905 the peasantry still remained for some purposes a separate class, an "estate" distinct from the rest of the tsar's subjects.

Production for a very low level of subsistence was still the dominant fact for most peasant households, and dependence on seasonal labor and on supplementary non-agricultural earnings, especially in the "consuming provinces," was even more widespread than in the past. Old features of the serf régime lived on in decay, and remnants of the old system of labor services still persisted, with the corresponding psychology. Conditions, as previously, varied immensely in different parts of the country, even apart from Siberia, which had never known agricultural serfdom to any extent, or the Cossack and other lands of the new South.

By 1916 perhaps as much as two-thirds of the cultivable area was in peasant hands, but it was very unequally distributed. In 1905 over a third of the peasant holdings in the communes was in the hands of only a tenth of the peasant households, with holdings of over fifty acres. This was the original nucleus of the kulaks. The process of differentiation among the peasantry was already marked, and it was greatly increased in the next dozen years. Above all, there were many more peasant mouths to feed. Between emancipation (1861) and the 1905 Revolution the peasantry swelled from 50,000,000 to 78,000,000, not counting another 6,000,000 peasants working in the towns or elsewhere away from the land. Land hunger and physical hunger were acute throughout wide regions.

"No rumors came to me about any little books [revolutionary propaganda]," a peasant said after the peasant outbreaks of 1902. "I think that if we lived better, the little books would not be important, no matter what was written in them. What's terrible is not the little books, but this: there isn't anything to eat." Five years later in the Duma a peasant deputy thundered: "Again we are told: property is sacred, inviolable. In my opinion it cannot possibly be inviolable; nothing can be inviolable, once the people will it. . . . Gentlemen of the gentry, do you think that we do not know how you staked us at cards and bartered us for dogs? We know that all that was your sacred, inviolable property. . . . You have stolen our land. . . . This is what the peasants who sent me here said: the land is ours, we have come here not to buy it, but to take it."

Ten years later they did so. In the meantime Stolypin, prime minister from 1906 until his assassination in 1911, the only man of big caliber, except Witte, to hold a commanding position under Nicholas II, hastened to initiate his agrarian reforms, his "wager, not on the needy and the drunken, but on the sturdy and the strong," men of the stamp of Lopakhin in Chekhov's *Cherry Orchard*. This policy was the answer to the wave of mass peasant strikes and outbreaks up and down the country during 1905 and 1906, with widespread burning of country houses and their equipment, which were fiercely suppressed by the army and specially created military field courts martial. Almost the whole empire between 1905 and 1908 was being governed under varieties of a "state of siege." Between 3500 and 4500 persons, not peasants only, are estimated to have been executed, apart from those killed in the Moscow and other armed uprisings and from "the pacification" of the Baltic provinces.

The growth of a new political consciousness among some at least of the peasantry was to be seen in the frequent conversion of the village communal assemblies into political meetings and the creation in 1905 of the Peasants' Union, an incipient agrarian party. It was also only too evident in the attitude of the peasant deputies in the first two Dumas, as illustrated in the speech just quoted. It was being said down on the Volga: "The government keeps us peasants jammed.

The fault is with the Romanovs; the tsar has sold Russia to Japan. For three hundred years the Romanovs have done nothing for the peasants, and the grand dukes do nothing but drink . . . as for us we have no one to set our hopes on, but we must take all by force." The dark, inscrutable peasant mass clearly was not the faithful, conservative bulwark which most of the authorities imagined when they gave it specially strong representation in the Duma.

Stolypin dissolved the second Duma (*cf.* p. 60) and drastically reduced the peasants' votes and deputies (1907). Immediately before he had begun his agrarian reforms, typically enough by government decree not by passage through the Duma.

Already before 1905 there had been much discussion of the advantages and disadvantages of the commune. Stolypin had expressed himself emphatically against it. "The natural counterweight to the communal principle is individual ownership. It is also a guarantee of order, since the small owner is the cell on which rests all stable order in the state." That, in a nutshell, was the policy of the 1906 and subsequent agrarian legislation.

The first object of the new policy was to break down the control of the commune over the peasant's life and methods of cultivation and to substitute consolidated holdings for the scattered strips in the common fields, strips that in some villages were held hereditarily, in most on a tenure involving redistribution at variable intervals among the members of the commune: in the case of these latter the initial aim was to convert them into hereditary holdings.

The second object was to facilitate the purchase or renting of land from the gentry, the state, and other non-peasant landowners and the establishment of separate, compact farms. To this end reforms were introduced in the working of the Peasants' Land Bank, which had been founded by the government in 1883 but had in fact done little to assist the purchase of land by individual peasants owing to its high rates of interest. Rural credit institutions were also encouraged, with conspicuous success in the South. In addition, migration to

Siberia and elsewhere and to the towns was made easier by provisions allowing peasants to abandon the commune altogether. At the same time, one vital step in the policy of disrupting the commune was completed by the full abolition of communal responsibility for taxation.

The results were remarkable even in ten years and despite the outbreak of the First World War; but in so short a time only a relatively small minority could be transformed into a "solid peasantry," and the commune showed greater vitality than its opponents expected. The kulaks, the richer independent farmers, increased considerably through buying or leasing the gentry's land and buying cheap the holdings of peasants leaving the communes. On the eve of the 1917 Revolution something like 1,300,000 peasant households (about a tenth of the whole) had been established on new consolidated holdings, and an even larger number were in process of such consolidation. 1905 and 1907 had been years of widespread crop failures, 1906 of famine in certain areas—a fact that had intensified the revolutionary spirit of the peasants—but the next ten years saw good or bumper harvests, except in the famine year of 1911, and there was a general advance in most branches of agriculture. More machinery, more artificial manures were being used: the crop acreage and co-operatives were extending. This improvement, however, was chiefly concentrated in the Ukraine, North Caucasus, and Siberia, and was in the main limited to the individual farmers, as contrasted with those still in the commune, and to the big estates. The material level of the great majority of the peasants still remained deplorably low, perhaps more comparable with India than with western Europe.

If one section of the peasantry was rising, the other—and much the larger—was only just managing to maintain its level, or was even sinking. It was still, in the main, illiterate. By 1917 the great majority of the peasants in European Russia were still working their scattered strips in the open fields of the commune, though most now held them hereditarily. Migration did little to ease the pressure of population, which was still intense in the central black-earth and the middle

Volga provinces, where the land was almost the sole source of livelihood and famine-relief records showed the highest figures of relief and indebtedness. As much as ever, the peasants looked at the gentry's estates: "You have stolen our land."

The land held by the nobility and the gentry in the Russian core of the empire was two and a half times less than what it had been before emancipation (1861). Many of their estates were small; many heavily mortgaged. There had been far more peasant buying of them in the ten years 1907-17 than in the previous thirty years. Yet big estates and latifundia still bulked large, and the fact remained that the nobility and the gentry, perhaps rather over one million all told with their families, still owned about a hundred million acres in contrast with the peasants, nearly a hundred times more numerous, but with just over four times more land.[1] Rightly or wrongly the peasants felt that the land was theirs and that they had been cheated of the fruits of emancipation.

The emancipation of the serfs in 1861 was the first of the great reforms under Alexander II which began the transformation of Russia into a modern state (*cf.* pp. 68-69). It meant the beginning of an economic, social, and psychological revolution, especially in the solid Russian regions that were the heart of serfdom.[2]

At the time of emancipation about 50,000,000 of the 60,000,000 inhabitants of European Russia, without the non-Russian fringes, were peasants of one kind or another. Of these just over 20,000,000 were the serfs of the nobility and gentry, the landlords' serfs. Rather under 20,000,000 were state peasants, whose position varied greatly but approximated to that of the former, though it had been considerably improved by various measures taken under Nicholas I (1825-55). The remainder belonged to certain other categories of serfs or non-serf peasants. The second and third groups were

---

[1] To realize the scale of the land and peasant problem in Russia bear in mind that the total acreage of Great Britain is only 57,000,000 and that in 1931 only 1,343,000 persons were classed as occupied in agriculture, though that did not include their families.

[2] The best introduction to emancipation and the peasants in the nineteenth century is Nekrasov's great poem *Who can be Happy and Free in Russia?* (1873), translated in the World's Classics series.

emancipated separately on very much more favorable terms than the first. These, the landlords' serfs, "bondmen," bound not so much to the land as to their owners, were the core of the problem.

Their major obligations consisted either in paying dues in money or in kind to their owner or in working his land or undertakings for so many days in the week, usually with their own stock and implements, or in a combination of both forms of service. In addition they worked their holdings in the open-field scattered strips as members of their commune or village. A considerable section of the serfs were landless household servants—in general a particularly miserable class —who were emancipated without any land. The emancipation edict liberated the serfs from their masters, but not from the commune, and gave them land, but at a price. Henceforward they were no longer legally debarred from taking up any occupation.

The land settlement was extremely complicated, varied substantially in different parts of Russia, and took twenty years and more to be completed. Its broad outline was as follows. The landlord kept the land he had farmed himself, henceforward to be worked by hired labor, as often as not that of his ex-serfs, who kept their cottages and garden patches. The communal open fields went to the ex-serfs (or those who had been state peasants), not as individual private owners in the Western sense of the term, but still organized in the commune. There were, it is true, provisions enabling peasants to separate from the commune, but they were so hedged about by restrictions as to be of comparatively little effect. For the most part their small strip holdings were not consolidated, but remained as before scattered and subject to periodical redistribution, save in the minority of villages where hereditary tenure was the custom. It was planned that the peasants should retain the holdings they had previously worked. This to a large extent was carried out, but, owing principally to arrangements made in favor of the landlords as to pasture, meadow, and wood, the holdings and subsistence rights of the peasants were diminished, except in the western and northern provinces, where the opposite was the case. Precisely where the pressure on the land was most severe, in the central black-earth and middle Volga provinces, the results of emancipation worked out worst for the peasants.

At the same time they had to pay for their holdings, mainly in the form of redemption annuities for forty-nine years to the state, which bought out the landlords at rates on the average much higher than the market prices of land, with the result that the redemption annuities were correspondingly high. In addition, until 1886, the poll tax remained in force and the commune was made collectively responsible for it.

Under serfdom the peasants said: "We are yours, but the land is ours." Now they no longer belonged to their masters, but the land still was not theirs. It ought to be. That, for most of the peasants, was the root of the matter. Emancipation was received with a wave of disorders almost throughout Russia, and a few actual risings; but there was no conflagration. Considering everything, the crisis was quickly overcome, and the new order with infinite pains began to take shape. The shape varied greatly in the very diverse parts of so immense a land, but there were certain features (some of them already noted) which were common to most of European Russia between 1861 and the 1905 Revolution.

(i) The abolition of serfdom greatly accelerated the decline of labor services and payments in kind and the spread of a money economy.

(ii) The technical backwardness of the open-field strip system became more and more pronounced.

(iii) The peasantry began to be differentiated into the richer kulaks, the middling peasantry, and a village proletariat with dwarf holdings and little or no stock or implements, who subsisted largely or solely as hired laborers, working not necessarily on the land. This differentiation was not by 1905 far advanced, partly because of the effect of the commune.

(iv) Emancipation of the peasants, and not merely of the landlords' serfs, was in the main based on the preservation of the commune (*mir*) and the family household, which continued to be regarded as immemorial Slav institutions safeguarding peasant Russia from the cut-throat competition of Western individualism. The obligations of the serfs to the state which had hitherto been controlled by the landlords, acting through their bailiffs and the village headmen, now mostly devolved upon the commune alone, with its general meeting of heads of families and its elected elders, and to some extent upon elected peasant officials of a newly created administrative unit, the canton, in which a number of communes was grouped. The communes of those who had been state peasants were retained and likewise received legal recognition.

The principal communal obligations were: collective responsibility for payment of direct taxes and redemption annuities; apportionment of direct taxes and recruiting; minor police duties; granting (until 1897 sale) of passports (a combination of the identity card and the labor book without which, since Peter the Great, peasants and most other classes could not legally move from their locality). Cantonal courts, composed of and dealing with peasants alone, decided minor civil cases and misdemeanors on the basis of local custom. In addition, the commune dealt, as it always had, with innumerable questions concerned with the working of the land, redistribution of holdings, and common village needs.

All this meant, both in theory and practice, a considerable amount of what may be called peasant self-government, at any rate for the heads of families. When the 1917 Revolution began the peasant communal and cantonal committees were the first means whereby the peasants took matters into their own hands. This self-government had operated within a narrow, but intimate and vitally important, range of subjects mainly on the basis of local custom; but it was also bound up with what was very irksome or unpopular, *e.g.* taxation, arrears, passports. Further, both the commune and the canton suffered heavily from the reaction in the eighties under Alexander III, when the powers of the police and the ministry of the interior were reinforced (*cf.* pp. 69-70).

Despite emancipation, the authorities continued in various

ways to treat the peasantry as it always had as a class apart: an attitude denounced by progressives and the left as responsible for widening the gulf between the town and the country, between enlightening influences and the dark, unlettered peasant mass, and as responsible for keeping Russia unknit together as one community and split between different classes with a minimum of interlacing ties.

(v) Industrialists and others needing new hands had supported emancipation as a long step towards mobility of labor. This proved to be a very important result of 1861 and there was a large outflow, in part seasonal, in part permanent, from the land to the new transport, mining, and industrial concerns that were changing the balance of Russian economy. Such permanent outflow, as well as that to new agricultural land in the south or the east, was, however, much hampered by the expense and difficulties of the passport system and by the ties of the commune, particularly as regards its joint responsibility for taxation which was not completely abolished until 1906.

(vi) The outflow from the land was far smaller than the natural increase of the peasants. Nor was the excess of peasant mouths sated by the steady passage of more land into peasant hands. The new holdings went chiefly to those who were already relatively better off.

(vii) By about 1900 the problem of the peasantry, especially in "the producing provinces," the so-called granary of Russia, was still more acute owing to this pressure of population, to the low standard of peasant farming, to the collapse of grain prices in the seventies and eighties, and to the great famine of 1891-92 (on a scale comparable to the worst Indian famines of 1876-78 and 1899-1900), followed by more local famines in 1898 and 1901. The salt tax went in 1880, the poll tax in 1886; yet arrears of other charges mounted. The redemption annuities had to be twice reduced, then three times deferred or in part canceled: finally, in the throes of revolution, they went by the board and there was what amounted to all-round cancellation (1905).

(viii) While many of the peasantry were on the verge of

revolution, their former owners, in general, had failed to adjust themselves economically or politically to the changes of the past forty years (1861-1905). Some were improving and successful landowners, but a great many of the gentry were either loaded with debt or practically divorced from the land. The gentry had been already heavily indebted before emancipation and much of their immediate profit from being bought out by the state went to meet those obligations. The efforts of the government under Alexander III to buttress up a resident landed gentry as the surest bulwark of state power, if they were temporarily successful in the political and administrative spheres, failed in the economic field. The gentry were parting with their land on an increasing scale, chiefly to the middle classes of the towns. The Nobles Land Bank, started in 1885 for the express purpose of their relief, succeeded only too well in one respect: by 1904 more than a third of their land was mortgaged to it. Economic power was more and more obviously passing to the new banking, industrial, and commercial interests, alien to the traditions and methods of the old landed class.

3. Serfs and Serf-owners

The emancipation of the serfs in 1861 took place four years before the final abolition of slavery in the United States, a dozen years after that of the remnants of serfdom in Prussia and Austria, seventy-two years after that in France. It came when it did because the breakdown of Russia in the Crimean war (1853-56), following the icy reaction imposed by Nicholas I after 1848, made imperative what was already overripe, namely, a general recasting of institutions, of which the most fundamental was serfdom.

For the previous quarter of a century, apart from the growth of humanitarian ideas, the economic disadvantages of serfdom were being prominently discussed among many of the serf-owners themselves, while the rising commercial and industrial entrepreneurs were only too anxious to sweep away serfdom and the restrictions imposed by the class system. During the reign of Nicholas I (1825-55) their factories, especially in the textile industry, worked by free hired labor, had strikingly increased, while those worked by serf labor had declined heavily. Yet their legal disabilities, although mitigated by Nicholas, remained galling and hampering. The labor market was greatly restricted by the exclusive privileges of owning serfs acquired by the nobility and gentry, and the level of internal consumption was deplorably low.

The serf-owners, officially estimated in 1851 at 262,000 males, were sharply divided among themselves, particularly according as to whether their lands were in "the consuming provinces," or in the black-earth provinces, or in New Russia. In Great Russia well over half of the serf-owners were small proprietors with less than ten male serfs apiece, whose interests and outlook were widely different from those of the large landowners, with anything from a hundred to many thousands of male serfs each, to whom over four-fifths of the serfs belonged. These divergences were increased by the great extension of wheat-growing, mainly for export, in the south and the middle Volga. Especially here more and more serf-owners were considering hired labor more satisfactory than serf labor, the technical backwardness of which was becoming acutely felt.

At the same time, serfdom was becoming more and more dangerous. There had been no mass revolt since that of Pugachov (1773-75; see pp. 152-161), but peasant outbreaks were increasing alarmingly. In the last ten years of Nicholas's reign there were at the least four hundred of them, and in the following six years alone (1855-60) the same number. In twenty years (1835-54) two hundred and thirty serf-owners or their bailiffs were killed; in three years before emancipation another fifty-three. The situation far exceeded in scale and intensity that in the most disturbed districts of Ireland in the eighties. It is no wonder that Alexander II said that he was faced with emancipation from above or revolution from below.

Serfdom in its fullness lasted longer in Russia than in

Western countries because its economic disadvantages did not earlier outweigh its advantages; because the increase of population did not cause sufficiently acute land shortage among the peasantry until the first half of the nineteenth century; because the middle classes were weak in comparison with the serf-owners; because humanitarian and other ideas of the value of the individual spirit were little developed; because the reaction against the ideas of the French Revolution strengthened the *vis inertiæ* inherent in any long-established institution; lastly, because serfdom was not merely the economic basis of the serf-owners but also a main basis of the Russian state in its immense task of somehow governing so many raw millions.

"Serfdom," Nicholas I recognized, "is the indubitable evil of Russian life, but I think it still more dangerous to touch it." Why he thought so was because he agreed with his chief of police who thus summed up: "The landowner is the most reliable bulwark of the sovereign. No army can replace the vigilance and the influence which the landowner continuously exercises in his estates. If his power is destroyed, the people will become a flood endangering in time even the Tsar himself. . . . The landowner is the most faithful, the unsleeping watchdog guarding the state; he is the natural police magistrate."

This ruling position of the serf-owners, *i.e.* the hereditary nobility and gentry, was the result of a long process that culminated in the eighteenth century, beginning with empress Anna in 1730 (*cf.* pp. 76-77) and reaching its full expression in Catherine the Great's explicit adoption of Montesquieu's maxim "point de noblesse, point de monarque," and in her charter of 1785 organizing them in an "estate."

Between 1731 and 1762 the landowners were made responsible for the poll tax from their serfs, introduced by Peter the Great and payable by all classes except the landowners and the clergy, and for the recruits from their serfs for the standing army organized by Peter the Great and continuing, whether in time of war or peace, to be a major, if necessary, burden that engulfed almost throughout the century far over half the state expenditure. In addition, under Catherine the Great they obtained in effect further control of local justice and administration, with the result that they were both the legal and economic masters of their serfs and their police and judicial rulers. Hence behind them they had the armed support of the state if required.

The serf-owners did not pay direct taxation, but they had previously instead owed service to the tsar, primarily military service. Peter the Great had reorganized and done his brutal best to enforce their lifelong service to the state, whether in the army and navy or in civil administration, and their compulsory education. The landowners reacted strongly, with notable success in their resistance to this last burden. After Peter they had their way. From 1730 service in the very unpopular navy was no longer compulsory. In 1736 a reduction of obligatory service to twenty-five years was granted, together with numerous grounds of exemption and other privileges. In 1762 they crowned their posthumous victory over Peter I by securing from Peter III the abolition of any obligation to serve at all.

This edict removed the formal justification of serfdom: the serfs had to serve the state directly by the poll tax and recruits, and indirectly by supporting their owners, who themselves had to serve the state directly by providing the officers in the army and civil service: if their owners no longer had to serve the state, why should the serfs have to serve their owners? So the serfs felt and argued—and revolted: there was a second edict freeing them from their masters, who had suppressed it and killed "the little father" for granting it (*cf.* p. 159). (Peter III was deposed and afterwards murdered in 1762 by court conspiracies, the first headed, the second connived at by his wife Catherine the Great.) But for the true emancipation edict the peasants had to wait another hundred years.

The edict of 1762 did not in fact result in the army or government service of one kind or another ceasing to be the usual career for most of the landowners. It was often lucrative, and it was in general considered "the right thing to do."

But the edict did result in government service occupying less of their time, and in many cases not being entered at all. It marked the beginning of the modern differentiation between the landowning class and the bureaucracy, and was also accompanied by the beginning of that critical spirit among the upper class which became so distinctive a feature of Russian cultural life in the nineteenth century.

From the time of Catherine the Great, in combination with her reforms of 1775 and 1785, a provincial society developed of a kind almost unknown before in Russia. It was too often a society of "backwoodsmen" or cardplayers and languid readers of French novels; but its better representatives were men of strong character and culture. It should not be forgotten that the serf-owning upper class in Russia, partly in service, partly in the two capitals, partly in their country estates, contributed more than any other class to the unmatched outflow of Russian literature in the nineteenth century and threw up an astonishing variety of outstanding personalities of the most diverse gifts and views, from Pushkin, Turgenev, and Tolstoy to Bakunin, Herzen, and Kropotkin.

Catherine the Great (b. 1729; reigned 1762-96), by her much-publicized ideas of "enlightenment" and by her encouragement of education and, until her closing years, of literature and the arts, greatly influenced the direction and standards of culture in Russia; but her reign in general must be accounted a capitulation to the landed class as regards serfdom, and her deliberate encouragement of the idea of separate "estates" of the nobility and gentry, of the merchants and townsmen, and of the peasants accentuated the divorce between each of them, especially of the first from the other two. The nobility and gentry failed only to win the concession that their "estate" should be a closed one, though enjoyment of its full privileges was severely limited, and to debar other classes from the legal acquisition of land, though these were not allowed to acquire new serfs for their factories and mines. On the other hand, they succeeded (1782) in securing full property rights in minerals and forests on their estates, rights which had been denied or limited by Peter the Great.

In her dealings with the peasantry, Catherine less deserves the title of great than Maria Theresa. She always realized the difficulty of translating into practice the pleasant intentions of her earlier letters and notebooks, when she recoiled against "the insupportable and cruel yoke of serfdom." After the terrifying experience of the mass peasant revolt in the Urals and the middle Volga lands headed by Pugachov (1773-75; see p. 157), crown and serf-owners were more closely bound together than ever in the indispensable task of maintaining social order. By the end of the century serfdom had achieved its final form, which was not in essentials altered by law until 1861.

Its general effect was portrayed in the most somber terms by Radishchev, the first prominent representative of the free-thinking "conscience-stricken" nobility, in his outspoken *Journey from St. Petersburg to Moscow* (1790), for which Catherine banished him to Siberia.[1] She herself summed up serfdom in one sentence, in a letter to Diderot: "Landowners do whatever seems good to them on their estates except inflict capital punishment; that is forbidden." Even so, they had almost unrestrained power of flogging which on occasion resulted in death. Although criminal offenses were reserved for the courts, other disputes between serfs were decided, directly or indirectly, by their masters without appeal. After 1765 they could send their serfs to hard labor in Siberia "for continued audacious behavior." They could both decide who should be sent as recruits to the army, which meant, until 1874, twenty-five years' service, and could sell their serfs as recruits. In 1767 the serfs lost the last shreds of any right of petition against their masters, and the loss of any such right, however ineffective and dangerous it had become, was bitterly resented. Marriage required the master's permission and normally payment in some form to him.

The serf was in one sense attached to the soil in that he could not leave his holding or the estate without his master's

---

[1] There is a German, but no English, translation (Leipzig, 1922).

consent; in another sense he was not attached to the soil in that he could be employed as his master thought fit on another estate, in his house, his stables, his offices, his factory or mines, his band or theater, if he had them. Where the serfs paid their services in money or produce rent, which was increasingly the practice in "the consuming provinces," they were left comparatively free to engage in whatever occupations they could and to work as hired laborers for other employers, provided they paid their dues and the poll tax. On the other hand, where the serfs performed their obligations to their master by working his land, the direct weight of serfdom was extremely heavy.

The master could not only move his serfs about as he liked; he could sell them at will, with or without land, by villages, by families, or (until Alexander I) individually. Public auction sales occurred, though by law not without land after 1771. Advertisements of serfs for sale appeared side by side with offers of Holstein stallions or books. Serfs were gambled with; betting debts were an affair of honor and must be paid.

The main essentials of serfdom were inherited by Catherine from the past, but under her and her son Paul (1796-1801) it was greatly extended and systematized in the Ukraine and the South (*cf.* pp. 37-38 and 219). In the Ukraine the sale of serfs without land was prohibited from 1798, but the customary two days a week work on the master's land was in effect raised to three. Elsewhere an effort was made to limit the number of days to three, which was in fact the most common, but four or five days continued often to be worked, and exceptionally even six: Sunday work of this kind was prohibited from 1797. Further, both Catherine and Paul far exceeded all previous bounds in the granting of land with serfs to favorites (800,000 of both sexes in thirty-four years; 530,000 in five years). Except in the Ukraine, however, this usually meant not the binding down of new serfs, but either the transference of court and state peasants, themselves serfs of a kind, to the generally harsher conditions of private ownership, or simply a change of masters through confiscations in the newly acquired Polish lands or elsewhere. From the time of Peter the Great a special type of serfdom was developed to ensure labor for the new mines and factories. It took the form of permanent attachment to them, under particularly onerous conditions in the Urals that led to frequent risings culminating in that of Pugachov (*cf.* p. 153).

Serfdom was hereditary and there were only two means of escape from it, flight and the gift or sale of freedom by one's master. This latter was rare, but Alexander I, who in his early liberal years was much exercised by the condition of the peasants, provided legal means (1803) for the voluntary liberation of serfs with land. The redemption rate was, however, high and not more than 50,000 serfs were thus emancipated during his reign (1801-25). In other respects under Alexander the weight of serfdom, though not the worst kind of cruelty, in general increased. In the Baltic provinces the personal emancipation of the Estonian and Lettish peasants from their German masters (1816-19), since it was finally sanctioned without any land, left them in continued economic subjection.

Conditions naturally varied much in different parts of the country and under different masters, and the picture was not as uniformly dark as the preceding summary may suggest. The most extreme cases of cruelty were regarded as such by contemporaries and met with punishment. Many individual serfs prospered at a variety of callings. Some were of the old family-servant type like Pushkin's beloved nurse immortalized in *Eugene Onegin*.[1] Others filled responsible posts in the communes or the management of their masters' affairs. A few exceptional individuals even made for themselves outstanding and famous careers.

Serfdom as described above was typical of the Russian core of the empire, but not of Siberia, the Far North or the new South. It applied in part to the Tatar-Finnish peoples of the middle Volga, but the nomad peoples remained with their own customs and social organization.

Rather under half of the peasantry were not bonded serfs

[1] There is a remarkable English translation by Oliver Elton (1939).

but various categories of state peasants (*cf.* pp. 21, 37-38, 45), who were subject to the poll-tax, recruiting, and rent payments, whether in money or in the form of very various labor services, such as transport, construction, and forestry work; but on the whole their condition was considerably better than that of the bonded serfs of the landowners, especially in the nineteenth century.

Still, with all allowances made, it remained true that serfdom was, as Nicholas I expressed it, "the indubitable evil of Russian life." "God, how sad our Russia is," Pushkin is said to have kept on repeating as he read the manuscript of *Dead Souls* (1842), Gogol's great novel depicting the life of the serfs, their masters and provincial officials.[1]

4. *Origins of Serfdom and the Commune*

In its modern form serfdom took shape in the sixteenth and seventeenth centuries as a mixture of custom, private contract, and governmental edicts on particular points, backed by force. Although it became the main basis of Russian society, there was never any clear formulation of its legal basis or any code or amalgamating legislation setting out the rights and obligations of masters and serfs. There was, for instance, no attempt at systematizing the position of serfs in the so-called code of 1649, a very important landmark, but despite its name a confused assortment of rules, mainly of procedure, some old, some new. Its general tendency, however, was to confirm the practice of attachment of peasant households to the land, notably by the new provision abolishing any time-limit for the recovery of future runaway peasants. The jurisdiction of masters over their serfs became more and more widely extended, and legally recognized, registered, hereditary bondage became established.

The opening chapter on the frontier has emphasized the continuous importance in Russian history of shifting population and migration. The hundred years between 1550 and 1650 was the century *par excellence* of runaway peasants,

---

[1] Translated in the Everyman series.

sometimes from one landowner to another, more often from any landowner whomsoever. Some did not move far; others took their chance in "the wild grounds," or swelled the class of "vagrants" which so much hampered and at times alarmed the government. This also was the century of the new serfdom.

Serfdom had long been one essential feature in the social structure of the Russian lands, but it had not expanded and hardened into the form that it later took. For many purposes, in Muscovy of the fourteenth and fifteenth centuries, comparison should be made with Anglo-Saxon rather than with Norman or Plantagenet England. Whatever feudal similarities there may be (see p. 86), there was nothing even in theory of "no land without a lord." Population was very thin and scattered; the family was the chief unit; the nucleated village and the large open fields were exceptions (*cf.* p. 15). The peasants, as much hunters, foresters, and craftsmen as farmers, had been both in law and in economic fact divided into a number of classes with differing obligations and rights, ranging from the unfree slaves, the full property of their masters and paying no dues to the state, to the independent "ownlanders" of Novgorod.

The line between freedom and unfreedom was wavering and blurred, but one usually distinguishing mark of the free was a burden, the obligation to pay dues in some form to the state. "The black lands" were those communities that owed such dues direct; those who were later called "black plowlandmen" were the free, taxpaying peasants, usually grouped for fiscal and administrative purposes in cantons of twenty or more hamlets or villages, which were collectively responsible for the detailed assessment of taxation and services. Other peasants lived on the lands of ecclesiastical and lay landowners on very various contractual terms as tenants, "commended men," metayers, serfs, "referred slaves" (a class of temporary slaves), or as full slaves. These last two classes were not free, but the others were, in the sense that they owed dues, directly or indirectly, to the state, though the jurisdictional and fiscal immunities granted by the grand-princes to big landowners, especially the monasteries, to a large extent removed those on their lands from direct contact with the state. In addition, there was an unsettled class of "men of diverse callings" and a class of casual laborers and artisans, usually landless, and not subject to state taxation.

Between about 1500 and 1700 there took place the great change—in part comparable to developments in much of western Europe between 1100 and 1300—whereby, roughly, one half of this variegated fluid peasant medley became transformed into a single class of landowners' serfs, "the bonded peasants," and the other half developed into various categories of state peasants, most of them more or less akin to serfs. The binding down of the landowners' serfs was first effected in the relatively small area of the central core of Muscovy, mainly between the Oka and the Volga and Novgorod. It seems to have been due partly to economic pressure, especially indebtedness, but especially to the effect of custom and the needs of the landowners and of the state backed by force.

From the time of Ivan the Great (1462-1505) both the power and the needs, above all the military requirements, of the state grew rapidly, and, as has been pointed out already (p. 87), there occurred a second great change, parallel with that in serfdom, the new conception of the state headed by the tsar as the regulator of obligatory service and the disposer of all land. For the new type of middling and lesser "men of service" (*cf.* p. 90) land grants were of little use without hands to work them. "Black lands" were made over to them. They also must be kept peopled. Those who owe taxation or service of any kind must be inscribed and somehow kept pinned down. To this end cadastral surveys had been developed since the late fifteenth century and a fair amount of evidence becomes available as to peasant attachment, either through privileges granted or confirmed to this or that landowner or through measures enabling a peasant "black" canton to prevent a drop in its taxpaying capacity owing to peasants leaving the canton without finding substitutes. The cadastral surveys and "inquiry registers" are extended in the sixteenth and seventeenth centuries and those inscribed in them become known as "old-dwellers," though the conception of "old" is variable and uncertain. They were probably a relatively prosperous section of the peasantry and their attachment was all the more valuable. Gradually between 1550 and 1650 this becomes the rule and the status of "old settler" hereditary. By then "the writer," who draws up the innumerable reports, inquests, and registers that are demanded by the government, has become a terrible figure in the eyes of the common folk: to be "written down" means trouble, obligations, some form of attachment.

Much of that same hundred years was a time of "dissension," of "sedition." The wars and violent struggles of the last twenty years (1565-84) of Ivan the Terrible's reign and of the first two decades of the seventeenth century reduced much of the center of Muscovy to desolation. Villages were abandoned and land reverted to waste. The pressure of taxation was increasing. The peasants made off on their own or "commended" themselves, seeking protection and economic support from the more powerful and bigger landowners. The hunt for hands became more and more intensive, and more and more limitations on free movement were imposed in the interest of the small and middling landed class, the men with the service fiefs, the backbone of the army. They had taken a large share in the expulsion of the Poles and the founding of the Romanov dynasty (1613), and in the next dozen years they reaped their reward in new land grants (*cf.* pp. 74-75).

The free peasants, for the most part, had had the customary right of departure from landowners each year at the Russian equivalent of Michaelmas, provided their dues had been met. That right had been recognized by the codes of 1497 and 1550, but thereafter it became challenged, especially by the lesser landowners, who could not offer the advantages of the big landowners, notably the monasteries. The *oprichnina* (1565-72; *cf.* p. 93) effected violent economic changes. As conditions grew more and more acute (1601-3 were years of very bad famine and plague) they clamored for full rights of reclaiming runaway peasants, for the prevention of further acquisition of peasants by the wealthier landowners, and for the abolition of any right of departure. From about 1580 onwards a series of edicts was issued regulating the time limit for the right of recovery and laying down "forbidden years" during which departure was temporarily prohibited. It is doubtful whether or not an edict of 1607 permanently abolished the right of departure, but in fact all years became "forbidden years," and after the Time of Troubles (1604-13) no more is heard of the right. But only too much continues to be heard of the *fact* of departure—flight. As we have seen, runaway peasants were a major problem of the seventeenth century, and finally in the code of 1649 no time-limit was set in general for the recovery of runaways thereafter.

Another factor which helps to explain the hardening and extension of serfdom is the influence of slavery. There had always been slaves in the Russian lands, though not in such numbers as to constitute a dominant element in the structure of society. They had been used mainly for domestic, managerial, or military purposes, but in the sixteenth and seventeenth centuries they began to be also used for working the land. Poverty and misrule forced men into a class of "referred," temporary slaves, and the unrestricted rights of a master over his slaves influenced his dealings with the nonslave peasants.

Slaves, however, were not "black"; they owed no taxation to the state. Hence the state did what it could to stop the growth of the slave class. After 1680 it levied taxation from those slaves settled by their masters on the land; just as from 1631 it began to sweep into its taxation net the swollen heterogeneous class of casual landless laborers and craftsmen. Similarly in 1649 drastic innovations were introduced whereby in the towns "self-pledgers," *i.e.* non-taxpaying "commended" peasants, were deprived of their *de facto* trading and handicraft privileges and subjected to inscription in the tax rosters of the towns.

None the less, on most questions the interests of the state and the landowner were fundamentally similar in that the one wanted settled taxpayers and settled providers of military and labor services, while the other wanted settled labor. Just as the "men of service," with their originally temporary land grants becoming more or less permanent estates, owed compulsory service to the state, so the peasants must owe compulsory service by assuring its economic foundation, agriculture; and the "men of service" became not only the officer class in the army and the bureaucracy, but also, as it were, the officer class in the great agricultural army of peasants.

The gradual transformation of the previously variegated classes of peasants into roughly two broad classes, the "bondsmen" serfs of the landowners and the state peasants, was advanced a long stage further by Peter the Great, especially by his imposition of a uniform poll tax on all males, except the nobility and gentry and the clergy (1718). This edict, with which was coupled a very searching new tax census, applied to the towns as well as to the country, but its effects were especially important in the latter. Peter, pushing further what had been begun by his predecessors, abolished all distinctions between slaves or various other categories who were still not taxpayers and the taxpaying peasantry, and merged them in the poll-tax payers either as bonded serfs, or state peasants, or registered townsmen.

As a consequence of the poll tax the whole relation of direct to indirect taxation was reversed. Ordinary direct taxation had formerly been based on a very complicated assessment computed on plowland and certain other sources of subsistence. Then in the course of the seventeenth century, when the state was making desperate efforts to raise more money, it gradually shifted over to taxation by households, which after 1681 became the ordinary mode of assessing direct taxation. The exact distribution of the assessment within each commune or district was left, as previously, to the locality itself. Direct taxation of various kinds, both ordinary and extraordinary, had increased greatly in the seventeenth century, but in 1680 it only accounted for about one-third of the total revenue.

Peter's poll tax, on the contrary, accounted for over half of the revenue, though it completely failed in one of its objects, the covering of the chronic budget deficit. It continued to be the main source of direct taxation right down to its abolition in 1886, but from the end of the eighteenth century it declined steadily in importance compared with the amount raised by indirect taxation, which resumed its earlier position in the state budget.

The further main consequences of the poll tax were threefold:

(i) Peter placed the general responsibility for its payment on the serf-owners, but its actual collection was first entrusted to the army, then to the provincial officials, with almost equally ghastly results. Finally, in 1731 the serf-owners were by law made responsible for the collection of the poll tax from their serfs, with comparatively little interference from government officials. Thereby the state became more than ever linked with the serf-owners. As a corollary, in order to prevent the exhaustion of so important a source of revenue to the state, the serf-owners were required (1734) to tide their peasants over bad times by practical assistance, "in order that the land should not lie idle." This remained a legal obligation, though its efficiency was, in the main, proportionate to the interest of serf-owners in keeping their peasants from too utter destitution.

(ii) The eighteenth century was marked by a great increase in the amount of land under cultivation. This was in part due to the increase of population, in part to other causes, but it was also due to one effect of the poll tax. Even though it bore much more heavily upon the peasants than previous direct taxation, they paid the same fixed sum however much land they plowed, however much money they made. There is no doubt that there was a growing increase in production and internal trade, which was much facilitated by the abolition of internal tolls (1753) and of restrictions on free internal trade in corn (1762). Contemporaries considered that this increase was due to serfdom, or at least was impossible without serfdom. In any case it was true that there was at one and the same time an extension and intensification of serfdom and an increase in production.

(iii) The working practice of the poll-tax system, in conjunction with the increase in population, was an important cause in the development of the commune both in its agricultural, economic aspect and its fiscal, administrative aspect.

The origins and development of the commune, or *mir*, have been even more hotly debated by Russian historians than those of serfdom, ever since the issue of the emancipation of serfs made the commune of central importance. As has been emphasized earlier in this chapter (see pp. 125-129), it was decided at the time of emancipation (1861) to establish the commune legally as an agricultural economic unit and as an institution for various fiscal and administrative purposes. The supporters of the commune belonged to various camps. Some, like the slavophils (see p. 232), saw in it an original Russian institution born of the people and capable of fending off the evils of Western individualistic competition. Others, like the populist socialist-revolutionaries, saw in it a means of achieving an agrarian socialism without passing through a long period of capitalist development.

At the time of emancipation most of the Russian peasantry were grouped in communes, of varying sizes, composed sometimes of one village, sometimes of parts of one large village, sometimes of groups of scattered settlements. The most essential usual features of the commune from the agricultural and economic standpoint were: (i) that its membership was hereditary, though newcomers could be admitted; (ii) that its members worked land by families, but (except in a minority of communes where holdings were hereditary) periodically redistributed their strip holdings scattered in the (usually three-course) open fields, in accordance with either working strength, or taxation and other obligations, or the number of "eaters" in each family; (iii) that the members of the commune regulated in common the use of meadows, pasture, fisheries, woods, etc., and the disposal of any communal land not already utilized and the acquisition of new land or working rights.

One school of historians took the view that the agricultural commune with periodical redistribution of land had been in various forms a continuous feature throughout Russian history, in sharp distinction from European development, and that the commune was a spontaneous, popular co-operative association which owed nothing, or nothing essential, to state action or influences from above. Another school of historians took the opposite view that the commune as known in the nineteenth century was the outcome of financial and administrative measures taken by the state since the late sixteenth century, combined with the effects of the rule of the serfowners.

Subsequent research during the last sixty years has shed much light on the problem of the commune, though its history before about 1550 still remains very obscure. It is now clear that the first view is untenable, and that the second requires much modification. In particular, the necessity has been shown of distinguishing between different types of communes which developed in different ways and at different periods in the very diverse natural and social conditions of different regions of Russia. Further, the importance has been shown of distinguishing between (i) the commune as an agricultural-forest community of working family units, combining in a great variety of labor and economic partnerships or associations, varying much in size and composition, developing diverse forms of land ownership and utilization of land and other means of subsistence, and (ii) the commune as an administrative and fiscal organization, of still more varying size, in dependence on state power and state needs.

It is clear that the agricultural commune was not the mere product of administrative action, though both the state and the serf-owners greatly influenced its development at least from the sixteenth century. Despite the comparative scantiness and the obscurity of the evidence before then, it seems certain that both in Kiev Russia and during the Mongol period one feature of society was the prevalence of collective arrangements by peasant communities (whether of the joint family, of groups of such families, or of wider groups) for regulating the transference of land and in many cases its utilization (for instance, meadows, bee or fishing grounds, or pasture), and for dealing with newcomers. Such agricultural communes must, in all probability, have been very different from their later successors (usually) with the nucleated village, the three-course open fields and periodical redistribution of holdings, since the present available evidence shows that still in the sixteenth century scattered settlements of not more than eight or nine households at a maximum were the usual form of agricultural village, and that the three-course open fields were only beginning to be usual in central Muscovy about 1500.

Periodical redistribution followed, but it did not become the outstanding feature of the agricultural commune throughout most of the Russian parts of the empire until the eighteenth century or even later. It was not by any means the sole mark of communal land-ownership or utilization, but it was of very great significance, and its encouragement (in some regions its introduction) by the state and the serf-owners assisted the growth of the peasant's idea that he had a right to be provided with some land. Periodical redistribution and the three-course open fields gradually developed owing to increasing pressure of population upon natural resources, to the tying down of the peasants through serfdom, to the weight of the services of the serfs to their masters, and to the increase in and methods of direct taxation by the state.

The practice of redistribution became slowly extended outwards from the more thickly settled portions of central Muscovy as these same factors, and especially pressure of population on natural resources, made themselves felt in this or that region. In much of the Ukraine and White Russia, however, this extension was far from regular, partly owing to the effects of Polish rule, and other forms of landownership and communal organization continued for long to persist. In New Russia (*cf.* pp. 37-39) the communal system was by no means general, and the frequent absence of the three-field system of necessity prevented the growth of land redistribution in the manner practiced in central Russia. Again, in the Far North and in Siberia conditions resulted in very different developments of the agricultural commune.

Here, as elsewhere, it grew up on the original basis of associated labor and of landowning and working by the joint family, usually composed of three generations; but the northern communes, nearly all of which were composed not of serfs but of those who eventually became state peasants, developed from joint family working through a complicated system of "share" landowning to individual private holdings, which in the eighteenth century led to wide variations in peasant wealth and a prolonged struggle between the poorer peasants and the richer peasants and landowning burghers. In the struggle the government, in its efforts to organize and ensure the dues and services of these state peasants, in effect took sides against the rich peasants, with the result that in the half-century or so following 1754 there came into being in the far northern provinces, under the influence of a series of measures taken by the state, a new form of equalitarian communal land system with periodical redistribution, much as in central Russia.

Thus, the agricultural commune, as far as it can be traced since the sixteenth century, developed in different ways and at different paces in different parts of the immense land of the Russians. Gradually, in most regions it became more and more influenced, directly and indirectly, by state action (especially in regard to taxation) and by obligations to the serf-owners.

Nevertheless, always behind this or that edict, this or that ruling of officials, this or that action by the serf-owners, there lay the reactions of the peasants themselves to the measures imposed from above; reactions that resulted in widely varying actual working practices in their continual struggle for and with the land. At the basis of the agricultural commune lay age-old folkways, the deep sediment of peasant customary law and practice, hinging on the principle of work applied to the land and the conception of a right to work land.

The commune in its second aspect, as a fiscal and administrative unit, has almost as long and quite as tangled and originally dark a history. In Kiev Russia and during the Mongol period, much as for instance in the hundred and shire in Anglo-Saxon England, certain responsibilities were placed on local groups or districts in regard to criminal offenses, the detailed assessment and collection of tribute or dues, and for certain other purposes. These responsibilities were met by headmen or elders or other local semi-officials. On this slowly evolving and overwhelmingly customary basis, the commune as a fiscal administrative community or district gradually took variegated shape.

Between 1450 and 1650 the Muscovite state was created, but it was too undeveloped not to continue in the main the traditional practice of dealing, not with the individual, but with the group. From the end of the sixteenth century the evidence multiplies and we can see in some detail the anthill Muscovite administration toiling away, above all with the task of raising taxation and providing for the army and defense work.

Assessment of taxation, primarily based on the plowland, was made by officials for each district, but they depended on information supplied by the peasants or the locality. The tax apportionment to the individual group of its share in the total assessment of a district continued to be made as previously by elected elders or others of peasant and borough communes, normally with no direct interference by the government. The collection of taxes was usually entrusted likewise to elected members of the commune, in the case of state peasants; but it was closely controlled by officials of the government. On the estates of the serf-owners, though they were not legally responsible for the state taxation due from their serfs until the eighteenth century (see p. 145), they, or their bailiffs, in fact were closely concerned with the collection, and to a varying extent with the detailed apportionment, of the taxation due from their serfs.

The commune or subdivisions of it, both peasant and borough, were collectively responsible for direct taxation, though it appears that (until after 1861) collective responsibility for arrears was not uniformly applied. Muscovite administration was always loth to lay down general principles; it worked piecemeal, from particular case to particular case, as often as not on the basis of the customary practice of a district, but also with a large dose of arbitrariness. In any case, the collective responsibility of the commune for tax apportionment was of the greatest consequence, and it was the development of this and other obligations in the course of the seventeenth and eighteenth centuries that resulted in the general coalescence of the commune as a fiscal administrative group with the commune as an agricultural, economic group.

The Muscovite officials of the sixteenth and seventeenth centuries found the utmost difficulty in establishing and applying any satisfactory unit of land-tax assessment. The units varied at different times and in different parts of the country. They were always exceedingly complicated and assessments were made at different intervals of time. The commune, being responsible for the tax apportionment among its members, was vitally interested in preventing at least any diminution in its numbers or the general amount of their income. The same applied still more after the introduction of the poll tax by Peter the Great, since the censuses, or "revisions," of males were taken only once in about every twenty years and the amount of the poll tax due from each commune remained the same between each "revision," no matter what changes occurred in that interval in the actual number of its "revision souls." This had an important effect in making continued membership of the commune in practice compulsory, at least as regarding payment of the poll tax.

Peter not only thus reinforced the communal system, taxed the peasants more heavily, and added to the weight of serfdom. The passport system (see p. 129), introduced by him and greatly extended by his successors, worked in the same direction; while, in addition to ruthless forced-labor levies for his new capital, his new fleet, his new canals, he imposed upon the peasants as a regular duty the very heavy burden of recruiting levies for his new standing army. As a consequence, the eighteenth century in one respect is similar to the seventeenth: it began, and continued to be, a century of peasant flight and peasant revolt.

5. *Peasant Revolts*

The reaction of the peasants, Russian and non-Russian alike, to increasing subjection to serfdom and to the rapacity of officials took two extreme forms—either flight from oppression or fight against oppression. The importance of flight as one great element in the history of Russian expansion and the frontier has already been sufficiently emphasized. The fight against serfdom in the central Russian lands was perhaps less determined than it might have been just because so many of the boldest and toughest spirits trekked away to the south or east. The bitterest fight against the expanding wave of serfdom was waged in the main from the frontier fringes, not from behind the wave itself. It was the fight of the frontier against the comparatively settled and expanding center, which was at the same time the seat of governmental power.

Four times, apart from revolts of non-Russians, the southeast and middle Volga frontier rose in great revolts, or better civil wars, which gravely shook the state; but, except to some extent for the first, they did not succeed in setting alight mass revolt in the central core of Muscovy. They are famous in Russian history from the names of their principal leaders, Bolotnikov (1606-7), Stenka Razin (1670-71), Bulavin (1707-8), and Pugachov (1773-75).[1]

In these civil wars certain characteristics appear, an analysis of which will help towards an understanding of the peasantry and of the social history of Russia during the two and half centuries before the ending of serfdom.

(1) Each of the great revolts, except that of Bolotnikov in its earlier stages, was headed by the Cossacks, of the Don or the Ural. They supplied almost all the leaders, and they were indispensable in firing the peasantry on a large scale and in providing some military organization and leadership.

---

[1] One of the best known of Pushkin's tales, *The Captain's Daughter* (1836; translated in the Everyman edition), gives a vivid picture of the setting of the revolt of Pugachov, who is himself portrayed in some respects in a curiously favorable light. Pushkin also wrote a valuable history of the revolt, which has not been translated.

But as they swept up northwards they dwindled in numbers and became less sure of themselves. Further, the most numerous element among the Cossack rebels were the needy newcomers and runaway peasants, "the bare backs," flocking south especially after 1650 to escape from serfdom, who, as has been seen (p. 43), had little in common with the privileged Cossack oligarchy of the lower Don, most of which held aloof from the rebels or even opposed them. Neither Razin nor Bulavin succeeded in establishing a secure base in the lower Don, and there was no rising on the Don to join Pugachov. Nor did Razin or Bulavin succeed in linking up with the Ukraine and the Zaporozhian Cossacks (*cf.* p. 218). Although many individual Ukrainians joined their bands, local differences and disputes were too pronounced for any combination against Moscow.

(2) The main seriousness of the revolts lay in the combination of Cossacks with the serfs and other classes of peasants (and not only Russian peasants). Bonded serfs and state or court peasants usually made common cause, and in the revolt of Pugachov a very prominent rôle was played in the Urals by the peasants ascribed to the mines and metal works. This new eighteenth-century class of serfs had their special grievances. The great majority of them had to work so many days a year at works far away from their own villages and were but unskilled industrial labor, half agricultural and sharing the traditions and interests of peasants. On the other hand, the small nucleus of skilled workers had a different outlook; for they lived permanently at the works and depended on them; hence they wanted their wretched working conditions bettered, but they did not favor the destruction of the works, and it was through them that Pugachov tried to secure the munitioning of his ill-provided bands.

(3) In addition to Cossacks and peasants, there were the very motley elements of the Volga and other garrison and trading towns—the boatmen and casual laborers, the small handicraftsmen and petty traders, many of the minor officials and reservist garrison soldiers. When the Cossacks were out

in strength there was ample enough discontented, downtrodden, and vagrant material in the frontier towns to swell the rebel forces.

This, however, did not apply to the towns of the older provinces of Muscovy. In the seventeenth century unrest was rampant in these towns, all of them except Moscow small, nearly all of them still owning some land and closely linked with agriculture, fishing, and the forest. In the history of seventeenth-century risings the towns figured almost as prominently as the peasantry (*e.g.* in Moscow and numerous other towns in 1648; in Novgorod and Pskov in 1650; in Moscow again in 1662; in Astrakhan in 1705-6). Yet townsman and peasant never really combined against the government and serf-owner. The very complex struggle in the towns was fed, for the most part, by causes that did not affect the peasantry, or did not affect them in the same way. The peasants did not to any extent make common cause with the townsmen when they "rioted." Nor did one town with another. Only once (1648) were there contemporaneous risings in a number of towns, and the result was the crisis of the assembly of the land of 1648/9 and the new code of laws.

(4) Three of the great revolts embraced non-Russians as well as Russians, and that of Bulavin coincided with a prolonged rising of the Bashkirs in the central Urals (1705-11). At the time of Pugachov the Bashkirs came out in force to join him in the fifth of their big-scale risings within a hundred years; while in the middle Volga many of the Kazan Tatars, Mari, Chuvash and Mordva (see map 4), revolted much as they had done at the time of Razin and Bolotnikov, both against the Russians and against their own upper class. Some of the rebel bands were mixed non-Russian and Russian in composition, and one of Razin's slogans ran, "For God and the Prophet, for the Sovereign and the Host" (*i.e.* the Cossack "host"). Thus the great peasant revolts were in part also colonial rebellions, the continuation of the long struggle against the Russian mastery of the Volga and the Urals.

In this respect, however, the attitude of the non-Russians

was broadly speaking the same to all classes of Russians, even though their relations with the Russian common people as individuals were generally none too bad. The Russian serf or petty trader or garrison rank-and-file spelled Russian penetration just as much as the Russian serf-owner or wealthy merchant or officer. The Bashkirs were specially stirred to struggle against the rapid intensification of Russian pressure on them when Peter the Great and his successors forced the pace of mines and factories in the Urals. Their attitude to the Russian peasants ascribed to the works is typical. "Go home," they said (1773), "your term is done: our fathers, who gave you land, are dead, and we don't want any more to let you have it." And they burned and pillaged to their hearts' content. Pugachov vainly attempted to limit depredations against the Russians, especially since he wanted the works to supply him with arms. During that revolt half the works in the Urals were more or less seriously damaged and it took half a dozen years before output reached the previous level of production.

The religious division between non-Russians and Russians was a further hindrance to common action between the two peasantries, and also a link pulling the non-Russians together. The mullahs, powerful among the Kazan Tatars and the Bashkirs, maintained intermittent connections with the Crimean Tatars and Constantinople, "for we are of one family and spirit with them." Communication, however, became increasingly difficult, and what was later to be called panislamism was never a very serious force in these parts, though in the nineteenth century it became so in the Caucasus and later in Central Asia. In the eighteenth century mass conversions to Orthodoxy (due to the tax exemptions and other privileges accorded to converts), the closing of mosques and other measures against the Moslems were important stimulants to anti-Russian feeling; until Catherine the Great reversed Elizabeth's support of Orthodox missionary militancy, returned to the usual earlier practice of religious toleration, and was stirred by the revolt of Pugachov to encourage a positive policy of favoring Moslem religious leaders.

Although Islam and defense against Russian colonization tended to draw the non-Russian peoples together, they were themselves increasingly rent by social divisions. For their own princelings and landowners and merchants the revolts of their own people usually meant revolt against themselves, as well as against the Russians. After the early seventeenth century they only combined in part with their own dependents against the Russians. Then, too, there were many "serving Tatars" in Russian employ who stood by the government and aided in suppressing rebellion, notably in the time of Razin.

Thus, two of the greatest motives for rebellion among the non-Russians—Russian colonization and defense of Islam—in the nature of things could not be shared by the Russians; while the motives that were common to non-Russian and Russian peasantry alike—the weight of serfdom and governmental misrule—were not in general shared by the most powerful sections of the non-Russian peoples themselves. Divided within themselves and divided from the Russians they could not combine with them on any scale in joint mass revolt.

(5) In the eighteenth-century risings the appeal to the Old Believers (see pp. 181 ff.) was pronounced, often combined with invective against the foreigners, "the Germans," who corrupt with novelties and grind the poor with oppression. "We stand for the old faith," one of Bulavin's henchmen proclaimed, "and for the House of the Mother of God and for you, for all the common people, that we do not fall into the Greek faith" (*i.e.* the reforms of Nikon; see pp. 179 ff.). On the Ural river, from which Pugachov started (1773), the Cossacks were mostly Old Believers, and they had had ten years' struggle with German officers sent down from St. Petersburg to impose a settlement of their local disputes and to reorganize them.

(6) The watchwords and the slogans in the four great revolts show the same primary characteristic, the appeal to elemental uprising against serfdom and oppression. The keynote of Razin was simple enough: "to remove the constables from the towns and to go to Moscow against the landowners," "to

kill the landowners." Bulavin's appeal was as simple: "to slay the landowners and the profiteers and the Germans"; our affair is against the landlords and those who do injustice. You barebacks, come all of you . . . on horse or on foot, naked and barefoot, come and do not fear: there will be horses and clothing and money for you. . . . And whosoever seizes the common people and does not let them pass, he shall be hanged to death."

Pugachov, masquerading as the emperor Peter III, poured out edicts admirably attuned to the variegated hopes and dreams of his diverse followers. Then the Ural peasants, for instance, "began to praise God that the bright sun, long hidden beneath the earth, is again risen over the whole world and can warm them once more. . . . They hope that the rebels will free them from wild beasts and cut the sharp claws of the malefactor landlords, officers, and factory owners." Above all, when Pugachov, after for a moment taking Kazan, crossed to the west of the Volga (1774) and seemed about to make for Moscow and set the central provinces alight in wild conflagration, he proclaimed far and wide the abolition of serfdom and war on the gentry:

"We grant to all hitherto in serfdom and subjection to the landowners . . . the old cross and prayers, heads and beards, liberty and freedom, always to be Cossacks, without recruiting levies, poll tax or other money taxes, with possession of the land, the woods, the hay meadows, the fishing grounds, the salt lakes, without payment and without rent, and we free all those hitherto oppressed by the malefactor landowners and the bribe-taker officials and judges. . . . Those who hitherto were gentry in their lands and estates, these opponents of our rule and perturbators of the empire and ruiners of the peasants—seize them, punish them, hang them, treat them in the same way as they, having no Christian feeling in them, oppressed you, the peasants. With the extermination of these enemies and malefactor gentry every one will begin to enjoy quiet and a peaceful life, which will continue evermore."

Small wonder that Pugachov, voicing thus the passions of

the underdog, "was for us, common people, no criminal, but our friend and protector"; much as Razin was heroized in popular song and folk-tale up and down Russia as the protector of the weak and needy, as well as the lusty conqueror and the magician, who flew on a carpet, whom no bullet could harm, who escaped from his chains through the eye of a needle. Small wonder either that over 1500 of the gentry, men, women, and children, perished at the hands of Pugachov's bands, besides another 1300 of other classes; that Catherine had to appoint one of her most prominent generals with dictatorial powers and send large forces of regular troops to round up Pugachov and restore government and the landowners in the Volga lands; that she hastened (1775) to refashion the system of local government; and, above all, that the governing classes looked back upon the revolt of Pugachov as the yawning chasm of social revolution, against which only the most ruthless upholding of the forces of law and order could avail.

(7) And yet the revolution of the peasant underworld was not thought of by that underworld in terms of revolution against the tsar. Except among some of the Cossacks and the Bashkirs, the rule of the tsar in some form was accepted as something given, like the sun and the moon. Two Russian proverbs are highly indicative. "Oppression comes not from the tsar, but from his favorites." "The tsar is gracious; not so his kennel-keeper." It is typical that Razin sallied out "to stand for the Lord Sovereign and to remove the traitors," *i.e.* officials and landowners. The great revolts, just like the small local risings, had hardly anything in the way of a political program with which they might combine their social program.

If need be the reigning monarch was declared to be no rightful ruler, or even Antichrist, but in his or her place was put another, the rightful ruler, falsely said to have been dead, actually alive and with the rebels, or soon to join them, his faithful subjects. Hence the long line of pretender tsars who appeared so frequently and at times with such alarming success ever since the first False Dmitry (1604; *cf.* p. 441), and who illustrate so forcibly the sway among the illiterate masses of rumor, child-like make-believe, and daring impersonation. The conduct of Pugachov and his associates best reveals the nature of the pretender idea.

Pugachov, who was actually a runaway Don Cossack wanted by the police, gave himself out as Peter III, Catherine the Great's husband who had been deposed and murdered in 1762. Rumors that he was still alive and near at hand had been rife, and there were at least four pretenders assuming his name before Pugachov, and at least one after him. Peter III enjoyed a certain posthumous popularity owing to the repercussions of his edict of 1762 absolving the gentry from compulsory service (see p. 134). This was believed to be either the work, not of the tsar, but of his enemies, or to be the harbinger of an emancipation edict for the peasantry that had been secretly suppressed. The belief took very confused forms, but always there was the idea that Peter had been about to save the serfs from their owners, when he was foully supplanted.

"There is great reason," Pugachov explained to his followers, "why I am not loved by the gentry: many of them, young men and others of middling years, so it happened . . . though fit to serve and given posts, went off into retirement and lived at their will off the peasants in their villages and quite ruined them, poor folk, and they alone almost ruled for themselves the whole empire. So I began to compel them to service and wanted to take away from them their villages, so that they serve only for wages. And the officials who judge suits unjustly and oppress the people I punished and wished to hand over to the block. And so, for this they began to dig a ditch for me. And when I went to take a row on the Neva river [in St. Petersburg] they arrested me there and they made up a false tale about me and they forced me to wander over the face of the earth."

But after many years in foreign lands Peter returned: "for I wanted to see how the common people were faring and what oppressions they suffered from the officials." Now he was come into his own again: he would soon join his poor son Paul (later emperor, at that time known by the Ural Cossacks to be on very bad terms with his mother, Catherine); and he would go to Kazan and to Moscow and to Piterburg, and he would send Catherine to a nunnery or back to her own country; but "if she meets me with bad words, I know already what to do then."

So the maze of rumor and make-believe was spread abroad from the headquarters of the impostor emperor and his war college, formed in imitation of that in St. Petersburg, and men galloped far and wide over the steppes bearing his imperial orders and imitation edicts, specially "beautiful and sweet-tongued" for the benefit of the nomad peoples. It mattered not that Pugachov himself was almost illiterate; that he had with him a wife from the Ural Cossacks (and another wife and family on the Don); that his closest confederates knew who he really was and many others suspected. A tsar at the head of rebellion would as it were legitimize it.

To an English observer it seemed (1764) that "the interior state of this country . . . appears . . . as one great mass of combustibles with incendiaries placed in every corner." Yet, in fact, the incendiaries were normally so local and disconnected that they could be stamped out by the powers on the spot or small-scale punitive expeditions. Only in the great revolts that have just been analyzed did it come to the pitch of actual warfare, even if of a guerrilla kind, and the employment of regular armies. Against isolated second-rate garrison posts the rebels were formidable, but against reliable troops they had no chance, for they were for the most part miserably armed (save for captured guns), usually short of horses, and very deficient in co-ordinated organization and discipline. They were generally always on the move, leaving a chain of fires, but without a solid furnace. Localism even in the case of the great revolts was a primary cause of failure. Most of the rebel bands would operate only in a comparatively small area. The largest of them at any one time were 15,000 to 20,000 strong, but their numbers ebbed and flowed with the utmost rapidity. Above all, none of the revolts, with the partial exception of that of Bolotnikov, succeeded in gaining a hold in the center of serfdom and governmental power.

CHAPTER IV

THE CHURCH

1. *The Revolution and Religion*

THE SOVIET UNION was unique in being the first state to be governed by a ruling party which proclaimed as part of its creed opposition to all and every form of religion, though the latest developments have culminated in a striking modification of this attitude. Dialectical materialism, as developed by Lenin, held fast to Marx's slogan, "Religion is the opiate of the people"; diagnosed it as an ideology based on fear of the forces of nature and of the prevailing powers that be; and attacked it as one of the allies of capitalism and as the inveterate opponent of science. The general attitude of enmity towards the official state church was shared by all sections of the revolutionary movement in Russia. They had always regarded the Orthodox church, which included the great majority of Russians, as so much a part of the organization of autocracy that the two blended together in a theocratic absolutism. Thus the fall of tsardom was bound to threaten the position of the Orthodox church, and shortly after the October Revolution a frontal attack on religion was begun, in the name of "genuine liberty of conscience."

The fact that many of the leaders of the church supported the Whites in the Civil War and Allied intervention gave further grounds for identifying Orthodoxy not only with reaction in the past, but with counter-revolution in the present. The Catholics in the Russian empire were mainly Poles and could not fail to be all the more suspect in view of the Soviet-Polish war of 1920, while the international character of Catholicism accentuated Soviet hostility. The Moslems, some twenty millions in all, though disunited, were subject to panislamic and anti-Russian influences, especially in Central Asia, the Communist reconquest of which involved a bitter struggle against Moslem vested interests, with some support from across the frontiers (*cf.* p. 286). Here there was, however, one notable change in that Turkey, under the new secularist régime of Mustapha Kemal, ceased to act as a powerful magnet for Russian Moslems.

The frontal attack against religion (mainly the Orthodox and Catholic churches) took various forms, ranging from cessation of all payments by the state to the clergy, prohibition of religious instruction in schools and theological seminaries, or closing of churches, to wide-spread, sporadic violence against the clergy, looting and confiscation of church property, or imprisonment and execution of the clergy and the faithful on political grounds as supporters of counter-revolution. Violent action against the churches declined after the early anarchic years and the Civil War, partly because the Soviet régime was more firmly established, partly because it was realized that, as Lunacharsky, commissar for education, expressed it, "religion is like a nail and the harder you hit the deeper it goes into the wood."

Lenin and the Communist party had always stressed that "the complete dying out of religious prejudices" could only be the result of complete reconstitution of society and of new education. Hence, the main methods of combating the influence of religion became less direct, and much more efficacious. Besides the ban on religious education in any schools, discriminatory taxation and the strict control of the printing press and licensing of churches, these methods concentrated on educating a generation on communist principles, unacquainted with and feeling no need for religion because bred up in a new economic and social order. Meanwhile some degree of accommodation with the churches was reached; advantage was taken of the divisions within the Orthodox church to weaken its hold, and there was some favoring of the Baptists and other Russian dissenters, whose social outlook in general had always been anti-monarchical and equalitarian.

In 1929 there was a return to militancy during the furious years of collectivization and the first five-year plan, and the whole weight of the state machinery backed the drive against religion, particularly through the secret police and the League of Militant Godless. In the same year the provision that had existed on paper in the 1918 constitution assuring freedom of both religious and anti-religious propaganda was rescinded by an amendment which left only the right of anti-religious propaganda. This was repeated in the new constitution of 1936, which, however, reflected an easing in the position of the churches by canceling the previous electoral disqualifications of "monks and priests of all religious denominations" and by specifically re-enacting freedom of religious worship. By then also the original attitude of vilification of marriage and the family had been completely reversed. Sunday was reinstated as a rest day. Except during the renewed attacks on the clergy in 1937-38, the general policy, at least towards the Orthodox, tended towards comparative leniency.

Since the early thirties it seems that the League of Militant Godless, despite a membership (1941) of three and a half million, has been apathetic and intermittent in its activities, and that religion has maintained a strong hold at the least in many rural parts of the country. In 1937 the president of the League estimated that in the towns about two-thirds of those over sixteen were unbelievers, but in the villages perhaps only about one-third. At the same time the fact must be faced that it is probable from Soviet figures that there were in 1941 ten times fewer Orthodox churches than in 1900 and at the very least six times fewer secular clergy, while monks and nuns have disappeared. Much the greater part of the drop seems to have occurred since 1928.

Since June 1941 the patriotic rallying of the churches against the German invasion of Russia has led to the elimination of one of the main causes of communist militant hostility, namely, the branding of the churches as the allies of foreign designs upon the Soviet Union. The result has been that the attitude of the government towards the churches has very significantly changed, as is most notably shown by Stalin's approval of the election of a patriarch (September 1943). Further, it is likely that the new Soviet patriotism, with its appeal to Russian traditions and the past, may contribute to a modification of outlook on religion and its historical forms in Russia.

That the coming of Christianity to Kiev Russia in the tenth century was a relative advance in civilization is now admitted by Soviet historians. During the Mongol period religious feeling was quickened and deepened by a new monastic movement and the Orthodox church became allied with the rising state of Moscow. From 1450 to 1650 Orthodoxy was a national and patriotic force, but at the same time the church became fatally tied to the new St. Petersburg autocracy. The Schism in the third quarter of the seventeenth century was followed by the complete subservience of the official church to tsarism, and on the other hand by the multiplication of dissenting sects in opposition to the ruling powers. Religion became increasingly divorced from the organized panoply of the Orthodox church, which was by 1917 in many ways a shell. Christianity remained, however, a living power, linked with the struggles of the Russian people for the last thousand years.

2. *Byzantine Christianity and Russia*

The latter part of the tenth century witnessed a sweeping advance of Christianity in the northern and eastern marches of Europe through the baptism of rulers followed by the adoption of Christianity as the state religion. Scandinavia, Poland, Hungary, and Russia entered the Christian fold. While the three first were converted by Rome, Russia owed her church to Byzantium. A century before Cyril and Methodius had earned their title of Apostles of the Slavs by their missionary labors among the Czechs and southern Slavs. Though they had come from Constantinople they themselves worked in close connection with Rome, and the final establishment of Christianity between Bohemia and the Adriatic was a Frankish and Latin achievement, while the Balkan

Slavs, after some oscillations, remained within the Greek Orthodox church.

"The conversion of Russia" was the complex product of the military, political, and commercial relations of Kiev Russia with the Byzantine empire and Bulgaria. It is dated from the baptism in 988 of Vladimir, grand-prince of Kiev, a slavized Varangian war leader, the Russian equivalent of the king-saints Olaf of Norway and Stephen of Hungary. Immediately afterwards he married the emperor's sister and set about destroying paganism and introducing Christianity. This he did both in Kiev and in the dependent Russian principalities, which his family, the descendants of the Viking adventurer Rurik (d. about 879), shared in ruling.

For half a century before Vladimir, Kiev had known Christianity, and known it as the religion of the rich and the powerful. His grandmother, Olga, and various individual leaders had been converted, and relations with the West had brought contacts with the Latins. These were later multiplied despite religious subordination to Constantinople through the frequent marriages, until the thirteenth century, of the house of Rurik with the reigning families of the West, marriages that were much more numerous than those with Byzantine princesses. Russia was indeed in more general touch with Europe during the eleventh and twelfth centuries than thereafter until the late fifteenth. Although "the conversion of Russia" took place at a time when the antagonism between Pope and Patriarch was widening into a breach between the western and eastern churches, for Russia the sharp cleavage between East and West was made rather by the Mongol conquest than by the adoption of Christianity from Byzantium.

Yet there was division, if not cleavage, in the earlier centuries. Russia, in contrast with the medieval West, knew no monastic orders, no canons regular, no friars, no crusades, no chivalry, no challenge by the spiritual power of claims to supremacy by the secular power, and no philosophic or scientific inquiry. Orthodoxy as inherited from Byzantium meant the preservation of what was already fixed, and the Russian church throughout its history has been weak in theological and philosophical creativeness.

As with the Roman missions to England four centuries earlier, conversion was primarily an affair of the princes and their retainers, but there was until the mid-fourteenth century little that was comparable to the Celtic missionary work which contributed so much to the christianizing of Anglo-Saxon England. Little organized resistance was encountered from paganism, since the Slav tribes had no common cult nor any solid equivalent to a priesthood, so that there was no powerful vested interest hostile to the new religion. The mass of the population, however, even when nominally Christian, for long retained their old customs and beliefs. Sorcery, magic, witchcraft, and omens still held sway almost as strongly, it appears, in the sixteenth century as in the thirteenth, when a church council (1274) had to insist that no one should be ordained priest who had previously practiced sorcery.

The organization and practices of the church inevitably followed those of Constantinople, of which it was a dependency. There were, however, considerable divergences owing to the great size and remoteness of the country and its very different social and political structure. While the newly arrived hierarchy were accustomed to strict monarchical rule and political centralization, they found neither in Kiev Russia. They were too few to attempt to remold the political fabric and in the main they contented themselves with struggling against the worst abuses, especially the internecine feuds of the princes, by exhortation and spiritual penalties, though the weapon of excommunication was not often used against the princes (see also pp. 77-80).

The metropolitan of Kiev, appointed by and under the jurisdiction of the Patriarch of Constantinople, was primate of the church, from 1037 onwards. The bishops, on the other hand, were appointed by the local princes (in Novgorod by the town assembly after 1156), but consecrated by the metropolitan. At first Greeks, they were soon for the most part chosen from Russians. In contrast, the metropolitans were for two hundred years all Greeks, with two contested exceptions. In the next two centuries (1238-1448) the Patriarch was less successful in resisting the claims of the grand-princes and the council of Russian bishops, but even so out of the ten metropolitans only three were Russians, while five were Greeks and two Bulgars or Serbs. As in the Greek church, the custom grew up, and finally hardened into invariable practice, of choosing bishops only from the monks, or black, clergy. Again as in the Greek church, the secular, or white, clergy were married. Monasticism spread rapidly to the chief towns, and under the influence of the famous Monastery of the Caves, in Kiev, the common-life rule of the great Constantinople monastery of Studius became generally adopted.

While the bigger churches and monasteries soon became dowered with tithe, land, and other grants, no regular provision was made for the lower clergy, who became in effect the hirelings of their parishioners or of the lords of the manor, who elected and dismissed them virtually at will, until appointment passed into the control of the bishops in the seventeenth and eighteenth centuries. Later the increasing number of unemployed lower clergy and nondescript monks constituted a serious religious and social evil, until reforms began in the eighteenth century. The lower clergy formed a hereditary caste, and were largely illiterate and little or not at all above the general level of the peasantry, but they did come from and live with the people: they shared their failings and their virtues, and when they were men of true religious feeling their influence was strong.

The adoption of Christianity increased the influence of Byzantine legal ideas, and parts of the civil and ecclesiastical law of the emperors were grafted on to Russian customary law. A system of ecclesiastical courts grew up with jurisdiction over clerics (defined even more widely than in the West) in all cases between them, except the gravest criminal offenses, and over all persons in matters of morals, belief, observance of church regulations, some matrimonial matters, and eventually inheritance. Other civil and all criminal cases involving a cleric and a non-cleric were settled jointly by ecclesiastical and lay officials. The limits of the two jurisdictions were dubious and they naturally varied much during the centuries. They occasioned much strife, but there was no such struggle as that between Henry II and Becket until Nikon, the Patriarch of Moscow, challenged the drastic curtailment of ecclesiastical jurisdiction and property rights sanctioned by the assembly of the land in 1649. Nikon partially succeeded, but the triumph of the secular courts was completed by Peter the Great.

Church jurisdiction had become from the fourteenth century onwards more and more important as a source of revenue in proportion as charters of privilege extended its scope. The monasteries and the episcopate in their capacity as great landowners acquired special, though varying, rights of jurisdiction over their tenants and peasants, as well as privileges in regard to taxation, trade, and service. Thus, when in the seventeenth century serfdom became generally established, they owned serfs in the same way as lay landowners, and had even wider powers over them. In this development the Russian church was not dissimilar to the Western church in the Middle Ages, but it was markedly different, at any rate from the medieval church in England and France, in that a large part of its administrative, judicial, and economic functions came to be exercised by laymen acting in its name, a fact which, while it mitigated the rivalry of church and state, also assisted the secularization of its courts and lands, to be mentioned later.

Byzantium brought to Russia five gifts: her religion, her law, her view of the world, her art and writing. The Cyrillic script commemorates the alphabet invented on the basis of the Greek in the ninth century by Cyril, the brother of Methodius. From the Bulgars, whose language was closely similar to that of the Russians, it was transplanted under Vladimir. Known as Church Slavonic, it was the written language until popular speech, governmental requirements, and the extension of writing to the laity gradually brought into being a written Russian (with the same script) more and more divergent from Church Slavonic, which continued always to be the language used in church services. As late as the seventeenth century written Russian was still to a large extent under Church Slavonic influence; by the next century it had ceased to be.

What was written in Kiev Russia was overwhelmingly religious, ecclesiastical, or legal, together with some chronicles.[1] Translations of the Bible, of the service books, and of Byzantine collections of the Fathers, church councils, and law books predominate. Extant original compositions, on Byzantine models, such as homilies, exegetics, or lives of the Russian saints, are all too rare before the thirteenth century: hardly any charters earlier than that survive. Legal enactments, law books, and chronicles are the main written sources for the history of Kiev Russia, apart from Arabic and Byzantine writers.

The transmission of the written heritage of Byzantine civilization was due partly to direct translation from the Greek, very largely to southern Slav versions of Greek originals. Bulgarian influence was specially important at the very beginning of Russian Christianity, and there was later, between 1350 and 1450, a notable revival of southern Slav literary, intellectual, and artistic influence on Russia, not only in the shape of various Greek ascetic and polemical works previously unknown in Russia and of new chronicles, but of secular tales and romances. For the first time, for instance, a few Russians then became acquainted with the tale of Troy and the tale of Alexander the Great through Serbian versions. Similarly southern Slav influence caused a change of handwriting in Russian manuscripts during that period.

Of earlier popular literature there is almost nothing left, with the stirring exception of the late-twelfth-century poetic lay *The Tale of the Host of Igor,* now best known in the West through Borodin's opera with the famous Polovtsy

---

[1] There is an English translation of the *Russian Primary Chronicle*, going down to 1110, by S. H. Cross (Harvard, 1930), and of *The Chronicle of Novgorod, 1016-1471*, by R. Michell and N. Forbes (London, 1914).

dances.[1] Such lays, folk-poetry, and songs of the universally popular bards were from their nature little likely to be recorded in writing, and the church frowned heavily upon them, as well as upon communal dancing and sports, as being wrapped up in heathen myth and non-Christian superstition. It was only in the last century that collections were made of the heroic poems then still recited or chanted among the peasantry, some of which derive in apparent origin from the golden days of "gracious Prince Vladimir . . . our Sun of royal Kiev," or of Sadko, "the trader, the rich merchant" of Novgorod—Newtown; "Novgorod, Novgorod, but older than the old."[2]

While the surviving literature of early Russia is all too scanty and suggests intellectual and creative poverty, enough remains (or did remain before the present war) of the Byzantine legacy in architecture, painting, and the minor arts to give some impression of the richness of the æsthetic and material effects of the introduction of Christianity, at any rate in Kiev, Novgorod, Vladimir and a few other centers. Until at least the sixteenth century religion shaped and dominated architecture and painting. Building in brick or stone was rare and almost a monopoly of the church, and skilled artificers were for long Greeks or Greek-trained. (The defenses of the Kremlin of Moscow were wooden until 1367, over two hundred years after the first mention of Moscow, and as late as 1600 there were, apart from monasteries, only ten stone or brick fortresses in the whole of Muscovy.) Architecture has been the outstanding Russian achievement in the arts, until the astonishing outpouring of literature in the nineteenth century. For its great periods it has three times borrowed from abroad; Byzantine, Renaissance, Baroque; but these alien forms were assimilated and blended with native elements, largely based on matchless skill in building in

[1] There is a literal translation in the edition of the Russian text by L. P. Magnus (Oxford, 1915).
[2] A representative selection of these heroic poems *(bylini)* is available in translation in N. K. Chadwick's *Russian Heroic Poetry* (Cambridge, 1932). Sadko, like Igor, is commemorated in opera, by Rimsky-Korsakov.

wood, and with other alien influences, for instance Armenian, Iranian, and later German, in such a way as to produce specific types of Russian and not mere imported architecture. Thus after a stage of copying Santa Sophia and other Constantinople churches in the eleventh century, there was developed in the next century a striking Russian version of Byzantine architecture (evolving in Novgorod the distinctive Russian "onion" dome). This flowered again richly between 1350 and 1450, and then, under the influence of Italian architects, best exemplified in the Moscow Kremlin, became transformed into the Moscow style (see illustrations facing p. 167). In a similar manner painting (on wood icons and in fresco on church walls), which inherited from Byzantium the far-reaching results of the iconoclast struggle, developed into independent schools, rich in color and harmonious grave beauty, from which Rublyov, the greatest master of medieval Russian painting, arose in the early fifteenth century.

3. Mongols and Monks

The Mongol conquest was a turning-point in all aspects of Russian life. There seemed a bare chance that the Mongols might accept Christianity, whether in the form of Nestorianism, or from the Orthodox, who were allowed a bishopric and made some highly placed converts, or from the Papacy, which multiplied attempts to enter into contact with them [1] and also to use the fears aroused by them as a means to win over the Russian Slavs. But by the beginning of the fourteenth century the die had been cast definitely in favor of Bokhara and Islam. Already for some four centuries the Volga Bulgars had been Moslem and Islam was politically desirable in view of the alliance of the Golden Horde with the Egyptian Mamelouks (themselves originating from the Black Sea steppes) against the rival Mongol dynasty in Persia. The

[1] Two of these efforts resulted in the well-known journeys of the Franciscans Rubruquis and Carpino to the Mongols through Russia, translations of which have been published by the Hakluyt Society (1903, and Second Series, No. 4, 1900).

khans continued indeed their tolerance of the Christian religion and repeated, with some modifications, their far-reaching grants of jurisdiction and exemption from taxation to the church in Russia; but the fact remained that after 1300 the whole region of the steppes was Moslem. Thus, when the Russian resurgence against the Tatars came, it took on something of the colors of a crusade in popular estimation and in the eyes of the church, though less so in those of the government.

While the Tatar hordes acknowledged the Prophet, to the west the Lithuanians—the last of the peoples of Europe to be christianized—in the same fourteenth century acknowledged the Pope. The Russian principalities were too shattered by the Mongol invasion and too divided among themselves to prevent the expansion of Lithuanian and Polish rule over the western Russian lands, including Kiev itself. The composite grand duchy of Lithuania for long remained largely Russian and Orthodox in character, but the adoption of Catholicism by the Lithuanians greatly increased Polish influence, which was further promoted by the fact that from 1386 the dynasty of the grand duchy and of Poland was the same (see p. 194). Thus Orthodoxy and Russian influence were losing ground on the west.

During the sway of the Golden Horde the church, like the rest of Muscovy, was to a large extent thrown in upon itself, but in its later phase there was a striking revival of religious life. Monasticism between 1350 and 1500 extended and flourished as never before or since. During the first three and a half centuries of Christianity in Russia we know of the foundation of rather over one hundred monasteries, most of them before 1200, and nearly all of them in the Kiev and Novgorod regions and in or very close to towns. Between 1340 and 1440 we know of no less than one hundred and fifty new monasteries in Muscovy, the majority in the forest wilderness, and their numbers continued to increase.

The most striking characteristics of the new monastic movement were these: it was no longer the follower but the leader of expansion; it sought the untamed wilderness, not as before the princes' courts and the bishops' seats; it recruited itself widely, from different classes and from the young as much as from the old; it was closely linked with the peasantry (not always amicably), in part preceding, in part following, the movement of the peasantry northwards beyond the Volga; finally, it threw up a series of remarkable religious leaders, fortified in the strength of their exceptional spiritual gifts by measured asceticism and practical application of the evangelical virtues.

Although many monks were for a time anchorites, and although the lonely ascetic and the wandering "man of God" (as well as the fitful, second-sighted "fool for Christ's sake" [1]) enjoyed right down to present times wide popular renown, Russian monasticism always preserved the Palestinian communal spirit of charity and support of the needy and outcast and did not extol as the one ideal the extreme asceticism of the solitary Egyptian or Syrian eremite. It was not pre-eminent either in learning or in works of religious devotion or thought, nor, despite the influence of Athos, did it produce many mystics. Its most conspicuously enduring characteristic was the striving for "the spirit of chastity, of humility, of patience, and of love," in the words of the prayer of St. Ephraim the Syrian, specially prized among the Orthodox; a characteristic that was in tune with the submissive endurance of a great part of the Russian people during much of their history.

In the fourteenth and fifteenth centuries the typical form was the small colony or brotherhood, inspired by the saintly power of an exceptional personality, at first living separately, then developing into a monastic community living a common life, from which again individual monks would depart to repeat the process in yet more remote spots. The peripatetic element was accentuated by the absence of any common or-

[1] "We are fools for Christ's sake, but ye are wise in Christ; we are weak, but ye are strong; ye are honourable, but we are despised" (1 Corinthians iv, 10). "But the foolishness of God is wiser than men; and the weakness of God is stronger than men . . . God hath chosen the foolish things of the world to confound the wise; and God hath chosen the weak things of the world to confound the things which are mighty" (1 Corinthians i, 25, 27).

ganization, such as Cluny or Cîteaux developed, linking daughter colonies with the mother foundation, and this later facilitated the growth of serious evils as monasticism decayed. Manual labor, the building of the chapel, the cutting of wood, the tilling of the ground, the catching of fish—very much the same hard round as that of the peasant—were part and parcel of the lives of the members of the new monasteries. Many of them became virtually the founders of peasant parishes, and the links of monastic expansion with colonization became increasingly close and far-reaching as the monasteries acquired wealth and privileges.

Three exceptional figures stood out for their Russian contemporaries of the fourteenth century, and stand out still today—Sergius of Radonezh, Alexis the metropolitan, and Stephen of Perm. Sergius (b. about 1314, d. 1392), the most generally popular of all the saints of Moscow, "the head and teacher for all the monasteries that be in Russia," was the most powerful single spiritual influence of his age, and the monastery that he founded, Troitsko-Sergievsky (see map 3), soon the largest and the richest in Russia, with its strictly ordered life on the basis of the Studite rule, almost at once became the mother or exemplar of numerous other monasteries.[1]

Sergius shunned the political arena, though he was credited with inspiring the victory of Kulikovo (see p. 30)—"go against the godless boldly, without wavering, and thou shalt conquer"—and he was the direct opposite of his admirer Alexis (b. about 1300, d. 1378), a many-sided, much traveled ecclesiastical statesman and administrator, the first metropolitan to be Moscow-bred, who for the last twenty-five years of his life was the central figure in the government of the grand-princedom of Moscow. The third figure, Stephen, first bishop of Perm (d. 1396), a man from the Far North, is again completely different, in that his monastic training and Greek learning led him to pioneer mission work in the wild north-

---

[1] One version of his life, written by a contemporary, is translated by N. Zernov in his *St. Sergius, Builder of Russia* (London, 1939).

east, where he turned his face against russification and invented a wholly new alphabet for the conversion of the Ziryanes, among whom he labored with bravery and devotion.

Between 1300 and 1500 the metropolitan "of Kiev and All Russia," in fact resident in Moscow since about 1300, was on most occasions the active supporter of the grand-princes of Moscow in their gradual extension and concentration of power at the expense of rival princes and feudatories. The very title of the metropolitans was a reminder of the old linking together of all the Russians through Kiev. Backed by Moscow, and usually by the Patriarch of Constantinople, they struggled for a century and a half, with varying success, to prevent the establishment of separate Orthodox metropolitans in Galicia and Lithuania, until late in the fifteenth century they were obliged to acknowledge the fact of division. It is significant, thereafter, that the Muscovite wars against Lithuania-Poland in the following century were in part waged in the name of Orthodoxy for the recovery of what was claimed as the patrimony of the heirs of St. Vladimir. Moscow, if it was "the third Rome," was also "the second Kiev."

4. *The Muscovite Church*

The long-attempted reunion of the eastern and western churches seemed for a moment to have been successfully accomplished in 1439 at the council of Florence, but it met with immediate repudiation in the Russian lands. "Blackblooded" Isidore, the metropolitan, who had played an active part at Florence in favor of reunion, was forced to flee the country in the face of the grand-prince backed by the Muscovite clergy. A prolonged series of papal endeavors to win over Muscovy proved fruitless, though ultimately in Poland the Jesuits won a pronounced victory by detaching a large section of the Orthodox there and forming the Uniat church under the Papacy (Union of Brest, 1596; see pp. 214-215).

In Muscovy, the effect of Florence in conjunction with the capture of Constantinople (1453) was to intensify the independence and nationalism of the church (*cf.* p. 79). Henceforward there was no question of the metropolitan being appointed from Constantinople or of his not being a Russian, though it was not until 1589 that he was raised to the dignity of Patriarch of Moscow. Thereby Russia set the example, followed in the nineteenth century by other Orthodox countries, of political independence dictating ecclesiastical autonomy.

The new Muscovite religious nationalism, which was further stirred by the advance against the Tatar khanates, linked together church and state yet more closely in the person of "the Orthodox Tsar." His position is reminiscent of the Russian version of the Tale of Prester John: "I, John, am tsar and priest, up till dinner priest, after dinner tsar, and I rule over three hundred and thirty tsars, and I am defender of the Christian Orthodox Faith." Moscow became not only, as has been already seen (p. 79), "the third Rome," but "the second Jerusalem" and "the second Noah's Ark," the sole guardian and repository of true Orthodoxy; and Russia became "Holy Russia," signifying the ideal of complete and unconditional loyalty to the faith accepted, a conception of orthodoxy somewhat akin to the orthodoxy of Communism. At the same time, while so strongly national, the Russian church continued to maintain the Byzantine tradition of the œcumenical church, a tradition of universalism which, long after the break-up of the rigid, ritualistic ordering of Muscovite life, gave birth to, or could be linked up with, the messianic appeal that has been so prominent in Russian thought and feeling during the past hundred years.

Russia never experienced the Reformation, but one of its great results, the emergence of national churches, was paralleled in Muscovy in the same period, and a second great result, the secularization of church or of monastic lands, was nearly paralleled. The religious revival of the fourteenth and fifteenth centuries was accompanied by a great extension of the wealth and the lands of the church, especially the monasteries, which contributed little to regular taxation and service. By the middle of the sixteenth century perhaps as much as one-third of the land was held by monasteries; they competed all too successfully with lay landowners in attracting peasants to their estates, and they played an important credit and financial rôle as being the largest possessors of ready money.

Hence there arose opposition to monastic landowning both from the laity and from a section of the monks themselves, who, particularly in the northern communities beyond the Volga, preserved the earlier ethos of the monastic revival. Led by Nil Sorsky (1433-1508), peasant-born, much influenced by Athos which he knew at first-hand, they stood for the purification of the church by the abandonment of all, or a great part, of the monastic lands and by concentration on the moral and spiritual needs of the individual. Against the "no property" school stood most of the hierarchy and the wealthier monasteries, by now largely recruited from the upper landowning class, from which came their champion, Joseph, abbot of Volokolamsk (b. about 1439, d. 1515). An erudite controversialist, a masterful disciplinarian and combative man of action, he openly supported monastic property on the ground, amongst others, that the monasteries were the necessary training grounds of the hierarchy, who must be of good birth; "if monasteries shall not possess lands, how shall a man of honor and noble birth assume the vows?"

The Josephines won the day in the church council of 1503, but the opposition both within and without the church continued. The state was urgently in need of inhabited lands to grant as payment for service, and it could not fail to be deeply concerned "to the end that there be not loss of service, and that lands do not pass from service." Ivan the Great had not hesitated, when he reduced Novgorod (1478), to deprive the monasteries there of over half their lands, but neither he nor his successors finally applied this precedent to Muscovy proper. They found no more active supporters in their work of national unification than among the Josephines, and Ivan the Terrible, though he had the metropolitan Philip deposed and (1569) murdered, did not go further than an increase in taxation and service from church lands and various measures to check the further acquisition of monastic property and circumscribe ecclesiastical jurisdiction and privileges.

These measures were in fact only to a limited extent carried out, but in the middle of the seventeenth century, as mentioned earlier (see above, p. 139), the needs of the government and the military, landowning class were met in the new code of laws of 1649. This drastically reduced and controlled the jurisdiction and economic power of the church, and the monasteries were subjected to a new, secular "department of monasteries." The Patriarch Nikon violently opposed "the accursed law book" and the new department was subsequently for a time suppressed, but Peter the Great, deeply impressed by the fact that about fourteen per cent of the peasantry were computed to belong to the church, in his usual piecemeal way brought church lands effectively into his recruiting and taxation net and reduced the ecclesiastical courts to a nullity.

After further transitional confusion, the final secularization of almost all the church lands was decreed in 1764, and there was a drastic closing down of monasteries, over half of the total of more than a thousand. Nearly a million male church serfs became in effect state peasants, under rather better conditions than before, and with substantially the same amount of land as they had previously occupied. Unlike the lay serf-owners in 1861, the church was not bought out by state purchase. The state simply kept for itself seven-eighths of the revenues from church lands and doled out the residue to the clergy.

This economic subjection of the church by the state was intimately linked with its political and religious subordination since the time of Peter the Great. The divorce between the official church and religion has at no period of Russian history been more marked than during the last two centuries. The reasons for this divorce and for the reduction of the church virtually to a department of the state lie in the great struggles in the third quarter of the seventeenth century for independence of the church and for reform, which resulted at one and the same time in the abasement of the patriarchate and in the Schism.

The claim to independence of lay control found its protagonist in the redoubtable Patriarch Nikon (1605-81), of a peasant family from Nizhni-Novgorod province, a disconcerting compound of asceticism, learning, pride, and imperiousness. Not content with reasserting the equality of, and equipoise between, the spiritual and temporal powers, Nikon eventually came to assert, in a manner hitherto unknown in Russia, the superiority of the spiritual power and even the subordination of the tsar to the patriarch. The arguments so familiar in the medieval papal armory of the sun and the moon, the two swords and the donation of Constantine appeared now in Moscow, not indeed as regards the last two for the first time, but extended and pushed to extremes.

Moscow had recently known one patriarch, Philaret, who had virtually acted as tsar (1619-33), but that was a novel exception due to the fact that he was the father of the weak and inexperienced tsar Michael, while himself for long only too deeply versed in affairs of state. Philaret's position had caused much dissatisfaction, and his two successors made no attempt to continue the rôle of "Lord Sovereign." Not so Nikon, who became patriarch in 1652.

He was overweening and highly autocratic, and by his reform measures, to be described in the following section, he aroused further antagonism from one section of the clergy. Thus he could rely only on his personal ascendancy over tsar Alexis for the paramount position in both state and church which for some years he occupied. This was not a secure basis upon which the predominance of the patriarchate could be built. The tsar finally became alienated from Nikon, and after a long and involved struggle he was condemned and deposed by a church council, attended by two of the Eastern patriarchs (1666). The same council pronounced that the tsar had independent authority in state, the patriarch in church affairs, and that neither should interfere with the other. Within less than forty years of this hopeful version of Justinian's sixth *novella* there was no patriarch at all, and a tsar who made a public mockery of the patriarchal office and stigmatized monks as "parasites" and "gangrene."

5. *The Schism and its Consequences*

Though Nikon as the overmighty patriarch fell, Nikon as the reformer succeeded, and in so doing he unwittingly changed profoundly the course of Russian religious and church history. The reforms were concerned solely with liturgy and ritual, involving the correction of the texts of the Bible and the service books and of various points of ritual in accordance (at least professedly) with the best Greek manuscripts and Greek practice. The reforms were denounced as Greek innovations by their opponents, though in fact they were a return to the old; but they constituted a challenge to the fundamental position of the Russian church, built up, as we have seen, for the past two centuries as the unique treasure house and guardian of the pure salvation of Orthodoxy against the Latins and the Turks, on the basis of an identification of religion with national feeling.

It was found, however, that the texts and practices of Russian Orthodoxy varied considerably and were in fact defective as judged by the essential appeal to antiquity, of which the Greeks had been the better preservers. The introduction of printing to Moscow in the second half of the sixteenth century added to the necessity of revision. This was quietly pursued for a generation before Nikon became patriarch, thanks to increased connections with Greek scholars and with the revived learning of Kiev, then still in Poland and in close touch with the Catholic world. Nikon as patriarch threw himself into the task of completing and enforcing the reforms unequivocally and ruthlessly. "I am a Russian and the son of a Russian," he declared publicly, "but my faith and convictions are Greek." That was what his opponents could not stomach.

The opposition, which was largely recruited from the white or secular clergy, called themselves the Old Believers. Both sides were at one in the fundamental importance they attached to ritual; religion was indissolubly reflected and experienced through the rites and worship that were for both not merely symbols but part and parcel of their faith. Hence the struggle concerned not mere minutiæ or formulæ, but an essential of life.

The Old Believers found an heroic, very human, deeply spiritual leader in Avvakum (b. 1621, burned 1681), like Nikon originally a priest from Nizhni-Novgorod province, a man of the people and the most impassioned and unwavering opponent of foreign importations of all kinds, whether from the south or the west.[1] Thus the opposition was strongly national and Muscovite; and, in addition to its religious origin, it assumed forms of an inchoate social protest against centralization and oppression whether by the church or by the state. But the religious leaders, if not the rank-and-file, of the Old Believers, in cleaving fanatically to their old Muscovite ways, were actuated primarily by intense religious feeling, not by patriotism or nationalistic obscurantism. For them Orthodoxy was not a national Russian form of religion: Russia was holy because she was, and in so far as she remained, the vessel of Orthodoxy.

The struggle was much complicated by the personality of Nikon and his claims as patriarch. As has been seen, he fell, but obedience to his ritual reforms was finally enjoined (1667) by the same church council that deposed him, and all those who continued defiant were anathematized as schismatic. This brought to the front the question of obedience to the highest ecclesiastical authority, and to the tsar, who enforced its decision by every means, including burning. The Old Believers held their ground against this persecution, by passive resistance, by self-burning, by flight, even by armed resistance. The schism became an accomplished fact.

Its results were twofold:

(1) The Old Believers constituted a considerable section

---

[1] There is a translation by Jane Harrison and Hope Mirlees (London, 1924) of *The Life of the Archpriest Avvakum written by Himself* (with his little black hen, in her day the champion egg-layer of Siberia), the most remarkable production of Russian seventeenth-century literature.

of the Orthodox, but after the first few years they included few of the upper classes: they were predominantly peasants and merchants. They were a disintegrating political force inasmuch as they identified tsarism with Antichrist owing to its relapse from Orthodoxy by its acceptance and enforcement of the reforms and to its encouragement of Polish and German importations. This idea of the state power as an evil tyranny was very strong before Peter the Great, but it was intensified by Peter's completely Western mode of living and the scale and energy of his drastic overhauling of Russian society. At the same time, the Old Believers were a disintegrated force in that to a large extent they were compelled to seek refuge in small communities on the frontier. They proved admirably sturdy colonizers, but their scattered distribution accentuated their disunion and diminished the danger of concerted action against the state, though they were dangerous allies of the discontent endemic along the lower Volga and Don.

The Old Believers originally held that either Orthodoxy, *i.e.* their Orthodoxy, the living church, would win through and Nikon's reforms be obliterated, or that it was a case of the end of the world, preceded by the reign of Antichrist. Since the reforms were not swept away and since, despite the coming of Antichrist, the world did not come to an end, they were faced with a series of new problems. The right wing, who clung to the priesthood and Orthodoxy, slowly evolved into a position of more or less compromise with the official church and the state, and, after varying fortunes, was eventually in 1905 allowed almost complete liberty. The left wing developed on quite new lines, without a priesthood, into sectarian groups mainly of a very individualistic kind, which became divorced from any pre-Schism basis and abandoned ritualism and tradition for independence of mind and extreme emphasis on the religion of the inner man. Thus the Schism introduced a phenomenon foreign to the old Russia, and to any other modern Orthodox country—a whole series of experiments in spiritual life entirely divorced from the official church.

At the same time other sects, especially in the South, came into being, or emerged from very doubtful origins, unconnected with the Old Believers. By the end of the eighteenth century there was a great multiplicity of Russian sects of evangelical, rationalist, mystical, or adoptionist colorings; and they were powerfully reinforced by German Protestant, and later Baptist, influences. Some of the dissenters held very extreme views on questions of vital importance to the state, such as payment of taxes and military service, and nearly all of them favored some brand of new social order in opposition to autocracy, and in part to any government.

Persecution and intolerance drove most of the sects underground and made migration frequent, so that information on them is difficult to check and opinion on them very diverse. In any case their fluidity and variety make generalization dangerous. On the whole, leaving aside the pervert and dissolute elements, the dissenters may be accounted a centrifugal and equalitarian force, often distinguished by much emphasis on education and equality of women, by self-reliance and self-organization, and by simplicity of life combined with considerable material prosperity. The numerical strength of the Old Believers and the sectarians cannot be accurately determined, though it is certain that the official figures were fantastically below the mark. They seem to have been continuously on the increase, and by the time of the Revolution they may possibly have numbered as many as twenty to twenty-five million all told. The sects remained, however, distinct and divided from each other, largely divorced from political action, and with local rather than wide-scale influence.

(2) The second great result of the Schism was that the official church, which had won the day largely through the backing of the state, became more and more dependent on it, and lost much of what was most living in the religious consciousness of the Russian people just at the time when it most needed cohesion and vigor in meeting the impact of western Europe upon Russia. This impact was making itself increasingly felt in Moscow and the upper circles of society during the two generations preceding Peter the Great. In the twenty

years before he took over power in 1694 the struggle for and against Western innovations was a burning question of the day, in which two patriarchs identified themselves with reaction (*cf.* p. 323). Hence when the second died (1700), Peter desired that no successor should be appointed, and it speaks much for the weakness of the church and for the strength of the position of the tsar that his desire was decisive. Opposition to Peter and all his ways continued to be strong, particularly among the monks, and centered its hopes upon Alexis, Peter's eldest son, but it was divided, without any leadership, and fatally handicapped by the Schism. Most of the ability and energy in the church came from bishops who owed their appointment to Peter. When finally he had beaten Sweden and had time for planned reconstruction he abolished the patriarchate and replaced it by one of his new collegiate boards of administration, the Holy Synod (1721). The highest body in the Russian church owed its very existence to the fiat of the tsar. The members of the Synod, appointed by him, were with one exception ecclesiastics, but they were expected to perform their duty—the moral education of obedient subjects—in the same spirit and manner as members of the college of mines and manufactures.

Henceforward the church became more and more a part of the administrative machinery of the state. There was a large element of truth in the accusation of a nineteenth-century Old Believer: "So-called orthodox faith is an appurtenance of the Crown and Treasury, an official badge. It rests on no basis of real life or sincere conviction, but just does its duty as a Government weapon for the defense of order." The Synod, after numerous changes, from 1824 onwards was ruled by its lay member, the chief procurator, who was in effect the tsar's minister for the state religion. Under Catherine the Great and Alexander I a tolerant spirit prevailed, but from the reign of Nicholas I (1825-55) any approach to freedom of conscience was almost continuously stultified by the policy of enforcing rigorously the old maxim that all Russians (including particularly Ukrainians) must belong to the Orthodox church, while its corollary, previously on the whole observed, that non-Russians could practice their own religion undisturbed was increasingly challenged, notably in Poland. The church became identified with reaction and its official trinity of autocracy, orthodoxy, and nationalism. Thus all the nineteenth-century revolutionary or socialist movements were, as in most European countries, bitterly opposed to the church, and the liberal elements, when not actively hostile, favored sweeping reforms. Within the church the gulf between the upper and lower clergy became a chasm, as in France before 1789.[1]

Moscow did indeed produce three remarkable metropolitans, and the eighteenth century produced a true saint (he was also officially canonized) in Tikhon Zadonsky (1724-83), the prototype of Father Zosima in Dostoevsky's *Brothers Karamazov*. But what the church most needed, a Leo XIII, it could not produce: it was given instead a Pius IX—Pobedonostsev (1827-1907), Procurator to the Synod from 1880 to 1905. The deepest currents of Orthodox religious life in the nineteenth century tended to flow in new channels, through the spiritual leadership of monastic elders, especially in Optyna monastery, and, in conjunction with them, through certain sections of the laity (above all the slavophils, see p. 230), to whom belonged the three greatest religious thinkers and writers of the century. The activity of the laity, not only in theology and learning but also in attempts at reform in the church, continued to be a conspicuous feature of Russian Orthodoxy during the 1905 and 1917 Revolutions.

When the storm of 1917 broke the Orthodox church was the one great institution in Russia which had remained unaltered either by the reforms of the eighteen-sixties or by the 1905 Revolution. Freedom of conscience for all religions in the empire had been granted in 1905 and thereafter to a large extent allowed in practice (with the glaring exception of the Uniats), but the far-reaching demands put forward in 1905 for reforms in the Orthodox church and a national church council were sidetracked by the reactionaries when they re-

---

[1] For an understanding of the life of the provincial clergy read Lyeskov's novel *The Cathedral Folk* (1872; English translation, New York, 1924).

gained command. Yet the position of the church was becoming more undermined through the weakness of Nicholas II, "supreme defender and protector of the ruling faith and guardian of orthodoxy . . . and in this sense Head of the Church," who notoriously yielded more and more to the magnetic influence, especially over the empress, of Rasputin, a Siberian peasant debauchee acting as "man of God" and healer, who came to dictate appointments, high and low, in church and state alike.

Rasputin was murdered in December 1916. Three months later Nicholas II was forced to abdicate. By the end of the year the Synod had been swept away. A national church council, elected predominantly by the laity, was set in its place together with the restored patriarchate. Disendowment and disestablishment were expected from the constituent assembly which was about to meet. Both came; but from the Bolsheviks, in the most extreme form; and they added prohibition of religious rites if they disturbed public order and of religious instruction in all schools. The new Patriarch Tikhon retaliated by excommunicating the whole Bolshevik party. In 1905 reform might have seized and strengthened the church; in 1918 revolution seized and rent it.

CHAPTER V

THE SLAVS

1. *Russia and Poland*

FOR THE LAST six hundred years the three major facts in the history of the Slavs have been the Ottoman conquests, the German expansion and power, and the struggles, military, religious, and cultural, dividing the Russians and the Poles. Until the eighteenth century the other Slavs meant for the Russians almost solely the Poles, who were their only immediate Slav neighbors. For both Russia and Poland their long and deep estrangement has been hitherto of greater weight than any of the various ties linking the Slav peoples together.

Since July 1941 Russians and Poles have been fighting in the common cause against Hitlerite Germany. Never before in history has it happened that all Russians and all Poles have been joined in struggle against a common foe. "Certainly," as a Soviet writer has put it (1941), "it was not easy to bridge the gulf which for ages divided Russians and Poles," but "the Russian people have a deep respect for sorrow and still more for courage." May this feeling, with its consequences, be reciprocated by both peoples.

What has thus divided the two countries in the past? Two different civilizations; disputed territory; the partitions of Poland and loss of independence (1795); subjection of the majority of Poles to Russian rule for a century after 1815. The last two causes after 1919 were memories, but bitter and long-festering memories, and in 1939 the Soviet-German partition transformed one of them into an actuality again. The first two causes of division have never ceased to be operative.

The Polish magnates and gentry, who together with the church shaped and controlled Poland, implanted on her a proud consciousness of being the bastion of Catholicism and European culture against what to them was a half-Byzantine, half-Asiatic barbarism. This feeling of representing superior civilization was fused during the partition period (1772-1919) with additional contempt, hatred, and fear of the Russian autocracy, after 1815 in possession of the solidly Polish central Vistula lands. When the Revolution replaced the Russian empire by the Soviet Union these feelings were transmuted into the idea of the new independent Poland as the upholder of civilization against the new barbarism of Bolshevism. The Bolshevik challenge of class revolution and interpretation of self-determination seemed to deny the independence even of ethnographic Poland and to make her eastern lands a strategical necessity even apart from other grounds.

The result of this combination of fear, pride, and hope was the Polish-Soviet war of 1920, begun by Pilsudski, himself from the eastern lands and always a fighter against all things Russian, when the Bolsheviks were in the trough of the Civil

War, though they had just beaten Kolchak in the east and Denikin in the south. The war brought the Poles to Kiev, then their defeat and headlong retreat; the Bolsheviks to the gates of Warsaw, then in turn their defeat and headlong retreat. A peace treaty was finally concluded in March 1921, but the war inevitably had deepened the antagonisms between the two countries. Poland, if no longer a spearhead, was to be the center of a *cordon sanitaire* against Bolshevism, the consolidation of which in the new Soviet Union it had proved impossible to prevent, doubly suspect to Poles as Communist and as Russian. To the Soviet régime Poland was equally suspect both on social, national, and historic grounds and as the ally of France and, in general, of the counter-revolutionary West. Nor were there any economic connections which might cut strands in the barbed-wire barrier between the two countries.

Russia and Germany, the two great losers of the First World War, the two historic enemies of the Poles, stood on either side of the Poland that had been restored so largely at their expense, again as in the past a composite state, with at the least one-third of her subjects Ukrainians, White Russians, Germans, Lithuanians, or Jews. For fifteen years they had been weak: by 1934 the Soviet Union had grown greatly in power and the new Nazi Germany under Hitler was taking ominous shape. France would take no decisive action with Poland to prevent the revival of the German menace. Great Britain still sheered clear of commitments in eastern Europe. Faced on the one side with the rising danger of Germany, on the other with the menace of communism to the structure and culture of Polish society and of the Russian past, Pilsudski with whatever misgivings accepted the proffered hand of Hitler with a ten-year pact (1934).

Later developments increased Moscow's impression that Poland substantially had opted for Germany against her. Despite a non-aggression pact (1932) and occasional easings of the very cold relations with Poland, the Soviet government became the more estranged when, at the same time as Hitler overran Austria, Poland seized the opportunity to demand of

Lithuania compliance to an ultimatum requiring the opening of relations, refused ever since the Polish seizure of Vilna in 1920; when, at the same time as Hitler broke up Czechoslovakia and imposed the Munich "settlement" to the exclusion of the U.S.S.R., Poland seized the opportunity to take from Czechoslovakia the mixed Polish-Czech coal and iron district of Teschen, disputed ever since 1919; and when in the summer of 1939, despite by now the extreme gravity of the German menace, Poland was (it seems) not prepared to run the risk of the Red Army as an ally.

Stalin, in deepest distrust both of Poland and of her allies France and Great Britain, and unable (it seems) to secure from them a free hand for the defense of the Baltic, considered Soviet interests least jeopardized by an agreement with Hitler, with whatever misgivings, at the immediate expense, so it proved, of war between Germany, Poland and her two allies, followed by the partition of Poland and Soviet occupation of the three Baltic states.

The lands which were so swiftly overrun by the Red Army (September 1939), in the rear of the broken Polish state and the gallant Polish troops battling against the German *Blitzkrieg* were promptly incorporated in the Ukrainian and White Russian S.S.R. after elections to national assemblies conducted according to the Communist version of self-determination. To these lands the Union had claims of close kinship and, as heir to Russia, historic title. They formed part of the disputed territory which was the second of the causes so deeply dividing Russia and Poland in the past; "the western lands" for Russia, "the eastern lands" for Poland.

"The western lands," roughly those west of the Dnieper and the Dvina and east of the Bug (see map 5), had been acquired by Russia by the three partitions of Poland of 1772, 1793, and 1795, and been ruled by her continuously until her breakdown in 1917. The outcome of the Polish-Soviet war of 1920 had been that they were approximately divided between the two, except for the northern portion which became Lithuania (but not Vilna, seized by the Poles in 1920) and part of Latvia.

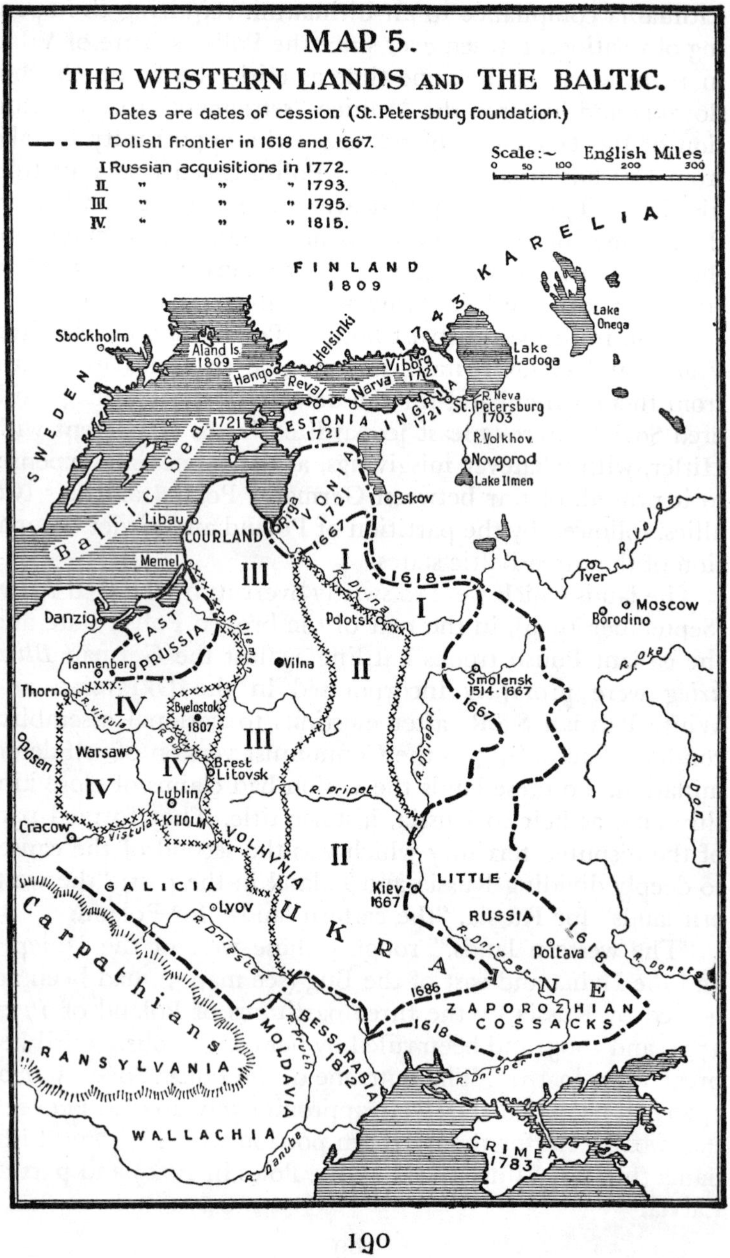
MAP 5.
THE WESTERN LANDS AND THE BALTIC.
Dates are dates of cession (St. Petersburg foundation.)
Polish frontier in 1618 and 1667.
I Russian acquisitions in 1772.
II. " " " 1793.
III. " " " 1795.
IV. " " " 1815.
Scale:~ English Miles
0 50 100 200 300
FINLAND
1809
KARELIA
1743
Lake Onega
Lake Ladoga
Stockholm
Aland Is.
1809
Helsinki
Hango
Reval
Narva
Viborg
1721
R. Neva
St. Petersburg
1703
SWEDEN
Baltic Sea
1721
ESTONIA
1721
INGRIA
1721
R. Volkhov
Novgorod
Lake Ilmen
LIVONIA
1721
Riga
Pskov
Libau
COURLAND
1667
R. Volga
Memel
III
I
1618
Tver
I
Moscow
Borodino
Danzig
EAST PRUSSIA
R. Dvina
Polotsk
R. Niemen
Tannenberg
Vilna
II
Smolensk
1514 · 1667
R. Oka
Thorn
R. Vistula
IV
Byelostok
1807
1667
III
R. Dnieper
Posen
Warsaw
R. Bug
IV
Brest Litovsk
R. Don
IV
Lublin
R. Pripet
Cracow
R. Vistula
KHOLM
VOLHYNIA
II
GALICIA
Kiev
1667
LITTLE RUSSIA
Carpathians
Lvov
R. Dniester
UKRAINE
R. Dnieper
Poltava
1618
R. Donets
1686
ZAPOROZHIAN COSSACKS
1618
BESSARABIA
1812
MOLDAVIA
R. Pruth
TRANSYLVANIA
R. Dnieper
WALLACHIA
R. Danube
CRIMEA
1783

The outcome of the German-Soviet partition of September 1939 was that the Soviet Union acquired the whole of "the western lands" and in addition eastern Galicia, which had never been included in the Russian empire, but had been under Austria since the first partition (1772) and then regained by Poland in 1919-20 by force of arms against the Ukrainians.

"The western lands" and eastern Galicia were, and always had been, non-Polish in the sense that, taken as a whole, the great majority of the inhabitants were Ukrainian and White Russian or Lithuanian.[1] Except for eastern Galicia, they had formed part of the grand-duchy of Lithuania since the fourteenth century, which itself was more and more closely linked with the kingdom of Poland, since 1386 through a common dynasty, since 1569 (the Union of Lublin) in a species of federated union. Thus the great Poland of the fifteenth to the eighteenth centuries was (like the Muscovite empire) a composite state, with the western half Polish, the eastern half Russian or Lithuanian. In this eastern half the Lithuanians were Catholic, but the Russian element (Ukrainian and White Russian) had been until the sixteenth century almost solidly Orthodox; after the Union of Brest-Litovsk (1596) which created the Uniat church as a half-way house to Catholicism, the Russian element was divided (*cf.* pp. 214-215).

The union with Lithuania did not represent conquest, nor on the other hand was it accompanied or followed by any considerable eastward colonizing movement of the Polish people, except eventually in the Lvov and Vilna districts. In this respect Polish eastward expansion was strikingly different from Russian eastward expansion, founded both on conquest and on colonization. The upper classes of "the western lands," and the centers of Vilna and Lvov, became Polish or polonized, and from the sixteenth century onwards the culture of the Lithuanian and White Russian regions was

[1] See the later section on the Ukrainian question. In this section I use the terms Ukrainian and White Russian to mean those inhabitants of "the western lands" who spoke what gradually developed into Ukrainian and White Russian.

Polish, though this was less so in the southeastern, Ukrainian regions.

The polonization of "the western lands" represented a remarkable achievement in assimilation, but it was vitiated by the fact that it was for the most part confined to the magnates and country gentry, while the great mass of the people remained a subject people of serfs for whom the benefits of Polish civilization meant almost nothing. As late as 1811 a friendly French observer lamented: "A great many more years will be necessary for people here to learn to consider peasants as human beings and to treat them as such." And this was written of purely Polish Poland, not of "the western lands" ruled by the Polish landowner minority. Polonization was, in the second place, vitiated by the immense extension of the Polish-Lithuanian state to the east, especially southeast into the steppes, where direct Polish rule after 1569 succeeded only in violently antagonizing the Ukrainians, as will be seen later (pp. 214-218). Finally, the whole eastward drive of the Poles was not accompanied by any diminution in their struggle for the Baltic or accommodation with the Germans on the west and north.

From the fifteenth to the seventeenth centuries the disputed lands were even larger than those described above, extending far to the east of the Dvina and the Dnieper. For these three centuries Muscovy stood against Lithuania and Poland in almost continual struggle, for one century unsuccessfully, for the next successfully, for the last again unsuccessfully, until (1654-67) the tide turned definitely in her favor. Muscovite foreign policy from Ivan the Great to Alexis Mikhailovich (1462-1676) was centered upon Lithuania-Poland and the Crimean Tatars, with Sweden a good third for the last hundred years.

It has been emphasized earlier that one major consequence of the Mongol invasion was the complete disruption of Kiev Russia. The principalities between the Oka and the Volga and, to the north, Novgorod and Pskov developed along their own lines in vassalage to the Golden Horde. The Russian principalities of the upper Dnieper and westwards, including Kiev itself, harried by and paying frequent tribute to the Tatars, slowly coalesced into the loosely knit grand-duchy of Lithuania. The rich Galician principality, likewise Russian, after a period of independent brilliance in the thirteenth century, sank into being an apple of discord between Lithuania, Poland, and Hungary and after 1350 fell to Poland.

Thus, between 1250 and 1450, before Muscovy became consolidated, Lithuania rose to be the major Russian state. By 1450 she stretched from the Baltic about Memel to the Black Sea, very insecurely at the mouths of the Dniester and the Dnieper; from the Bug on the west, eastwards well beyond the Dnieper and Smolensk and Kiev. She was within a hundred miles of Moscow and doing her best to prevent the growth of Muscovy: she was pressing hard upon Novgorod and expanding to the upper Oka and into the wooded steppe beyond the Dnieper.

This was a joint Lithuanian-Russian achievement; for except in the north, where the Lithuanian tribes formed a solid block, the grand-duchy was peopled by Russians, developing into White Russians and Ukrainians. It had been built up by the energy and adaptability of four outstanding Lithuanian military leaders, in part by conquest, in part by marriages, treaties, and purchase. The state language (to some extent even down to the early seventeenth century) was a variety of Russian approximating to White Russian, and Orthodoxy the religion of the bulk of the people. The culture, institutions, and law of the old western Russian principalities remained until about 1450 little affected by the formation of the new state, the capital of which was Vilna. Relations with the other Russian principalities to the east, at any rate as regards the princes, the military landowners, and the upper clergy, were constant and not always bellicose. There was much intermarriage, and individuals were ready enough to pass from Muscovite to Lithuanian service or *vice versa*, and back again.

At the very time, however, when this predominantly West Russian state of Lithuania was at its height and was expanding eastward at the expense of the other Russian lands, it was being drawn westward into the orbit of Poland. The common danger on the north from the German knights in East Prussia and Livonia (see p. 247) brought the "union" of 1385 with Poland and Catholicism for the Lithuanians. The first-fruits of the "union" were the decisive common victory of Grünwald or Tannenberg over the German knights (1410). The constitutional relations of Lithuania with Poland thereafter were a thorny ground of controversy, but, although it took a number of further "unions" before the final one at Lublin (1569), the results of that of 1385 proved to be of as great final consequence as the contemporaneous Union of Kalmar (1397) for Norway and Denmark (though not for Sweden).

The joint, elective, Jagellon dynasty, given by Lithuania to Poland—justly the most renowned of Polish dynasties—and above all Catholicism, given by Poland to the Lithuanians, resulted in the eventual polonizing of the upper class in most of the grand-duchy and the gradual confinement of Russian and Orthodox influence to the unlettered peasant masses and the frontier lands. This process of acquiring the privileges, institutions, and outlook of the Polish magnates and country gentry was exceedingly slow. Until 1569 Lithuania preserved its separate institutions and administration: then, faced by the threat of Ivan the Terrible, it was compelled at Lublin to abandon to direct Polish rule its southern, Ukrainian provinces and to agree to a closer union, though even then the curtailed grand-duchy continued to have an army of its own, its own autonomous provincial diets, on the Polish model, and other centrifugal features.

By 1569 the balance of forces was very different from a hundred years before, when Lithuania-Poland stretched from the upper Oder to the upper Oka and "from sea to sea." The consolidation of Muscovy under Ivan the Great (1462-1505) and his successors, the striking power of the Crimean Tatars (in alliance with Muscovy until 1507), and the extension of the Ottoman Empire made the grand-duchy more and more dependent on the richer and more powerful Polish kingdom.

Within that hundred years Muscovy forestalled Lithuania and the German Order in Livonia by the annexation of Novgorod and Pskov, thrust Lithuania back from the Oka to the Dnieper, and captured the key-fortress of Smolensk (1514). Already Ivan the Great was declaring that "all the Russian land, Kiev, Smolensk and other cities [a conveniently vague expression] . . . by God's will are of old from our forefathers our inheritance." This claim of Moscow as the heir of Kiev Russia to reunite "the western lands" in one Orthodox Russia became the more pronounced as Polish Catholic influence in Lithuania grew decisive and transformed what had hitherto been in the main an inter-Russian rivalry into a deeper Russo-Polish conflict.

Ivan the Terrible, after his sweeping successes to the east against Kazan and Astrakhan (1552-56), turned to the west and plunged into a twenty-five years' struggle for an outlet to the Baltic (1558-83), which involved him in war with the Livonian Order, Sweden, and above all Poland (see also pp. 250-251). For a time he made striking gains, but he could not press them home. He strained his country to the uttermost, and failed. Poland, thanks to the leadership of king Stephen Bathory and his reorganization of the army, in the end had the ascendancy.

While Muscovy was plunged into the impotence of the Time of Troubles (1604-13), Sigismund III of Poland, on the crest of the Counter-Reformation, moved forward with an eastern policy that might ultimately achieve another and even greater union than that of Poland with Lithuania. First one pretender tsar, then a second, each with the same Polish wife, were set up with Polish armed support; great stretches of Muscovy were occupied or overrun; Smolensk was captured, after a twenty-one months' siege; twice the Poles seized Moscow itself. Finally Sigismund's son and heir, Vladislav, was installed there as tsar, with the help of one section of the Muscovite magnates (1610-12). He was eventually driven out by the wave of national resistance organized by Minin and Pozharsky from the Volga and northern districts, and young Michael Romanov was elected tsar (1613). This period of Polish ascendancy and humiliation for Moscow left the bitterest memories, and the names of Minin and Pozharsky have been honored by Russians ever since as the symbol of patriotic rallying against "our enemies and outragers of Christian faith the Polish and Lithuanian men."

Though Moscow had been regained and the Polish tsar evicted, Muscovy was too weak to reconquer Smolensk and other territory lost to the Poles, and on the northwest to the Swedes (see p. 250). She had been thrust back to where she was before 1500. Her first attempt to win back the lost ground failed ignominiously (1632-34). Twenty years later she had recovered strength and the Ukrainian Cossacks under Bohdan Khmelnitsky were in revolt against Poland (see p. 216). Their appeal to the Orthodox Tsar was accepted. Little Russia, or the Left-bank Ukraine, *i.e.* that on the left bank of the Dnieper, came over to Muscovy, and tsar Alexis renewed the struggle with Poland for "the western lands" (1654).

The next dozen years are known in Polish history as "the deluge," a parallel to "the sedition" in Muscovy in the first two decades of the century. Moscow emerged in 1667 with the prizes of Kiev (ceded permanently in 1686) and Smolensk and most of the left bank of the upper and middle Dnieper, including the rich steppe lands of Little Russia (see map 5).

There the political boundary remained for a hundred years. The Black Sea and the Baltic, Turkey and Sweden, took the place of "the western lands" and Poland as the main directions of expansion and the principal enemies of Russia. "The western lands" could wait: they were not attractive economically, save for the Dvina water-route and the Polish Ukraine; and these could only be securely held by Russia after the power of Sweden and Turkey had been reduced. Further, there was a change of attitude in regard to Poland, then likewise the enemy of Sweden and Turkey. Above all, she was no longer feared: she was terribly weakened by "the deluge": her internal weaknesses, intensified by the divisions within the one politically privileged class, the nobility and the very numerous petty gentry, and by the centrifugal and growing power of their provincial diets, were only too apparent by the close of the seventeenth century. At a time when Sweden, Prussia, and Russia were building up new, modern armies, the Poles, for all their splendid military tradition and the brief glory of king John Sobieski, the savior of Vienna (1683), scarcely even attempted to do likewise until too late.

Peter the Great entered into his dramatic contest with Charles XII of Sweden in alliance with Poland, and they fought the Great Northern War (1700-21) up and down the country, each supported by his rival king of Poland (see pp. 252-254). The final Russian victory ensured the position of Peter's protégé, Augustus II, Elector of Saxony. It brought to Russia a new consciousness of her power, and throughout the rest of the century Russian diplomatists and armies behaved as they had learned to do in the later years of the war, marching about Poland as if it were their own land and playing off with plentiful gold the rival aristocratic factions and their client gentry against each other and the crown. There was a great revival of schemes for dismembering Poland, but Peter, though he seems to have played with the idea at one time, favored keeping her as she was, weak, nominally independent, and subservient to Russia.

The election of a successor to Augustus II resulted in the War of the Polish Succession (1733-35), in which Russian armies successfully placed his son upon the throne to the discomfiture of his rival, Stanislas Lesczinski, previously the protégé of Charles XII, now supported by France. Henceforward, for two hundred years, France stood out as the consistent, but distant, supporter of Poland and the Poles, and for a hundred and forty years as the opponent of Russia, save for occasional interludes.

One such interlude was the Seven Years' War (1756-63). Poland remained nominally neutral, while in fact Russia used her as a base of operations, faithful to her Habsburg alliance but now turned against the Prussia of Frederick the Great, until on the death of the empress Elizabeth in 1761

Russia changed sides. The change was decisive both for the issue of the war and for the future of Poland. A generation after the victory of Frederick the Great Poland had ceased to exist.

2. *Partition and After*

Frederick the Great and Catherine the Great (1762-96), for all their divergences and hard bargaining, were in fundamental agreement as to maintaining a feeble Poland and preventing any reforms which might weaken their hold. On the death of the king (1763) the usual electoral struggle was decided this time without fighting. Catherine, in agreement with Frederick, imposed Stanislas Poniatowski, the last king of Poland (1764-95); a Polish nobleman, then but little known save as an ex-lover of Catherine, who proved to be a man of great cultivation and well-meaning endeavor, but shackled by indecision and enormous debts that made him doubly the pensioner of Catherine.

The Russo-Prussian veto on reforms was not absolute: one type of reform was not only allowed but demanded, and finally enforced by arms; namely, the re-establishment of the dissidents, the Orthodox and Protestants, "in the free exercise of their religion, their rights and their immunities." From this time (1766) the question of the Orthodox in "the western lands" became again a cardinal feature in Russian policy and attitude.

Two centuries earlier the Counter-Reformation and the Jesuits had imported into Poland a militant aggressiveness that swept away the old Polish tolerance. The Uniat church (see p. 215) had been created (1596) as a weapon against the Orthodox and had prospered. In the eighteenth century the position of the Orthodox, the underdog in eastern Poland, grew worse, and there is no doubt that radical changes were needed. The religious grievances were a symptom of seething social discontent, especially in the Polish Ukraine, where the renewed extension in the eighteenth century of Polish landlordism and the Uniat church drove the Ukrainian peasantry into jacqueries in alliance with the popular Cossack frontier bandits known as *haidamaki* and with some unofficial Russian support. At the same time, it is certain that Catherine used the condition of the Orthodox to suit her own ends, and that some of the appeals that poured in to her from them were in part stage-managed.

The Russian demands in favor of the dissidents and other requirements amounting to a virtual protectorate were forcibly imposed upon the Polish Diet (1767-68), but the Polish reaction was bitter and many took to arms. They found a ready ally in Turkey, who promptly went to war with Russia (1768-74), and some support from France, also the ally of Turkey. None the less they failed. The Poles were divided, and there was always a party among the magnates which favored accommodation with Russia. The Ottoman empire was not strong enough to avoid serious defeats, not weak enough to suffer full defeat. Hence Prussia in conjunction with Austria was able to make Poland pay part of the price of the Russian victories over Turkey, and the first partition took place in 1772.

Russia's share was the northeastern corner of "the western lands" (see map 5), largely White Russian, relatively poor, but strategically and commercially important for Russia since she now secured the whole eastern bank of the Dnieper and the northern bank of the Dvina, so that Riga, Russian since 1721, was linked directly with Smolensk. The eventual annexation of this region had been approved by Catherine ten years earlier in secret conclave with her counselors, and the usual view that in this first partition she was duped by Frederick is incorrect, though she may have had her hand forced. Panin, her foreign minister, was certainly opposed to partition.

The Polish element in the region was very weak, and taken by itself the loss to Poland was not serious and its acquisition by Russia could be justified. But what was extremely serious was that its acquisition, unlike the gains of 1667, was the result of a deal between the three eastern powers. Henceforward the solution of the question of "the western lands" in a sense favorable to Russia was tied up with Prussian and Austrian designs, which unlike the Russian had little or no religious, national, or historic backing. It was no longer an inter-Slav problem, but a catspaw of European diplomacy.

Twenty years later, in the second and third partitions (1793 and 1795), the whole of "the western lands" fell to Russia, while Prussia and Austria divided the remainder of Poland. For the first time their frontiers were contiguous with those of Russia. The Russians, and to a lesser extent the Prussians, had hard fighting against the Polish army, in the end nobly led not by any of the magnates but by one of the minor gentry, Kościuszko, like so many foremost Poles by origin from the disputed eastern territory, an engineer veteran of another War of Independence, across the Atlantic. The mass of the Polish peasantry proved unreliable when it became clear that the fight for national independence was not to be accompanied in fact by their own liberation from their Polish masters. In the final struggle (1794), despite striking initial successes, the Poles were soon overborne once the Russian command was given to Suvorov. Thus Polish independence in the eyes of Poles was extinguished primarily by Russian arms (stained by one wholesale massacre), even though the Polish heart of their country was carved up between Prussia and Austria.

The destruction of Poland was a crime against the Polish people and the best standard of international morality of the age, and it proved a curse for each of the partitioning powers. Frederick the Great was mainly responsible for the first, Catherine the Great for the other two partitions, though Prussia sooner or later would in any case have insisted on seizing the Polish province of Posen and the German towns of Danzig and Thorn.

The decisive rôle in Russian policy was played by Catherine herself (b. 1729; reigned 1762-96). She had courage, self-reliance, and great skill in diplomacy. With many strings to her bow, with her versatility and with her cunning, she disliked cut-and-dried schemes and professed to rely rather on "circonstance, conjecture, et le conjoncture." It is correspondingly difficult to judge her Polish policy with certainty, and the estimates of it have varied sharply.

Almost from the outset she rejected the policy of favoring a stronger, moderately reformed Poland, friendly to Russia and capable of being of aid against Turkey in place of Austria. This policy was urged by her first minister for foreign affairs, Panin, but Catherine yielded to Frederick's arguments and some of her own advisers and Panin was overruled. One obvious difficulty was that Poland might not remain friendly to Russia and being reformed and stronger would then be the more dangerous. Further, Panin's policy involved the virtual abandonment of any forward policy in "the western lands," which would have been very unpopular in various influential Russian circles.

After the first partition, Catherine did not plan further partitions until the determined Polish revival (1788-91), which was accompanied by a temporary rupture between Prussia and Russia. She then felt herself threatened and defied and the policy gained the upper hand in St. Petersburg of shearing Poland of most of her territories, or even of complete dismemberment. Her closest advisers during her later years, though they were at odds with one another, all favored the inclusion in Russia of the Polish Ukraine: one of them was a Ukrainian, another, Potemkin, the viceroy of New Russia (*cf.* p. 38), entertained the most ambitious schemes at the expense of Poland. Catherine herself too by then had become much more of a Russian nationalist and far less of a purveyor of cosmopolitan enlightenment, and she was quite ready to extend her empire on any grounds.

The three partitions gave to Russia the whole of the long-disputed "western lands," the old grand duchy of Lithuania, with over 6,000,000 new subjects. The western frontier, after the further acquisition of the mainly Polish district of Bialystok in 1807, was almost exactly the same as the new Soviet frontier in the autumn of 1939, apart from eastern Galicia. Except for the Polish or polonized upper class and the Catholic and Uniat clergy, the eastern part of these lands was almost solidly White Russian, the southern Ukrainian, both of them mixed Orthodox and Uniat: efforts to raise them in the final struggle for independence, or later, had hardly any success. In the western part the Poles were more numerous, especially in Vilna, and Polish influence was deeper. In the northern part illiterate, Catholic Lithuanian peasants predominated. On the whole, if the question of "the western lands" could have been separated from that of partition, the Russian gains in the first and second partitions were justifiable, those in the third much less so.

For the main mass of the people the Russian annexation for some time made little difference, save in two respects: Orthodoxy had full scope, and there were better conditions for the towns. In these Russia for the first time came in contact with the Jewish problem on a large scale and with anti-Semitism, which, with its strong economic roots, was already locally virulent, though a century later it was deliberately intensified by the worst elements in reactionary tsarism. Serfdom remained as before; very onerous, though perhaps less arbitrary than in the rest of the empire. Law and custom likewise remained substantially as before. The Catholics were tolerated, and the Jesuits even favored. The Polish upper-class minority, in addition to the actual fighting, suffered in many cases individually from repressive measures, but most of them kept their land and the large grants made to Russian nobles were made chiefly at the expense of state and church lands. The Poles of course ceased to be the rulers of the country, but they retained much of their position in local government, except in the region acquired in the first partition which was handed over to Russian officials and rapidly assimilated to the rest of the empire.

Apart from this region the great bulk of what was acquired in the other two partitions was governed during the reigns of Paul (1796-1801) and Alexander I (1801-25) under a special régime, which, especially under the latter, reflected his friendly attitude towards the Poles. The local administration was mainly in the hands of Poles, and a special army, "the Lithuanian Corps," was created, linked with Warsaw, not St. Petersburg. Czartoryski, scion of one of the greatest of the Polish noble families, the confidant and early foreign minister of Alexander, was allowed to build up at Vilna a university which for twenty years (1803-23) was the center of education and Polish culture for "the western lands" and in fact nourished a new generation on the aspirations of Polish nationalism.

This last was the cardinal fact. The Polish state had been extinguished in 1795, but not Polish national feeling. Hitherto Russia and Poland had been divided by two different civilizations and by disputed territory; now there was added a third cause of division, loss of independence; after 1815 a fourth, inclusion of the majority of Poles in Russia and after 1830 their subjection to Russian oppression.

Polish hatred of the partitioning powers was intensified by the fact that they had destroyed Poland just when, and because, an effort at all-round reform was being made which culminated in the new constitution of 1791. The influence of French ideas was strong in Warsaw and Catherine made good the opportunity of publicly denouncing the Polish patriots as "hateful enemies of social peace, imitating the godless, rabid, criminal, and cut-throat gang of French revolutionaries." In fact the attitude of the Poles to the French Revolution was very mixed, but after 1795 France and Napoleon acted as a magnet for the fighting spearhead of *émigrés* patriots. They had some reward after Eylau and Friedland when Alexander could not prevent Napoleon from establishing under his control the grand-duchy of Warsaw (1807-13), composed of the Prussian and part of the Austrian share in the partitions, not of any of the Russian, but none the less doubly dangerous as a military outpost of the Napoleonic empire and as a possible nucleus for a future independent Poland that would owe nothing to Alexander (*cf.* p. 391).

The Polish question, as much as the Continental System and even more than the Turkish question, caused Napoleon's 1812 campaign, which was a reply to a projected campaign of Alexander through the grand-duchy in the previous year. Napoleon himself began by calling 1812 "the second Polish war." As soon as it opened the Diet in Warsaw proclaimed the restoration of Poland and summoned "the western lands" to rise: 1812 was to be a war of national reconquest. The summons was none too successful; but in the Grand Army there were 85,000 Poles, and none excelled them in enthusiasm and bravery.

Three years later Napoleon was in St. Helena and Poland for the fourth time partitioned, after a long and almost violent tussle between the powers at the Congress of Vienna. Posen, Thorn, and Danzig returned to Prussia, while the rest of the grand-duchy went to Alexander as his "Polish Kingdom," in official style, unofficially known as "Congress Poland." Austria remained in possession of Galicia, except for Cracow, which was erected into a tiny free state, until Nicholas I insisted that an end be made of this "hotbed of a vast new conspiracy whose ramifications embrace all the former Polish provinces," and it was accordingly annexed to Austria in 1846.

In 1815 for the first time Russia was joined with the core of Poland, the central Vistula lands centered on Warsaw, with some 3,000,000 Poles (and two to three hundred thousand Jews). This "Congress Poland" was originally entirely distinct from the empire, with a separate crown hereditary in the house of Romanov. Like the grand duchy of Finland, conquered by Alexander from Sweden in 1809, his "Polish Kingdom" had a constitution of its own, drawn up in 1815 by Poles on moderate liberal lines (except as regards the Jews), which gave them a parliament, full internal self-government with separate finance and tariffs, and an army—"a snake spouting its venom at us," as a Russian official protested. Under this régime the Poles organized considerable economic prosperity for fifteen years. But the constitution was not adhered to by the Russians. They felt—and they were right—that the "Polish Kingdom" would be used as a stepping-stone to the incorporation in it of "the western lands." The Poles had fought for that in 1794 and 1812, and they were to fight for it again in 1830 and 1863.

The cleavage between Russian opinion and Alexander as Polish king was fundamental. Alexander may have been a mask, but he was not, as his grandmother Catherine thought, a mask of wax. He possessed much obstinacy and he never showed it to more effect than in his Polish policy, even though in the end he gave way. Under the influence of his early friendship with Czartoryski, Alexander sincerely aimed at the reconstruction of a Poland—provided that it was his own handiwork. At the Congress of Vienna he tried to include the largest possible number of Poles in a restored kingdom. A compactly Polish state composed of the grand-duchy of Warsaw and Galicia, *i.e.* the Prussian and Austrian share of the partitions, might perhaps have led Polish nationalism to renounce its old eastern mission. Any such possibility was wrecked on the jealously of Prussia and Austria and the general fear of an overmighty Russia with Poland as her pawn.

Even so, Alexander had granted a general amnesty to Poles despite 1812, set up his "Polish Kingdom" on liberal and national lines, and deliberately left the door ajar to its possible expansion eastwards. As has been pointed out above, he favored what was in substance a polonophil régime in the greater part of "the western lands." For a decade or so after 1815 there seemed a possibility that a compromise solution might emerge whereby a part of these lands might be added to "Congress Poland" and the remainder definitively absorbed into the empire. In all this Alexander was maneuvering continuously against all his Russian advisers and the great bulk of Russian opinion.

Russians distinguished sharply between "the western lands" and "Congress Poland." The former, as not being Polish, must never return to Poland and must be governed quite differently from it. As regards "Congress Poland" opinion differed. Many would have preferred that Russia should have stayed on her frontiers when Napoleon had been driven out in 1812 and should have left the grand-duchy to its fate and washed her hands of the Poles. This solution was later wistfully contemplated from time to time even in the very highest quarters. It had two great defects: after 1815 it meant abdication on the part of the tsar as Polish king, an almost impossible step; and it meant also the almost certain aggrandizement of Prussia and probably Austria and incalculable international complications.

To most Russians the constitutional régime given to "Congress Poland" not only opened the way to most dangerous influences in "the western lands," but was incompatible with the position of the tsar in the rest of his dominions. Most, though not all, Russians were not prepared for a transformation of tsarism into some kind of constitutional monarchy along Western lines. Nor for that matter was Alexander himself. The rising tide of conservative nationalism, which found full expression under Nicholas I, was already by 1815 very strong where Poland was concerned. The only antidote to the anti-Polish chauvinism current in most sections of Russian society that counted for anything could have been a growing liberal movement in Russia. But this sole support for his Polish policy Alexander no longer encouraged. In his own way as much an autocrat as his father Paul, he was sympathetic towards liberal reforms only in so far as he himself granted them; and they must be gratefully received without criticism. The last of the enlightened despots, and therefore fundamentally at odds with the spirit of liberalism, he substantially agreed with Madame de Staël when she said to him: "Your soul is the best constitution for your people." At home, and in Poland, he swung more and more to the right, "wrapped in some moral fog," and his closing years (1820-25) seemed as "the darkness of a prolonged eclipse."

Already from 1820 the cloven hoof appeared in Alexander's dealings with his "Polish Kingdom." He yielded ground to the worst enemies of the Poles. The constitution was twisted out of shape and Russian control insidiously introduced. From 1825 Nicholas I set a new course in "the western lands," and, although he himself was both scrupulous and at pains to win some popularity in Warsaw, he was at loggerheads with his brother Constantine, brutish and erratic, but with a Polish wife and devoted to his Polish and Lithuanian troops, of which he was in command. Russian interference in "Congress Poland" became more and more critical. In 1830. spurred by the revolution in France and Belgium and fearing that the Polish army was destined to be sent to the West in the cause of reaction, the Polish nationalist societies and the army rose, declared Nicholas deposed, and made their bid, not for their full rights under the 1815 constitution, but for an independent Poland that should include "the western lands."

The 1830 rising was not merely a revolt of the upper- and middle-class nationalists, but, unlike the guerrilla struggle of 1863, a full-scale war owing to the existence of a well-trained Polish army and the Lithuanian Corps. The Russians, however, were bound to win in the end unless assistance was forthcoming from abroad. None came. Polish hopes of French aid, as always, were far too sanguine.

While the Polish revolt prevented any effective intervention by Nicholas I in the settlement of the Belgian revolution, that crisis equally prevented any effective intervention on behalf of Poland. As in the case of Napoleon III's diplomatic campaign against Russia in the 1863 revolt, French and British sympathy with the Polish cause merely intensified Russian national feeling against the Poles and "the calumniators of Russia," presuming to intervene in "this contest of Slavs with Slavs, this ancient domestic contest," that did not concern and could not be understood by Europe. England in particular had better remember Ireland.

Nevertheless, the Polish question between 1830 and 1863 was a stormy petrel of European international relations, and the Polish *émigrés* and their quasi-government in Paris were a perpetual preoccupation for Nicholas. In any case, even apart from the West, the Polish question could not be a purely internal problem simply owing to the existence of a Prussian and an Austrian Poland. In 1830 the three eastern powers, and in 1863 Russia and Prussia, though not Austria, marched literally hand in hand.

The Russian reaction to 1830 was to treat "Congress Poland" as a conquered country, though still distinct from the rest of the empire. The 1815 constitution was swept away and until the death of Nicholas in 1855 the Russian hand lay heavier and heavier upon the country. In "the western lands" full assimilation with the rest of the empire was henceforward the order of the day: a long series of anti-Polish measures was introduced and a powerful campaign launched against the Uniat church. 1848, the year of revolutions, and the Crimean War (1854-56) somewhat strangely saw no revolt in Russian Poland: the collapse of a rising in Prussian Poland, the strength of the Russian army and the absence of a lead from Warsaw or from the West prevented any move. But the defeat of Russia in the Crimean War brought a change.

The internal crisis in Russia during the early years of Alexander II had its effect on policy towards "Congress Poland." Under the Polish nobleman Wielopolski a number of reforms were made which gave some scope to Polish development, and there seemed a chance of an understanding between Polish and Russian conservative adherents of moderate reform. It proved impossible. The blunders of the government incited the nationalist societies to rebellion. They declared Alexander deposed and an independent Poland with "the western lands."

Alexander (and Russia was behind him) refused to return even to 1815, for he feared that it would be but a stepping-stone to 1772. "There can be no question especially of a constitution or a national army," he wrote just before the revolt, in private instructions to his brother the viceroy of Poland, "I will allow neither the one nor the other in any form. To agree to them would be to abdicate from Poland and recognize its independence with all its baneful consequences for Russia, namely her deprival of all that was in the past conquered by Poland which Polish patriots continue to regard as belonging to them."

The rebellion was crushed in blood, and the Russian reaction to it was even more severe than in 1830. Everything that was regarded as tainted with "polonism," *i.e.* the identifying of the Polish people with "the armed propaganda of Latinism in the midst of the Slav world," was systematically attacked. There was ruthless repression by an administration that was now, as it had not hitherto been, almost purely Russian in personnel. The extreme was reached when Russian was required to be taught even in village schools and religious teaching in Polish was prohibited. At the same time

Russian policy in certain respects deliberately favored the peasantry and industrial development as a means of countering "polonism."

The Polish, even more than the Irish, cause was weakened by social and political divisions among the Poles themselves, both at home and in the *émigré* camp, divisions that had been accentuated by the effect of the French Revolution. Above all there was the fact that most of the Poles in "Congress Poland" were a backward peasantry, thirty to forty per cent of them landless in the middle of the nineteenth century, in technical methods and general standards not much above the Russian peasantry. The Napoleonic edict of liberation of 1807 and earlier attempts at peasant reform had led in practice to little change in the rule of the Polish landowning class.

This failure gave the Russians the opportunity to adopt a land reform policy, from 1846 onwards, which aimed at representing the Russian tsar as the friend of the Polish peasant, in opposition to the Polish landowner. The peasantry took little part in the 1830 rebellion and on the whole a secondary part in 1863, though the revolutionary government did then, in contrast with 1830, make far-reaching promises to them. As an offset to these and a pendant to the emancipation of the serfs in Russia, the Russian government enacted a land law (1864) in "Congress Poland" directed against the Polish landowners, whereby the peasantry received about four times as much land as the Russian in the central Russian lands and under very much easier conditions.

The small, but growing, Polish professional and small bourgeois class supplied together with the lesser gentry the driving force of the 1863 rebellion, whereas in that of 1830 they had been subordinate to the nobility and bigger landowners. After 1863, again in contrast with 1830, there was no large emigration, and the Polish (and Jewish) urban working class and professional middle class increased steadily with the industrial development (mainly textiles and coal) of "Congress Poland." This was favored by the abolition in 1851 of the customs frontier between it and Russia and the consequent opening of the large Russian market to Polish manufactures. At the same time there was a wide opening in Russia for Polish skill in railway building, engineering, and other professions. All this was the economic basis for the post-1863 generation of so-called "organic work" or "Warsaw positivism" in contrast with the previous generation of militant nationalism and messianic romanticism typified by the great triad of *émigrés* patriot poets, Mickiewicz, Krasiński, and Słowacki.

By 1900 resigned caution and economic betterment no longer sufficed for the younger generation, but both the National-Democrat party which grew up under the leadership of Dmowski and the much smaller and divided socialist groups were strongly influenced, in different ways, by the change in the economic structure of Poland and its very close economic ties with Russia. Further, the increasingly anti-Polish policy of Germany in her Polish lands, especially in the form of their colonization by Germans (a policy never attempted by Russia in her compactly Polish lands), encouraged Dmowski and many Poles to choose as the lesser evil temporary collaboration against the common enemy with Russia, where it was hoped that the liberal and revolutionary movements might extract from the government concessions to Poland.

The 1905 Revolution did extract concessions; but Polish hopes of any material change in the Russian régime were dashed when reaction set in again after 1907 and withdrew or emasculated most of the reforms undertaken. The tsarist government still further antagonized Polish feeling when in 1912 it separated from "Congress Poland" the district of Kholm, a battleground between Poles and Ukrainians, Uniats and Orthodox, the first and only alteration of the frontiers of "Congress Poland" since 1815.

The outbreak of the war in 1914 found the Poles necessarily divided. The response of the Russian Poles was far more favorable than might have been expected, in part thanks to a moving proclamation issued under the signature of the commander-in-chief, the grand-duke Nicholas. But reactionary Russian nationalism remained the dominant influence with the tsar, and, despite discreet pressure from France and Great Britain, nothing of any value could be extracted from him in favor of Poland. On the other hand, though both the liberal and the revolutionary parties in Russia were prepared to recognize the freedom of ethnographic Poland (as they did after the Revolution of March 1917), they did not interpret this as including any large part of "the western lands." Meanwhile, by 1917 most of these and all "Congress Poland" had been conquered by the Central Powers. But for their conflicting rivalries they might have presented the Allies with the *fait accompli* of an Austro-German solution of the Polish question. As it was, Pilsudski proved right in the judgment attributed to him in the summer of 1914: "The Polish question will be decided in our favor if Germany is victorious against Russia, but is herself defeated by France."

3. *The Ukrainian Question*

The major fact in the relations of Russia with the other Slavs, her conflict with Poland, was largely due to the division of the eastern Slavs after the Mongol conquest into two groups. One came to be called the Great Russians and expanded, after much intermixture with Finnish tribes, from the Oka-Volga region and the North into the Muscovite state and empire, later into the Russian empire. The other developed differently during about four centuries within Lithuania and Poland. By the sixteenth century this second group had become roughly differentiated into those speaking what came to be called White Russian (the origin of the name is unknown), who occupied approximately the eastern central portion of "the western lands" between the upper Dnieper and Dvina and the Bug, and those speaking what came to be called Ukrainian, who occupied part of and later the whole of the southern portion of "the western lands." [1]

[1] I use the term Ukrainian in this section to mean those inhabitants of the Ukraine (taken in its widest sense, *i.e.* the territory in 1941 forming the Ukrainian S.S.R.) who spoke what came to be called Ukrainian, Little Russian, or Ruthenian.

The Ukrainians until the nineteenth century usually styled themselves simply Russians, some of them Cossacks, in contrast with the "Moskals" or Muscovites, although in the seventeenth century they called the land they lived in (then roughly the western part of the present Ukrainian S.S.R.) the Ukraine or Ukraine-Russia. By imperial Russia they were usually called Little Russians; by Western writers Ruthenians, particularly in eastern Galicia under Austria. The name the Ukraine means literally the borderland, and the Ukrainians have always dwelt with indeterminate frontiers in a land of mixed forests merging into woodland steppe merging into open steppe, a meeting point and a battleground of different powers and ways of life, Muscovite, Polish, Tatar, and Turkish. The fluidity and uncertainty that have marked so much of their history are to a great extent due to this fact, combined with the further fact that they proved unable to combine the freedom of the frontier with the discipline and stable authority necessary for the creation and maintenance of a state.

The Ukrainians developed in the last hundred years a nationalist movement which, like that of the other resurgent Slav peoples in the nineteenth century, was based on the conceptions of a common Ukrainian language and folk-tradition, of a distinct Ukrainian history, and of a lost birthright of Ukrainian national independence.

The question whether Ukrainian was a separate language or only a dialect of Russian was hotly disputed, and became, owing to persecution by the tsarist government, a political issue. It was assumed that, if there were a Ukrainian language, it followed that there was a Ukrainian nation: and the converse was also at the same time held. It seems difficult, however, to avoid the conclusion that the present literary Ukrainian was, like Jugoslav and modern Bulgarian and Czech, the creation of a nationalist intelligentsia to serve as the standard form for the Ukrainians, who hitherto had developed their vivid folk-literature in closely related but differing dialects, and in print had used either these or Church Slavonic or Russian.

Within the last eighty years an active school of Ukrainian historians, working under many difficulties but with great assiduity, has developed a scheme of Ukrainian history fundamentally at variance with that of most Russian historians. The Ukrainians are represented as a separate branch of the eastern Slavs with a separate language and history of their own, and as having achieved an independent Ukrainian statehood twice in the past: first, in the form of Kiev Russia embracing all the eastern Slavs of which the later Ukraine was the inheritor, not Muscovy, which represented a new start and a quite different development, part Russian, part Finnish, part Tatar; secondly, in the seventeenth century when Bohdan Khmelnitsky and the Cossacks headed the national rebellion against Poland and sought the aid of Moscow in preserving Ukrainian independence under the guise of loose vassalage to the tsar. This independence was lost in the eighteenth century and the Ukrainian nation subjected to Great Russian despotism.

It is quite true that Russian history until recently has usually been written too much from the angle of Moscow and imperial Russia, with the consequence that the special development of "the western lands" and the distinctiveness and achievements of the Ukrainians have been belittled or ignored; and it is also true that Ukrainian nationalist historians have contributed a large new fund of knowledge by their researches. Nevertheless the emphatic warning must be given that, just as it is impossible to prove the present existence of a nation by appeals to past history (though such appeals may do much to create or revive a nation), so it is a falsification of the past to write it in terms of the nationalist and political ideas of the last hundred years.

Soviet historians give a more reasonable general outline, when, while emphasizing the very marked differences in the development of the Ukrainians from that of the other Russians, they also emphasize the common influences drawing the two peoples together, notably in the conquest and colonization of the steppe regions, the modern industrialization of the South, and the common reaction against tsarism. They further hold that the social and economic divisions between the Ukrainians in the seventeenth century made it impossible for them, placed as they were between three comparatively well organized states, Poland, Muscovy, and Turkey, to establish an independent statehood of their own, and that the lesser of three evils was absorption in Russia. Certainly it seems that Ukrainian popular antagonism to the Poles has been much deeper and more continuous than hostility to the Great Russians.

The fact has to be faced that none of the Ukrainians have ever established a truly independent national state. After being for some three centuries under Lithuania-Poland, in the middle of the seventeenth century they fought for independence from Poland and, much less unitedly, from Muscovy. In the result they were divided between these two states and Turkey. From the partitions of Poland until 1918 they were divided between Russia and Austria. From 1920 to 1939 the great majority of them were included in the Ukrainian S.S.R. as part of the Soviet Union, but a very important minority, chiefly in eastern Galicia, were under Polish rule, until their incorporation in the Ukrainian S.S.R. in the autumn of 1939. A submerged half-million south of the Carpathians in sub-Carpathian Ruthenia were included in Czechoslovakia until the Munich disruption of September 1938, some months after which they were reacquired by Hungary, under whom they had always been prior to 1919. Finally, a more considerable minority in Bessarabia and northern Bukovina formed part of the new Roumania (1919) until the Soviet occupation of these provinces in the summer of 1940. Thus on the eve of the German invasion of the U.S.S.R. in 1941 all the Ukrainians in Europe, except the handful in Hungary, were united in one state.

The Ukrainians have not only been politically divided, but religiously divided; since the Union of Brest-Litovsk in 1596, when the Uniat church was created, composed of those Orthodox who, while keeping their rites and liturgy, accepted the Papacy. This arm of the Counter-Reformation and the Jesuits for a time had great success in "the western lands," and it served its purpose as a powerful means of spreading Polish, Catholic influence, of winning over most of the nobles and gentry, and of thus weakening the Ukrainians. Much later, in the course of the last hundred years, however, the Uniat church in eastern Galicia, where alone its roots were deep, proved to be a boomerang against the Poles, for it then became a main center of the Ukrainian nationalist movement.

Orthodoxy had sunk very low in "the western lands," but after 1620 there was a spirited revival and the Orthodox fought back with some success. Kiev replaced Lvov as the leading center of Orthodox life in the Ukraine and enjoyed a century of remarkable intellectual and educational activity, which had in addition marked results upon culture in Muscovy (see pp. 320-322). Above all, Orthodoxy now became linked up with the social and economic struggle headed by the Cossacks against Polish rule.

The Ukrainian Cossacks developed under the same frontier conditions as the Cossacks in Muscovy (see pp. 40-42 and note); but they were much more numerous than those on the Don. In the wooded steppe, in constant strife with the Tatars, a free Cossack society of hunters, ranchers, and farmers had grown up, which the Polish government strove to control as "registered" Cossacks for military service. In advance of them, out in the feather-grass steppe, by the late sixteenth century the boldest spirits had formed the Zaporozhian "host," beyond the cataracts of the Dnieper, buccaneers by land and sea, living much as the Don Cossacks, closely linked with the "registered" Cossacks, and in semi-independence of Poland. The Cossacks proved useful enough to the Poles on various occasions, particularly during their overrunning of central Muscovy in the Time of Troubles. But the Polish government, unlike the much weaker Muscovite in its relations with the Don Cossacks, attempted to regiment them and control their daring raids on the Tatars and Turks around the Black Sea coast.

Above all (again in contrast with the slower Muscovite expansion towards the Don), the transference of the southern, Ukrainian portion of the grand duchy of Lithuania to the

direct rule of the Polish crown by the Union of Lublin in
1569 was followed by a great extension there of Polish estates,
serfdom, and Polish administrative and military measures.
Thus, in addition to the Cossacks, the Ukrainian peasantry
were further alienated and either swelled the Cossack ranks
or looked to them as the military leaders of social revolution.
Five times between 1593 and 1648 there was armed struggle
between the Cossacks and the Polish troops, and though the
Poles had the upper hand and cut down the privileges of the
"registered" Cossacks, the feeling against the rule of the Polish or polonized nobles and gentry, if not against the Polish
crown, ran high and deep.

In 1648 the great Ukrainian revolt against the Poles began,
led by Bohdan Khmelnitsky (b. about 1595, d. 1657), a "registered" Cossack officer-landowner and a skillful, experienced
diplomat-warrior; "our dear leader," in the words of his funeral oration ascribed to his secretary, "an old Russian
Odonacer [? Odoacer], a celebrated Skanderbeg, Hetman of
the whole glorious Zaporozhian Host and of the whole Cossack-Russian Ukraine." For six years he battled and negotiated with the Poles, first for the full autonomy of the
Ukrainian steppe lands, then for a wider Ukraine independent even of the Polish crown.

It proved impossible to secure independence without the
armed support of either Muscovy or Turkey. After involved
moves and counter-moves, including alliance with the Crimean Tatars, Khmelnitsky in 1654 gained the agreement of
the Cossacks "to ask for the protection of the Tsar" in defense of their liberties and the Orthodox faith. The resultant
"treaty" with tsar Alexis was an ill-defined mixture of the
idea of mutual contractual obligations and that of the tsar
granting some of the petitions put forward by the Cossacks,
his new "subjects," who took the oath to him. The terms
of the agreement were imperfectly known by the Cossacks at
the time, and its nature both then and in modern times has
been the subject of much controversy. It is clear, however,
that for the next half-century the actual conditions prevailing

in the Ukraine prevented either party from extracting from the "treaty" what each had originally intended.

After the death of her great leader Khmelnitsky in 1657, the Ukraine entered upon her "period of ruin," at the same time as Poland her "period of deluge." For twenty-four years rival groups of Cossacks, on both sides of the Dnieper, alternately fought and leagued with each other, Muscovy, Poland, the Crimean Tatars, and Turkey. In Little Russia or the Left-bank Ukraine, *i.e.* the eastern side of the Dnieper and Kiev, alliance against Muscovy was not generally popular; on the contrary, there was much migration eastwards into the Muscovite frontier land of Slobodskaya Ukraine (see p. 37). In the Right-bank Ukraine alliance with Turkey became very unpopular. The result of "the ruin" was that the Ukraine was divided: Kiev and the Left-bank (later also the Zaporozhian Cossacks) were recognized as being under Muscovy; the Right-bank Ukraine was partitioned between Poland and Turkey, but continued to be violently restless and disturbed for many years to come.

The main reason why the struggle for independence failed was because it became a struggle less for the independence of the Ukrainians as a whole than for the privileges of the military element, the Cossacks, who were themselves not united, and in addition never made common cause with the rebellious spirit among the Don Cossacks. Hence it was possible for Muscovy to play off the conflicting interests and gradually establish effective hold on the Left-bank Ukraine, though the Cossacks under their hetman (ataman, commander) kept their own financial and military autonomy and their own traditional forms of self-government, and the hetmans only too often conducted foreign relations independently of Moscow.

The Cossacks were divided, somewhat as on the Don, between the richer, officer governing class, the rank-and-file, and the Zaporozhian Cossacks well to the south "in the wild grounds." Most of the Ukrainians were peasants, formerly serfs of Polish masters, now free of them, closely linked with the Cossack rank-and-file, but with little save religion in common with the Cossack aristocracy, which wanted their labor and taxes. The townsfolk disliked Cossack rule, had their own rights, and were encouraged by Moscow to gravitate to her. The upper clergy, heavily endowed with land, for a time stood out strongly for ecclesiastical independence of Muscovy, but became at one and the same time increasingly subject to her and increasingly powerful as a cultural influence on her. As a result, Little Russia developed with very wide Cossack autonomy, but with Muscovite influence extending and garrisons and officials in certain towns, and with a growing concentration of land in the hands of the privileged Cossack upper class at the expense of the peasants, who were being reduced to serfdom.

These main lines were twisted by the rebellion of Mazepa at the crisis of the Great Northern War which culminated in Peter the Great's complete defeat of Charles XII of Sweden at Poltava in Little Russia (1709). Mazepa, the very un-Byronic hetman since 1687, was a great builder and patron of the church and education, but he was also a *rusé*, wealthy man of affairs, representative of the new, grasping Ukrainian upper class and an enemy of the old Cossack equalitarian traditions. Distrusting Peter and fearing to be on what seemed to be the losing side, he went over to Charles XII, aiming at a more or less united Ukraine under Swedish or Polish protection. Despite bitter discontent at Peter's heavy hand little support for Mazepa was forthcoming from his fellow-countrymen, and the battle of Poltava decided the issue.

Thereafter, Little Russia was governed either by puppet hetmans or by a board nominated by St. Petersburg. Its autonomies were more and more curtailed until Catherine II, true to her centralizing policy, completely absorbed it into the administrative, financial, military, and ecclesiastical system of the rest of the empire (1781, 1783, 1786), and facilitated the further extension of serfdom. The Zaporozhian "host," now a shadow of its former power, was broken up (1775) and its much-reduced lands granted to new settlers. New Russia began to take shape (see pp. 38-39). The Zaporozhian Cossacks themselves, after various peregrinations, were mostly re-employed on frontier defense along the Black Sea coast by the Kuban.

This absorption of Little Russia was effected largely through the assimilation of the Ukrainian Cossack officers, who, even more than in Slobodskaya Ukraine (see p. 37), developed into a serf-owning aristocracy, only too anxious to receive, as they did in 1785, the same privileged status as the Russian gentry. Just as earlier the upper class of the western Ukraine had become polonized, so in the eighteenth century the upper class of the eastern Ukraine became russianized. Henceforward Ukrainians played a prominent part in all sides of Russian life.

The Ukrainian peasantry under Russian rule, which was extended to the Right-bank Ukraine by the second partition of Poland (1793), multiplied to such an extent that these provinces became the most densely populated rural areas in the empire and one of the main centers of agrarian discontent and of migration. While retaining for the most part their distinctive ways of speech, building, living, and farming, the Ukrainians shared with their Great Russian kinsfolk in the colonization of the Volga, North Caucasus, and Siberia, and took the leading part in that of the Black Sea steppes (see p. 37). The economic links of the Ukraine with the rest of the empire were further strengthened in the nineteenth century by the great development of the new sugar-beet industry, of grain exports through the Black Sea ports, and finally of the coal and iron-ore deposits of the Donets basin and Krivoi Rog (see map 1).

This amalgamation of the Ukraine with Russia brought many advantages to both, but it also involved subjection to the bureaucratic centralizing state-power of tsarism so alien to the particularistic traditions of the Ukrainian past. After 1863 russifying measures increased, notably for example the prohibition (1876) of most publications in Ukrainian. These greatly intensified feelings against tsarist rule and provided ample fuel for the new Ukrainian nationalist movement.

This had grown up since about 1840, originally centered

in Kiev, later driven over the Austrian frontier to Lvov. It had two bases: first, grievances, economic, social, and cultural, against the ruling powers; secondly, the Western idea of nationalism, blended with a glorification of the seventeenth-century Cossack struggles against oppression, which inspired the national poet, Shevchenko (1814-61), himself a freed serf, in his appeal to Ukrainian peasant traditions.

The politically minded nationalists were a small minority, chiefly drawn from the professional classes of the towns and municipal and *zemstva* workers. They strove first for the revival of Ukrainian studies and culture, but with the ultimate political aim of some form of local autonomy, which might eventually lead either to a reconstruction of Russia on more or less federal lines, or even to an independent Ukrainian state; in either case it was hoped by some means to include the Ukrainians within Austria-Hungary.

The 1905 Revolution was preceded and accompanied by violent outbreaks in the Ukraine, though not of a distinctively nationalist coloring, but the widespread demands for liberal reforms and decentralization gave a further impetus to the Ukrainian nationalist movement. It was allowed the possibility of more open development in Russia, and the reaction after 1907 did not go the whole length, being prepared to favor Ukrainians against Poles (*cf*. p. 210).

None the less the tsarist government, if it was less repressive of everything Ukrainian, continued to be fundamentally opposed to anything in the nature even of cultural autonomy for the Ukrainians, as being likely to prove but a stepping-stone to some kind of home rule, which in turn might encourage separatist ideas. Owing to the immense importance of access to the Black Sea and of the new industrial south all Great Russians, and not the government only, viewed with suspicion the development of a specifically political movement among the Ukrainians; and these same two factors were of cardinal importance for the Provisional Government in 1917 and, still more so, for the Soviet régime.

How wide and how deep the political nationalist movement was by 1917 is a matter of acute controversy. On the whole, the tangled history of the next few years supports the view that the solid basis behind the Ukrainian nationalist movement in Russia lay rather in the administrative and cultural fields than in the politico-national. What was widely and deeply resented seems to have been tsarist misgovernment and oppression rather than the idea of a continued common life with the Great Russians. The Ukrainians in Russia may have been a nation in the making, but scarcely a nation made. Events suggest that their politicians were nationalist, but not national leaders.

The Ukrainian question was further complicated by its international aspects and the rivalry between Russia and Austria-Hungary, with Germany behind her. The Austrian electoral reform of 1907 *(cf.* p. 236) gave a further outlet to Ukrainian political activities in eastern Galicia, where a well-organized nationalist movement had grown up and the Ukrainian majority, mostly Uniat but with some Orthodox, were united against the Poles though divided in their attitude to Russia. Austria was willing enough to use Ukrainian nationalism against Russia and up to a point against the Poles, but she could provide no solution of her own Ukrainian problem without a complete alienation of the Poles and a contest with Hungary, which was by then herself disturbed by the russophil tendencies of the tiny groups of intelligentsia among her illiterate Ukrainians in sub-Carpathian Ruthenia.

Germany was interested even before 1914 in using the Ukrainians if possible as a means of weakening Russia and of furthering the eastward expansion of her own power. The War and the Revolution in 1917 gave her a good chance. They opened the floodgates of autonomy or separation to the peoples of the Russian empire. An autonomous Ukrainian government was set up in Kiev, which after the Bolshevik *coup d'état* in November 1917 declared independence and turned to the Central Powers for assistance against a rival, Bolshevik Ukrainian government operating from the industrial center of Kharkov. The Central Powers forced Soviet Russia to sign away the Ukraine by the treaty of Brest-

Litovsk, drove the Bolsheviks out of it, and proceeded with their army of occupation to extract from the guerrilla-infested country the utmost possible in the way of much-needed supplies. From March to November 1918 Germany was able to carry out her Brest-Litovsk policy of creating a zone of client states, of which a nominally independent Ukraine was one, under a monarchist-inclined puppet government. Defeat in the West ended the German-controlled Ukraine.

For the next two years the Ukrainian lands were the scene of civil war and chaos exceeding even the time of "the ruin." A revolutionary, but anti-Bolshevik independent government under Petlyura was formed in Kiev. The Russian Whites remained hostile to Ukrainian nationalism. The Bolsheviks were equally hostile to it, but not to the new form the Ukrainian Bolsheviks were giving to it. France and England eventually backed the Russian Whites under Denikin, not Petlyura. Both Denikin and Petlyura, however, were defeated in savage civil war by the Bolsheviks, who received much assistance from the industrial working class in the Ukraine and (for a time) from anarchical peasant bands stimulated by the semi-legendary guerrilla leader Makhno. Petlyura was driven ultimately to make terms with the Poles. Despite Allied efforts to hold them back, the Poles crushed by force of arms (1919) an independent government of western Ukraine, which had seized power in eastern Galicia and had proclaimed a federal union with Petlyurist Ukraine. A year later Polish fears of Bolshevism and designs on "the western lands" led to the Soviet-Polish war, as already explained (pp. 187-188).

The outcome was that, as before 1914, the Ukrainians were divided. Poland, taking the place of Austria, regained eastern Galicia, and in addition Volynia (see map 5), while the Bolsheviks were left with the great majority of the Ukrainians and their half-ruined land, formed into the Ukrainian Soviet Socialist Republic. Groups of Ukrainian nationalists took refuge in western Europe and did their best to keep alive the cause of a free Ukraine, in which task they received considerable assistance from the numerous Ukrainian immigrants in North America.

The success of the Bolsheviks had been due to their own energy and ruthlessness, but especially to the divisions among and mistakes of their opponents and the divisions among the Ukrainians themselves. The appeal of social revolution to the bulk of the Ukrainians, *i.e.* the peasants, proved to be much stronger than that of nationalist slogans, especially since the Bolsheviks were quite prepared to give the widest latitude to the use of Ukrainian in schools, and in all other ways, and to staff with Ukrainians the new administration which painfully took shape on Soviet lines.

The Ukrainian S.S.R. included substantially all the contiguous areas in the Union compactly inhabited by Ukrainians and something like three-quarters (23,000,000) of all the Ukrainians in the Union (1926). In the Ukrainian S.S.R. itself they then formed nearly eighty per cent of the population, and a still larger proportion of the peasantry which at that time was more than four times as numerous as the townsmen.

For some ten years Ukrainian Communists and those prepared to work with them had a comparatively free hand, even though the main lines of policy were laid down from Moscow. From 1928 onwards, however, Moscow adopted more and more stringent measures against what was denounced as Ukrainization and right-wing nationalism, and heavy reprisals were carried out. Autonomy was drastically curtailed and the formula "nationalist in form, socialist in content" rigorously applied. Above all, the drive to enforce wholesale collectivization of agriculture in a land where individualistic peasant farming was strongly rooted and the N.E.P. period (see pp. 117-120) had favored private initiative led to violent resistance, mass deportations, and the famine of 1932-33. Mass party purges, which affected the rest of the Union equally with the Ukraine, followed, together with the great Moscow trials of 1936-38, in which a prominent place was given to German designs on the Ukraine, in line with the refurbishing of schemes for eastward expansion by Hitler, Rosenberg, and the "geo-politicians."

The opposition to Communist policy and rigid control from Moscow did not, however, prevent collectivization being carried through and the great agricultural resources of the Ukraine being mobilized as in the rest of the Union. At the same time, in addition to the famous Dnieperstroi electric-power station, the development of heavy industry under the five-year plans was enormously extended. Despite the building up of new industrial centers in the east of the Union, the South in 1940 was still producing from fifty to sixty per cent of the Soviet output of coal, iron, and steel, and the economic interdependence of the Ukraine with the rest of Russia was more marked than ever.

The character of the Ukraine was very considerably changed by the influx of new workers to the factories and mines: by 1939 more than a third of the population of the republic was classed as urban, and Great Russians and Ukrainians were much more intermixed than previously. There was a heavy decline, both absolute and relative, in the numbers of the Ukrainian peasants, partly owing to deportations and high death rate, partly to migration to industry and elsewhere; and there was perhaps a diminution even in the total population of the republic in 1939 (31,000,000) as compared with 1933.

However ruthless and uprooting the revolution has been in the Ukraine during the last dozen years, it does not seem to have engendered a separatist nationalism in reaction to it. Ukrainian cultural activities and the use of Ukrainian have continued to be encouraged, if in revised forms. The incorporation of the Ukrainians of eastern Poland and Roumania in the Ukrainian S.S.R. in 1939-40 was hailed as the reunion of blood-brothers and the accomplishment of Ukrainian unity. The Communist party in the Ukraine is as numerous proportionately as in the other Soviet republics. The Ukrainians have supplied conspicuous leaders to the Red Army. Soviet patriotism has been spread amongst them, recalling the exploits both of their Bohdan Khmelnitsky and of their guerrillas against the German oppressor in 1918. The second German conquest has not brought in its wake any puppet Ukrainian administration or any apparent revulsion against the long and close intermixture with the rest of Russia or the sharing in the destiny of the Soviet Union. Revulsion there is in plenty—against the brutal exponents of the Nazi "new order."

4. *Panslavism*

Today, more openly than ever before, Germany declares herself the enemy of the Slav peoples, at their throats in immense contest on the Russian battleground or trampling on the bodies and souls of the "sub-human" slave folk in the occupied territories. Today, as in the First World War, Polish, Czech, and Jugoslav contingents are joined in arms with the Russians in common struggle against the German and the Magyar. In August 1941, in 1942, again in 1943, all-Slav conferences met in Moscow to denounce "the Fascist enslavers" and to declare "the historic mission" of the great Russian people "in the gigantic and heroic struggle of all Slav and freedom-loving nations against the German Fascist curs." This was not, it was emphasized, a revival of panslavism, which was repudiated as the tool of tsarism and reactionary chauvinism. But it was an evocation of a century and more of Russian history in which slavophil sympathies and the tradition of "oppressed Slav brothers" had been a force among the Russian people; and it was a new departure in Soviet policy.

The October Revolution replaced the idea of the solidarity of the Slav peoples by that of the solidarity of the working class in all countries. After the Soviet defeat by Poland in 1920 and the agony of the Civil War, Allied intervention, and the famine, the Communists were too weak and too engrossed by internal problems to pay much attention to the Slav states, except for a time Bulgaria. Soviet energies were turned to the East and to the vast hinterland of Soviet Asia rather than to the old mosaic of the Danube basin and the

Balkans. In the building of a new Soviet world there was no thought of old conceptions of a Slav world or the common links between Slavs.

In the First World War Germany and Russia were the losers, the other Slav peoples (except the Bulgars) the victors. Victory was theirs on an unprecedented scale. They owed its possibility to the valor of the Russian armies, but its achievement to the valor of the Western allies. Inevitably the new Slav states looked to the West and the League of Nations: Communism was a nightmare or a bugbear to them: the Soviet attack on religion violently antagonized the Orthodox churches, previously one of the strongest sources of russophilism: the old appeal of "Holy Russia" to the Orthodox Slavs was gone: White Russian *émigrés* reinforced anti-Soviet feelings, particularly in Jugoslavia where the dynasty persisted in its refusal to have any dealings with the assassins of the tsar and of the monarchical idea in Russia. In Bulgaria, where the traditional links of the very radical peasantry with Russia were powerful, the Communist party found its strongest foothold outside the Union, but its attempt at revolution and its terrorism (1923-25) led to violent reprisals which reduced it for a decade to a nullity.

The Nazi seizure of power (1933) soon set in motion a change in Soviet policy towards the West and in the mutual relations of the Soviet and the new Slav states. With Czechoslovakia, which had always been well disposed towards the U.S.S.R., an alliance was concluded (1935), in dependence on the contemporaneous Soviet-French alliance, and the Munich tragedy strengthened the bonds between the two peoples. Bulgaria changed course and recognized the Soviet régime (1934); in the result Soviet influence grew so strong that it seems nearly to have brought about alliance against Germany in the winter of 1940-41 and, despite German dominance since then, the Bulgarian government has not dared to involve its people in actual war against the too popular Russians. Jugoslavia, when at the last moment (March 1941) she revolted against subservience to the Nazis, at once turned to Moscow and found a ready welcome. Poland, when the

Nazi attack on the Soviet Union was launched, likewise made alliance against the common enemy. Among all the Slav peoples only some Slovak troops and a handful of Croats are to be found aiding the Germans against the Russians. Hostility against the common foe has drawn almost all the Slav peoples together as never before. The same bond, common hostility, against the Turk, against the Magyar, against the German, has always been the strongest force linking the other Slavs to Russia. For over a century before 1917 Russia, as the only powerful Slav state, was the liberator magnet for the Slavs under Turkey, the Serbs, Montenegrins, and Bulgars, all Orthodox. For half a century before 1917 she had something of the same attraction for the Slavs under Austria-Hungary,[1] part Orthodox, but mostly Catholic, and much divided.

Russia had had important religious and cultural links with the Bulgars and the Serbs under the Byzantine Empire (see pp. 168-170), but connections became very thin indeed under the Ottoman Empire and it was not until the eighteenth century that continuous Russian relations of any importance with the Balkan Slav peoples were re-established. Even then, during that century the Roumanians in the Principalities (Moldavia and Wallachia) and Bessarabia, Orthodox but not Slav, were the main center of Russian political and military interest, since they lay nearest to Russia. Five times within a hundred years (1711-1812) they had experience of Russian armies; five times again within the next hundred years (1828-1918); and they did not like it.

Peter the Great publicly denounced "the yoke" imposed by "the barbarians" upon the Balkan Christians, and initiated two centuries of very close relations with the Montenegrins; but his defeat on the Pruth (1711) by these "barbarians" destroyed his schemes (*cf.* p. 263). It was reserved for Catherine the Great to assume definitely the rôle of "protector of the faithful" and "champion of Orthodoxy." Her

---

[1] Except the Poles. To save wearisome repetition I shall use the term "other Slavs" throughout the rest of this section in the sense of "the other Slavs except the Poles."

first Turkish war was signalized by the first appearance of a Russian fleet in the Mediterranean (1770), sailing round from the Baltic, and by the launching of ill-prepared revolts in Greece. These were promptly crushed, but the destruction of the Turkish fleet in the Ægean, the victories on land, and the treaty of Kuchuk-Kainardji (1774) made a lasting impression. The treaty gave Russia special rights in the Principalities and until her defeat in the Crimean War (1856) was the basis for her claims to interfere throughout Turkey on behalf of the Orthodox.

Catherine's later Balkan policy expanded rosily in "the Greek project" (1782), whereby Russia and Austria were to partition Turkey in Europe, with something thrown in for Venice. It was not designed, however, on a Slav basis. In any case, the Austrians were not easy to square, and above all the Turks to shatter. Beaten again (1787-92) by the Russian armies under their magnetic leader of genius Suvorov, but themselves beating the Austrians, the Turks had to yield ground to Catherine, but their hold on their Balkan provinces was far from dissolved.

When Alexander I resumed the struggle for the Principalities (1806-12) the Russians were assisted for the first time (apart from the Montenegrins) by a really serious rising, the Serbian peasant rebellion led by Black George (Karageorgevich, the forefather of the present king of Jugoslavia). The Serbs were ready enough to receive arms and money from any source, preferably the Russians, if need be from the Austrians, if needs must from Napoleon. Russian agents were very active amongst them, but material assistance was erratic and policy vacillating. For a brief moment (1812) Alexander planned a league of the Balkan Slavs as a great diversion in the rear of Napoleon and his nominal ally Austria, but this chimera faded into cloudrack in face of the Grand Army, and the Serbs were left to the tender mercy of the Turks.

When victory over Napoleon was finally won, Alexander was determined that the Congress of Vienna should not concern itself with the Ottoman empire. He remained deaf to the Serbs and the Greeks, unlike the Poles, and the Turks were wrong in fearing that his Holy Alliance was designed to prove its holiness by some crusade against themselves. It proved rather to be the father of a crusade for conservatism.

At the very time when the Slavs outside Russia were reviving their past and molding their future in the new crucible of nationalism, autocracy in Russia under Nicholas I (1825-55) was playing the part of "the gendarme of Europe" and the upholder of thrones and constituted authority against "the demagogic hydra." The days of Czartoryski, the Pole, and Capodistrias, the Greek, as foreign ministers of the tsar were past. The latter's successor, Nesselrode, of German parentage, foreign minister continuously from 1822-56, frowned severely upon any Slav movements which might infuse a further dose of revolutionary principles. For Nesselrode and his closest associates the Serbs were "these brigands"; complete emancipation of the Orthodox from Turkey was no part of their policy; still less any encouragement of movements that might infect the Habsburg empire.

These generally conservative directing lines of official policy were, however, modified by three facts, which account for the acute distrust or hostility of the West, above all Great Britain. Nicholas I himself spoke with two voices (see pp. 264-269). Many minor Russian officials, often themselves Balkan by origin, maintained a quite different attitude to that of their superiors. Thirdly, it was impossible for the Russian government to take no notice of Turkish misgovernment and the risings of the Orthodox Christians and their appeals to Russia. Even if it did not encourage revolution, it could but encourage, or demand, concessions and thereby to some extent appear as the protector of revolution.

No raising of the Slav banner was possible without serious repercussions in Vienna, for there were more Slavs under the Habsburgs than the Ottomans. Nicholas to the very last and to his cost remained convinced of the solidity of his alliance with Austria. In the war of 1828-29 against Turkey he had made no resounding appeal even to the Orthodox oppressed: there was no incitation of the Serbs and hardly any use made of the Bulgars. Nicholas, only as a last resort on the very eve of the Crimean War, hoping to spike the guns of the English, yielded to slavophil desires and favored the arming of the Christians in Turkey and an appeal to them to rise in defense of Orthodoxy, but not of Slavdom; even so, the appeal should not be launched until his armies had crossed the Danube. But they crossed the Pruth not the Danube, back into Russia. The scene shifted all too rapidly from Silistria to Sebastopol.

The Crimean War (1853-56) brought cruel disabusement. Austria in malevolent neutrality sided with France and Great Britain and ended with an ultimatum to St. Petersburg which caused Russian acceptance of peace. This was a vital turning-point. Russia never forgot, nor truly forgave, what she regarded as the treachery of Austria. Henceforward Russo-Austrian rivalry, though at times patched over, corroded the dynastic community of conservative interests, introduced a new element in Russian relations with the other Slavs, and kept the Balkans a nerve-center of European diplomacy.

Under Alexander II (1855-81) and his foreign minister, Gorchakov, official Russia waveringly began to reflect the influence of those currents of national opinion which had always hailed the other Slavs as "little brothers" and believed in the mission of "Holy Russia" to save them from the infidel Moslem and the contaminating West.

The slavophil movement, which grew up during the two decades before the Crimean War, had neither any organization nor any definite political program; but the slavophils represented in their own way a deep, popular nationalism in their emphasis on the high destiny of Russia, the uniqueness of her historical development, and her radical difference from the West. They reconstructed Russian history in terms of Orthodoxy, Muscovy, and the native Slav heritage of the commune (*mir*), the *artel,* and folk-tradition, and foretold that Russia "would give the world a *new culture,* a new Slav-Oriental civilization, in place of the declining Romano-German European civilization."

The slavophils were first and foremost steeped in Orthodoxy, and, although they were well acquainted with and influenced by Western thought and literature, their fundamental opposition to the westernizers, such as the great critic Byelinsky or the revolutionary Herzen, lay in divergence of approach—they profoundly religious, the westernizers primarily rationalistic. Their leaders were closely bound to the Russian land and were born and bred as patriarchal serf-owners. Moscow was their capital, St. Petersburg the washpot for the vials of their wrath. They were deeply conservative, but at the same time radically opposed to the governmental machine, which they denounced as an alien incubus imposed by Peter the Great and controlled by Baltic Germans and other bureaucrats entirely alien to the true genius of Russian national life. When the catastrophic failure of this bureaucracy in the Crimean War led to the reform period of 1856-67 the slavophils entered the lists prominently in the ensuing struggle, especially over the emancipation of the serfs. For them internal reforms were the first essential: only a healthy, cleansed Russia could come forward as the savior of Slavdom.

Prior to the Crimean War the slavophils, with some exceptions, had taken little sustained interest in the other Slav peoples, whose linguistic and cultural revival was then in full swing. After 1856 a change set in. Slavonic Benevolent Committees were set up with official approval and there was much cultural interchange and educational work, particularly among the Bulgars. In 1867 a Slavonic Ethnographic Exhibition was held in Moscow, the first of its kind, which was loudly advertised in Russia and much commented upon abroad as a thin cultural cloak for political propaganda. In fact, it did not result in much more than a platonic declaration of common Slav sympathies, and it was not repeated until after the lapse of forty years. The absence from it of the Poles underlined only too acridly the divisions within Slavdom. "When the Russians behave like Tatars," a Pole summed up in that same year, "can they complain if they are despised? If Russia is really our Slav brother, she is as Cain to Abel."

Slavdom, as a contemporary Russian critic of panslavism complained, was "a sphinx, an enigma," something "amorphous, elemental, unorganized, rather like the appearance of distant and spacious clouds out of which . . . the most varied forms may emerge." This was precisely why it could be a dangerous force, especially in the eyes of the West. Panslavism was neither a definite creed or party, nor a clear-cut policy, but on the one hand a form of Great Russian nationalism, on the other hand an aspect of the rebirth of the other Slavs and of their struggling for a changed future.

The earlier slavophils had dreamed poetically of a "great Greco-Russian Orthodox Empire," headed indeed by "the Pan-Slavonian Tsar," but with their prime emphasis on the redemptive powers of Orthodoxy and Russia's messianic calling as the savior of humanity at large. Most of the later slavophils and the panslavs confined this messianic calling either to the Orthodox Slavs or to the Slavs in general.[1] As long as Orthodoxy and religion took first place, it was inevitable that Russian panslav ideas could find a strong echo only among the Bulgars and the Serbs: more than half the Slavs outside Russia dwelt within the bounds of the Habsburg empire and the great majority of these were Catholics and had been for centuries deeply affected by Western influences, especially the Poles and the Czechs.

Between 1856 and 1878, when the next Near Eastern crisis came to a head, there grew out of Russian slavophilism a much more active and strident form of Russian nationalism, panslavism. This no longer put the main emphasis on Orthodoxy, but on the general community of Slav interests, particularly their common hostility to the Germans and the Magyars, as well as to the Turks. "The eastern question can be solved only in Austria, not in Turkey; the way to Constantinople lies through Vienna." The panslavs were bitterly critical of official Russian foreign policy during the first half of the century. They believed in an independent, anti-European policy of force and in utilizing the growing nationalism of the other Slav peoples so as to facilitate the disruption by

---

[1] An exception is Dostoevsky, whose mixture of slavophilism and panslavism is very well illustrated in his impassioned *Diary of a Writer* (1876-78; various translations).

Russia's own might of both the Ottoman and the Habsburg empires: in their stead there would arise a southeastern Europe linked in some form of union under Russian protection and control: above all, Constantinople and the Straits would be under the control of Russia or actually in her hands.

Such ideas, in confused alliance with the older, slavophil outlook, found influential adherents in the imperial family (though not in Alexander II himself), the church, the army (though not in his war minister), and the foreign office (though not in his foreign minister, Gorchakov). They had a very able, ingeniously flexible, and powerful proponent in Ignatyev, from 1864 to 1877 ambassador in Constantinople, who incurred the merited suspicion and hostility of all the powers, in particular of Austria-Hungary.

In 1876 Russia became deeply stirred by the revolt of the Christians in Bosnia-Herzegovina, the Bulgarian massacres and the outbreak of war between Serbia and Montenegro and Turkey (two of which owed something, and the last a great deal, to panslav intrigues). There was a prolonged outburst of nationalist feelings on a scale even greater than that against the Polish revolt of 1863; and now for the first time opinion and assistance found an organization, in the panslav committees. Volunteers and money poured in to aid the Christians against the Turks.

There was much that was shoddy or ephemeral in the movement, as the closing pages (originally censored) of Tolstoy's *Anna Karenina* bear witness, but, both at that time and later, beneath the turgid and often chauvinistic externals of panslavism there lay a popular appeal to two deep motive forces. In its call to action, to self-confidence, to a belief in Russia as a mighty power destined to shape the history of the world and to fulfill a mission of her own, panslavism responded to a craving for national recognition, all the keener when the humiliation of the Crimean War was set in such sharp contrast with the achievements of Italians and Germans in reshaping their future, just as later the humiliation of the war with Japan in 1904-5 and of the Bosnian crisis of 1908-9 stimulated feelings both against tsarism at home and

Germanism abroad. The second motive force lay in the reaction, so explicit in all forms of slavophilism and panslavism, against the claim of western European civilization to set up as the one true civilization which all other peoples were or should be adopting, a reaction which in very different form has been a potent force in the new Soviet Russia.

The dualism of Russian policy during the crisis of 1876-78 was impossible to conceal: the official policy of the tsar and Gorchakov publicly working in concert with Austria-Hungary (and in secret agreeing to hand over to her the Slav province of Bosnia-Herzegovina); the unofficial policy of Ignatyev and the panslavs urging the Balkan Slavs to fight and Russia to join them and settle the Eastern question for herself.

The Serbs in fact broke down and the panslavs quarreled with them and transferred their favors to the Bulgars, with very serious consequences for the future; the two peoples became estranged and Serbia for the next twenty-five years revolved in the orbit of Austria-Hungary (1878-1903). But the strength of nationalist feelings pushed Alexander II into war with Turkey (1877) and caused the final crisis of 1878 when in face of the armed opposition of Great Britain and Austria-Hungary the tsar had to substitute for Ignatyev's triumphant treaty of San Stefano the treaty of Berlin, the handiwork of European intervention, cutting down Russian gains and lowering Russian prestige.

Although in fact the gains remained considerable, there was passionate disillusionment in Russia, all the bitterer since the splendid feats of the Russian soldiery had stopped just short of the actual capture of Constantinople (*cf.* p. 272). Soon the Russian diatribes were no longer concentrated on Great Britain and Austria-Hungary, but directed at "the European coalition against Russia under the leadership of Prince Bismarck." The new German empire as the bulwark of Germanism against Slavdom came to the front for the panslavs: for them the road to Constantinople henceforward led through Berlin.

Already in 1878 the internal crisis was acute which culminated in the murder of Alexander II in 1881, and the discomfiture of Russian hopes in Bulgaria completed the decline of panslav influence. Bulgaria proved a striking illustration of the difficulty already emphasized as inherent in the position of Russia as a liberator; for Russia was also an autocracy and a strongly conservative one, even after the great reforms of the eighteen-sixties. Tsarism was fundamentally antipathetic to most of the nationalist movements in the other Slav countries, which were strongly influenced by Western radical thought and by peasant social-revolutionary ideas. The latter current had indeed much in common with Russia, but with the opponents of tsarism, the populists or *narodniki*, who later developed into the social-revolutionary party. Gorchakov, always an opponent of panslavism, was right in saying: "I find it difficult to believe in the sympathy of the Slav peoples for *autocratic Russia*."

Hence the paradox of Bulgaria which owed almost everything to Russia both in her national regeneration and her liberation from Turkey. A generation of Bulgarian nationalists was trained in Russia at her expense (1856-78), but half of them brought back not sound Orthodoxy and belief in the beneficent might of tsarism, but on the contrary disgust at its oppression and belief in armed revolution and a democratic republic of a very equalitarian kind. When Russian generals and reactionaries tried to impose their will on the infant Bulgaria (1878-86) they found to their cost that enough of the Bulgars were determined "to breathe free air and not through Russian nostrils," with the result that Bulgaria caused a first-class international crisis (1885-87) that ended in the complete discomfiture of Alexander III.

Increasingly after 1878 the internal problems which festered into the 1905 Revolution and the new Asiatic imperialism, which ended by launching out into the disastrous war with Japan (1904-5), distracted attention from the other Slav lands, though not that of the government from Constantinople and the Straits. Panslavism as such was in decline. In its place there flourished its twin brother pan-russianism, with the government at its head. Both Alexander III (1881-94) and Nicholas II (1894-1917) intensified russifying measures at home, not only in the Ukraine, "the western lands," and "Congress Poland," but in the Baltic provinces and finally Finland (*cf.* pp. 105-106). Anti-Semitism was now deliberately encouraged by the police, while in the Caucasus the old feuds between Armenians and Tatars were exacerbated. Thus when the Revolution came in 1905 it was marked by the violent reaction of almost all the non-Russians in the empire against Great Russian chauvinism.

The Revolution was marked by revived connections with the other Slavs, including now the Poles, and by what was known as neoslavism. Liberal, and some conservative, elements stood for a change of policy within the empire towards those who were not Great Russians, and for a time concessions were granted. The reaction from the Far East turned opinion again to Europe and the Balkans, and neoslavism was encouraged by Russian foreign policy, now directed by Izvolsky (1906-10), whose ambitions were directed to the Straits.

Above all, neoslavism, in which the Czechs took a specially prominent part, was the result of new developments in southeastern Europe. Austria-Hungary changed its ten-year policy of combining with Russia to keep the Balkans on ice and embarked on a new forward policy, signalized by the annexation of Bosnia-Herzegovina in 1908. At the same time the grant of universal manhood suffrage in Austria (1907), with its inevitable repercussions in Hungary, rendered yet more serious the problem of their Slav nationalities. These now represented a formidable, though still divided, challenge to the German-Magyar domination which was the basis of the Dual Monarchy ever since its birth in 1867.

The Jugoslavs were the greatest danger, since across the frontier Serbia, after the bloody *coup d'état* of 1903, restored the russophil Karageorgevich dynasty, broke with Austria-Hungary, linked up closely again with Russia, and drew towards Bulgaria. The Young Turk revolution of 1908, the Bosnian crisis of 1908-9 resulting in the humiliation of Russia and Serbia by Austria-Hungary and Germany, the making of the Balkan alliance and the two Balkan wars (1912-13), first against Turkey, then against Bulgaria, made the Slav lands a storm center of international relations and the object of intense interest and feeling for Russia.

Neoslavism gave birth to the striking novelty of a series of annual Slav conferences (1908-12), in Prague, St. Petersburg, Sofia, and Belgrade, but not in Warsaw; attended by Russians and representatives of various parties from all the Balkan and Austrian Slavs, though not from those of Hungary or Germany. Orthodoxy was definitely abandoned as the keynote of neoslavism (except in eastern Galicia). Plans were made for an extension of Slav cultural and economic links. What political form their common links might ultimately take remained very dubious, but the essential was the belief in the early break-up of the Dual Monarchy, almost certainly through war, in which the aid of Russia would be indispensable for the other Slavs.

Berlin figured as even more the enemy of Slavdom than Buda-Pest or Vienna. Anti-Germanism was in the forefront and was the one tie which inclined Poles to initial co-operation in the Slav conferences. Later, the Balkans and the mutual relations of the Serbs and Bulgars bulked large, both for the Russian foreign office and for unofficial agencies. They were at first successful in linking Serbia and Bulgaria together, with Greece and Montenegro, in the Balkan League (1912), but they were unable to prevent the second fratricidal war in the following year, or the third in 1915 (*cf.* p. 408).[1]

In Russia neoslavism, though supported by some individual liberals, was closely connected with various trends of conservative opinion and with the government. The contrast between tsarist reaction after 1907 and some form of new Danubian democracy under Slav leadership such as discussed by Czechs could not fail to cast a deep shadow over neoslavism. Common Slav endeavors were weakened not only by the old stumbling-block of Russia as an autocracy and by the poisoned relations between Serbs and Bulgars, but also by the

[1] The first Serbian-Bulgarian war had been fought in 1885 and ended in the victory of Bulgaria, the only one of the three to do so.

old feud between Russians and Poles. A reconciliation of this feud had been the first object of neoslavism, but it failed. In the Russian foreign office under Sazonov (1910-16) it was recognized that "the road to Constantinople lies through Warsaw." But Sazonov was not a man who could enforce his conciliatory views, least of all against the ministry of interior. He secured the proclamation to the Poles issued under the name of the grand duke Nicholas in August 1914, but no tangible concessions.

Yet, despite the various divisions among the Slavs and the few concrete results produced by neoslavism, the mutual links between Russia and the other Slavs (even perhaps including the Poles) were more numerous and stronger in 1914 than before, and Russia was more widely conscious of the clash between Slavdom and Germanism than at any time until 1941.

CHAPTER VI

THE SEA

1. *The Baltic*

THE IMMENSE LAND mass of the Soviet Union, like that of the Russian empire, is washed by five seas—the Baltic, the Black Sea, the Caspian, the Arctic, and the Pacific. The first three are landlocked. All are, in whole or in part, icebound for varying portions of the year, as are the great river systems draining into them that have played so large a part in Russian history. No other power shares the fifteen thousand miles of polar coastline of the Arctic, but the four other seas have always been controlled or disputed by other peoples, Greek, Turkish, Iranian, Scandinavian, German, Chinese, or Japanese.

The coastlands of the White Sea have been Russian settled for some nine centuries. Those of the other seas have either been never effectively Russian settled or only so within the last two hundred years (with certain exceptions). On the far

Pacific shores, Russian settlement from the mid-seventeenth century was almost confined to a few fur and fishing outposts until the acquisition from China of the lower Amur and Vladivostok as late as 1860 (*cf.* pp. 24 and 289). The Black Sea steppes, after the sustained but unsuccessful challenge of Kiev Russia to the nomads, were lost to the Russian people for some six centuries, during which the Black Sea was in the main a Tatar or a Turkish lake, save for privileged Genoese and Venetian merchantmen and later the pirate "seagull" galleys of the Cossacks. It was only from the time of Catherine the Great (reigned 1762-96) that the Russian southward expansion swept over the Black Sea steppes, from the Danube to the Caucasus. The Baltic coastlands, won between 1700 and 1809, almost entirely lost to the Soviet Union in 1919, mostly regained in 1940, have never been Russian settled but always peopled by Lithuanians, Letts, Estonians, and Finns, for about seven centuries with a German or Swedish dominant minority.

These influences—climatic, geographic, demographic, and military—have combined with the still greater influence of the immense land spaces of Eurasia to make the sea a secondary feature in the life of the mass of the Russian people. It could never play the rôle that it has with the Norwegians, Dutch, or British. And yet, though the Russian "urge to the sea" has often been exaggerated, it has been of decisive weight in state policy since the foundation of Peter the Great's new capital (1703), and at times earlier, and it has been the indispensable avenue of foreign trade and connections. Still by 1914 three-quarters of Russia's exports went by sea; almost half her imports came by sea; and these proportions have risen greatly under the Soviet régime, though the quantity of foreign trade is far smaller.

The incorporation in the Soviet Union in 1940 of the three Baltic republics, Estonia, Latvia, and Lithuania, and, after a bitter war, of portions of Finland was the pendant to the Soviet incorporation in the autumn of 1939 of eastern Poland. Both were reversals of the First World War and of the 1919-20 frontier settlements with which the Bolsheviks struggling for bare life perforce had to content themselves. For the Soviet Union the Baltic coastlands hold the same importance as for the Russian empire, principally as outlets to the West and for strategic defense. The heritage of Peter the Great was avowedly resumed, and the dangers of the First World War and the Civil War were only too well remembered.

The First World War had emphasized clearly enough the importance of the Baltic; on the one hand, the German closing of the Sound to Russia, the strategic advantages of the Kiel Canal (opened in 1895, for Dreadnoughts in 1914), and the Baltic as, so to speak, the left wing of German advance against Russia; on the other hand, the value of the holding power of the Russian fleet with its excellent minefields, and the value of the Baltic provinces, especially the line of the Dvina, as a kind of glacis in front of the true Russian lands and of St. Petersburg. Riga and the coastline north fell to the Germans only when in 1917 revolution had broken down the army and navy. The treaty of Brest-Litovsk (March 1918) left the door wide open for German designs in the Baltic provinces, which the Bolshevik government had to cede, and in Finland, where independence had already been proclaimed and German troops landed to aid General Mannerheim, the leader of the Finnish Whites, in implacable civil war against the Reds, in part Russians, but mostly Finns themselves.

Defeat in the West ruined German designs in the Baltic lands, but the Bolsheviks now had to face national independence movements and Allied intervention in place of German. The Russian Whites in Estonia, assisted by British men-of-war, organized two most dangerous attacks upon Petrograd at the height of the Civil War (1919). Allied forces under British command were in occupation of Murmansk (as well as Arkhangel), Russia's one ice-free port, and of the railway to it from Petrograd, until early in 1920 they were forced to evacuate. The Finns strove to make good in border warfare their claims in Karelia, which at their maximum

involved the cutting of the Murmansk railway (see map 1).
The Bolsheviks were too exhausted to continue their efforts to enforce their own interpretation of self-determination in the Baltic states and Finland, and they recognized their independence and the new frontiers in 1920. The Soviet foothold on the Baltic was confined to a narrow, ice-bound loophole at the eastern extremity of the gulf of Finland, all the more difficult to defend with the rapid growth of air-power. The Estonian boundary was less than ninety miles from Petrograd, the Finnish but twenty-three. The Bolsheviks could not forget that it was first Germany that had split off the Baltic provinces and Finland and used them as stepping stones for the defeat of Russia and the Revolution, then Great Britain and France that had aided their independence and used them as bases for counter-revolution or the *cordon sanitaire*. They could not forget the dangers that had beset Leningrad during the maelstrom years.

Leningrad, thus renamed in 1924 on the death of Lenin, ceased to be the capital since early in 1918 when, in fear of a further German advance, the government was moved back to Moscow, a momentous reversal of two centuries of history. But Leningrad remained a key center and the symbol of the triumph of the October Revolution, even though Moscow dwarfed her as the central focus of the Soviet Union. Revivified and refortified under the rigorous sway of two of Stalin's right-hand men, Kirov (b. 1886, murdered 1934) and Zhdanov (b. 1896), the present leader of her heroic defense, Leningrad became again an industrial and cultural center of the first rank, and again far the largest port for foreign trade. Her seasoned cadres of skilled workers turned out from her restored and expanded shipyards, engineering, munitions, and other works over a tenth of Soviet industrial production (1939). Once again one of the great cities of the world, with over three million people, she stood in emulous rivalry of Moscow. Now, tragically scarred, she is doubly enshrined for the Soviet peoples as the epitome both of the October Revolution and of indomitable resistance to the Nazi onslaught.

For twenty years (1920-39) Soviet relations with the new

independent states on the Baltic, though uneasy, in particular with Finland, were disturbed by few major incidents. The four states, each overwhelmingly composed of its own people, developed with remarkable rapidity, especially Finland, in close economic connection with England and to a lesser extent Germany. This was nothing new for Finland, which had always been in every way orientated towards the West. But Estonia, Lithuania, and particularly Latvia, with the great port and manufacturing town of Riga, were now cut off from their former markets in the Russian empire on which they had largely depended. Lithuania, in addition, was plunged in continuous feud with Poland over her medieval capital, the Polish-Jewish town of Vilna, occupied by Poland since 1920. Her one outlet to the sea at Memel had been taken from Germany and cast a permanent shadow over her relations with Berlin. Hence Lithuania was drawn more closely to the Soviet Union, though the two countries were separated territorially by the northern wedge of Poland.

The development by Litvinov, commissar for foreign affairs, of the Soviet policy of non-aggression pacts with her immediate western neighbors, coupled with attempts to revive trade with them on some scale and with the Soviet entry into the League of Nations (1934), seemed to augur more hopefully; but this proved to be more than offset by the threats to the stability of the Baltic states from the consequences of the world economic depression and the Nazi revolution in Germany. If their very close connections with the Western powers had been suspect in Soviet eyes, fears of the growth of German influence could not fail to make them yet more suspect and intensify memories of the First World War.

By the spring of 1939, when Hitler occupied Memel at the same time as he entered Prague and completed his destruction of Czechoslovakia, the position of Lithuania (2,800,000), Latvia (2,000,000), and Estonia (1,100,000), and to a smaller extent Finland (under four million), was precarious in the extreme; less because of their internal difficulties than because of their strategic situation between two of the strongest powers in the world. Already two years before they had been raspingly warned against "the bestial howling and gnashing of teeth of Fascism which is preparing war against the Soviet Union. . . . It does not pay small countries to be dragged into great adventures" (Zhdanov, December 1936). Already three months before the outbreak of the Second World War Molotov had publicly emphasized the likelihood of such small states "being powerless to defend their neutrality" (May 1939).

Whether or not Soviet requirements in regard to the Baltic states and Finland were the main reason for the breakdown of the negotiations in Moscow with Great Britain and France during that same summer, the Soviet Union apparently extorted from Germany in September what was in effect for the time being a blank check drawn on the Baltic states. Within two months of the Soviet-German treaty and the beginning of the Second World War not only had eastern Poland been overrun by the Red Army, but Estonia, Latvia, and Lithuania had been compelled to conclude close alliances with the U.S.S.R. and grant the establishment of naval and military bases. Lithuania at the same time was richly rewarded by the Soviet gift of Vilna, which had just been acquired through the Soviet-German partition of Poland. There was no introduction of the Soviet régime in the three countries, though Soviet cultural and economic activities were energetically forwarded, and the discipline of the Soviet garrisons, which kept almost entirely to themselves, appears to have been excellent.

In June 1940, at the same time as the collapse of France, for reasons that can at present be only surmised as imperative on military grounds, the Soviet policy of occupation of key points and dominant influence was suddenly abandoned for the policy of inclusion in the Union. There was full-scale military occupation; new left-wing governments were set up; the election of national assemblies was rushed through under Communist control, which proceeded to vote for incorporation in the U.S.S.R. This was formally ratified in Moscow in August. For ten months the three countries suffered the cruel pangs inevitable in the initial stages of sovietization; but land redistribution on an individual basis took the place of collectivization of agriculture, which was not introduced here (unlike eastern Poland) in what was, since the dispossession of the German landowners twenty years before, a stronghold of peasant farmers.

When the German battering ram was turned against the Soviet Union in June 1941, the outer defenses of the Union, if none too strong and weakened by hostility among the Baltic peoples, were at least well forward of the vital centers. None can say whether the Germans would not have entered Moscow and Leningrad had not the Red Army been in possession of the Baltic states and eastern Poland, and as well of Viborg and the Karelian isthmus on the side of Finland.

In the same autumn of 1939, when the Baltic coast from Tallinn (Reval) to Libau was secured by Soviet bases, strategic demands were made upon Finland, principally for the cession of part of the Karelian isthmus between the sea and Lake Ladoga (the Mannerheim line) and for the lease of Hangö as a naval base, which would make possible full Soviet command of the gulf of Finland (see map 5). The Finns refused to budge sufficiently. Moscow precipitated war (December) and proclaimed a rival puppet Finnish government, headed by a Finnish communist refugee who had long held a high post in the Communist International. After a bitter mid-winter campaign, Moscow jettisoned her puppet government, while Finland was forced to yield the original Soviet demands and in addition Viborg and other territory that the Red Army had conquered (March 1940). The frontier was now a hundred miles from Leningrad.

The Soviet-Finnish war had other important consequences. The Red Army, though it began badly and the world at large derided its performance, proved to be a formidable engine of modern war in its final capture of the extremely strong Mannerheim defense lines, and to be possessed of the same sterling fighting qualities as the Russian armies of old. In the light of this experience of modern, winter warfare under Western conditions the high command set to work with the utmost energy to remedy its defects. The Finnish army covered itself with glory in a struggle that could but end in defeat against so overwhelmingly stronger a foe, unless help came from outside. The sympathy of the world was demonstratively extended to Finland. The international position of the Soviet Union was deeply prejudiced. She was expelled from the League of Nations; and France and England, in addition to supplying some munitions to Finland, went to the brink of intervention in her support. That could be directly effected (apart from Petsamo on the Arctic) only through Norwegian Narvik and the north of Sweden, at that time a vital supply region of iron ore to Germany. The blasting power of the Red Army and the negative attitude of Sweden in face of Germany perhaps prevented a contortion in the Second World War that might have sealed the fate of western Europe.

On the Soviet side, bitterness and yet more suspicion towards the Allies were engendered, all the deeper if Moscow, with her memories of 1918, was convinced that sooner or later Finland would, willingly or unwillingly, open her ports to Hitler. On the Finnish side, exhaustion and recrimination did not oust the fixed resentment felt by so many Finns against the Soviet Union, whether feared as the old Russia in thin disguise or as well as the propagator of social revolution. Additional fears were aroused now that (March 1940) the Karelian autonomous republic was enlarged to include Viborg and raised to the status of a constituent republic of the Union with the ominous title of Karelian-Finnish Soviet Socialist Republic (see map 1) and with a government headed by Finnish Red refugees from the civil war period. The German conquest of all Norway (April-June 1940) completed the isolation of Finland and gave yet further opportunity for Germany to assume again, as in 1918, the rôle of savior of Finnish independence. She did so with only too much effect fifteen months after the first Soviet-Finnish war, when in June 1941 Finland joined with her in "a holy war against our national enemy" (Mannerheim).

Both Finland and the Baltic states, so intimately bound

up with the Russo-German struggle of the two World Wars of this century, had come to be under Russia as a result of another struggle for the Baltic, that between Russia and Sweden. This reached its maximum intensity in the Great Northern War (1700-21), when Peter the Great won the coastlands from Viborg round to Riga. It was finally concluded in 1809 when Alexander I conquered and retained the whole of Finland. The struggle with Sweden in turn was the protracted climax of seven centuries of intermittent, unsuccessful Russian efforts to secure or enlarge an outlet to the Baltic in opposition to Swedes, Poles, or Germans.

The Baltic was of continuous trading importance to the eastern Slavs for at least a thousand years before 1700. The Varangian Vikings coming across from Sweden in the ninth century, at the same period as their western kinsmen were overrunning western Europe and the British Isles, played a famous rôle as the welders and military spearhead of Kiev Russia (*cf.* pp. 16 and 27-28) and greatly strengthened the connections of the Russian lands, especially Novgorod, with the Baltic and beyond. Scandinavian, and later German, ships and traders distributed westwards the wares of Novgorod and the other Russian principalities and the luxuries of Byzantium and the East that came up the ancient water-routes of the Volga and the Dnieper, the "way from the Varangians to the Greeks."

The southern Baltic coastlands from Holstein to the Vistula had been in the hands of the western Slav peoples and then in the course of the three centuries following Otto the Great (936-973) were for the most part subjugated by German expansion or made tributary to the Danish empire. The eastern Slavs, on the other hand, had always been cut off from the sea by the Baltic peoples (Prussians, Lithuanians, Letts) between the Vistula and the gulf of Riga and by the Finnish tribes stretching round the gulf of Finland.

The two main routes for Russian access to the Baltic were by the western Dvina or by the waterways to the southeastern corner of the gulf of Finland (what was later called Ingria, see map 5), especially from Novgorod on Lake Ilmen by the

Volkhov to Lake Ladoga and thence by the mighty Neva to the sea, where now stands Leningrad. The mouth of the Dvina was never mastered by the Russian principality of Polotsk, but Novgorod was closely linked with the Estonian tribes and succeeded in subjecting to regular tribute those of them on the Ingrian coast and their Finnish neighbors in the lake region stretching away to the northeast to the White Sea. Thus Novgorod secured a narrow outlet to the gulf of Finland.

Three decisive events in the thirteenth century prevented any Baltic expansion of "Lord Novgorod the Great," with its turbulent dependency Pskov (the most westerly of the Russian bastions, after 1348 independent of Novgorod): the conquest of Estonia, Livonia, and East Prussia by the two German crusading orders of the Knights of the Sword and the Teutonic Knights; the conquest of Finland by the Swedes; thirdly, the Mongol conquest of the Russian lands, which destroyed the possibility of Novgorod, herself subject to Mongol tribute, receiving combined assistance from the other Russian principalities in a Baltic drive. Three great fortresses and trading centers, Riga (founded 1201), Reval (Tallinn; 1219), and Viborg (1293), symbolize the barring of the Baltic to the Russians. These Baltic lands were gradually won by fire and sword for Catholic (from the sixteenth-century Protestant) Europe, and their civilization ever after developed on quite different lines from that in the Russian Orthodox lands.

On the other hand, neither the Swedes nor the German Order succeeded in depriving Novgorod of any but small portions of her dominions. Two of their offensives were decisively smashed by Alexander Nevsky, grand-prince of Vladimir, patron saint of Peter the Great and his successors, now again in Soviet times heroized as the patriot deliverer, who beat the Swedes on the Neva (1240), whence his epithet, and above all the Germans (1242) by the lake of Pskov, "by the ravens' rock"; "and there was great slaughter and the clash of spears shivering and the clang of swords hewing as they strove on the frozen sea: the ice could not be seen; it was covered with blood."

During the two following centuries border warfare was continual and Novgorod remained hemmed in from the Baltic with only her narrow Ingrian outlet, but she kept intact, and extended, her river empire of the pine forest zone stretching away to the Arctic and the Urals (*cf.* pp. 18-19). On this was built her great prosperity as a trading center, which reached its highest pitch in the fourteenth and early fifteenth centuries. The dominating fact was her economic alliance with the Hanseatic towns, which established in Novgorod an almost complete monopoly of Western trade.

Power rested with a governing oligarchy of magnates—*"molt grans seigneurs"* (for two hundred and seventy-five years the two most important offices were filled from not more than forty families)—with the merchant guilds and with the archbishop and a cluster of wealthy monasteries. This power was rudely tempered by the violence of class divisions, and the unruly city mob found some effective organization, at least in times of crisis, in the traditional popular assembly that was formally the sovereign body of the city. The powers of the local prince had soon been closely curtailed: after 1272 he was dispensed with altogether. Thus, both politically and socially, Novgorod, and Pskov, developed very differently from the other Russian centers during the Mongol period. She acknowledged the suzerainty of the grand-princes of Vladimir or Moscow and paid tribute to the Horde, but acted as an independent state. There was, however, one essential element of weakness: she was usually dependent for food supplies on the Volga-Oka region.

In the latter part of the fifteenth century the Baltic question began to be transformed and the days of Novgorod were numbered. The growth of Lithuania-Poland and the consolidation of Muscovy under Ivan the Great (reigned 1462-1505) were the overriding facts. Novgorod (1471, 1478) and Pskov (1510) fell, not to Lithuania-Poland, but to Muscovy. The Hanseatic League was everywhere in decline, and in 1494 Ivan canceled its privileged position: henceforth rival trading interests—Scandinavian, Dutch, finally English—competed for Muscovite trade through the Baltic. Poland had had the upper hand of the Teutonic Knights since her great victory at Tannenberg (1410) and was now re-established on the Baltic at the mouth of the Vistula. German power was also weakening fast in Livonia and Estonia. Ivan the Great's new fortress of Ivangorod over against the German key center of Narva, his heavy defeat of the Order in 1501, and his alliance with Denmark and war with Sweden (1493-96) foreshadowed the new shape of things to come. During the next three centuries Russians and Swedes were pitted in war against each other for the Baltic lands nine times: five times the Danes were in alliance, ineffectually, with the Russians. But first, for both Muscovy and Sweden, Poland was the major foe.

Half a century after Ivan the Great the issue was fully joined for the possession of the Baltic lands, decided first in favor of Poland, then of Sweden, finally of the Russia of Peter the Great.

Sixteenth-century Muscovy needed open access to western Europe for three main purposes: supplies of firearms and munitions of war; artificers, engineers, and mercenaries; general trade. Poland-Lithuania, the Livonian Order, and Sweden blocked or impeded direct communication with the West; often to great effect, as for instance when (1547) a band of a hundred and twenty-four specialists, hired for service in Muscovy, were successfully stopped by Lübeck and the Livonian Order. There was an alternative to the Baltic, the newly discovered White Sea route (1553; see p. 20), which was in fact rapidly developed by the English and the Dutch. But it was a poor alternative, for it was roundabout and remote and ice-bound for much longer than the Baltic. The ice-free outlet at Murmansk (see map 1), where there was already a Russian colony and some trade, was too hard of access from Moscow and it was of no importance until the present century, with the building of the railway (1915) and the great Soviet development of the North. Intercourse with Muscovy was a major matter of diplomacy. After the capture of Narva by Ivan the Terrible (1558), the king of Poland summed up his fears thus, in protest to Queen Elizabeth against English trade: "We know . . . the Muscovite, enemy to all liberty under the heavens, dayly to grow mightier by the increase of such things as be brought to the Narve, while not onely wares but also weapons heeretofore unknowen to him, and artificers and arts be brought unto him; by meane whereof he maketh himself strong to vanquish all others."

The Livonian War (1558-83) had begun. It was part and parcel of the long contest of Muscovy with Poland-Lithuania (see pp. 193-196), but it was also the first big-scale effort of Muscovy to win through to the Baltic by way of the Dvina; whose banks, in Ivan the Terrible's saying, were worth their weight in silver, whose waters in gold. The internal weakness of the Germans in the Baltic provinces was by then so acute that Ivan had good hopes of forestalling their acquisition by Poland, Sweden, or Denmark. The outcome was twenty-five years of tangled warfare and diplomacy, which ended in the disastrous failure of Ivan. In part alliance with the Danes, he had had to contend ultimately with the Swedes as well as with the Poles, in combination with the Crimean Tatars. He could not maintain his early successes at Polotsk and in Livonia or at Narva and in Estonia, where Reval (Tallinn) gave itself over to Sweden and proved impregnable. In the end Ivan was compelled to acknowledge Poland as master of Livonia, Sweden of Estonia. He had gained nothing and was forced back to where he had started from, the narrow Ingrian outlet.

Even that was lost as a result of the Time of Troubles (1604-13), when internal disintegration opened the way to the competition of Sweden and Poland for the spoils and the very throne of Muscovy. All the northwest, including Novgorod and Pskov, fell for a time into Swedish hands. In the end the patriots rallying round the first Romanov tsar, Michael, rescued Muscovy from both Poles and Swedes, but peace with the latter was not obtained until 1617. Though Novgorod and Pskov were regained, Ingria had to be ceded. Muscovy was deprived of even a foothold on the Baltic.

After the Time of Troubles it was forty years before

Muscovy could move westward again with success, and when she did so she moved first against Poland (1654). By then the situation in the Baltic had been radically altered by the ascendancy of Sweden, thanks to Gustavus Adolphus, and the rise of Prussia, thanks to the Great Elector. Livonia was in Swedish hands; the Treaty of Westphalia (1648) had recognized the dominating position of Sweden in northern Germany; and she was about to dislodge Denmark completely from the eastern side of the Sound (1658).

In the resultant "period of deluge" for Poland (1654-67)—a deluge not only of Muscovites and Ukrainian Cossacks, but of Brandenburgers and above all Swedes—as has already been explained (p. 196), Muscovy made great gains against Poland—Smolensk, Kiev, and Little Russia. But there had been divided counsels in Moscow, and Sweden and the Baltic had been far from forgotten. One of the most experienced of the counselors of tsar Alexis, Ordin-Nashchokin (d. 1680), a lifelong westernizer, who hailed from Pskov, then on the Swedish frontier, argued that Sweden was a greater danger than Poland and that the Dvina and Riga were better prizes than the Dnieper and Kiev. There was a brief, and in the end fruitless, war against Sweden (1656-58); then the policy of concentrating against Poland won the day again: "It is not meet," tsar Alexis wrote, "for a dog to eat even one morsel of Orthodox bread." In the Ukraine but not in the Baltic lands there were Orthodox to be redeemed. In contrast with Ivan the Terrible Alexis avoided challenging Sweden and Poland at one and the same time. Forty years later Ordin-Nashchokin's idea of alliance with Poland against Sweden bore fruit with Peter the Great.

Peter had begun facing towards the Black Sea not the Baltic, having inherited the new offensive policy against the Crimean Tatars and the Turks, which was combined with alliance with Poland—another legacy of Ordin-Nashchokin—and Austria (*cf.* p. 197). But his famous first visit to the West (1697-98) showed him that Austria was now thinking mainly of Louis XIV and the Spanish succession question, not of the sultan, and that Poland's new king, Augustus II, elector of

Saxony, was concerting with Denmark an elaborate combination against Sweden. Into this Peter entered. Within a fortnight of concluding a hasty peace with Turkey he began the great reckoning with Sweden that was to drag on for twenty-one years and be known as the Great Northern War (1700-21).

No great war seemed so easily won before its start. Sweden stood alone, assailed by Denmark, Saxony, Poland, and Russia. Her empire included all told not more than about 2,500,000, and of them only 1,500,000 were Swedes, whereas Russia alone had a population of perhaps eight million Russians, apart from others. A generation of absolutism at the expense of the nobles had aroused bitter internal conflicts, not least in Sweden's Baltic provinces where the interests of the German barons had been attacked by the Vasa land policy. Her new king was only a stripling of eighteen. But he was Charles XII; and where he led in person the Swedes were the Swedes of old.

No great war seemed so nearly won after its first year. Copenhagen had been captured and the Danes perforce had sued for peace. The Saxons had been driven reeling back from Riga; the Russians ignominiously overwhelmed at Narva. A meteor had blazed forth, the most magnetic captain of his age, even of the age of Marlborough and Eugène.

Years later Peter frankly acknowledged his blindness and miscalculations. But he first showed his true metal when he refused to be deterred by the disaster of Narva. Charles met his match in Peter; for he combined equal tenacity with more many-sided and even more tempestuous energy, and in the end he learned how to organize the greatly superior resources of Russia.

While Charles was deeply engaged against Augustus II in Poland and Saxony, Peter, doing what he could to maintain the resistance of Augustus, concentrated on building up new armies on the Western model. With these he won back Ingria and avenged Narva by capturing it (1704); and he set about the creation of a Baltic fleet at his newly founded St. Petersburg (1703). He was hard pressed at home: there was a revolt in Astrakhan (1705-6), Bulavin's rebellion on the Don (1707-

8), a long sputtering civil war with the Bashkirs (1705-11). But by the time Charles was able to turn east once again (1708) the worst of Peter's difficulties were surmounted. He skillfully prevented intervention by the Crimean Tatars and the Turks on the side of Charles, who was also unable to draw any military assistance from the Poles. Peter's armies were by now large and well-equipped. They had their reward in the crowning victory of Poltava (1709).

The Poltava campaign was not, as has often been represented by critics of Charles XII, the reckless fling of an impolitic gambler. Mazepa, the Ukrainian hetman of Little Russia (see pp. 218-219), was in league with Charles and, had he succeeded in rallying the mass of the Ukrainians to his standard, the issue might have been different. As it proved, the campaign ended in annihilation. Charles himself almost alone, wounded and sick, escaped south to the Turks. Poltava was decisive in the sense that thereafter the strategic initiative lay with Russia. Although it was twelve years before Sweden was forced to sign peace, she was continually on the defensive and her strength exhausted in so unequal a struggle. The odds against her became still more heavily weighted. Denmark and Saxony-Poland now re-entered the war in alliance with Russia. Prussia and Hanover followed suit later (1714).

Poltava was immediately followed by the Russian conquest (1710) of Estonia and Livonia, Sweden's main provider of rye, hemp, and flax, and of Viborg, "the pillow of St. Petersburg." Peter's rashly executed and disastrous campaign against the Turks in Bessarabia (1711; see p. 263) proved to be of no relief to Sweden. In 1713-14 the whole of Finland and the Åland inlands (within raiding distance of Stockholm) fell to the Russians, and Peter's new galley fleet, which revolutionized naval warfare in the northern skerry-fences, won its first resounding success off Hangö (see map 5).

At the same time the treaties of Utrecht (1713) brought to an end the war of the Spanish succession and enabled the Western and German states to pay greater attention to the Baltic. Henceforward the struggle became even more diplomatic than military and as much between the members of the coalition against Sweden as against Sweden herself. Operations in and rivalry for the Swedish possessions on the North German seaboard involved Peter more and more deeply in the politics of northern Germany, where for the first time in history Russian armies made their unwelcome appearance. Russian designs in Mecklenburg and in the Holstein question (for the next fifty years a major issue in the politics of St. Petersburg) became central knots in the entangled diplomacy, strategy, and economics of the closing period of the Great Northern War, when the elector of Hanover had become as well George I of England and the Duke of Holstein Peter's candidate for the throne of Sweden, and later his son-in-law.

The emergence of Russia as a great military power and of her fleets on the Baltic created universal apprehension and widespread alarm. Thus, after Charles XII had met his death before a Norwegian fortress (1718), Sweden found it relatively easy to make peace with the other powers. But she paid dearly for renewed stubbornness in yielding to Peter's peace terms. In the final years (1719-21) the Russian galley fleets and raiding parties wreaked savage havoc in Swedish coastal districts, even as far as the outskirts of Stockholm, to the contumely of the armed mediation of a British fleet in those waters.

When at long last peace was signed at Nystad (1721), Peter was hailed by his subjects as "the Great" and "Father of the Fatherland." He had won for her the Baltic coastlands from Viborg to Riga, both inclusive, a far larger window than he had dreamed of in earlier years. He had wrenched Russia westwards, for good and ill, and had raised up his new capital and its guardian fortress Kronstadt as the enduring agents of Russia's new orientation and her new position as a Baltic power. Henceforward Russia bulked as one of the major powers of Europe. She not only displaced Sweden, but for a century vied with France, Prussia, and England in controlling her politics and ultimately (1809) succeeded in depriving her of Finland. These were the main results of the Great Northern War. Of them the most important for Russia were the economic and cultural effects of the Baltic doorway through the new capital.

St. Petersburg, begun in 1703, was built under appalling conditions by massed labor armies; in four years alone about 150,000 men were drafted to work in the Neva swamps. Immediately after Peter's death the old capital made a counterchallenge and Moscow was for a few years again the capital, but St. Petersburg won the day, and never lost it again until 1918. It grew to be a majestic city of superb Russian Baroque and Classical architecture, thanks largely to a long line of Italian architects and especially to the genius of Bartolomeo Rastrelli (1700-71); and it soon became the center of the learning and culture of enlightened absolutism borrowed from the West. Through the Baltic doorway the West flooded into Russia, whereas before it had but seeped through joints and cracks. Unlike other newfounded capitals such as Washington or Ottawa, Canberra or Pretoria, St. Petersburg was not merely the center of government but as well the financial and commercial capital. Peter immediately concentrated foreign trade in his new foundation. Arkhangel was deprived of her special privileges and already by the end of his reign was reduced to insignificance. Riga absorbed what St. Petersburg did not take of foreign trade, though her acquisition did not result in her becoming a great emporium for the Russian empire until after the partitions of Poland (*cf.* pp. 199-200).

Russian foreign trade with Europe expanded very rapidly in the eighteenth century. It was overwhelmingly by the Baltic, and about two-thirds of it passed through St. Petersburg. The economic primacy of the Baltic in foreign trade did not decline until the middle of the nineteenth century. By then overland trade with the West was growing steadily in importance and the new Black Sea grain trade claimed a third of the sea-borne exports (*cf.* p. 266). By the beginning of the present century the balance had tipped heavily against the Baltic, though she still carried much the greater share of sea-borne imports. Even so, the Baltic remained an essential artery for Russia, despite the great development of the South, which had changed its relative economic importance to the advantage of the Black Sea. An indication of Russia's economic weight in the Baltic can be seen from the fact that, when in 1857 the Sound dues were abolished by international agreement, the Russian share of the compensation paid to Denmark amounted to nearly a third of the whole, and was only very slightly smaller than that of the largest contributor, Great Britain.

Until sail had definitely yielded pride of place to steam after the mid-nineteenth century, the Baltic countries were the main providers of naval timber and stores to western Europe. From this angle the emergence of Russia on the Baltic had immediate and long-continued economic and strategic consequences. On the one hand, the rapid expansion of Russian trade was a golden opportunity for British and Dutch skippers, which in the almost complete absence of a Russian merchant marine they utilized to the full throughout the eighteenth century. On the other hand, the creation of a Russian navy, however technically inferior the sea-going fleet was to the Swedish, Danish, or British, transformed the balance in the Baltic owing to Russia's command of enormous resources in naval material and munitions and to Peter's novel employment of galley fleets on a large scale. Already in his lifetime Russia on the Baltic was regarded by the British as an unpleasant novelty "which would disturb the world."

In 1716 a British secretary of state could write: "it is our misfortune at this juncture, by the knavery of the Muscovites . . . , to have our navall magazines so ill provided with stores, particularly with hemp, that if the fleet of merchant men, now lading in the Baltick, should by any accident miscarry, it will be impossible for his Majesty to fitt out any ships of war for the next year, by which means the whole navy of England will be rendered perfectly useless. . . ." The particular entanglements of Great Britain with Russia during George I's reign were due mainly to his North German interests as elector of Hanover, partly to Peter's harboring of Jacobites; but in any event Great Britain was bound to be deeply involved with Russia and the Baltic on account of supplies for her navy and marine. These Baltic supplies were indispensable to her, and she was also greatly concerned to prevent them reaching her principal enemy France. The later history of the Anglo-Russian commercial treaties of 1734 and 1766 and of the Armed Neutrality of 1780 and 1800 bears telling enough witness to the continued importance of timber and naval stores. The fear of a Danish closure of the Sound, backed by Russia and France, was one of the principal reasons for the two British attacks on Copenhagen (1801, 1807).

While most of the timber, except for the first-class Riga mast-pools, was supplied by Poland, Norway, Sweden, and Finland, outside direct Russian control, the newly acquired Baltic provinces and Russia proper were essential for naval stores (hemp and flax, cordage and sailcloth, pitch and tar), long before the partitions of Poland and the acquisition of Finland still further strengthened the position of Russia. At the end of the eighteenth century Great Britain was still overwhelmingly dependent on Russian hemp and only slightly less so on Russian flax. When in 1807 Napoleon forced Alexander I to join the Continental System against England, one result was that hemp and flax prices in England more than doubled within a year. Baltic timber prices soared, and until the reversal of Russian policy in 1811 England was desperately hard put to it to obtain sufficient naval supplies.

If the deepest result of the Great Northern War was the economic and cultural effects of Russia's Baltic doorway, another great result was the changed relation of Russia to Sweden during the century that closed with the conquest of Finland (1809).

It has often happened that war, far from setting up watertight barriers, has acted as a conduit of influence. Russia in the past had gained much from prisoners of war, and Peter the Great not only made the very most of his Swedish prisoners but closely studied Swedish governmental and military organization for the purpose of his own internal reforms. As has also been pointed out in an earlier chapter (p. 76),

Swedish oligarchic constitutional ideas had their repercussions in Russia after Peter's death. On the other side, Russian influences upon Sweden were almost solely confined to political influence. This was one of the outstanding issues in Swedish history during the half-century after the death of Charles XII, known as "the period of freedom" (1719-72), when Sweden abruptly changed from one of the most absolutist of monarchies to one of the most limited, and rival oligarchies in the estates of the *Riksdag* disputed for power with the lavish aid of foreign subsidies—Russian, French, Prussian, and British.

Russia, usually in alliance with Prussia and almost always in opposition to France, worked very much as in Poland to maintain the impotence of the monarchy and to secure the position of her Holstein candidates to the throne. At one moment (1743-44) Swedish political dissensions were so severe that a Russian fleet and army were called in to suppress the opponents of the Russophil party. During the first ten years of Catherine the Great's reign (1762-72), when her foreign minister Panin was maneuvering his "northern system," the stream of Russian gold reached its high-water mark in successful rivalry with French subsidies.

Russian influence was, however, shattered in 1772 by the *coup d'état* of the new king, Gustavus III, which restored much of the old power of the monarchy, and by Gustavus's attachment to all things French. Catherine the Great was too deeply involved in war with Turkey and in Poland to take effective counter-action, but she did all she could to win over the opposition in Sweden and Finland that developed to Gustavus III, who was more and more given over to a reckless foreign policy, and in particular war against Russia.

Since the peace of Nystad Sweden had made only one actual bid to regain her losses by renewing war with Russia (1741-43). That war had been largely due to French diplomacy, anxious to prevent Russia from joining Austria in the war of the Austrian succession. It entailed a series of defeats for Sweden who was lucky not to have to cede more than a small strip of Finland, which brought the Russian boundary to almost exactly the same line as that in 1940 after the Soviet-Finnish war.

Catherine's second Turkish war gave Gustavus the chance he wanted to attack her (1788). Ill-prepared in the north, Catherine at first succeeded in staving off the new enemy with the help of a Swedish-Finnish conspiracy against Gustavus. But the situation grew more and more critical for Russia, when Denmark, her one ally, proved a broken reed. Great Britain was arming against her, and Prussia seemed about to enter the war. "Only a miracle," Catherine wrote, "or the mercy of God can end matters satisfactorily." In fact the internal difficulties of Gustavus were even greater and, after the Swedish navy had reasserted itself by a striking victory, both sides were glad enough to make peace (1790). Within little more than a year later Catherine had won the unstable Gustavus to secret alliance "for the restoration of European equilibrium [against Prussia and Great Britain] and of the French monarchy."

The French Revolution and the Napoleonic wars caused frequent shifts and changes in Russia's Baltic policy, and in the end her final reckoning with Sweden over Finland. The two wars of 1741-43 and 1788-90 had been waged there and on the sea, not in the Baltic provinces. In Russian eyes the continued dangers arising from the proximity of Finland to St. Petersburg and the Swedish possession of the north coast of the gulf of Finland had been amply enough demonstrated. The peace of Tilsit (1807) between Alexander I and Napoleon marked down Sweden for inclusion in the Continental System and deprival of Finland.

Separatist tendencies existed among the dominant Swedish upper class in Finland and had long been made use of by the Russians. One of the leading Swedish-Finnish renegades to Russia in 1788 led the way twenty years later in the Russian acquisition of Finland with an autonomous status. It involved a brief war (1808-9), in which the Russians conquered the whole country. Sweden, who failed to concert any operations with a British expeditionary force under Sir John Moore, was compelled to cede it, including the Åland islands.

The long struggle between Russia and Sweden was completed. Ever since 1809 they have been at peace. During the last stages of Napoleon's downfall (1813-15) Russia and Sweden, with Bernadotte heir-presumptive, were even leagued together in the grand coalition against him. But the heritage of the past and Sweden's dislike of Russian autocracy, and latterly Soviet communism, have perpetuated fear and suspicion of her colossus neighbor and have drawn her, in combination with other influences, to Germany or to England.

After the Napoleonic period Russia had to measure herself in the Baltic mainly against England, until from the end of the nineteenth century the German empire altered the balance of power. British fleets had sailed into the Baltic time and time again in the earlier eighteenth century and during the Napoleonic wars. They have only once (1808) fought a full-scale action there, inside the Sound, but Russia has often had to face such a possibility. Twice since 1808 she has suffered from British naval operations, in the Crimean War and in 1919.

When Anglo-Russian rivalry was put to the test in the Baltic in the Crimean War (1854-56), the greatly superior British and French fleets swept the sea but made little showing against the new and powerful Russian coast defenses. They did, however, reduce the Åland islands (see map 5), and the Russians were increasingly nervous that the enticements of France and Great Britain would bring Sweden into the war. It did not come to that; but Palmerston, who for twenty years past had been highly suspicious of Russian alleged designs on the far northern ice-free Finmark coast of Norway (then joined with Sweden), concluded in company with France a treaty with Sweden (1855), pledging armed assistance against any Russian designs on the integrity of Sweden and Norway.

This "work of injurious mistrust towards Russia" was followed by the much more serious "servitude" imposed on her at the end of the war in the treaty of Paris (1856), whereby she was forbidden to maintain any bases or fortifications on the Åland islands. This "servitude," coupled with the public guarantee of Sweden against Russia, rankled deeply and was of serious practical inconvenience. Thus, when Norway separated from Sweden (1905), Izvolsky, the new foreign minister, seized the opportunity to launch out into an active Scandinavian policy (1906-8)—what he called "a new edition of Catherine the Great's 'Northern Accord' "—and he did his best to secure Swedish and German consent to refortification of the Åland islands. Izvolsky's maneuvers had no practical effect, but when the First World War broke out Russia inevitably proceeded to fortify the islands.

By the time the war had finished Russia was in revolution and Finland, to which the islands, though admittedly Swedish in population, had always been attached, was independent. A dispute with Sweden for their possession was settled by the League of Nations (1921) in Finland's favor, but with the proviso that the islands be once again unfortified. Their strategic importance, so close to Stockholm and lying across the entrance to the gulf of Bothnia with its iron ore ports, has probably been increased by the advent of the submarine and the airplane. Certainly the islands have been very far from forgotten by the Soviet government. When Finland, Sweden, and the Western powers reached agreement on their refortification the Soviet government promptly reminded the world (May 1939) that the U.S.S.R. was a Baltic power and must be consulted, with the result that the project had to be dropped. Events since then suggest that the Soviet Union feels little less concerned with the Åland islands than did the Russian Empire, which possessed them.

2. *The Black Sea and the Straits*

Prior to the Mongol conquest in the thirteenth century the Black Sea was far more important as a cultural route than the Baltic, and for most of the period of Kiev Russia trade with the South was probably of greater consequence than trade across the Baltic. Thereafter the Baltic was infinitely more important as an economic route until the later nineteenth century. From 1700 it was the main route for the europeanizing of Russia, while the Black Sea as a cultural channel had long shrunk to almost nothing. Yet since the middle of the eighteenth century the rôle of the Black Sea in Russian history has been in its different way as prominent as that of the Baltic, and in the nineteenth century more prominent; and the Sound has never figured in Russian history as have the Straits.

Whereas the Baltic coastlands, except the narrow strip of Ingria, have never been colonized by the Russians, the northern coastlands of the Black Sea, from the Danube round to the Caucasus, have been since the last two hundred years the scene of the final stages of the southward expansion of the Russian people. This historic expansion from the mixed forest into the steppe zones and the immense transformation of New Russia along the north of the Black Sea have been sketched in Chapter I (see pp. 30 ff. and 41-43). This is the cardinal fact in regard to the Black Sea in modern Russian history.

The advance was in part planned, in part one of the independent groups acting for themselves. In either case it involved an armed struggle against the Tatar peoples, above all the Crimean Tatars, grazing and raiding from the steppe lands. The Tatar peoples were the subjects or vassals of the Ottoman empire; and the two outstanding features of the Russian conquest of the Black Sea steppes were that it was both the triumph of the agriculturist over the nomad and the triumph of the organized Russian state over the organized Ottoman state.

In the late seventeenth century Muscovy turned to the offensive in the south. Seven times between 1676 and 1812, for over thirty years in all, Russia and Turkey were openly at war. By 1812, with the acquisition of Bessarabia (see map 4) and the Turkish strongholds near the modern Novorossisk, Russia was mistress of the great arc from the Danube to the Caucasus.

She began with costly failure. Peter the Great indeed scored a notable success by capturing Azov, at his second attempt (1696), and scared the Turks with the portent of the first

Russian fleet in what hitherto had been regarded as their own lake; but thereafter the international situation and other Russian interests diverted Peter to the Baltic. When Charles XII after Poltava fled to Turkey, and urged her to renew war, Peter suffered a catastrophe on the Pruth (1711), which but for the venality of the grand vizier would have eclipsed Narva. Azov and the other gains of Peter had to be retroceded.

This first foothold on the Black Sea was regained after four years of war (1735-39), in which the Russian armies had won, though with terrible wastage of life, success after success, only to be rewarded with the shameless burlesque of the treaty of Belgrade (1739). The treaty was a triumph of French diplomacy, in its regular support of the Sultan. In the end the Turks yielded nothing but Azov and maintained their veto on Russian ships appearing in the Sea of Azov or the Black Sea.

None the less, the Ottoman empire was now permanently on the defensive. The Russia of Catherine the Great won the whole coast from the Dniester to the Kuban (see map 4; 1768-74, 1787-92), including the Crimea (1783). Under Alexander I Bessarabia and the Principalities (Moldavia and Wallachia, the eastern half of the present-day Roumania) were again conquered (1806-12), and, although owing to the imminence of Napoleon's invasion Russia was unable to force Turkey to cede more than Bessarabia, she was now established at the mouth of the Danube.

The conquest of the Black Sea steppes was a great achievement, studded with famous feats of arms, linked with famous commanders, Suvorov and Kutuzov in the van. Three times Russia had Austria as an ally (1697-1700, 1735-39, 1787-91). Three times Turkey had active assistance from the Poles (1768-72) or the Swedes (1711, 1788-90); once almost from Prussia (1790) or England (1791). Always she had aid, often to great effect, from France. Yet in the main the struggle was a Russo-Turkish contest.

Distance, difficulties of supply and munitions, and deficiencies of organization cost the Russians extra heavy losses and too often robbed them of the fruits of individual victories. The resilience of Ottoman power and the doggedness of Ottoman armies could not finally stay the Russian drive to the Black Sea, but they did prevent the Russian retention of the Principalities. It was only the northern steppe fringes of the Ottoman empire that were as yet lost. A Russian soldiers' saying goes to the bone: "The Turks are falling like skittles, but, thank God, our men stand fast, though headless."

The eighteenth-century struggle for the Black Sea was primarily a struggle for its northern steppe lands, not for the Balkans or Constantinople and the Straits, and only latterly for the Caucasus. The schemes and dreams of some partitioning of Turkey, of Catherine the Great's "Greek project" (1782; see p. 228), of risings of the Balkan Christians, of championship of the *rayahs* in the name of Orthodoxy, remained for the most part schemes and dreams, though pregnant with the future. Ottoman power was still too strong, Russian still too remote, until a solid southern base could be established in the Black Sea steppes. These two facts, even more than the rivalry with Austria, the diversions of Poland and Sweden, the policies of Prussia and Great Britain and the French support of the sultan, explain why European Turkey did not fare as Poland did in the eighteenth century.

In the nineteenth century the Black Sea changes its place in Russian history. The rise of New Russia transforms the economic position of the Black Sea and the Straits and threatens to put the tsar's army and fleet within striking distance of the heart of the Ottoman empire. The conquest of Transcaucasia transforms the eastern Black Sea coast and neighboring lands. Russia becomes far more than before a magnet for the Balkan Christians, now in the throes of rebirth as modern nations. Under the impact of this last challenge and of the Western world in other forms, the Ottoman empire becomes more and more deeply shaken. Leaves of the artichoke are peeled off: the core itself is questionable.

Some diagnose that "Turkey is a dying man. We may endeavor to keep him alive, but we shall not succeed. He will, he must die"; that it is essential therefore for the powers to be ready in advance with some "ulterior system . . . and not allow events to take us by surprise" (Nicholas I, 1844 and 1853). Others hold that "no empire is likely to fall to pieces if left to itself, and if no kind neighbors forcibly tear it to pieces" (Palmerston, 1838). Diverse suspicions and rivalries aggravate the central problem of Constantinople and the Straits. To Russia the Straits figure as "the gates to our house": the questions of ingress to and egress from the Black Sea and of the defense of her coasts are vital issues. But for Turkey the Straits mean not so much gates to her house as the very center of her house, her capital, Constantinople. Thus the Black Sea and the Straits become a perpetual plague-spot of European controversy, since they involve the heart of the Ottoman Empire.

From the standpoint of Russia, her relations with Turkey during the century closing with the First World War involved four different, but overlapping, problems: the Balkan Christians and later the Slav states, the attitude of the other great powers, Constantinople and the Straits, and (often forgotten or minimized in the West) the Caucasus.

First and foremost, the Straits, quite apart from any political designs of Russia, were of essential and ever-increasing economic importance to her. The development and prosperity of New Russia depended on secure access to the West, through the Straits. This was a primary concern of Russian policy ever since Catherine the Great extracted by the treaty of Kuchuk-Kainardji (1774; *cf.* p. 228) the right of Russian merchantmen to navigate the Black Sea and pass through the Straits, together with various trading rights within the Ottoman Empire. Thereby the Ottoman monopoly of the Black Sea had been broken into. But it took roughly half a century before Russia secured in practice that Turkey should not requisition at will cargoes coming through the Bosporus and that the navigation and commercial stipulations of a series of Russo-Turkish treaties should be actually operative. She was also active and successful in supporting the claims of other countries to the same right of commercial passage of the Straits. This was an essential complement since her own merchant marine was diminutive. Her object was attained by the treaty of Adrianople (1829). Henceforward the unhindered passage of unarmed ships through the Straits has not been called in question, while Turkey has been at peace.

The new wheat lands of the South already under Alexander I (1801-25) were receiving great attention from the government. Until late in the century they continued to be the principal source of the phenomenal rise in Russian grain exports, which came to occupy such an exceptional place in Russian economy. During Alexander's reign grain exports, hitherto quite secondary and mainly rye, jumped up to third place, coming next to flax and hemp. They were now chiefly wheat, which was exported solely from the South, through the Straits.

Russian (and Soviet) grain exports have always varied sharply in different years, and other factors also complicate the available figures. None the less, it is broadly true that by about 1850 grain exports had risen to almost a third of total Russian exports; by about 1875 to well over half; while about 1910 they were not much under half. Wheat, practically all shipped from Black Sea ports, constituted in most years much the largest share of the grain exports, until after 1870. Then its share declined; but its absolute quantity remained very large and much of the other grain shipments were also made via the Black Sea.

In the first decade of the present century Russia had regained her position as the largest grain exporter in the world and the largest wheat supplier of Europe (29 per cent of European wheat imports—mainly to Germany and Italy); positions which she had lost to the United States in the seventies. She supplied about a quarter of the world's wheat exports, nearly half of the oats, over a third of the rye, three-quarters of the barley. The bulk of this huge trade was carried across the Black Sea.

To this must be added the effects of the uprush since the eighties of the Caucasian oil and South Russian coal and metallurgical industries, which yet further increased the independence of Russia on passage of the Black Sea and the Straits. The foreign minister Sazonov scarcely exaggerated when he reported to the tsar in 1913: "The Straits in the hands of a strong state mean the full subjection of the economic development of southern Russia to that state."

The effect of war with Turkey (1828-29, 1853-56, 1877-78, 1914-18) was bound to dislocate Russian economy most gravely; even if it were not combined, as it twice was (1853-56, 1914-18), with the closing of the Baltic at the same time. The threat of a blockade of the Dardanelles by Italy in 1911 during her war with Turkey called forth the most active, and successful, diplomatic pressure by Russia. Even while Turkey herself remains at peace, the enemies of Russia may control the Ægean, as now (June, 1943), and thereby close the Dardanelles. Once again, as in the First World War, Russia has no access to her allies either through the Straits or through the Sound.

The economic importance of the Black Sea and the Straits has been interwoven for Russians with strategic needs of defense and political and religious ideas and claims centering round the conception of Russia as the protector of the Orthodox in Turkey, and, later, as the champion of the Slavs (see pp. 225-238). Catherine the Great in her last years had enlarged her expansionist policy against Turkey to include the acquisition in some form of the Principalities and in general the disruption of European Turkey. It was rightly regarded as significant that her second grandson was christened Constantine. This general line of policy ever after had powerful adherents, both in the country at large and in St. Petersburg. It was adopted for a time (1806-12) by Alexander I and, hesitantly, by Nicholas I (1844-54). In changed form, it was part of the gospel of the panslavs. From the end of the century, with the growth of the new Balkan states, it became more than ever concentrated on the Straits.

Already, however, under Paul and Alexander I the contrary policy of the maintenance of a weak Turkey with Russian influence dominant at Constantinople had been formulated and acted upon, in connection with Napoleon's expedition to Egypt and the new position of Russia between 1799 and 1805 as the ally of Turkey against France. Russia was only once again in alliance with Turkey, for a few years after 1833; but this policy, with varying adaptations, continued in governmental circles to compete with the other, expansionist policy. It found its most effective exponent in Nesselrode, foreign minister continuously from 1822 to 1856. Still in the dozen years before 1914 there were influential spokesmen in certain Russian camps who argued in favor of "the maintenance of Constantinople and the Straits in the hands of the Turks" and of some close understanding with them as best suiting the interests of Russia. The problem of what was to happen to Constantinople and the Straits if the Turks were ejected raised such "a labyrinth of difficulties and complications each more inextricable than the other" (Nesselrode, 1829) that it could be effectively urged that it was a lesser evil, or even a positive gain, to leave things as they were. In any case, the Turks had first to be ejected, which they never were.

In 1829, for the first time, the Russian armies swept across the Balkans, captured Adrianople and seemed to have Constantinople at their mercy. Look behind the scenes at this critical moment. Nicholas I was prepared, if the Turks refused his terms (which in fact they did not), to seize their capital and the Dardanelles and deny them to any fleet, but he professed no desire to see himself "master of Constantinople and in consequence of the disposition of the Ottoman empire in Europe." On the contrary, he endorsed the views of an imperial committee that the advantages of the preservation of Turkey outweighed the disadvantages. Russia was already vast enough and needed no further extension. The acquisition of Constantinople and the Straits might indeed deny the Black Sea to an enemy fleet, but it would only be at the price of a general partition of the empire and it would not ensure Russian exit into the Mediterranean, since no doubt France and Great Britain would seize or dominate the Ægean islands. Russia would be faced with their power and efficiency in place of the weakness and incompetence of Turkey. Moreover, the far-seeing suggestion was made that a Turkey thrust out of Europe back into Asia Minor might solidify as a much more compact state and a graver danger to the Caucasus. If and when, however, the final hour of Turkish rule struck, Russia would have to negotiate a new settlement with the other powers, but she must be ready to seize on her own account the northern entrance to the Bosporus so as to close the Black Sea.

This last recommendation often reappeared in Russian projects when conditions in Constantinople and suspicions of other powers, usually Great Britain, raised the bogey in St. Petersburg of a complete breakdown of the sultan's power. It brings out a central fact in Russian policy towards the Straits. Russia was always weaker at sea than Great Britain or France; hence, as long as they were her chief potential enemies, she was primarily concerned to keep hostile fleets outside the Black Sea rather than to open the Straits for her own fleet, since this was almost bound to involve as well opening them to other fleets. It is true that a closed Black Sea meant that the Russian fleet there had to be self-contained and could not be used elsewhere, for instance in the Far East during the war of 1904-5 with Japan. But it meant some additional defense of her Black Sea lands, provided of course that Turkey herself was not at war with her.

On the other hand, if Russia could secure the alliance of Turkey in war, all could be well; both Straits would be opened to her warships alone. This happened in practice only once. In 1799 Russia made alliance with Turkey against France, when Napoleon was in Egypt, and Russian warships sailed through the Straits to operate in the Mediterranean and contest the Ionian isles.

Thirty years later Egypt, then under the sultan's semi-independent vassal Mehemet Ali, again threw him into the arms of Russia. In 1833, on the reluctant invitation of the sultan, for the first and only time a Russian expeditionary force landed at the Bosphorus, to defend Constantinople against threatened Egyptian attack. The result was the Russian triumph of the treaty of Unkiar-Skelessi (1833). A defensive alliance was concluded for eight years; Russia undertook to assist Turkey to the full if she were attacked, though she was careful not to guarantee the territorial integrity of the empire; in return Turkey promised to keep the Straits closed to all foreign warships. Palmerston, who denounced the alliance with extreme asperity, was wrong in believing that the treaty gave Russia the right to send warships through the Straits in peace-time. It did not explicitly do so. Nesselrode in fact interpreted the treaty defensively and held that it would be neither legal nor politic to send warships through the Straits in peace-time, though his own admiralty differed and did on one occasion send a squadron through.

In any case, Unkiar-Skelessi was a resounding success for Russia. She had not only given a single-handed and sensational set-back to Mehemet Ali (though it proved only temporary). She was for the time being in the position for which she was always striving and which she never again attained: "the treaty," Nesselrode wrote, "will justify, if occasion requires, the presence and employment of our forces and will allow us to place ourselves again, before any others and in superior strength, in the theater of events in such a manner as to remain always masters of the situation, whether one admits the maintenance of the Ottoman empire as possible or its dissolution as in the end inevitable."

In the face of British and French opposition it proved impossible for the Russians to remain thus "masters of the situation" for more than a few years. When the second Mehemet Ali crisis came to a head in 1839 Nicholas I realized that he could not repeat his single-handed intervention and settlement of the Straits question. He swerved round to the policy of dividing Great Britain from France and joining with the former and Austria in supporting the sultan against Mehemet Ali. He knew that Unkiar-Skelessi was dead and in the circumstances was well enough pleased to substitute for it the London convention of 1840, next year acceded to by France. Thereby, foreign warships, with certain minor exceptions, were banned from both the Straits while Turkey was at peace: Russia could not get to Constantinople or the Mediterranean; the other powers could not get to Constantinople or the Black Sea.

The London convention was a milestone in the history of the Straits. For the first time they were regulated by international agreement between the powers and Turkey, whereas hitherto the sultan had always treated them as his own territorial waters. Russia had recognized the Greek question to be of European concern, as she had shown most notably in her victorious treaty of Adrianople (1829); but her other interests in the Ottoman empire had been regarded by her as matters to be regulated by herself and Turkey alone. Now she admitted the Straits as of European concern. Defeat in the Crimea and the treaty of Paris (1856) compelled her to admit all Ottoman questions as of European concern (see also pp. 404-405).

Shortly before the Crimean War Nicholas I, communing with himself, had sketched "the least bad of all bad combinations"; Constantinople might be a free city with a Russian garrison on the Bosphorus and an Austrian on the Dardanelles. Later in the same year (1853) he suggested to the emperor Francis Joseph Constantinople as a free city and the razing of the fortifications at the Bosphorus and the Dardanelles. The bitter arbitrament of war ended with the razing of fortifications; but they were Russian not Turkish.

The treaty of Paris (1856) signalized the nadir of Russian influence in Turkey. Until Sedan (1870) France was preponderant at Constantinople, with Great Britain running a good second. The Russian naval stronghold, Sebastopol, had been captured and her fleet scuttled or destroyed. The treaty forbade her to build another in the Black Sea or to construct any arsenals on its coast. Turkey was similarly shackled in the Black Sea, but since she could keep a fleet in the Sea of Marmara or the Mediterranean and, in case of war with Russia, pass it through the Bosphorus, it was obvious that the shackles on Turkey were light. As regards the Straits, the London convention of 1841 was renewed, but a secret alliance between Great Britain, France, Austria, and Turkey (known to the Russians) virtually opened them to the Western powers in case of Turkish need. Russia was forced back from the mouths of the Danube by the cession of southern Bessarabia. Over against Transcaucasia, the commanding fortress of Kars, which had been brilliantly stormed for the second time (1855, 1829), had to be restored. Russia had to renounce all her previous rights or claims in regard to the Principalities, Serbia, and the Orthodox subjects of the sultan.

The neutralization of the Black Sea and the cession of southern Bessarabia were specially onerous and humiliating. Alexander II (1855-81) was determined to rid himself of "these two nightmares," as he styled them. He regained the lost territory in the war of 1877-78. Within a few years of 1856 the impossibility of continuing indefinitely the veto on a Russian fleet in the Black Sea came to be privately recognized in all quarters. Gorchakov, Alexander's foreign minister, wanted to denounce the veto in 1866, but was overborne in St. Petersburg. He seized his chance four years later after Sedan. The Gladstone government reacted stiffly against the unilateral abrogation by Russia, but did not dispute that the veto should be removed. At the London conference (1871) the powers and Turkey agreed to this and renewed the previous (1856, 1841) ban on the passage of the Straits by warships. But an involved clause was added empowering the sultan to allow warships to pass the Straits even in time of peace if it was necessary to uphold the independence and integrity of the Ottoman empire guaranteed by the powers, including Russia, in 1856.

The war of 1877-78 went even nearer than that of 1828-29 to settling the question of Constantinople and the Straits by a Russian capture of them. In the end the Russian commander in the field, to the disgust of Alexander II and Russian opinion, stayed his victorious but almost exhausted troops on the outskirts of Constantinople and the approaches to the Dardanelles. Meanwhile a British fleet went up through them to the Golden Horn, with the reluctantly extracted consent of the sultan, and for some months Russia stood on the edge of war with Great Britain and Austria-

Hungary. Yet the treaty of San Stefano (March 1878), which marked the high-water mark of its maker Ignatyev, did not change the Straits régime. Ignatyev did his best to force the sultan to accept an arrangement whereby the Straits should be open to Russian warships and closed to all others; but Gorchakov was ultimately successful in his insistence that the Straits must be left to international settlement.

At the Berlin congress (July 1878; see also p. 233), which revised the treaty of San Stefano, Russia did not improve her position in regard to the Straits. The treaty of Berlin simply renewed the 1871 convention. But at the congress the Russian and British representatives each made official declarations which showed that the two governments differed entirely in their interpretation of the involved additional clause in the 1871 convention. The British declaration gave the Russian government excellent ground for thinking that, if the appropriate moment came or the situation in Constantinople were out of hand, the British would again send their fleet through the Dardanelles, as they had done a few months earlier.

For the next twenty-five years (especially during the Central Asian and Bulgarian crises of 1885-87 and the Armenian massacres of 1896-97), when Anglo-Russian hostility was extended from the Near and Middle East to the Far East (see later pp. 290-294), suspicions were rife on both sides that the other would make some coup in Constantinople. The Russians in the eighties were only beginning to recreate their Black Sea fleet and in fact were not ready to take the initiative, but they were determined, if possible, to forestall a British control or European intervention at Constantinople, by preparing as well as they could for a rapid descent at least upon the Bosphorus.

The emperor Alexander III (1881-94) was fully aware that Russia was not yet in a position to act, but he hoped that sooner or later it would be possible: "the principal thing is *not to lose* time and the favorable moment." "In my view," he also wrote (1885), "we ought to have one principal aim, the occupation of Constantinople, so that we may once for all maintain ourselves at the Straits and know that they will remain in our hands. That is in the interests of Russia and it ought to be our aspiration. Everything else that takes place in the Balkan peninsula is secondary for us. There has been enough propaganda to the detriment of the true interests of Russia. The Slavs must now serve Russia, and not we them."

These secret avowals of Alexander III sum up what was, perhaps, the main Russian attitude towards the Straits in the thirty years before the First World War. On the other hand, there were influential, but divided, currents in Russia which pulled her in other directions, to the Far East, to agreement with Austria-Hungary, even to some form of *entente* with Turkey. And there were always serious technical difficulties in a Russian descent upon the Bosphorus, which, whatever the optimism at certain moments of the experts, made it extremely hazardous, even if the possibility of its igniting a European war could be discounted.

The expansion of Russian imperialism in the Middle East and especially the Far East, culminating in the Russo-Japanese war of 1904-5 and followed by the 1905 Revolution, prevented a forward policy in the Balkans until 1908. By then Russia, fortified by the new (1907) *entente* with England as well as by her alliance with France (1893), was no longer bent mainly on parrying the British at Constantinople or content with keeping foreign warships out of the Black Sea, but desired some change; if possible, in the sense that the Straits should be open to her fleet while still closed to others; if that were not possible, in the sense that the Dardanelles should be open to all warships but the Bosphorus only to Russian.

Such were the lines upon which the active and ambitious Izvolsky, foreign minister from 1906 to 1910, began to work. Despite the internal weakness of Russia in consequence of the Revolution of 1905, he strove by diplomacy for "the realization of Russia's historic aims in the Near East," though he was emphatically warned by Stolypin, the very powerful prime minister, that he could count on "no support whatever for a resolute policy."

After concluding the Anglo-Russian conventions of 1907 (which did not themselves touch upon the Straits), Izvolsky believed (rightly) that the British government favored a strengthening of the position of Russia and (wrongly) that it would at once lend support to a change of the Straits regulations to her advantage, without regard to the Young Turk revolution which had just taken place in Constantinople (July 1908) and which seemed to Izvolsky to give Russia the requisite opening. He thought that he could square Austria-Hungary by bartering an eventual annexation by her of Bosnia-Herzegovina (September 1908). In actual fact Austria-Hungary proclaimed annexation at once, while Izvolsky secured no agreement on the Straits with any of the powers or the Young Turk government. He was arraigned at home for having abandoned the Slav cause in return for nothing at all, and he aggravated the most dangerous Bosnian crisis that ended next year in the humiliation of Russia and Serbia by Germany and Austria-Hungary (*cf.* pp. 407-408).

Izvolsky's failure did not mark the end of the efforts of Russian diplomacy to achieve a new Straits settlement. The Italo-Turkish war of 1911 gave a further opportunity which was taken advantage of by one section of the Russian foreign office to return to a turcophil policy and negotiate with the Turks for an agreement allowing Russian passage of the Straits. The negotiations came to nothing, largely because of the strong opposition of the Russian panslavs, who were backing the opposite policy of a Balkan League under the ægis of Russia.

The league brought the Balkan wars (1912-13) and a further disruption of European Turkey. Russian relations with Turkey went from bad to worse in 1913-14 owing to the crisis caused by the mission of the German General Liman von Sanders to take command virtually of the Turkish army, and owing to Turkish fears of Russian reform projects for the Armenians and Russian fears of pan-turanian and pan-islamic propaganda.

By the beginning of 1914 the problem of the Straits was regarded by the Russian government as soluble only in case of a European war, which now seemed lowering. As in 1886-87, the way to Constantinople was thought to lie through Berlin. At the same time it was admitted in secret councils in St. Petersburg that Russia would, until 1916, be inferior at sea to Turkey and would be unable to make any combined descent upon the Bosphorus. The army chiefs held that Russia's western front was all in all and would determine the issue of the Straits, if war there had to be.

European war came in August 1914; and therewith the *Goeben* and the *Breslau* to Constantinople. The Young Turk government clinched its compact with Germany and at the end of October entered the war. Russia was cut off from her Western allies and remained so until the end, despite the great venture of the Gallipoli campaign.

The immensity of the conflict and the inestimable value of Russian man-power set the future of Constantinople and the Ottoman empire in a wholly new perspective. Russia was to gain "the immemorial and sacred dream of the Russian people," as her prime minister publicly announced three months before the Revolution of March 1917. Her allies had agreed (1915) to her acquisition of Constantinople and the Straits, together with eastern Thrace and two islands off the Dardanelles. In addition (1916), Russia was to annex great stretches of northeastern Anatolia, the Armenian provinces, including the fortress of Erzerum and the port of Trebizond, both already captured by Russian arms.

The nineteenth century had seen the slow partition of the Ottoman empire in Europe between the Balkan peoples. The twentieth century should see the partition of the Ottoman empire in Asia between the Allied powers, the reduction of the Turks to their Anatolian homeland, the restoration of the Cross upon Santa Sofia, and for the first time in history the Tsar of All the Russias reigning in the city of Constantine the Great.

All this was dependent upon the proviso "if the war were brought to a successful conclusion." It was, for the Western allies; not for Russia. The Revolution cared not a jot "for the immemorial and sacred dream of the Russian people."

When the Bolsheviks overthrew the Provisional Government they denounced and renounced all the tsarist secret treaties, all annexations and indemnities. They were impotent to affect the destiny of Constantinople and the Straits.

When Turkey collapsed in the autumn of 1918 control of the Straits and the Black Sea passed into the hands of the British and French, and the Bolsheviks were faced with Allied intervention against them in support of General Denikin and other anti-Bolshevik movements. While the tortuous struggle (1919-23) to agree upon and carry out a peace settlement with Turkey coiled and uncoiled, the new régime in Russia was fighting for its life and did well to regain the vital Baku oilfields and most of Transcaucasia. The key fortress of Kars, but not Batum, the terminus of the pipe-line and railway from Baku, was ceded to Turkey (March 1921), and the same peace treaty laid the ground for an entirely new relationship between the Turkey of Mustapha Kemal and the Soviet Russia of Lenin, who had always denounced the aggressive designs of tsarist imperialism and preached the liberation of Asiatic peoples from the thrall of the West (*cf.* p. 297).

The Soviet-Turkish treaty of March 1921 indicated Soviet ideas as to the future of the Straits. They were to be open to the commerce of all countries, but the regulations as to passage of warships were to be decided upon by international agreement between the states bordering the Black Sea only, without prejudice to the independence of Turkey and the security of Constantinople. These were mere hopes. The actuality proved to be a settlement that could scarcely be more unfavorable to the Soviet Union, namely the treaty of Lausanne (1923) concluded between Turkey and the Western powers in the face of violent Soviet protests.

The treaty of Lausanne left Constantinople and the Straits to Turkey, but demilitarized them under international supervision. This solution ran counter to the almost invariable Russian view in the past that it was better to have fortifications at the Straits, even though in Turkish hands, which might at least deter or stop intruders, rather than to have nothing barring the way to the Black Sea. In view of Soviet naval weakness this old view that the primary essential was to prevent entry into the Black Sea rather than to secure Russian exit was bound to be uppermost. Thus no comfort was found in the fact that the treaty of Lausanne gave Soviet warships of all types full right of passage through the Straits in peace or war, if Turkey were neutral. For at the same time it gave substantially the same right to non-Black-Sea states, subject only to the condition that in peace-time no *one* such state should send into the Black Sea a force larger than the Soviet navy; a limitation that was in Soviet eyes in any case illusory in view of the likelihood of another coalition against the revolutionary republic of the proletariat.

The treaty of Lausanne was both a complete reversal of previous international regulations governing the Straits, and a settlement that was as displeasing to Turkey as to the Soviet Union. By 1936 the international and internal position of both states had changed fundamentally. Germany was Nazi; Italy Fascist and bent on empire. France (by now in alliance with the U.S.S.R.) and Great Britain were ready enough to win Turkish and Soviet support by radical changes in the Lausanne treaty. The result was the Montreux convention of 1936 which still juridically governs the Straits.

At the Montreux conference Turkey regained her full right to the fortification of the Straits and the Constantinople district, while Litvinov in effect gained what Izvolsky so resoundingly failed to obtain in 1908. Non-Black-Sea states were narrowly limited in the tonnage of light warships they could send through the Straits in time of peace, and they could not send any large vessels, submarines, or aircraft carriers. If belligerents, they were in most contingencies excluded altogether. On the other hand, all types of Soviet warships, except submarines and aircraft carriers, were allowed through the Straits while non-belligerent: if belligerent, they were in most contingencies excluded. Turkey, if she were a belligerent or believed war involving her to be imminent, was to act as she chose. As had always been the rule, commercial vessels, whether of belligerents or non-belligerents, were to enjoy free passage, so long as Turkey herself was not at war.

At present (June, 1943) the Straits are closed to the United Nations though not to the Axis states. But the great fact stands out that this is due to Axis command of the Ægean—not, as in the First World War, to the hostility of Turkey. In addition to the treaty of Turkey with Great Britain (October 1939), the great fact stands out that this is the only war (save one) which Russia has fought in the past two hundred and fifty years in which Turkey has not been either fighting against her or at least definitely hostile. For this striking change there are various reasons, not the least of which has been the Soviet policy of friendship with Kemalist Turkey.

Latterly Soviet-Turkish relations have been clouded with mutual suspicions, particularly from the Turkish side, where the old fears of ultimate Russian demands upon the Straits have been revived and played up by German propaganda. It is hardly to be expected that the memories of the long past of contest, ill-will, and rival intrigue could be sloughed off in twenty years, however radical the revolutions that have transformed both countries; the long past, with its eleven Russo-Turkish wars (1676-1918), which spelled the historic contest not only for the northern Black Sea lands, the Balkans, and the heart of the Ottoman empire, but also for the eastern seaboard, the Caucasian bridge lands between the Black Sea and the Caspian.

3. *The Black Sea and the Caspian*

The Caucasian lands—the great isthmus linking Eurasia with western Asia, immemorial crossroads of culture, trampling ground of urgent armies, and refuge of riven peoples—had been since the sixteenth century a cockpit between the Turkish Osmanlis and the Persian Safavids. Ottoman power and influence reached out from the eastern Black Sea to the Tatar or Moslem peoples of Eurasia in process of engulfment by the Muscovite and Russian empire. The long duel for the Black Sea became also a contest for the Caucasus; but it was a triangular contest; both Turkey and Russia had to face Persia.

Russian connections with the Caucasian peoples had been considerable in the middle of the Kiev period; thereafter they were almost entirely severed until the capture of Astrakhan in 1556. That made the Caspian trade and relations with Persia (arbiter of the much-coveted silk trade) of continuous importance to Moscow. A generation later Cossack settlements along the Terek (see map 4) pushed Muscovite interests to the foothills of the eastern Caucasus. Muscovy was too weak and too far distant until the eighteenth century to extend this outlying Cossack fringe or to do much more than spy out the land with, at frequent intervals, exchange of embassies with the Christian Georgian principalities, lying beyond the immense massif of the central Caucasus between the hammer of the Turk and the anvil of the Persian.

The Russia of Peter the Great moved forward against the derelict Persia of the last Safavids. Peter, whose reckless energy was unspent even by the Great Northern War, had pushed out expeditions towards Central Asia in quest of Eastern marts and Indian trade routes (1714-17), and he himself in person led a campaign against Persia (1722-23) by the age-old route along the narrow coastal strip between the Caucasus and the Caspian. He lost a fleet and there were the usual appalling losses from sickness, but he imposed his will upon the tottering shah, who ceded Baku and all his western and southern Caspian seacoast in return for help against his hereditary foe, the Turks.

The Russian forward bound was too great. Communications and climate were fatally weakening. The two ancient Christian peoples of Transcaucasia, the Georgians and Armenians, were in constant touch with the Russians, but they were far too divided among themselves and too beset by the Turks to be of any direct assistance. The Armenian merchants were closely bound up with Persian trade, and Georgians, usually as converts to Islam, had played a notable part in Persian administration for a hundred years past. Far away at the other end of Russia Peter's immediate successors were otherwise engrossed and in any case were of a very different kidney to the new ruler who had appeared in Persia, Nadir Shah (d. 1747), the last of the great Persian conquerors. In 1732 and 1735 all Peter's Caspian gains were retroceded to Persia. The Russian frontier was once again the Terek.

Russian aims in one respect, however, had been attained. A contemporaneous Turkish bid for the eastern Caucasus and the Caspian had been frustrated. Tiflis and the eastern Georgian lands together with Armenia and Azerbaidzhan (see map 1) remained in the Persian sphere of influence; western Georgia and the Black Sea coast and hinterland in the Turkish. The continuance of Persian-Turkish rivalry in the Caucasus was always a major aim of Russian policy. In conjunction with the disparateness and animosities of the Caucasian peoples themselves, it operated as a deciding factor in the permanent Russian conquest of these lands that began in the late eighteenth century. In all the fifteen wars that Russia has fought with Turkey and Persia, only once (1806-12) did she have to fight both of them at the same time.

During Catherine the Great's reign the Russian drive against Turkey for the northern Black Sea coastlands was also a drive southeastwards for their continuation in the Kuban and North Caucasus steppes. Her two wars with Turkey (1768-74, 1787-92) were, on the eastern side of the Black Sea, the climaxes of a generation of energetic military colonization of these steppes, of challenge to the Turkish forts on the coast, to Turkish slave supplies, and to Turkish suzerainty over the warlike Moslem mountaineers. Among them for the first time (1785) a "holy war" was successfully preached against the infidel northerner: their eighty years' struggle against subjection had begun.

Beyond the giant range of the Central Caucasus, the Georgians, long since disunited and rent by social cleavages, multiplied renewed appeals for Orthodox assistance against the competing overlordship of Turkey and Persia, and in 1783 the eastern Georgian kingdom accepted the protectorate of Catherine. Three times Russian troops, marching through the key Dariel Pass in the central Caucasus, entered Tiflis, only to be later withdrawn. At last in 1799 they came to stay. The eastern Georgian kingdom, under threat from its suzerain Persia, expired into the arms of Russia (1801).

This led on to the final reckoning with Persia. It was long drawn out, principally because Alexander I was heavily engaged at the same time in the West both with Napoleon and with Turkey, additionally because at times Napoleon, at times the British, did what they could to bolster up Persian resistance. By 1813 Persia was compelled by force of arms to recognize Baku and most of eastern Transcaucasia as Russian. A second war, this time short and decisive (1826-28), settled the fate of the Azerbaidzhan highlands and Persian Armenia: the Russian frontier was advanced to the Araxes, where it has stayed ever since, only a hundred easy miles from Tabriz, the second city of Persia (see map 1).

The final acquisition of Tiflis in 1801 also led on to thirty years of contest with the Turks for the western Caucasus. Pushing westwards from Tiflis the Russians engulfed the other Georgian principalities (by 1810), and from the north gradually succeeded in reducing the Turkish strongholds on the inhospitable Black Sea coast and in cutting their communications with the Caucasian mountain peoples. By 1829 (treaty of Adrianople) Russian ascendancy was definitely won. The Turks were left with nothing north of Batum (see map 1).

Although the Turks had lost control of the Caucasus littoral, the Russians took another thirty years to master it. While Transcaucasia fell to the Russians between 1801 and 1829, behind, ensconced in forest and crag, the mountain peoples of the Caucasus continued a desperate resistance, and their subjection could not be called complete until by 1864 the Circassians had been levered out of their fastnesses above the Black Sea and had migrated *en masse* to their protector Turkey, where many of them were to win sinister notoriety as the Bashi-Bazouks.

The duration and vigor of the resistance of the Moslem mountaineers, even though they were much divided among themselves, were mainly due to the combination of a new puritanical religious fervor with the economic, social, and political struggle against the infidel invader, and often against his local client khans or begs. The combination was effected above all by the striking personality and all-round ability of Shamil (b. 1798 or 1800, d. 1871), "the Imam, ruler of the righteous, destroyer of the unbeliever, mighty and victorious governor." Religious, military, and political leader in one, for nearly thirty years Shamil defied the Russians and even imposed a considerable degree of united action upon many of the diverse peoples of the eastern Caucasus. It is a tribute to him and typical of his captors that, after he was at last brought to bay and surrendered (1859), he and his family were treated with every consideration in Russia, though kept under close surveillance, and that he himself was officially ennobled.

The mountaineers were in constant connection with the Turks. Gun-running and contraband trade along the wild Black Sea coast were perpetual preoccupations for the Russians. Unofficial British agents were active among the tribesmen and, notably in the thirties, aggravated the very strained relations between Great Britain and Russia. For long, British opinion was fed on stirring accounts of the Circassians battling for independence against the Cossack and the knout. Naturally enough, during the Crimean War (1853-56), Russian fears of a large-scale expedition to the western Caucasus ran high; but in fact the Turks and their allies signally failed to take advantage of their command of the sea and nothing beyond small-scale operations was attempted in that region. Twenty years later during the war of 1877-78 two serious mountaineer risings threatened the Russian rear, but they were only incidents. The fortress of Kars was again captured from the Turks, and this time retained; Batum, the Black Sea outlet for Transcaucasia, was at last ceded (1878). Russia had conquered and a new Caucasia was about to take shape.

The century of struggle for the Caucasus spelled campaign after campaign, astonishing feats of arms, yet more astonishing feats of endurance; it spelled massacre, burning villages, raided herds, devastation. There was indeed all too much fire and sword, especially in the grim contest with the mountaineers.[1] But the conquest meant other things as well. In the North Caucasus steppes it meant security for Russian colonization, the victory of the farmer settler and all that follows (*cf.* p. 44, note). In Transcaucasia, for the upper few it brought from the first excellent opportunities, readily taken, of service, often high service, in the Russian army and administration; for the, largely Armenian, middle-class minority it brought expansion of trade and industry; for the many, some relative security and less oppressive taxation. Above all, the Russian domination set in motion the slow, painful, but ultimately liberating transition to a modern life.

The new contacts with Russian civilization and the West bore varied and positive fruit. Caucasia herself has left a rich and many-colored mark on three generations of Russian literature,[2] has contributed distinctively to Russian music, and has attracted a continuing line of Russian scholars in many fields. The economic transformation of Caucasia has been due to Russia, begun under tsarism with the aid of Western skill and money, grandiosely revolutionized under the Soviet régime, with more and more active participation of the Caucasian peoples themselves. The rebirth of the Georgians and Armenians took place under Russia, and though this owed nothing to the heavy hand of tsarism neither people could have developed as they did had they remained under the far more erratic and benumbing rule of Turkey or Persia.

There was no comparison between the Transcaucasia (or the North Caucasus steppes) of 1900 and that of 1800, except that Georgians, Tatars, and Armenians still predominated and still were fatally divided. Population had greatly in-

[1] Read Tolstoy's *Hadji Murad*, an episode in the struggle against Shamil; finished in 1903; published only in 1911 after Tolstoy's death, and then heavily censored owing to his unbridled invective against Nicholas I; various translations, including the World's Classics series.

[2] Most notably for instance in Lermontov's work, *e.g. A Hero of Our Times* and some of his best-known poems, *The Novice, The Demon, The Dispute* (1839-41) (various translations, including B. L. Tollemache, *Russian Sketches* [London, 1913]).

creased. The influence of Western science and capitalism was changing the life of much of the country. Railways had come: Batum was linked with Baku in 1883; and in 1900 by pipe-line (now doubled). The modern development of Baku oil and Georgian manganese was well under way, like that of irrigation and the various specialized crops of Transcaucasia to be immensely extended under the Soviet five-year plans.

A new Georgian literature and culture were developing fast with the growth of a modern middle-class national movement. This found varied political expression, notably in a social-democratic party of Menshevik coloring which supplied a handful of the most prominent leaders of the Petrograd Soviet in 1917 and of the struggling, nominally independent Georgia of 1918-21. Beneath, the mass of the Georgian peasantry rose in jacqueries in the 1905 Revolution. Underground, a tiny group led by Stalin conspired and battled indomitably for the Bolshevik cause.

The Armenians, divided between Russia and Turkey and with important foreign colonies, much divided also amongst themselves, had a wider range of contacts than the Georgians, all of whom were included within Russia. While in the eyes of the Turks they figured as the tools of Russian expansion in Asia Minor and paid a terrible price in repeated massacres, the Russian Armenians were far from united in accepting a tsarist Russia as the best means of attaining a reunion of the Armenian people. Although many prospered in business and the professions or Russian service, revolutionary movements were strong among them, and their principal party, of a social-revolutionary brand, looked largely to the West.

The Tatars of Azerbaidzhan were already beginning to be dislocated by the effects of the Baku oil industry. Still mainly an illiterate reservoir of unskilled labor, by 1914 they yet had produced a local press and their first local millionaire. They were mostly Shiahs; hence pan-islamic propaganda from Constantinople had never been dangerous. But pan-turanianism had a breeding ground and in the twenty years before the Revolution of 1917 their links with Turkey were being strengthened.

The curse of Transcaucasia had been the centuries-old feuds between these three main peoples. The Russian conquest did little or nothing to allay them. On the contrary, the darkest side of tsarism was to be seen in the at times deliberate fostering of animosities by the authorities during the forty years before 1917. The Revolution of 1905 was marked by terrible excesses in Transcaucasia. Nowhere in the Russian Empire was the nationality problem both more envenomed and more complex. After 1917 it proved to be an insoluble obstacle to independence and the most difficult task confronting the Communists in their refashioning of the land.

In 1917 the Revolution turned Caucasia into a vortex of dissolving and insurgent armies, class struggle, and conflicting national claims to independence or autonomy. The Bolsheviks, having lost control of the Black Sea, abandoned Georgia to the Germans, and Batum and Kars to the Turks by the treaty of Brest-Litovsk (March 1918). Georgia entered upon a checkered period of three years' independence of Russia, but of dependence first on Germany, then after November 1918 on the Allies. Baku oil was a prize contested between the Germans and the Turks, while the British attempted to deprive both of them of it.

The victory of the Allies seemed to give them the final say, and the British, dominant in both the Black Sea and the Caspian, occupied Georgia and again Baku. But in fact they were too hard-pressed by other problems elsewhere to enforce their say, except that Baku should not remain in the hands of Turkey (her forces had succeeded in reaching as far a month before her final collapse). The reality proved to be the swaying turmoil of local combinations and local civil wars, not Allied recognition of Georgian independence and Allied endeavors to redress the wrongs of the Armenians. The deciding issue was the great Civil War in Russia proper. Whether Red or White won, Baku oil and communications by the Caspian and the Black Sea were vital to any Russia. The final defeat of Denikin's White Russian forces north of the Caucasus was followed by the Bolshevik capture of Baku (April 1920).

Turkey, likewise coping with revolution and intervention at one and the same time, turned to a policy of peace with the new anti-imperialist Soviet Russia and was ready enough to receive assistance, though not communism, from her. The treaty concluded between the two in March 1921 decided that Batum should be given up by the Turks, and that the future of all Transcaucasia, except Kars which they kept, should lie with Moscow. A month earlier Georgia had ended her brief interlude of precarious independence: she too was reattached by force to the Red phœnix of the north.

4. *The Pacific*

After Transcaucasia had been won, to the east beyond the Caspian the Revolution was also ultimately triumphant in Central Asia, where British intervention faded away, as it had in Baku, and Russian Red troops and railwaymen succeeded in breaking up the challenge of the local conservative forces under the banner of Islam; a challenge, both to the Revolution and to Russia, that was the more formidable owing to the pan-turanian ambitions of Enver Pasha, the former Turkish leader, who had fled to the Oxus (killed 1922). In the end the red flag flew throughout Central Asia wherever the imperial standard had waved.

Again to the east, far to the east, three thousand miles away on the Pacific, the red star likewise followed wherever the imperial eagle had gone. The Soviet Union became a Far Eastern and Pacific power, the heir to three centuries of Russian expansion across Asia.

There, in contrast with the relatively civilized and thickly populated Transcaucasia and Central Asia where Russian conquest was not followed by Russian colonization on the land, the expansion had been in the long run that of the Russian people across the waste immensity of northern Asia. An earlier chapter has sketched its origin and development since the days of Yermak at the end of the sixteenth century (see pp. 19-24). It was there pointed out that, though Russian outposts were maintained on the northern Pacific coasts from as early as about 1640, the Chinese Empire successfully prevented the Cossacks from establishing themselves farther south on the middle and lower Amur (see map 2). For the next two centuries, Russia, though she spread across to Kamchatka under Peter the Great and thence to Alaska, remained for the most part confined to the ice-bound fur and sealing grounds of the northernmost Pacific. Then, in the middle of the nineteenth century there began the three great changes that have transformed the Far East for our day.

From the south, the British as a result of the first Anglo-Chinese war (1839-42) compelled China to admit foreigners on special terms, besides setting a possible precedent by the acquisition of Hong Kong. A new door into China was opened for the influence of Europe and America, small at first but soon to be widened, with far-reaching consequences both for China and the world.

A dozen years later (1853-54) the United States compelled Japan to open certain ports to her. This action led immediately to contacts with other foreign states and to the great reversal of Japanese isolationism that had been the national policy since the early seventeenth century. In 1868 the policy of self-modernization on the basis of Western technique was deliberately adopted, with decisively rapid results. Within forty years the Pacific had a new great power in the modern sense.

The third great change in the Far East was the forward movement of Russia, beginning in the middle of the century, which brought her to the Amur and Vladivostok, and within forty years to Port Arthur (see map 2).

The initial impetus was due to the ambition and vision of Muravyov-Amursky (1809-81), one of the most outstanding figures in the long line of Russian pro-consuls. He foresaw Siberia as the great field for Russian colonization in the century to come: therefore "in order to preserve Siberia it is necessary now [1853] to preserve and strengthen for us Kamchatka, Sakhalin and the mouths and navigation of the Amur and to obtain solid influence over neighboring China." Otherwise, the British, always his special bugbear, would forestall Russia. As governor-general of eastern Siberia from 1847 to 1861 he overrode the obstructive caution of the foreign minister Nesselrode and others of his opponents in St. Petersburg and launched out with well-prepared energy on the consolidation and expansion of Russian power in the Far East.

Muravyov had the satisfaction of bloodily repulsing a British expedition against Kamchatka during the Crimean War, and the triumph, in company with Ignatyev, of extracting bloodlessly from China (1858, 1860) her nominally subject Amur region and the seacoast down to the Korean boundary, near which on a splendid site he founded Vladivostok, "the domination of the East" (*cf.* p. 25). There was a long dispute with Japan over the island of Sakhalin, but finally (1875) she acknowledged it as Russian.

Muravyov fully realized that there were two essentials for the new-won lands, and indeed for all Siberia—communications and colonization. The difficulties of overland communication with the Russian Pacific stations on the other side of the world had been so great that the ocean route, from the Baltic round Cape Horn, had been usual. The opening of the Amur to navigation improved matters. The opening of the Suez Canal in 1869 shortened the sea-route, now from the Black Sea instead of the Baltic; and this continued to be a very important auxiliary for Russian, and Soviet, communications with the Far East even after the building of the railway. But railways were essential, as Muravyov urged, both for strategic and for colonizing purposes. The Trans-Siberian did not come for another thirty years; until then his work bore little fruit.

When he left the Far East there was said to be a population of 630,000 (perhaps half of them Russians) east and north of Lake Baikal, and of these a mere handful of some 50,000 were in the territory he had added to the empire. Less than eighty years later instead of 50,000 there were (1939) nearly two and a half million, and instead of 630,000, four and a half million, the great mass of them Russians. This was the result of the new development policy which was begun in the eighteen-nineties with the Trans-Siberian railway (see pp. 47-48), and was transformed and greatly intensified under the Soviet régime.

The Russian achievements in this gigantic and hitherto virgin land have been grimly dramatic, especially in industrial development during the last fifteen years. Emptiness remains, however, one great characteristic, and until latterly Russian colonization was very small in the Amur region and on the Pacific compared with the growth of Siberia proper, west of Lake Baikal. South of the Amur Russian settlers did not penetrate into Manchuria. On the contrary, in the eighteen-nineties, at the very time when Russian imperialism was thrusting southwards here, Manchuria, largely a vacant land, was beginning to fill up with wave upon wave of Chinese peasants at a rate more rapid than the Russian outflow to Siberia and the Far East.

The Trans-Siberian railway was at last begun in 1891, when a much-advertised visit to Vladivostok of the heir-apparent, soon to become the emperor Nicholas II, boomed the "manifest destiny" of Russia on the Pacific. The railway was due to a combination of economic and strategic interests, both of which came increasingly to the fore in the eighties, when Great Britain and France seemed to be heading towards a virtual conquest of China. Russia must not sit idly by. The military were united in demanding the railway. The construction and heavy industries stood to gain largely by a big railway program, and various commercial and industrial interests were urging the necessity of securing in time markets in the Far East and of building up a solid base for Russian power on the Pacific. Almost all shades of vocal opinion in Russia joined in backing expansion in the Far East. After the turn of the century economic conditions and prospects changed abruptly for the worse and the government no longer had such backing; revolutionary unrest was admittedly swelling, and the Manchurian adventure which caused the war with Japan in 1904 had by then lost any real basis of popularity.

The ablest and most powerful representative of the economic interests which in the nineties were transforming Russia at home and giving a new cast to Russian imperialism abroad was Witte, who in 1892 entered upon his ten-year tenure of the ministries of communications and finance. In Witte's eyes the Trans-Siberian would open "a new route and new horizons not only for Russia but for world trade . . . resulting in fundamental alterations in the existing economic relations between states"; it also would open "the possibility of being in direct relations with the United States"; and it would immensely strengthen the position of the Russian Pacific fleet and serve as the arm for political and economic alliance with China against England or any other power.

The opportunity of attaining this last aim was taken in 1895 when Japan defeated China in a war caused by their clash of interests in Korea, a semi-independent country over which China had long claimed suzerain rights. By the treaty of Shimonoseki, Japan, in addition to other gains, acquired the peninsula on which Port Arthur stands (see map 2). Russia, in company with her ally France and Germany, intervened diplomatically and forced Japan to restore it to China. Witte immediately followed up this support of China by guaranteeing a loan to her, by founding the Russo-Chinese Bank, one of the most important first-fruits of the Franco-Russian alliance, and by concluding (1896) an alliance with China against Japan. This included the concession for a Russian broad-gauge railway straight across northern Manchuria just under a thousand miles to Vladivostok.

The new railway, called the Chinese Eastern, cut off the great loop of the Amur and thus saved about three hundred and fifty miles on the original trace of the Trans-Siberian, which was to run entirely through Russian territory to Vladivostok, across very difficult country, and which was not completed till 1917. The Chinese Eastern, on the other hand, was pushed ahead very rapidly, and a year before the outbreak of war with Japan there was through connection between Vladivostok and Russia, except for the heavily tunnelled section round Lake Baikal. Like the Russo-Chinese Bank, the Chinese Eastern was in fact a government concern, originally the preserve of Witte as finance minister. It had "the absolute and exclusive right of administration" over a large railway zone, which was substantially turned into Russian territory.

Witte had from the first intended to secure economic dominance in southern as well as northern Manchuria, and in 1898 China was compelled to grant an extension of the Chinese Eastern railway, with the same rights, due south to Port Arthur, which she had to lease to Russia at the same time. The acquisition of Port Arthur, long mooted in certain Russian circles, took place as a result of the German occupation of Kiaochow a few months before. It was immediately followed by the British acquisition of Weihaiwei, lying over against Port Arthur, while in the south France gained a similar lease of Kwangchow. The rivalries between the Western powers, particularly Russia and Great Britain, were becoming more and more openly accentuated, and what was about to prove a new power was rapidly emerging in the near-at-hand island empire of Japan.

The set-back administered by Russia in 1895 to Japanese interests and ambitions on the mainland had not been forgiven, and her activities in Korea and occupation of Port Arthur after having deprived Japan of it added injury to insult. Port Arthur was promptly turned into a powerful fortress and naval base, unlike Vladivostok, open all the year round. It was, however, a thousand miles from Vladivostok, the nearest Russian territory, and the Russian admiralty, which for this reason had always preferred an ice-free Korean port, continued to alarm the Japanese with the specter of another Russian naval station, this time in the strategic straits of Tsushima.

Russian power in Manchuria was alarmingly extended as a result of the anti-foreign "Boxer" outbreak in 1900. This led to joint armed intervention by the European powers, but

Russia as well acted on her own and occupied the whole of Manchuria with regular troops. This action, as also the acquisition of Port Arthur, had not been approved by Witte, who held to his original policy of gradual economic dominance in Manchuria, in agreement with the Chinese government, through his bank and railway, with the military kept well in the rear.

Henceforward Witte's influence was definitely on the decline, and in the summer of 1903 he was relieved of his ministries. His extremist rivals triumphed, by their capture of the tsar's private ear and privy purse. They also triumphed over the moderating influence of the foreign office and the changed views of the war minister, who by 1903 was advocating a more conciliatory policy. In that year Far Eastern affairs were taken out of the hands of the departments and concentrated in those of a new viceroy at Port Arthur and of a special committee headed by an extremist adventurer who had won the tsar's confidence. Perhaps at no time was the chronic rivalry of government departments and the lack of a concerted ministerial policy (*cf.* pp. 99-100) more fatal than in Far Eastern affairs between 1898 and 1904.

The extremist standpoint may be summed up in the words of one of its most influential exponents: "Russia has been made by bayonets not diplomacy, and we must decide the questions at issue with China and Japan by bayonets and not by diplomatic pens." What was needed was, not Witte's step-by-step schemes of economic supremacy in northern China, but "a nice little victorious war," not least in order to provide an antidote to the revolutionary movements which were by now shaking the confidence and the nerves of the government. In consequence, Russia refused to evacuate Manchuria completely, strengthened her military and naval forces on the Pacific, and initiated a new penetration of Korea, under the thin disguise of a timber company.

To the Japanese it seemed that she was determined to block them completely on the mainland of Asia. In the summer of 1903 the war party in Tokyo won the day, at the same time as the extremists in St. Petersburg. Japan was fortified by the alliance with Great Britain, concluded and published to the world in 1902, which assured her of British friendship and of armed help if another power joined Russia in war against Japan. Nevertheless, to challenge a power with such prestige and apparently superior strength was a very grave step for a country which was only in the first generation of self-modernization. Ito, one of the greatest of modern Japanese statesmen, had done his best to prevent the alliance with Great Britain and the abandonment of accommodation with Russia.

Japan struck without warning—as she did at Pearl Harbor —with a surprise night attack on the Russian fleet in Port Arthur (February 1904). Command of the sea was won at the outset, and the war resulted in a series of hard-fought successes for the Japanese in southern Manchuria, including the capture of Port Arthur. The Russian high command failed badly. The Trans-Siberian worked far better than might have been expected but could not compensate for the fact that Russia was fighting beyond the farthest outskirts of her immense empire. Above all, nothing could compensate for the fact that she was on the verge of revolution. Three weeks after the fall of Port Arthur (January 1905) "Red Sunday" occurred in St. Petersburg, which may be taken as the opening of the 1905 Revolution.

At the end of May 1905 the Russian Baltic fleet, after its voyage round the world, was annihilated in the straits of Tsushima in the most dramatically decisive of modern naval battles. It was immediately followed by a crescendo of revolutionary outbreaks and demonstrations in Russia, and by peace proposals from President Theodore Roosevelt, after approaches from Japan.

The Japanese, hard put to it financially, feared an exhausting war of attrition farther and farther from their bases and set their hopes on the revolution in Russia so developing as to make the continuance of war impossible. Their hopes were justified. Peace was signed at Portsmouth, New Hampshire, in September. Within two months the Revolution extorted from the tsar the October manifesto (see p. 60).

The defeat of the Russian colossus by an Asiatic state had profound repercussions in Asia, in Europe, and in Russia herself. At home it had similar effects, in certain respects, to defeat in the Crimean War, and it still further discredited tsarism as a system of government. By the terms of the treaty of Portsmouth Russia gave up Port Arthur, and in effect southern Manchuria, to Japan, acknowledged Japanese control in Korea (it was annexed in 1910), ceded the southern half of Sakhalin island (the oil deposits in the northern half were not known at that date), and accorded fishing rights along the Russian coast, a matter of special importance (and still so today) owing to Japanese dependence on fish supplies and the great richness of the fisheries in question.

The blow to the prestige and power of Russia was great, but she still remained in possession of the Chinese Eastern railway across northern Manchuria to Vladivostok, and the war did not create a gulf between the two governments. On the contrary, for ten years, 1907-17, they collaborated in opposing the American policy of "the open door" in China, and in creating two exclusive spheres of influence in China north of the Great Wall, a Russian comprising northern Manchuria, Outer Mongolia, and Sinkiang (see map 2), and a Japanese comprising southern Manchuria and Inner Mongolia. The Chinese revolution which began in 1911 greatly assisted them.

One of the first results of the deposition in 1912 of the Manchu dynasty in Pekin was the success of an anti-Chinese revolt which had been taking place in Outer Mongolia. This was an almost purely Mongol, nomad, and Lamaist-Buddhist country, fringing the Russian Empire, geographically almost cut off from China proper by a great desert belt, and with connections with the Buryat Mongols under Russian rule. The Russian government extorted from China the full autonomy of Outer Mongolia with freedom from Chinese colonization and the reality of predominant Russian influence, a policy which pointed the way towards the eventual Soviet transformation of Outer Mongolia, after Russia had succumbed in the First World War and the Soviet Union had emerged staggering but triumphant from the Civil War.

The First World War fully proved the value of the Pacific to Russia, when exit from the Baltic and Black Sea was closed to her. Vladivostok became a vital, though terribly distant, supply base. The Civil War proved the danger of the Pacific to the Bolsheviks. Vladivostok became the eastern port of entry for Allied and American intervention in 1918.

Undertaken as a check on separate Japanese initiative, joint intervention was originally intended to prevent a German penetration of Siberia, to safeguard the great stocks of stores, and to extricate the Czech prisoners of war, who had been formed into a separate force and were to be evacuated via Siberia to the Western front, but had become embroiled with the Bolsheviks. Soon, however, the main object of intervention came to be support of the Russian Whites in the Civil War.

Both the anti-Bolsheviks and the Allies proved too divided among themselves to prevent the general drift into local and sectional anarchy and to withstand the unflagging offensive of the new Red Army. After almost losing the middle Volga, it drove its opponents from railway center to railway center right across the Urals and Siberia to Lake Baikal. The Allies had recognized as head of the Whites throughout Russia the right-wing government in Siberia of Admiral Kolchak, a distinguished naval officer of great personal bravery but with nothing else to recommend him. Its reactionary policy alienated almost all sections of the anti-Bolsheviks and at the end of 1919 it utterly collapsed. Kolchak himself was handed over to the Bolsheviks and shot (January 1920). Siberia was theirs.

The Far Eastern region, from Lake Baikal to the Pacific, hung in doubt for another two years while different brands of Pinks, Reds, and various Cossack adventurers contended for local mastery, alternately supported and opposed by the Japanese. The American, British, and French troops, all of them very few in numbers, had been withdrawn early in 1920, but the Japanese remained in large force on the coast, suspected on all hands of aiming at the permanent exclusion of Russia from the Pacific. At length, in 1922, they did evacuate the mainland, largely owing to American pressure, leaving the field clear to the Bolsheviks.

Three years later Japan recognized the Soviet régime and evacuated the Russian half of Sakhalin (1925). In return she gained important fishing rights and oil concessions in the newly discovered Sakhalin oilfield, both of which became fertile sources of dispute in the subsequent years. Almost at the same time the Soviet government secured from the Chinese special agreements (1924) in regard to the Chinese Eastern Railway which brought it on modified terms largely under Soviet control. Everywhere the Soviet Union was back where the Russian Empire had been. Four years before, at the time of the Washington Far Eastern conference, the new Soviet state was so exhausted and disunited that she was ignored. Now she appeared as a Far Eastern power to be reckoned with.

If in one sense she was the heir of the Russian Empire, in another she was the very opposite. A wholly new feature in Far Eastern relations was introduced by the links between the Revolution of Lenin and the Revolution of Sun Yat-sen.

Lenin, one of whose main additions to the gospel of Marx was its application to Asia, had from the first hailed the Chinese Revolution of 1911 (as that of Persia and Turkey and the Indian nationalist movement) as the beginning of the upsurge of the peoples of "advanced Asia" in their unconquerable millions against "backward Europe," which did nothing but plunder China and bolster up the enemies of her freedom. The October Revolution was to be the opening of the world revolution, an anti-imperialistic revolution in which China, in common with the rest of Asia, in winning her freedom would thereby aid the Russian vanguard of the proletariat in its struggle against counter-revolution.

The Asiatic activities of the Communist International, founded by Lenin early in 1919, at once became pronounced. Red Russia appeared in the rôle of the liberator of Asia. Above all in China the Communists reaped a harvest. They appeared not as the Russian foreigner of old, but as the one ally of Chinese nationalism, ready to renounce "the unequal treaties," if not "special interests," the champions of unity and equality, of science and the welfare of the common man, summoning China "to escape the destiny prescribed for it at Versailles in order to transform it into a second Korea or a second India" by joining with "its only allies and brothers in the struggle for liberty . . . the Russian worker and peasant and the Red Army of Russia."

Sun Yat-sen (1866-1925), the semi-deified apostle of "National Revolution" and of the Kuomintang, "the People's Party," had hailed the Russian Revolution as marking the breakaway of the Slavs from the white races and had in the end looked to the land of the Soviets as the principal helpmate of China in her struggle for freedom. His famous testament and *Three Principles of Democracy*, with their blend of Lincoln and Lenin, were accepted as the gospel of Chinese nationalism, but their interpretation and application remained to be fought out in swaying conflict.

The Bolsheviks were at first far too hard-pressed at home to be able to influence China on any considerable scale. By 1923 they were strong enough to extend their activities in support of the Kuomintang, which since 1917 had repudiated the central government in Peking and had set up its national republic under Sun Yat-sen based on the great southern port of Canton. Soviet military instructors, experts in mass propaganda, and money were accepted, while the Kuomintang organization was recast in close imitation of Russian experience and young Chinese were sent to Russia for training. At the same time a Chinese Communist party was formed, which for some time permeated the Kuomintang with its adherents and sympathizers. An uneasy alliance was, with much difficulty, maintained between the left (Soviet influenced) and the right elements in the very heterogeneous nationalist movement.

The crisis came when in 1926 the Kuomintang forces marched northwards against the quasi-independent provincial military governors and the more and more nominal Peking government, and against the foreigners, particularly the British, in the Yangtse treaty ports. The sweeping success of the northward advance brought to a head the divisions among the revolutionary left and the moderates and conservatives.

The period of communist collaboration in the "bourgeois-democratic revolution . . . directed entirely against the imperialistic yoke" had ceased; the time had come "to promote the agrarian revolution, arm the workers and the poorer among the farmers, prepare the way for the hegemony of the proletariat in the Revolution and look for a decisive trend towards democratization of the Kuomintang." Within a month of this resolution of the Executive Committee of the Communist International (July 1927) the principal Soviet advisers with the Kuomintang on the Yangtse were on their way home, and there had previously taken place a complete rupture with the Soviet embassy in Peking.

Throughout the first six months of 1927 the situation had been growing more and more out of hand. The Chinese Communists were heading for out-and-out social revolution. The left-wing Kuomintang was vacillating. The right could at least combine to crush the left. Chiang Kai-shek and other generals and the leaders of the right had reluctantly used Communist help only up to a point: they were not prepared, if they could help it, to tolerate the incitement of class-war and "red spears" among the peasantry or of such extreme violence against the foreigners as would cut their own purse-strings and endanger the attainment of Chinese unity.

Ferocious reprisals were launched against everything that could be branded with the name of Communism or Soviet influence. By the beginning of 1928 the rout of the Left was complete, except among the peasantry in certain regions. In Manchuria, where Russian White *émigrés* added to the complexity of local politics, the anti-Communist drive threatened the Soviet position on the Chinese Eastern railway and resulted in an armed clash (1929) when a Chinese attempt to oust the Russians was rebuffed by force.

Whether the *débâcle* of the Communist International in 1927 in China was primarily due to Chinese Communists themselves or to the policy of Stalin or to that of Trotsky and other exponents in Moscow of extreme tactics, it was the most severe blow that it suffered in any country, with the possible exception of Germany. The tactics to be pursued in the Chinese Revolution had caused much dispute in Moscow, and the events of 1927 in China added to the bitterness of the struggle which was being waged at this time on other vital issues between Stalin, Trotsky, and various groups.

Notwithstanding the rout of 1927, Communism of an indigenous, agrarian brand was a power in certain of the south-central provinces where peasant soviets established control and maintained a long guerrilla war against Chiang Kai-shek. Even when finally defeated there (1934-35), this "Chinese Soviet Republic" was transported by the now famous "long march" of its Red army towards the northwestern region, far nearer to Soviet territory, and Soviet influence began to revive. However different Russian and Chinese Communism may be, it remains significant that China is the only country in the world, apart from the Union, where a large and influential Communist party continues in being.

The repercussions of the Japanese occupation of Manchuria (1931-32) started a realignment of forces, and the Japanese invasion of China within the Great Wall in 1937 resulted in the U.S.S.R. supporting Chiang Kai-shek and his Kuomintang government by an alliance. The Chinese Communists had been leading the way in all-out resistance to the invader and combined, despite frequent rifts and jockeyings, with Chiang Kai-shek in the present (1943) "national united front." In effecting this rapprochement Soviet influence was instrumental, and the Soviet material and moral aid provided to Chiang Kai-shek refashioned in new form the links between the two countries.

As has just been seen, the complete change between the Soviet-Chinese rupture of 1927 and the Soviet-Chinese alliance of 1937 was due to the unleashing of Japanese continental imperialism.

In 1931-32 Japan overran the whole of Manchuria, which she erected as the nominally independent state of Manchukuo, and in effect deprived the Soviet Union of the Chinese Eastern Railway. Instead of a few miles along the Korean boundary, Japan now faced the Union along 1500 miles of frontier. Soviet strength was greatly impaired by the crisis of collectivization and the first five year plan, and Japan seemed about to seize what she had relinquished in 1922, the Soviet Maritime Province with Vladivostok, and thus to remove the threat from Soviet air bases. No such attempt was made, if only because she was deflected by an explosion in Shanghai of anti-Japanese feeling over the rape of Manchuria.

The Soviet government remained on the defensive and cut its losses in 1935 by selling its rights in the Chinese Eastern Railway to Manchukuo-Japan. This was a notable withdrawal but the government was pressing forward with renewed energy in its policy of all-round strengthening of the military, naval, and economic defenses of the Far Eastern region. A frontier dispute that led to a pitched battle in 1938 showed that Moscow did not intend to retreat farther. The doubling of the Trans-Siberian, the start on the construction of a second rail connection with the West running far in the rear of the Amur frontier, intensive colonization and industrial and mining development—these and other measures have gone far towards solidifying the Pacific base of the U.S.S.R.

At the same time, on the western side of Manchuria, Soviet policy towards Outer Mongolia was firm and decided. The Anti-Comintern pact between Japan and Germany, signed in 1936, seemed to be directed towards an encirclement of the Union, and the opening of the full-scale Japanese invasion of China within the Great Wall in 1937 led to an increased Japanese hold on Inner Mongolia. Japan must not be allowed to extend her power to Outer Mongolia and be in a position to threaten the whole of the Soviet Far East by cutting its neck along the Trans-Siberian somewhat east of Lake Baikal (see map 2).

Outer Mongolia, after three years of blood-curdling phantasmagoria, had developed after 1921, as before the war, within the Russian not the Chinese orbit, even though the formula of Chinese sovereignty over it "as an integral part of the Republic of China" was acknowledged by Moscow. In fact, a Mongolian People's Republic was set up (1924) under

Soviet control. The Soviet determination not to let slip this strategic key was publicly shown in 1936 by the announcement of a close guarantee alliance. The guarantee was effective. In the summer of 1939 the disputed frontier between Outer Mongolia and Manchuria caused several months' large-scale operations between the Red Army and the Japanese which ended in the discomfiture of the latter with admittedly heavy losses (and with the discovery of the present Marshal Zhukov as a first-class tank general). Hostilities, however, remained localized, and the Soviet-German agreement and the outbreak of the war in Europe brought about an immediate armistice.

Two years of uneasy watchful waiting followed: the Japanese continued "bogged" in China, who was assisted by Soviet war material; then after the collapse of France they turned south to Indonesia; while the Red Army fortified itself on the Pacific, and on the Baltic against Germany, who was assisted by supplies sent by her ally Japan across the continent by the Trans-Siberian. In April 1941 Japan, in preparation (it seems) for total war in the South Seas, covered her rear by a neutrality pact with the U.S.S.R., in which the latter recognized the Japanese position in Manchukuo and the former the Soviet position in Outer Mongolia but did not obtain the promise of cessation of aid to China.

Two months later Hitler launched his armies eastwards. In October 1941, when the fate of Moscow was in the balance, it appeared possible that his Far Eastern ally soon might stab his adversary in the back. Two months later the Japanese air fleet rained down upon Pearl Harbor, not Vladivostok.

CHAPTER VII
THE WEST

1. *Russia and Europe*

UNTIL THE LAST hundred years Russia has been broadly speaking a recipient; first, mainly from Byzantium and the steppe peoples; then from the West, on a very small scale since the late fifteenth century, on a large scale since Peter the Great. During the last hundred years Russia has continued to be a great recipient, but at the same time she has been a mighty giver. She has given one of the world's great literatures, and much in music and the art of the theater; she has shared conspicuously in the creative achievements of the sciences; and, for good or ill, she has given the successor to the French Revolution, the Soviet Revolution with its new trinity of communism, the one-party state, and economic planning.

Communism was born out of the West, out of Marx and Engels, and the October Revolution was international in its philosophy and appeal. But what has triumphed has been the Revolution in Russia and Russian Communism. Thus the international influence of Communism has been twofold. On the one hand it is the re-export to Europe, and the world, of Marxism as formulated by Lenin and propagated through the Communist International, which he founded early in 1919; on the other hand it has become the export of a specifically Russian achievement.

The elements of moral and apocalyptic appeal to social justice and to a new man refashioned in a new world, which were implicit in Marxist Communism, became fused in Russia with something that was perhaps akin to the messianic, œcumenical trends of thought and feeling that have been so conspicuous in past Russian social and religious thought. Various writers have found in the Russian Communist party with its absorption of the individual in the whole, its ascetic discipline, and its attitude to dogma, parallels with the Orthodox church, which molded so much of Russian life throughout the centuries. At any rate, the new revolutionary Russia was to cleanse the world, remake it, purge it of the suffering of the past.

> "Beat on the street the march of rebellion,
> Sweeping over the heads of the proud,
> We, the flood of a second deluge,
> Shall wash the world like a bursting cloud." [1]

In the ten years following 1918 the Marxist gospel of world revolution was a major problem in most parts of the world, and the Communist International a major factor in Soviet foreign relations. Both have everywhere engendered fierce and continuous controversy. "The Bolshevik peril" has been used in the most various quarters, pre-eminently by the Nazis, not only now in 1943. They and others have linked to it virulent anti-Semitism, on the ground that the Bolshevik Revolution and all that has come out of it was the handiwork of a gang of international Jews. It is in fact true that Russian Jews played a large part in Russian revolutionary movements before 1917 and that a number of the most important Bolshevik leaders in the early days of the Revolution were Jews. It is equally true that during the last fifteen years Jews have occupied very few of the chief positions in the Soviet hierarchy, and there can be no doubt that revolution in Russia was not "made" by the tiny minority of Jewish socialists of various brands.

On the other flank, the hostility between Labor and Socialist bodies and Communists has been constant. It was mitigated after 1935, when the Communist International was preaching "the united front" and favoring national defense. But the change of policy in September 1939 and the sabotage tactics of the Communist parties in Allied or friendly countries down to June 1941 inevitably re-aroused the bitterest feelings. Now (May 1943) the Communist International has

[1] Mayakovsky (1893-1930), *Our March* (1917). I have quoted the translation in *Mayakovsky and His Poetry,* compiled by Herbert Marshall (London, 1942).

been disbanded. Whatever may be the immediate or far-reaching significance of this important step, it is likely that Marxist Communism as an article of re-export to other countries has been less influential than the example of "socialism in one country," the specifically Russian achievement of the Soviet Union.

The victory of the October Revolution had been regarded by millions throughout the world as the victory of the underdog, the hewers of wood and drawers of water. They had known how to cast down the mighty from their seats and to fight and win in the face of heavy odds, against the privileged and the entrenched. Whatever might be the truth about the terror, the Cheka, the concentration camps, the persecution of religion; however dubious or repellent might be the forms of government and conduct in the land of the dictatorship of the proletariat, it was now their land, the land of the outcast millions. Let them at least be left to themselves to make or mar it. To these general feelings of unanalyzed sympathy towards the republic of workers and peasants there has been added in the last dozen years the growing realization that a new society and state has taken shape, however brutal the methods or fearful the cost; that collectivization of agriculture, however violently imposed, has constituted another revolution only second in importance to that of October; that the five-year plans, whatever their shortcomings, have radically transformed the productive power of Russia; and finally, in the last two years, that the new Soviet Russian state has succeeded in organizing an army on the vast, all-round modern scale, imbued with the new Soviet patriotism, an army which unlike that of any European country has shown itself capable of withstanding the heaviest blows of the major military power in the world.

The two main characteristics of the Soviet state which have already in diverse forms influenced Europe and the world are the rôle of party and total planning. An attempt has been made earlier to sketch some salient features of the Communist party in Russia (pp. 48 ff.). Here it is not necessary to do more than emphasize again that party itself is in a sense a misnomer; that it is rather, as Lenin planned it, a rigorously disciplined *élite* corps of men and women inspired by and trained to the vocation of governing, administering, and in the broadest sense educating others towards socialism and ultimately communism. As an English observer has written, the party is the "Priesthood of a Religion which is of this world, not of the next."

The Soviet single-party state is totalitarian. Education, propaganda (and hence the arts), press and wireless, health and science, must be planned and strictly controlled. Youth must be molded, shaped, and given the utmost incentive and opportunity. Even before November 1917 the Bolsheviks had their eyes on the new generations, and within a year of their overthrow of the Provisional Government they had begun the foundation on a national scale of the Communist League of Youth; a body that proved, until its reorganization in 1936, by no means always readily subservient to the central organs of the Communist party.

Finally, the single-party state must plan, organize, and "run" its economic life. Probably in no other field have the practical results, if not the theory, of the Soviet Revolution had a more world-wide, percolating influence than that of economic planning, even though it was practiced by most of the belligerents in the First World War and was to the fore in the Germany of the Weimar Republic. Its history and main essentials in the Soviet Union will be outlined later (pp. 361-379) as part of the Soviet revolution in industry.

In the hundred years prior to the Revolution, as has been stated at the beginning of this chapter, Russia, while continuing to draw more and more from Europe, became for the first time a giver. She gave one of the world's great literatures, and much in music and the art of the theater, and she shared conspicuously in the creative achievements of science. All the world has at least heard of Mendeleyev (1834-1907), the great chemist, and Pavlov (1849-1936), the great physiologist and pathologist. All the world of science knows of Lobachevsky (1793-1865), the pioneer of non-Euclidian geometry, Timiryazev (1843-1920), the plant biologist, and

Joffe (b. 1880), the physicist; to name only three outstanding representatives. Soviet Russia inherited from the old Russia a great tradition in scientific research and, in the best centers, standards in learning and training fully equal to those of the West. Such centers were, however, far too few, and neither science nor other branches of learning were endowed on a scale that could meet the needs of more than a very small minority. In striking contrast, the Soviet Revolution has concentrated on an immense extension of scientific research and the widest diffusion of scientific knowledge and training.

In the arts, Russia in the last fifty years has transformed the art of the theater and the ballet, and the Soviet cinema has won similar renown. In music, Russia has given Tchaikovsky (1840-93), the most Italianate and the most elusive figure among Russian composers, one of the three or four most widely popular composers in the English-speaking world; even though his greatest gift, that of lyrical and elegiac song, is almost unrecognized outside Russia, where *Eugene Onegin* still retains its pride of place among operas. A very different appeal has come from Russian folk-music as transmuted, together with quite other musical elements, in Rimsky-Korsakov (1844-1908) and Borodin (1834-87), or in the profoundly original—and incurably erratic—realistic genius of Musorgsky (1839-81). If one of the marks of vitality of music in a country be the number of her composers who, without being accorded the highest rank, yet stand high, Russia has done well even within the first century of her musical creativeness.[1]

Russian nineteenth-century music has often been divided into two schools, "the cosmopolitan" and "the national." The latter also is European music; it could not have been written without the West. Yet there is much in it that is not-Europe. The same deep, in part hidden, conflict or admixture that runs throughout Russian culture for the last two hundred and fifty years appears in Russian literature from Pushkin (1799-1837) to Gorky (1869-1936); the incomparable century

[1] For instance: Glinka (1804-57), Balakirev (1837-1910), Glazunov (1865-1926), Rachmaninov (1873-1943), Scriabin (1871-1915), Stravinsky (b. 1882), Prokofiev (b. 1891), Khachaturian (b. 1904), and Shostakovich (b. 1906).

in which Russian literature has rivaled (all would admit), has outshone (many would hold) that of any other country in the world during the same period; the century of Pushkin and Lermontov, Gogol, Turgenev, Dostoevsky, Tolstoy, and Chekhov, and of clusters of stars some only a little less brilliant than these great planets.

It is not possible in this brief introduction to Russian history to give even a bare summary of the development or the main characteristics of Russian literature.[1] All that can be attempted is to indicate some aspects of its relations to the West in connection with one of the central problems of modern Russian history, the rôle of European civilization in Russia and the internal cleavages which caused the revolutionary movements of the past hundred years.

Russian nineteenth-century literature is Russian through and through, but it is also European. Nearly all Russian writers were deeply versed in French, German, and English literature; mostly in the originals, partly in translations; and probably in no country was the range or quality of translations wider or higher. Greek and Latin were a mainstay of the upper-class schools of the first forty years of the century, and again of its last quarter. Similarly, Russian social thought and philosophy developed from European thinkers and were subject to the influence of the same trends as were dominant in the West. The one great exception was the counter-influence of Orthodoxy and the Greek fathers.

On the other hand, despite the fact that Russian literature was part and parcel of the great European heritage, there was in it, and still more in Russian social and religious thought, a persistent and often violent insistence that Russia was not and would not be Europe. Was not Peter the Great himself reputed to have said: "Europe is necessary to us for a few decades, and then we can turn our backs on her"? Russian civilization was regarded by many as a separate civilization, with its own basic foundations either in Orthodoxy or in the unique spirit of her people or in both combined, and with a

---

[1] See appendix, Note on Books, pp. 449-450, for some suggestions for introductory reading on the history of Russian literature.

glorious future before it. The Western conceptions of individualism and private property, the primacy of rationalist and scientific thought, the democratic and atomic ideas of government and society popularized by the American and French revolutions, the ideas and results of the industrial revolution, capitalism, and *laissez faire,* with their unbridled competition and class conflicts—all these forces at one and the same time were becoming more and more influential in Russia through the rapidly increasing economic and intellectual impact of Europe, and on the other hand were being criticized, attacked, or repudiated in protest against the assumption that Europe was "the *sine qua non* of historical progress in the future." The protest was made, in varying degrees, by a very wide range of Russian writers and thinkers. It was not a peculiarity merely of the slavophils, whose outlook was in general based on an antithesis between East and West, the Greco-Slavonic and the Romano-German worlds, an antithesis grounded in the nature of Orthodoxy and hostility to Catholicism (*cf.* p. 230).

It is true that the radical "westernizers" of the thirties, forties, and fifties looked to the West as in many ways the exemplar of Russia; but it is significant that Herzen (b. 1812, refugee from 1847, d. 1870), the greatest and most influential of the "westernizers," became bitterly disillusioned after the 1848 revolutions and inveighed against the half-measures of parliamentarism, the smug complacency and bourgeois decorum of Western life. In the end he turned away from the West, where he spent his later life, and looked "with faith and hope to our native East, inwardly rejoicing that I am Russian," to the Russian peasant masses in their communes and *artels.*[1]

The later generations of the populists and social-revolutionaries denied the necessity of Russia following the path of Europe. Many of them opposed industrial development of the Western type; all of them believed in the peasantry as

[1] Herzen's views are well illustrated in "Ends and Beginnings" and "The Russian People and Socialism," in vol. 6 of the English translation of his *Memoirs.* He is a master of Russian Prose.

the talisman of Russia which alone could remake her on a model new to the world. They were haunted, as all the intelligentsia during the second half of the nineteenth century, by the problem as to whether Russia could escape capitalist development along European lines. Only the social-democrats, who were growing from the eighties onwards, unreservedly welcomed this development in accordance with Marxist analysis and believed in an identity of interest between revolutionary Russia and revolutionary Europe; but even in their ranks there was recognition that Russia, with her illiterate peasant millions, was *sui generis,* and none were louder in their denunciation of the bourgeois culture of the West.

The very conception of culture (except in so far as it was limited to science working for the needs of humanity) was widely questioned and by some repudiated. The "nihilists" of the sixties and seventies,[1] who were politically radical or socialist revolutionaries, in their materialism and worship of natural science were not libertine skeptics, but on the contrary ascetics of dogmatic faith, however much they agreed with Bakunin's denunciation of the church as "a heavenly dram shop." The two most influential "nihilists" were sons of priests and had been brought up in religion and Orthdox seminaries. A third began as a believing Catholic and had been trained for the priesthood. Just as ascetic Orthodoxy was always doubtful as to the justification of culture and art, so were nihilism and indeed most strands of Russian radical or revolutionary thought.

Byelinsky (1811-48, the great critic and "westernizer," went to the heart of what was so gnawing a problem for so many Russian intellectuals, when he exclaimed: "I do not want happiness even as a gift, if I do not have peace of mind about each of my blood brothers, bone of my bone and flesh of my flesh. They say that disharmony is a condition of harmony;

[1] The word "nihilist" was first coined by Turgenev (1818-83) in *Fathers and Sons* (1862; translated by Constance Garnett), one of the best, and in Russia most controversial, of his novels, delineating the cleavage between the new free-thinking revolutionary youth and the older generation.

it may be so, and that is very advantageous and delightful for devotees of music, but it is naturally not so for those who are fated to express the idea of disharmony as their share of life." "What right had I," cries Kropotkin in his *Memoirs*,[1] "to these higher joys [his research work on the southern limits of the ice age] when all round me was nothing but misery and struggle for a moldy bit of bread." In the same vein the outburst of Verkhovensky in Dostoevsky's *The Possessed*[2] is typical: "Down with culture.... The thirst for culture is an aristocratic thirst." So too, it seemed to Tolstoy (1828-1910) that "a pair of boots is more important than all your Madonnas and all your refined talk about Shakespeare." So, in the second half of his life, he repudiated the greater part of European civilization, preached that "religious perception" and "the union of mankind" were the sole purpose of art, and strove to find in service of the Russian peasant the one justification for his inexhaustible creative gifts.

The most fundamental reason for this tendency towards repudiation or questioning of Europe and her civilization was the Russian thirst for social justice, stimulated by the consciousness of the abyss between the so-called civilized and the so-called uncivilized, the tiny educated minority and the vast uneducated mass. One Russian nationalist summed up in extreme form thus (1874): "There are two layers of Russian people distinguished from each other not so much by privileges as by the fundamental difference that each represents a different epoch of history—the upper the nineteenth century, the lower the ninth." A hostile French critic, with similar exaggeration, expressed the same contrast (1839): "Le

---

[1] *Memoirs of a Revolutionist* (1899; written in English). Prince Kropotkin (1842-1921), born and brought up in the old, aristocratic quarter of Moscow, joined the revolutionary youth, was arrested in 1874, but escaped two years later, and spent the remainder of his life abroad, largely in England, as the apostle of his own version of anarchism, until 1917 when he returned to Russia.

[2] First published in 1871 (translated by Constance Garnett); one of the profoundest studies of revolutionary ideas and mentality. As in all the novels of Dostoevsky (1821-81) the foreigner must beware of looking upon them as giving a typical picture of Russia and must allow for a large element of psychological autobiography.

Kamchatka et Versailles à trois heures de distance, voilà la Russie."

The magnitude of the problem and political conditions in Russia bred among many despair of gradually bridging this abyss through the extension of education and progressive reforms on the model of western Europe, such as those introduced under Alexander II during the sixties. To many of the intelligentsia revolution of some kind seemed the only way out. Others, acutely aware of their helplessness, lack of scope, or social displacement, drifted irresolutely, feeling themselves "superfluous men"; a type that has figured again and again in Russian literature; epitomized, from different angles, most lastingly in Oblomov [1] in his eternal dressing-gown and in the plays and short stories of Chekhov (1860-1904), himself conscious already before he was thirty of "a sort of stagnation in my soul . . . the stagnation in my own personal life."

Such passivity or pessimism was but one form of reaction to the governmental régime and economic and social change. The intelligentsia, whether "conscience-stricken" gentry or "men of the mixed class," were also capable not only of terrorist conspiracy, but of attempting to bridge the gulf between themselves and the majority of their fellow-countrymen by such a stirring example of inchoate, revolutionary enthusiasm as "the going to the people" (1873-75); when the revolutionary youth sallied forth to the villages to merge themselves in their masters and enlighten them as to their true, revolutionary and socialistic interests.[2] The movement was almost entirely lacking in cohesion and the program preached was vague and varying. The usual essentials were that the land was to belong to those who worked it, the land-

---

[1] *Oblomov* (1858; translated in the Everyman edition) is the best-known novel of Goncharov (1812-91). Oblomov has passed into the Russian language in a form meaning "the imperfective state incarnate," very properly a term of obloquy both in pre-Revolution and particularly Soviet Russia.

[2] It is the subject of Turgenev's last novel, *Virgin Soil* (1877; translated by Constance Garnett), written abroad and in opposition to the movement, but not to be dismissed as an out-of-touch criticism, and containing some excellent characters and scenes.

owner to be expropriated, and the commune to be the basis of a socialist utopia, in which the dissonances between the West and Russia would somehow disappear.

Those who thus "went to the people" themselves confessed that they were met with bewilderment, hostility, or apathy by the peasants, and the movement failed almost completely among them. But it made a deep impression on all thinking Russia, not least on the government, which was frightened into mass arrests and mass trials. These yet further stirred opinion and accentuated the divorce between the bureacracy and the bulk of educated opinion, not then itself revolutionary but dangerously infected with indifferentism towards the government and sympathy towards its opponents.

The failure of "the going to the people" caused a split in the ranks of the populists (*narodniki*). One small section formed a conspiratorial organization, "The People's Will," which conducted a terrorist campaign against the government ending in the assassination of Alexander II in 1881. The rest of the *narodniki* sought to construct revised versions of their agrarian socialism, which eventually (1901) took a more or less organized form in the Social-Revolutionary party. This was both in 1905 and 1917 in closer touch with the peasantry than any other party and was consequently the most dangerous rival of the Bolsheviks.

All parties, all groups of opinion in Russia felt that, at least ultimately, the deciding factor in revolution, reform, or the maintenance of autocracy was the hundred-million-headed peasantry, still even by 1917 in the main illiterate. One of the deepest students of Russia has written of "the inevitable spell exercised by the immensity of Russia's peasant population with characteristics as definite as those of the ocean. It is almost impossible not to connect a specific meaning with a phenomenon so great and unique." The contrasts between "the dark people" and the few for whom European culture was available remained glaring. Even though in the course of the century between 1815 and 1917 the few had ceased to be drawn almost entirely from the landed gentry and had multiplied many times over, the recurrent notes persisted of divorce between two worlds, divorce also within the educated minority, and of impending revolution. The scale of Russia and the feeling of the abyss help to explain both the maximalism and the catastrophic and apocalyptic strains that are so prominent in Russian thought.

This contrast between Russia as part of Europe and Russia as a world to herself, with different values and different roots, became all the more acute by the end of the nineteenth century, when the educated minority was deeply divided within itself and the basis of civilized rule as earlier understood, *i.e.* European absolutism, was being more and more heavily attacked. Tsarism, as a system of bureaucratic absolutist rule, with all its dark evils represented none the less Europe; for its enemies the Europe of reaction or a Europe alien to the best past and the true genius of the Russian people.

In the eighteenth century the situation had been completely different. Then tsarism and European civilization on the whole went hand in hand with the privileged upper class. Despite the opposition to Peter the Great and continued xenophobia, the eighteenth century, viewed in the large, meant the europeanizing of the bulk of the upper class. Since the culture of "the age of enlightenment" was in the main based on privilege and absolutism, or at least aristocracy, Europe in this respect did not bring Russia much that need fundamentally divide the educated minority. "Enlightened despotism" after a time found a ready soil in Russia because there were no radically divergent views as to what constituted European civilization.

The effects of the French Revolution and the Industrial Revolution altered the balance. New European values and ideals appealed to some sections of the educated minority in Russia; but one section of it, the government and bureaucracy, for the most part clung to the old Europe, and became more and more divided from the rest of educated opinion, by whom it was regarded as "official Russia, the parade-Tsardom, the Byzantine-German government." Thus, educated opinion in the half-century following 1860 became divided, broadly speaking, between supporters of the government, moderate progressives or liberals (the left wing of the *zemstva*, the left-center of the Duma, the men of the Provisional Government of 1917), and, thirdly, the socialists and revolutionaries of various schools (*cf.* pp. 62 ff.).

In the sixteenth and seventeenth centuries the situation had been different again. There had been in Muscovy a great gulf between rulers and ruled, but the gulf was economic and social rather than cultural. Europe, in almost all ways, was equally alien to both rulers and ruled. Muscovite civilization, until the Schism in the later seventeenth century (see pp. 180 ff.), had a certain unity of its own. Subsequently, Russians have advanced sharply opposed views as to the character and value of Muscovite civilization, but they have almost all agreed that it had homogeneity and that then with Peter the Great something happened (whether catastrophically from a clear sky, or, the truer view, at a violent pace in continuation of a process already set in motion), which eventually split Russia into two worlds. In this divorce many have seen the fundamental cause of the ills of Russia since Peter's day and of the Revolution in this century. This is the reason why Peter the Great is the most debated of Russian sovereigns, not excluding Ivan the Terrible.

2. *Europe and Russia*

What did Peter do which cleft the soul of Muscovy? He opened wider with sledge-hammer blows fissures which had already been spreading in the half-century before 1700. Ever since the late fifteenth century intercourse between Muscovy and the West had been increasing; between 1650 and 1700 intercourse began to grow into influence; after 1700 influence became imitation; after 1800 came absorption.

Muscovite civilization of the sixteenth and seventeenth centuries was, in the main, unlettered; it was devoid of science, sorely lacking in intellectual accomplishments, but much more productive, though within a limited range, in the realm of art. It was unlettered in the sense that literacy was regarded as a specialized, professional requirement, necessary up to a point only for the clergy (though by no means all of them were literate) and for administrative purposes. Schooling, where there was any at all, was a family or monastic affair. The hand of God was everywhere, and religion, nationalized in the Orthodox church, powerfully shaped and colored men's outlook and actions. Despite the social disparities and the effect of the frontier, the Muscovite way of life had a certain unity, in so far as it was based on a common attitude to life and Orthodoxy, a common ethical code, a common acceptance of the place and meaning of rite, ceremonial, and tradition, and a common patriotic pride.

This Muscovite way of life, that grew out of Byzantine and steppe grafts on Slav institutions and lore, was until the later seventeenth century very little affected by Western culture (except in architecture), but it was exposed very much earlier to Western technical and economic influences.

Ivan the Great (grand-prince 1462-1505) had inaugurated a new period in the history of Russian relations with the West by his multiplication of contacts with it, notably as a result of his second marriage, to Zoe Palæologus (1472; *cf.* p. 79). Henceforward the borrowing of Western technical and material knowledge became a regular policy, while Muscovy became known to the West thanks to a long series of envoys and adventurers.

The borrowing was for long on a small scale and almost entirely for the military needs of the state or the requirements of the court. Ivan the Great called in a handful of Italian architects and engineers, led by Aristotele da Fioraventi from Bologna, to refortify and embellish Moscow. Their work had much influence on building in Muscovy, and produced the unique architectural blend of the Kremlin, part fortress, part shrine of churches, part cluster of palaces. The need for artificers, gunfounders, engineers, and specialists of various kinds became more and more felt. It was met by importation, by hook or by crook, of all sorts and conditions of foreigners, not by any methodically organized training of Russians at home, still less abroad.

Ivan the Terrible (reigned 1533-84) greatly increased the

use of firearms, mercenaries, and foreign technicians. Thus, for instance, his capture of Kazan (1552) was largely due to a Danish engineer in his service, "a messenger sent on a sudden by God to the Tsar Autocrat like as He sent His angel to Joshua, the son of Nun, to destroy the walls of Jericho." Direct intercourse with western Europe became a major issue for Ivan and one of the main objects of his Livonian War (1558-83; *cf.* p. 250). His defeat did but increase the need for European techniques, and Boris Godunov (regent from 1587, tsar 1598-1605), by temperament and interests a westernizer, did his utmost to encourage foreign influences. He planned a university and accomplished the novelty of sending a dozen or so young Russians of high birth to study in the West. Unlike Peter a century later he did not himself go abroad, and his experiment was a complete failure; not one returned.

The Time of Troubles, when Muscovy was rent by civil wars and overrun by Poles and Swedes (1604-18), had a double effect. On the one hand, it put a premium on reorganization and re-equipment of the army, if Muscovy's Western neighbors were ever to be made to disgorge their gains. On the other hand, it gave rise to feelings of nationalism and xenophobia, both against the foreigners who flooded the land and against those Russians who "kept not fasts nor Christian rites" and went a-whoring after Polish fleshpots.

For the next fifty years the remodeling and training of the army on Western lines were among the main tasks of the government. Regiments began to be enrolled on a permanent basis, especially those trained entirely with firearms. The artillery, taken in hand by a Dutchman, was greatly extended and the state arsenal of Tula was founded (1632). Mercenaries, for whom the Thirty Years' War provided an admirable recruiting ground, were employed in larger numbers, but after humiliating experience in the Polish war of 1632-34 chiefly as officers and experts, not in compact units.

At their head appeared the Scots soldier of fortune, Alexander Leslie, the first prominent representative of the long line of Scots soldiers, sailors, doctors, and others who did so much for Russia; witness the names, for instance, of Menzies, the Gordons, Bruces and Keiths, Ogilvie, Grieg, Elphinstone, Cameron (Catherine the Great's architect), or the doctors Erskine, Rogerson, and Wylie.[1]

The military made up the largest category of foreigners in seventeenth-century Muscovy. The foreign merchants, mostly British and Dutch, introduced a taste for English cloth and various Western goods, but perhaps their main effect was to arouse in the small Russian merchant class a nationalist conservatism in defense of its own interests and customs. This won the day in the new trade regulations of 1667 and persisted, partly owing to the effects of the Schism, right down to the late nineteenth century. There were, however, other foreigners who played an important part in Russian economic development, notably the Hamburg family of Marselis and the Dutch family of Vinnius, who became virtually Russians and exercised great influence in governmental circles, partly as diplomatic agents in Denmark and elsewhere, and especially *e.g.* in the development of the iron industry on a larger scale and with better technique in the Tula and Onega districts. The activities of these entrepreneurs and of certain other foreign specialists led to a better utilization of the natural resources of Muscovy and paved the way for the hectic economic expansion under Peter.

Moscow was naturally the main center of the foreigners, who were concentrated, after 1652, in "the German colony" just outside it, to the number of at least 1500. There had been three earlier "German colonies" (German was used to describe any westerner) since the early sixteenth century, but they had at various times been sacked. Lutherans and Calvinists, being heretics but not schismatics, had been allowed to have their own churches and schools, but Catholics

[1] Many of the Scots, as also of the other foreigners, served in Russia only for a short time, but many also settled for good and became russified; for instance, besides some of those mentioned above, a certain Learmonth who came over into Muscovy from Poland in the seventeenth century and from whom the great poet Lermontov claimed descent; or Barclay of Towy, in Aberdeenshire, whose family settled in Riga, later became ennobled in Russian service, and produced Barclay de Tolly, one of Alexander I's best-known generals.

(save for a few Scots) were until late in the century as far as possible excluded, mainly because Catholics were synonymous with Poles. This boorish, hard-drinking "German colony" was, despite its rapscallions, in a way a little fragment of industrious, ingenious, Protestant Europe. Here Peter the Great from an early age disported himself, intellectually and physically, poles removed from the forbidding associations of the Kremlin or the congested, tumultuous *Streltsy* quarter of Moscow. Here in the "German colony" he thoroughly imbibed Europe several years before he actually visited the West (1697).[1]

Tolerance of foreigners came from the top, from the court and a few favored personages. The mass of the clergy and the populace at best looked askance at them, at worst raged against them, swallowing with superstitious credulity any tale bruited abroad in their disfavor or that of Russians who associated with them. When the Moscow mob was out, it was dangerous to be a foreign doctor, fatal to keep a cuttlefish in your house.

Nevertheless, together with the technical, economic, and military innovations introduced by foreigners, western manners and customs began to filter into the court and the houses of a few of the upper class, followed by the deeper cultural effect of western ideas. Here the two main influences, from about 1650 onwards, came through Poland and the Ukraine.

Despite the heritage of conflict, Poland in the second half of the seventeenth century came to be regarded in a rather different light at least in some of the leading circles in Moscow. Tsar Alexis (b. 1629, reigned 1645-76), impulsive mixer of the old Orthodox way of life and western innovations, had three of his children taught Polish and Latin (his son Peter's children seventy years later will be learning French), and the fact is typical of the little groups of outward-looking men in Muscovy of that generation. Po-

---

[1] There are vivid scenes depicting Peter's early contacts with "the German colony" in Alexis Tolstoy's novel *Peter the Great* (1930-34; English translation, New York, 1932). Alexis Nikolaievich Tolstoy (1882-1945), one of the foremost Soviet writers, and Alexis Konstantinovich Tolstoy (1817-75), the dramatist and poet, were only distantly related to the great Tolstoy.

lish dress and furniture began to appear. The influence of Polish verse and chronicle writing made itself felt. Through Poland there now flowed a rivulet of secular western literature, largely antiquated, but also including geographical and other utilitarian works, such as Mercator.

Polish cultural influences were also operative indirectly through the close relations established between Moscow and Kiev as a result of the political and social struggles of the Ukraine against Poland, which culminated in the cession of Kiev and Little Russia by Poland to Muscovy in 1667 (see pp. 214-216). Many of the Ukrainians, both ecclesiastics and laymen, were well acquainted with Jesuit education and the culture of the Polish gentry; for them the defense of Orthodoxy against Catholicism and the Uniat church required the use of their enemy's armory.

Thus, the ambitious, western-educated metropolitan of Kiev, Peter Mogila (b. 1596, d. 1647), a Moldavian nobleman by birth, who played an outstanding part in the history of the Polish Ukraine, founded in 1631 the Kiev academy "for the teaching of the free sciences in the Greek, Slavonic, and Latin tongues." This became the intellectual center of the Ukraine, and it soon sent a number of learned Ukrainian ecclesiastics to Muscovy, where they initiated a cultural reformation.

In the Ukraine education was both more advanced and much more organized than in Muscovy. Under the influence of the Kiev academy, which continued to flourish well into the eighteenth century as a center both of lay and ecclesiastical education, other colleges were founded, notably in Kharkov (1731), and in the left-bank Ukraine a system of parochial schools became fairly widely spread. This higher standard largely explains the prominence of Ukrainians in government, church, and cultural activities in eighteenth-century Russia.

Meanwhile, in the second half of the seventeenth century, the Ukrainian, and to a lesser extent the direct Polish, cultural and religious influences had a fourfold effect on Muscovy. They brought home the lack of education, even among the clergy; they broadened what education there was, especially through emphasis on Latin; they invigorated religious life by emphasis on preaching; they spread in some degree western secular literature.

In "the western lands" printing, which had begun forty years earlier than in Moscow (Vilna, 1525; Moscow, 1564), was more widely extended and less strictly ecclesiastical than in Moscow. Translations of western books, in manuscript, remained few in seventeenth-century Muscovy, but they were increasing, and they included secular writings. From "the western lands" also versions of medieval collections of romantic tales began to penetrate. These later became widely popular in russianized forms, as the chap-books and woodcuts of the eighteenth century testify. Likewise in the second half of the seventeenth century the so-called "alphabet books," a species of composite elementary grammar and cyclopædia, changed character and contained a wider and a western range of information.

Yet, while making full allowance for the significance of such innovations and of the Ukrainian "Latinist" influence on the culture of Muscovy, it must be recognized that in the main this influence (in the first generation, *i.e.* roughly to 1690) meant the percolation of the methods and knowledge not of seventeenth-century Europe, but rather of medieval scholasticism. In the age of Bacon, Galileo, Kepler, and Descartes, Muscovy was first introduced to translations from Albertus Magnus, Raymond Lull, and Michael Scott. Arabic numerals made their first appearance only in the middle of the century. The elements of Euclid were not studied until Peter hired a Scotsman to teach them in his first "navigation school." The Copernican system was unknown until late in Peter's reign, and still in 1757 was considered by the censorship at the Moscow printing-press to be "dubious."

Muscovy in the sixteen-fifties and sixties was in the throes of the ritual and liturgical reforms which resulted in the great Schism (see pp. 180 ff.). These reforms were due to foreign influence; but Greek, not western. The Schism was felt as a very alarming symptom. The high Greek ecclesiastics, who had come to Moscow to resolve the dissension in the church, agreed in finding the root reason for the Schism in the absence of any proper education of the clergy, and consequently of the people. A prolonged struggle followed over how the clergy should be educated. It largely took the form of a struggle between the "Latinists" (mainly from the Ukraine) and the "Greeks" over the foundation and control of an academy in Moscow similar to that in Kiev. After initial successes for the "Latinists," the "Greeks," headed by the Patriarch Joachim (1674-90), won the day and the leading "Latinist" was hanged (1691), it is true ostensibly on political grounds rather than on account of his reputedly western views on the eucharist.

The Old Believers had rebelled against the church, backed by the state, in the name of ancient custom and national tradition. In the same name, though necessarily not in alliance with the Old Believers, a large section of the official church fought against western, but not southern, *i.e.* Greek, innovations, whether in questions of education and religion or in those concerning contacts with "Germans" and western importations. In so doing the Patriarch Joachim and his adherents fought against the strongest tendencies in the government.

The struggle for power between the rival families of the first wife of tsar Alexis (d. 1676) and his second wife, the mother of Peter the Great (b. 1672), was the main political thread between 1676 and 1694. Both groups in fact looked to the West, but both had to maneuver cautiously, especially in face of the reactionary nationalism of the turbulent *streltsy*, the privileged Moscow garrison.

In 1682, Sophia, half-sister of Peter, having won over the *streltsy*, effected a *coup d'état* and seized power, proclaiming herself regent. Peter never forgot that day when, as a boy of ten, standing by the side of his trembling mother on the great red flight of open stairs in the Kremlin, he had to face the reeking *streltsy* as they bore off on their pikes the gory heads of his supporters. He had to face them again in 1689 and in

1698, when they revolted against him. Then they were crushed without a shred of mercy, broken on the wheel as only Peter could break men.

The rule of the regent Sophia (1682-89) and her favorite Prince Golitsyn, despite the events of 1682, was in many ways tolerant, except of Old Believers, and it actively favored westernizing influences. Golitsyn (b. 1643, banished to the Arctic 1689, d. 1714) was a cultivated nobleman of enlightened views, both in internal and external affairs, but without any executive or military abilities. He was the foremost representative of that handful of men who, like Ordin-Nashchokin (*cf.* p. 251), looked away from the old Muscovy to the West and were the precursors of Peter. Golitsyn himself entertained a reform program which was anticipatory of Peter and included full freedom of conscience and religion and foreign education.

In 1689 a second *coup d'état* was engineered, mainly on political grounds, partly in opposition to concessions that had been made to Catholics. Peter's mother and the Patriarch Joachim took the place of Sophia and Golitsyn. Peter continued to devote himself to his widening circle of friends in the "German colony" and to his mechanical, military, and naval "diversions," and he did not direct policy until the death of his mother in 1694. Joachim had already protested, unavailingly, against the employment of foreigners in high military posts and had fulminated against the imitation of the Polish fashion of shaving the beard. He died in 1690, but his will, which was a violent anti-foreign manifesto, showed clearly enough his intentions, and these were fully shared by his ignorant and reactionary successor Adrian, elected in opposition to Peter's candidate, who was branded with the reputation of too much book-learning and addiction to foreigners. The tide turned when Peter took power to himself in 1694. When Adrian died, six years later, the patriarchate, identified as it was with opposition to the West, lapsed.

Such were the main currents and counter-currents swirling within seventeenth-century Muscovy and creating the fissures that Peter widened with sledge-hammer blows.

It has been seen in an earlier chapter (pp. 184-185) that Peter rode roughshod over the opposition within the church to westernizing, harried unsparingly the similar opposition of the Old Believers and sectarians, and made an end of the patriarchate. The division caused by the Schism prevented any common religious front against the West. And further, a new generation of able, modernist Ukrainian ecclesiastics were prepared to collaborate with Peter, at least in part, and were raised to high office.

The most eminent of these was Feofan Prokopovich (b. 1677 or 1681, d. 1736), in his own day and subsequently a very controversial figure. Born and trained in Kiev, he was for a time a Uniat, and he spent three years studying in Rome. But he returned to Kiev and Orthodoxy, and his later foreign connections were mainly with the Protestant world. He was a man of great learning and many-sided gifts and an opponent both of scholasticism and of the Muscovite version of Byzantinism. His energy as a writer, preacher, and educator drew Peter's attention. After 1716 he became his most trusted ecclesiastical adviser and was mainly responsible for his *Spiritual Regulation,* in accordance with which the Synod was established in place of the Patriarchate (1721) and a church secondary school set up in each diocese.

Peter's struggle against Muscovite nationalism within the church and his general policy of the subjection of the church to the state were of lasting importance. Still more so were his direct methods of westernizing Russia, for they deliberately involved the secularization of life and education. He employed three main methods: use of foreigners in Russia, learning from foreigners abroad, and lay education. The first was but an extension on a very large scale of what had been increasing during the previous hundred years. The novel elements in it were the closeness of Peter's own companionship with foreigners, and the much greater responsibility they were given. The other two methods were new, save for the fruitless attempt of Boris Godunov mentioned earlier.

One prominent trait in Peter was that he believed that the sovereign should set the example by showing that he could himself do what he called upon his subjects to do. This was a natural corollary of his insatiable curiosity and his physical and intellectual energy and dexterity. Hitherto no Russian sovereign had ever been outside the western bounds of his realm. In 1697 Peter himself went off as a member of "the great embassy" to the West, three hundred strong, which was to introduce to the young Russian aristocrats the science and technique of the German lands, the Netherlands, England, and Venice. It was followed by other, more or less forced, educational assignments abroad. Peter himself paid a notable visit to Paris in 1717, after which more Russians were sent to France, partly for general education, specially (as elsewhere) for naval instruction. The subjects prescribed for study were for the most part directly utilitarian, in connection with the army and navy. But languages necessarily figured as well, and in his later years some outlet was given to the polite arts and general culture. Already in 1717 there appeared in Russian *The Honorable Mirror of Youth,* to be reprinted five times within fifty years, one of the most popular guides for teaching the young gentry how to behave like courtiers instead of country bumpkins.

Probably more important than forced studies abroad, which in too many cases resulted in little permanent gain, were the effects of the great extension of Russian diplomatic and business connections with the West and of the fact that Russian armies and missions spent so much time in North German Baltic lands during the later part of the war against Sweden. Regular contact with foreigners in their own countries, as well as now on a much larger scale in Russia herself, bred up a generation of officers and officials the best of whom were deeply influenced by such contacts and took pride in their nickname of "fledgelings" of Peter, to whom they gave their full loyalty. And loyalty was the first and last requisite for Peter in his treatment of men.

Peter's third method of westernizing was the organization in Russia for the first time of lay, secular education. It was on a small scale, but it started from nothing. The object was to give a rudimentary technical or professional education for state service of various kinds. The names are significant: the "school of mathematics and navigation," a number of "ciphering schools," which taught the three R's and geometry, a few "admiralty schools" and "war department schools," and some others in the new metal works in the Urals.

At the top, the main instrument of secular education was the Academy of Sciences, opened in 1725. It was the fruit of much correspondence with Leibniz and others and of inquiry into the Royal Society and the *Académie des Sciences*. There was no educational ladder leading up to it, and it failed to develop into a university, as originally intended, but a secondary school attached to it later had valuable results. Its primary importance was that it soon became the center of research in the natural and physical sciences and of exploration of the resources of Russia. After 1748 it did much to encourage the translation of foreign books. Despite its early deficiencies and internal feuds, it was until the extension of universities under Alexander I (1801-25) almost the only organized center of higher learning in the empire.

The attempt of Peter to impose some compulsory schooling on the children of the nobility and gentry was impracticable and broke down after two years. Nevertheless it cannot be classed with other reforms, which bore no fruit and were scrapped after Peter's death, such as his far too elaborate expensive local government system, his army quartering plan, or his inheritance law. The requirement of a minimum of education to rise in the grades of the new "table of ranks" (see p. 98) had some effect, particularly when, after Peter's death, a cadet school was founded (1731) in St. Petersburg, from which the nobility and gentry passed into state service.

The general effect of Peter's westernizing, however superficial in many respects in his lifetime, had the deepest consequences. It is significant that a generation after Peter the upper class, who in his day had usually to be more or less conscripted for educational service abroad, were beginning to go abroad of their own free will, and that at least the outward appearance of European culture was becoming the requisite symbol of belonging to the privileged class.

This was not the intention of Peter himself. He had aimed at inculcating upon all classes (except the serfs, though they were not expressly excluded) the Western outlook, initially in regard to material technique and science. He succeeded posthumously in inculcating western customs and ways of living and eventually western ideas among the upper class, but almost solely among that class.

This was the beginning of the cultural divorce between the minority, European Russia, and the great majority, non-European Russia. It was largely due in the last resort to the character of education.

Primary education, even in the towns, was not developed from Peter's small beginnings. It was only slightly furthered by the educational reforms of Catherine the Great and Alexander I, and it was not until Alexander II (1864) that it began to receive continuous, widespread attention. On the other hand, secondary education on European lines eventually became relatively well developed among the upper class, and to a lesser extent the children of the clergy; while, from the early nineteenth century, universities, very few in number but on the whole high in standard, drew a very mixed class of students.

Nicholas I (1825-55) acted on the principle that "children belonging to different social groups must not be educated together," and that as far as possible education should be confined to the gentry and the civil service. It could not be entirely confined, even in theory, to the upper class, if only because the enormous needs of the administration could not possibly be met by that class alone. Hence Nicholas adopted the principle, in his decree of 1827, that schooling was to be such "that nobody should aim at rising above that position in which it is his lot to remain." That meant as regards primary education that, except for the state peasants, nothing was done by the government, and it continued to be left to the usually nominal initiative of the clergy and local bodies.

The period of the great reforms of Alexander II necessarily involved a comprehensive recasting of education (1863 and 1864). Considerable independence was restored to the universities; the limitations on the numbers of students at them were abolished, and the prohibition (since 1848) on study abroad was removed. A large section of the university students, however, were now composed of "conscience-stricken" gentry and "men of mixed class" imbued with "nihilism" and social revolutionary populism. Hence the government soon retreated towards the practices of Nicholas I. A prolonged, and at times savage, struggle was waged with the student youth, especially after the murder of Alexander II in 1881. Secondary education also became a battleground. Primary education was slowly extended from 1864, with a three-year course and Russian compulsory as the means of instruction; but the special attention of the government was given to church schools, most of which were of a very low standard.

The 1905 Revolution set free the universities, though there was reaction again from 1911. At long last the immense problem of illiteracy was recognized as a leading issue. Strenuous opposition, above all from the supporters of the church schools, prevented the Duma from carrying into effect its full projects, which aimed at slowly instituting compulsory primary education; but considerable progress was made, and for the first time the central government assigned comparatively large sums to primary education.

Since the reforms of Alexander II much had been done in education, particularly through the provincial and district councils (*zemstva*) and in higher specialized education, even despite the reaction under Alexander III and Nicholas II. In 1881 there were 1,300,000 pupils in elementary schools, and 9,300 university students; by 1914 the corresponding figures were nearly 6,000,000 and 35,500.[1] Yet illiteracy remained very widespread, especially among women and in Asiatic

[1] These figures exclude Poland and Finland, but include the Baltic provinces, where education was much more extended than in Russia proper. They also include the church primary schools, mostly of a very low standard. Of the university students, 70 per cent were classed in 1880 as belonging to families of the gentry, officials, or clergy, 46 per cent in 1914. Besides the 35,500 students in the state universities in 1914, there were about 40,000 students in other higher educational institutions.

Russia. According to the most favorable calculations over forty per cent of those over ten were literate in 1914; according to less favorable figures only about twenty-eight per cent. In addition, the quality of education was very variable, and the use of Russian as the sole language was still a burning question. There was no greater task for the Soviet régime to cope with than education, and perhaps in no other field has it displayed more energy and achieved greater results, notably among the non-Russian peoples. Compulsory primary education has been made a reality, illiteracy reduced to under twenty per cent of those over nine, and great expenditure devoted to higher education.

Literacy in itself is no infallible test, and illiteracy in itself no badge of inferiority in character or many skills. But it was broadly speaking true of Russia that Europe impinged on the great bulk of the illiterate masses primarily in the form of blind economic forces and in the form of war. On the other hand, since Peter the Great's day the influence of Europe, which he so vehemently furthered, had led to the creation at the top of a minority European civilization of a distinct Russian type. By 1917, as has already been emphasized (see pp. 63-65 and 313-315), this minority was so acutely divided between its three sections that the disasters and blunders of the First World War resulted in the collapse of the government section of the minority.

The influence of Europe had been immensely extended during the hundred years following Peter's death. During that century (1725-1825) foreigners of all descriptions played an outstanding part in the army and navy, in the administration and diplomacy, in learning and education, in medicine, in mining and industry, in foreign trade, in the arts, and as purveyors of the luxuries of aristocratic life. After half a century of raw and frequently superficial adoption of the externals of Western culture, the Russian upper class began to absorb the main developments of European literature and thought.

While in literature, the arts, and fashion France became, until the close of the eighteenth century, the predominant influence or the main intermediary, in other fields German influence was, and remained, more important. This was due to four reasons: the proximity of the German lands, the original partiality of Peter to German ways, the long series of Romanov marriages with the German courts, beginning with Peter's children (*cf.* pp. 76-78), and above all the consequences of his acquisition of Livonia and Estonia and his virtual protectorate of Courland, with their predominant German upper class (see map 5).[1]

The Baltic Germans began very badly with Biron (1690-1772), the Courlander favorite of the empress Anna (b. 1693, reigned 1730-40), a daughter of Peter's half-brother Ivan V and by marriage duchess of Courland. Biron has earned for himself the reputation of the most unpopular German in Russian history. Throughout the reign of Anna he headed the mainly German court oligarchy which in most respects shamefully misgoverned Russia. He paid the penalty by twenty years' exile in Siberia. The emperor Peter III, a Holsteiner, paid an extremer penalty. His obsession for Holstein and Prussia cost him both his throne and his life (1762).

The privileged position of the Baltic Germans within their home lands has been mentioned in a previous chapter (see p. 105). However somber the record of their rule there, in the empire at large they supplied a valuable nucleus of hardworking administrators, diplomats, and officers. They had important influence at court, above all under Nicholas I. None were perhaps more loyal, or more bureaucratically conservative, servants of the Romanovs, but their loyalty was essentially dynastic. They rarely became russified, and they retained their Lutheran religion, their own distinct culture, and an aloofness from, often a hostility to, many of the most potent currents in Russian life. This was also true of most of the numerous Germans who came from Germany proper.

In consequence, Germans were the target of constant at-

[1] The Duchy of Courland was a vassal of the kingdom of Poland, but for the greater part of the eighteenth century was in effect a Russian protectorate, until its definite incorporation in the empire in 1795 as a consequence of the third partition of Poland.

tack by various sections of Russian opinion, notably the slavophils and the panslavs (*cf.* pp. 231, 235). The accusations made of their virtual monopoly of the higher posts in government service were exaggerated, but it was true that in proportion to their numbers the Germans were very influential, whether from the Baltic provinces or (as for instance Osterman in the eighteenth century and Nesselrode in the nineteenth) from the German lands proper. The extreme case was the London embassy; between 1812 and 1917 there were nine ambassadors; four of these were Baltic German barons, who between them occupied the post for eighty-three out of the hundred and five years.

Both through the Baltic Germans and from Germany herself Russia absorbed much of Western technique and thought. Study in Germany and the employment of German teachers, professors, naturalists, and scientists, even though many of them at first were very secondary or unsuitable persons, led already by the second half of the eighteenth century to a new era in the sciences, geography, mathematics, and history. Catherine the Great and Nicholas I borrowed, indirectly or directly, from Prussian educational practice. Alexander I founded or re-founded four universities on the German model. The Academy of Sciences in the eighteenth century was predominantly German: only a quarter of its members were Russians. In the nineteenth century the position was reversed; seventy per cent were Russians, but Germans accounted for two-thirds of the remainder. Throughout that century, except for a break after the 1848 revolutions, Russians frequented German or German-Swiss universities far more than any others.

In literature and thought, apart from masonry and religion (see p. 337), Goethe, especially *Werther,* Schiller, the German ballads, and Hoffmann combined with the English pre-romantics, Scott and Byron, to oust French pseudo-classicism in Russia in favor of romanticism and the cult of the past. In philosophy, Schelling's romanticist idealism found ardent devotees in the twenties and thirties, until his predominance was challenged and in the forties replaced by that of Hegel, the most ramifying influence that has been exerted upon Russian thought by any single European philosopher. The "left-wing Hegelians" (Feuerbach and others) spread abroad in Russia nineteenth-century materialism, and its transformer Marx in the generation before 1917, directly and indirectly, exercised profound influence.

These German influences and contributions, which were accompanied from about 1850 by increasingly close economic relations with Germany, were accepted or absorbed without a corresponding friendliness of feeling towards Germans themselves. Large sections of the educated minority resented or girded at German civil servants and officers and often attacked the foreign policy conducted from St. Petersburg on the score of its control by foreigners who thought in terms of European equilibrium or German interests instead of the true needs and aspirations of Russia. The mass of the people knew Germans more than any other foreigners, but they knew them only as the overseers of their masters, whether in field or factory, or as meticulous, flint-skinned officials. The very virtues of the Germans appeared in Russian eyes to be turned by excess or inadaptability into the vices of pedantic routine and cold-blooded or cruel superiority. Europe through the Germans gave Russia much, but far too often as the exacting and inhuman schoolmaster or the rigid and alien disciplinarian.

These diverse and widespread feelings against Germans helped to give powerful, if incoherent, backing to the growth of a new Russian nationalism in the forty years before 1914. They also gave backing to the political, diplomatic combination which linked up Russia with France and eventually Great Britain, and to the patriotism initially evoked by the war of 1914 as a retributive contest of the Slavs against the German taskmaster or overlord. These feelings were strongly reinforced by Russian experience of German occupation, above all in the Ukraine in 1918. Now in the present war they have been surcharged with the far greater waves of popular hatred loosed by the Nazi outrages; now the watchword is "execration and death to the German Fascist invaders, their state, their army, their 'New Order in Europe' " (Stalin).

The second greatest, and a very different, agent of Europe in Russia has been France. Peter the Great had very strongly reinforced the connections of Russia with the non-Catholic, northern European lands. As a result the predominance of French culture was delayed until the middle of the eighteenth century. The reaction against German favorites, which came to a head with the palace revolution that placed Peter's daughter, Elizabeth, on the throne (b. 1709, reigned 1741-62), told in favor of French fashions and the beginnings of deeper French influence, for instance, in drama and poetry and the foundation in 1757 of the Academy of Fine Arts in imitation of that in Paris.

In any case, since Russia had now been drawn into regular, multiple contacts with Europe, she could not fail to be swayed by the dominance of French culture which she met in almost all western countries, even apart from her relations with France herself. The French language, since it was the international language of eighteenth-century Europe, was adopted by the Russian upper class as its second language, in later generations often as its first. The private tutor was a principal means of education, and the French tutor (with however little qualifications) rapidly became from about 1750 an essential among the aristocracy.

Not only did French literature become a staple, but French translations or versions of English, German, or other writings were for long the chief means whereby these became known in Russia. Largely through French culture Russia was introduced to ancient Greece and Rome, and thanks to their French exemplars the first two periods of modern Russian literature, those of Elizabeth and Catherine the Great, were pre-eminently those of pseudo-classicism. Above all, the best of French culture introduced Russia to a new clarity of thought and expression, a new spirit of criticism, analysis, and sensibility, a new conception of education as distinguished from the mere acquisition of skill or useful information.

French style and French thought profoundly influenced Russian as a literary language and the technique and content of Russian prose and poetry. Molière, Racine, Corneille, La Fontaine, and Fénelon exercised a prolonged sway. Montesquieu and the Encyclopædists, above all, Voltaire, had their great days between 1760 and 1790, and Voltaire continued long an influence. Rousseau lasted even longer, as his effect on Tolstoy shows. After the French Revolution other currents swept into Russia; France continued to the fore, but she was never again the almost undisputed mistress.

The great period of the dominance of French literature and thought coincided, not by chance, with the reign of Catherine the Great (1762-96), which marked a watershed in the relations of Russia with Europe.

Catherine (b. 1729), more gifted and more filled with vitality than any woman who has sat upon a throne since Queen Elizabeth, climbed to her empire from a paltry German princedom over the body of her deposed and murdered husband (1762). She was a courageous adventuress, an accomplished blue-stocking, and an admirable actress. On her own admission she was without creative originality, but she was a ready and assiduous absorber of the ideas of others; a third-rate authoress, but a first-rate propagator of the ideas of the age of reason and enlightened despotism. Catherine regarded herself and her court as the main channel for europeanizing Russia, a civilizing mission that ranged from satire to paper money and vaccination. She combined the energetic patronage of literature, art, education, and the press with important internal reforms and sweeping successes against the Turks and the Poles. The general renown of her reign has won for it in Russian history the title of "the age of Catherine."

The result of "the age of Catherine" was that a large part of the upper class became infused with Western culture, whereas previously the West, except for small groups at court and in service, had spelled little more than material innovations and a gauche imitation of externals. Russian literature had grown to its second generation, still largely imitative of

France, but now capable of holding up to scorn mere aping of Paris as well as backwoods boorishness.

Already in the reign of Elizabeth the closer contacts with Europe had stimulated a polymath of genius, Lomonosov (1711-65), the son of a peasant-fisherman from the White Sea. His exceptional natural gifts were allied to untiring determination and energy, which brought him to Moscow, to study in Germany (not France), and to the Academy of Sciences, and he became almost as eminent in literature and history (and even the craft of mosaic) as he was in the sciences (especially physical chemistry, of which he is the father).

By the eighties there had come into being small circles who had learned from the West to apply criticism and rationalism critically and in reason; who reacted against slavish acceptance of anything and everything that professed to have the hall-mark of France, against adulation of Peter the Great and contempt of religion and the old Russia, and against mute acceptance of existing conditions and institutions in Russia, above all serfdom.[1] By the end of the century "the conscience-stricken" gentry had been born, and the beginnings are to be found of the division of educated Russia between the government and a critical opposition.

Catherine herself had encouraged criticism and public discussion, provided she could guide them. When she could not, she frowned upon or suppressed them. Her early addiction to the Encyclopædists, especially Voltaire, gave a great vogue to rationalism and skeptical free-thinking, and her dissolute amours and the spendthrift luxury of her court still further demoralized the aristocracy. She kept up a long correspondence with Voltaire (*cf.* p. 70, note), Diderot, D'Alembert, Grimm, and other reigning intellectuals abroad, largely as a means of propaganda, partly as a form of self-flattery. She and her associates invited the great French lights of the day to view with their own eyes the splendors of "the Semiramis of

[1] See p. 136 for Radishchev. One of the most interesting conservative critics of Catherine and Peter and the effects of Europe on Russia was Prince Shcherbatov (1733-90). One of his writings is translated into German, but not English, *Ueber die Sittenverderbnis in Russland* (Berlin, 1932; written 1786-88; first published in 1858 by Herzen in London, in 1859 in Russia).

the North" and her mighty realm. The only one of the major lights to come was Diderot, "ambassador and minister plenipotentiary of the Republic of the Encyclopædia," who professed to find in Catherine "l'âme de Brutus avec les charmes de Cléopâtre."

The influence of the extreme rationalism of the Encyclopædists did not go long unchallenged. Rousseau did much to break their spell. Catherine found herself better suited by the measured moderation of Montesquieu and was by no means an admirer of all things French. It was the cosmopolitan, humanitarian enlightenment of the great opposition writers that spelled to her France. Politically she was hostile, or at best cool, towards the France of Louis XV and Louis XVI, and her general predilections were towards England and the German lands.

Peter the Great has been called a germanized Russian, Catherine the Great a russianized German. From the first, when she came to Russia at the age of fifteen (1744), she was at pains to show herself a good Orthodox and to learn the language, history, and ways of her adopted country. What had begun as duty and artifice became more and more part of herself, and in her last years she may be classed as a Russian nationalist. She plunged into Russian chronicles, encouraged the writing of Russian history, and herself composed two dramas, in imitation of Shakespeare, in the national setting of *Rurik* and *Oleg*. At the end, partly in reaction against the French Revolution, her outlook was closely similar to that of the best-known Russian dramatist of her age, when he wrote: "All the tales of the superiority of this country [France] are arrant lies; people are the same everywhere; a really wise and deserving man is everywhere a rarity; in our fatherland it is possible to live as happily as in any other country."

Catherine's nationalism naturally did not mean a renunciation of Peter and Europe. It sought to fuse them with the historic past and distinctive characteristics of Russia. It was of a piece with the confident pride of so many of the dominant landed gentry in the prowess of Russian arms and the achievements of Catherine's reign. It linked on to the still more pronounced nationalism that was to be bred from 1812 and the final triumph over Napoleon.

In her later years a very different current began to act as a powerful influence coloring Russian thought between 1780 and 1825. This was the influence of masonry, pietism and mysticism, deriving especially from England and Germany. Russian masonry owed something to the Frenchman Saint-Martin, and more to the German Rosicrucians, but most to the English model. It became of importance from the early eighties, especially through the activity of Novikov (b. 1744, imprisoned 1792-96, d. 1818), who devoted his life, until he fell under Catherine's final ban, to the extension of true education, the serious periodical press, and social relief. In conjunction with other groups, small in numbers but mostly very highly placed, masonry declared war on the rationalistic free-thinking and loose-living skepticism typical of the Voltairean society of the capital. These groups preached a new, sober spirit of criticism—"the moral rebirth" central in masonry—a new feeling for religion and a new consciousness of toleration and of duties towards one's neighbor and humanity.

Such ideals of upright virtue found a ready welcome with Alexander I (b. 1777, reigned 1801-25). He had first imbibed them from two of his tutors, the earnest, lofty-minded Swiss republican, La Harpe, and a Russian priest from the Ukraine, who had been long in England, had married an Englishwoman and combined a devotion to improved farming methods with the gospel of evangelical fraternity and simple piety. Alexander's later liking for Lutheran pietism and German mysticism reinforced his liberal attitude on toleration and influenced his combination of religion and politics which inspired the Holy Alliance in 1815 (see pp. 395-396). It is significant that after 1812 Alexander was never without the Bible, and typical that he should combine religion and education under one minister, should befriend the Quakers, and should encourage an offshoot of the British and Foreign Bible Society in Russia.

The first years of Alexander's reign were filled with liberal hopes, which linked up with Novikov and Radishchev. They were encouraged both by Alexander himself and by his intimate advisors, two of whom were enthusiasts for the English fusion of aristocratic and monarchical institutions which Catherine herself had studied with approval in Blackstone. Bentham (who came to Russia to visit his brother in 1786) and Adam Smith aroused interest in the highest quarters, though to little practical effect. After 1815 the political ideas of England of the unreformed Parliament were felt to be too radical or alien by the conservative nationalists, too aristocratic or reactionary by the generation influenced by the French Revolution and the wars in the West.

The French Revolution had soon brought into drastic play Catherine's censorship and police, but neither it nor the Napoleonic wars caused a general revulsion from France. There were so many different Frances. Where the Revolution was taboo or Napoleon an ogre, there was the France of the *émigrés,* of the Jesuits (allowed in Russia between 1772 and 1820), of Chateaubriand and Madame de Staël. And there was always the France of the seventeenth-century classics. Many royalist *émigrés* figured prominently in the Russian army and navy, and New Russia owed a great debt to her governor-general, the Duc de Richelieu, later Louis XVIII's prime minister, and to his French collaborators (*cf.* p. 38).

1812 and the burning of Moscow caused an explosion of national feeling against "the barbarians, the Vandals," "the modern Tamerlane," but the catastrophe of the Grand Army and the part played by Russia in the final overwhelming of Napoleon changed the outburst of hatred to mixed feelings of pity, condescension, and superiority. The events of 1812-15 gave a most powerful impetus to the Russian nationalism that had thriven on the Great Northern War, the Seven Years War, and the all-round prestige of "the age of Catherine." It was reinforced by a recrudescence of militant xenophobia in the Orthodox church and by the patriotic, literary conservatism best represented by Karamzin's phenomenally successful *History of the Russian State* (1816).

On the other hand, the campaigns in the West and the occupation of France (1815-18) made Russians far better acquainted with Europe at first hand than ever before. Many officers, especially in the Guards, became impregnated with, or sympathetic towards, liberal or radical ideas. The glaring contrasts between Russia and the West inspired feelings of the necessity of wholesale reform, beginning with the autocrat's throne and reaching down to the serf's hut. From small circles of mostly well-born officers secret societies were formed, partly under masonic influences. They were spared despite the reaction during Alexander's last five years, and on his death (December, 1825) they took to arms in the Decembrist rising (*cf.* pp. 76 ff.).

The rising was promptly, but bloodily, suppressed. The effect on his successor, Nicholas I (b. 1796), was that he became even more of a parade-ground martinet and believer in the necessity for strong, inquisitorial, if ostensibly paternalistic, rule. The severity of the punishments meted out, not only to the participants but to all who were suspected of the slightest collusion or sympathy with liberal ideas, created a gulf between the autocracy and a large section of the intellectuals.[1] This was steadily widened during his reign (1825-55), in proportion as Nicholas strove to abolish "the pernicious luxury of half knowledge" and succeeded in transforming Russia into the "police state" *par excellence* (*cf.* p. 103), which culminated in the ice cap of repression following the 1848 revolutions.

The policy of Nicholas was primarily negative in character, and it was not until 1848 in all directions carried to extremes. Its positive aspect, the official creed of "Orthodoxy, autocracy, and nationality," had a wider appeal than often allowed, but it bred nothing but repulsion in the young in-

[1] A vivid picture of the post-Decembrist generation of radicals is given in the first three volumes of Herzen's *Memoirs* (translated 1924), describing his early life in Moscow and the university, his two exiles to the provinces, and Moscow in the forties (written 1852-53; 1859). Herzen is a master of Russian prose. The two-volume translation by J. D. Duff (New Haven, 1923) is first-rate, but it goes only to 1838.

telligentsia of all classes, especially because it was based on a repudiation of the idea of progress. In consequence, the effect on the young generation was not to banish independent thought and exclude the virus of "dangerous" Western ideas, but to drive them underground, to make literature the cryptic medium of social and political thought, and to put a premium on extreme views.

Between 1830 and 1860, apart from the great influence of German thinkers already mentioned, the French "utopian socialists," Saint-Simon, Fourier, Proudhon, and Louis Blanc, and the novelist George Sand, gained a very wide, surreptitious popularity among the intelligentsia, which became only too manifest in the much freer atmosphere of the sixties and seventies. By then the ideas of J. S. Mill, Buckle, and, above all, Darwin were competing, together with Comte's positivism and later Herbert Spencer's sociology; to be succeeded by Nietzsche, and, above all, Marx's dialectical materialism.

By then, Russia had long been too advanced, too complex, and too conscious of her individuality and of her own creative originality to look to any one foreign country for enlightenment. Whether in literature or in social thought she was a sharer in all sides of European civilization, not as she had been in the eighteenth century for the most part a mere imitator now of this, now of that country. Both the revolutionary [1] and the liberal-progressive movements, which grew so powerfully from the sixties onwards and by the time of the 1905 Revolution had created a new political climate in Russia, drew from very varied European sources; but they transmuted them into new forms under the pressure of the great social transformations that were taking place as a result of the emancipation of the serfs (1861) and rapid economic westernization.

[1] No attempt is here made to trace the development of the revolutionary movements in Russia, beyond what has already been said on pp. 313-315 and 48-51, since they have been comparatively fully treated in English, particularly by Masaryk, Maynard, Mavor, and Berdyaev (see pp. 451-453 in the appendix, Note on Books).

3. Economic Westernization

During the half-century between emancipation and the First World War industrial revolution profoundly changed the economic structure of Russian life, and in so doing westernized it to a far larger extent than previously, even though Russia still remained a predominantly peasant country, with the most varied contrasts in ways of life and technique.

By the beginning of the present century certain of the most obvious features of the Western capitalist and industrial world were among the dominating influences operating in Russia: a "free labor market," the absorption and utilization of capital accumulation (both home and foreign) through developed banking, company and stock exchange systems, the close interlocking with world prices and the world money market, the application of modern science to communications and industry, the concentration of power-driven machinery in large-scale factories. All these features were to be found in Russia even before the eighteen-sixties, but only in rudimentary forms or on a very small scale. From the sixties onward they became marked; from the nineties dominating.

The emancipation of the serfs (1861) and the other reforms of the sixties marked the watershed between the old and the nineteenth-century Russia, much as the reign of Peter the Great marked that between the old Muscovy and a new Russia. Prior to the sixties Russian industry had been technically backward and to a large degree based on handicrafts and domestic industry. The two biggest exceptions were the iron and textile industries, into which especially Peter had injected new life.

As has already been emphasized (pp. 107-108), the industrial development that began in the early eighteenth century was initially almost entirely, and for a long time very largely, bound up with the needs of the state, above all the army and navy; hence the primary attention given to metallurgy, munitions and military supplies, including the new cloth factories. Foreign, especially German, technical skill was largely drawn upon; but not foreign money to any extent. Peter relied chiefly on the Russian merchant class, not on the landed class, for his economic developments, but there was insufficient capital accumulation available for the new merchants' factories without state aid in various forms. The state directly worked many of the mines and some factories, and where it did not work them itself it had first call on their output.

Russia in the eighteenth century was substantially self-supporting in munitions. She was not so, however, in cloth, despite Peter's efforts. Russian army contracts for Yorkshire woolens continued to be, as in the seventeenth century, far and away the largest single item in British exports to Russia, save during one period of successful Prussian competition. The advance in iron-ore production and metallurgy was most striking. In the third quarter of the eighteenth century Russia supplanted Sweden as the largest iron exporter to England. By 1750 Russia was smelting perhaps four times as much pig-iron as England. The main center of this new heavy industry was now the Urals, where there were abundant supplies of high-quality ore, charcoal and water-power.

The lead of the Urals began to decline after about 1800. By then British production of pig-iron was on a level and it soon far outstripped the Russian output, thanks to the substitution of coke for charcoal and a long series of inventions in iron and steel manufacture. These were only very slowly or very sparsely introduced into Russia. Puddling, for instance, was not experimented with until 1836, fifty years after the invention of Cort's process, while smelting with charcoal predominated in the Urals right down to the late nineteenth century.

On the other hand, the first half of the nineteenth century saw the expansion of the cotton textile industry, mainly concentrated in and near Moscow. Its growth was assisted by high protective tariffs after 1822 and by the impetus given by the break with England when Russia joined Napoleon's Continental System (1807-10). Between 1820 and 1860 raw cotton imports (entering free of duty from the United States via England) increased over thirtyfold by weight, and the workers in the cotton mills were much the largest group of factory operatives. English machinery was used in some factories, but cheap English yarn was imported in increasing quantities down to 1842. In that year Great Britain repealed the prohibition on the export of machinery. As a result the Russian cotton-spinning industry began rapidly to be mechanized, and, much more slowly, the weaving industry followed suit. A prominent part was played by Ludwig Knoop, Bremen-born and Lancashire-trained, a proverbial figure in mid-nineteenth-century Russia, and by a few large-scale British-Russian manufacturers; but in the main the cotton and linen industry was in the hands of Russian merchant-manufacturer dynasties, many of them Old Believers, some of them freed serfs, a few of them ennobled merchants.

The cotton, and to a lesser extent the flax, industry worked chiefly for the general Russian market and was not closely bound to the state. There was some concentration of certain processes in factories, but the bulk of the weaving in particular was done in villages between Moscow and the Volga as a domestic industry, organized through capitalist manufacturers and master middlemen. The cotton and flax industry was also distinguished by the fact that it drew its hands mainly from a heterogeneous class of hired labor or from serfs owing money dues but not labor services to their masters. In contrast, the cloth and heavy industries depended on ascribed serfs, whose productivity was extremely low.

On the basis of this serf labor the landed class from the middle of the eighteenth century had combined agriculture with manufacture, based on their own raw materials, whether concentrated in workshops or distributed among their serfs on a "put-out" system. There was keen competition for labor with the state mines and foundries and with the enterprises of the merchant-manufacturers. This led to the landed class under Catherine the Great demanding various privileges prohibiting or limiting the further acquisition of peasants by any undertakings other than their own. They were for a time successful, and they also secured (1765) the valuable monopoly of distilling.

Nevertheless, subsequently between 1815 and 1860 the

share of the landed class in manufacture steadily diminished. Their serf labor was being found more and more unsatisfactory. The legislation of Nicholas I (1825-55), however politically reactionary, favored in certain respects the extension of the merchant-industrialist class, which together now with some sections of the landowners favored emancipation of the serfs (*cf.* pp. 131 ff.).

By the middle of the century the economic links of Russia with the West had so multiplied that radical legal and social, if not political, changes could hardly be delayed much longer. For a century she had been borrowing abroad, mainly through Amsterdam, though not on a large scale. For a century she had been in the toils of paper money and had been developing a rudimentary banking system. Between 1800 and 1850 foreign trade had more than doubled. Wheat exports and world wheat prices by now were vital issues. The effects of the industrial revolution in the West were beginning to be felt in Russia.

Yet prior to the Crimean War (1853-56) industrial development along the lines of western Europe was looked askance at by those most influential in government circles. Hopes were pinned to patriarchal manufacture, with its roots in the native Russian handicrafts which were still the main suppliers of domestic needs. Some of them were in the hands of serf-owners, but many were the long outgrowth of specialized peasant craftsmen, organizing themselves on co-operative lines in what were called *artels*.[1] Thus different groups of villages became widely famous, for instance, for their knives, locks, or nails, for their tea urns (*samovars*), for their bast shoes, their felt boots, or their icons. So far from dying away in the nineteenth century, these peasant industries developed strongly in its first half, owing to their comparative cheapness, their flexibility, and their close touch with their market. Machine-made factory goods did not kill them or drive them to reorganization with machinery until late in the century.

[1] One of the very best of Lyeskov's short stories, *The Sealed Angel* (1873), has as its subject a bridge-building *artel* of Old Believers. It is translated in B. L. Tollemache, *Russian Sketches* (London; 1913).

Internal trade had developed steadily, and the formation of an all-Russian market had been much assisted by the abolition in 1754 of internal tolls and by the proclamation in 1762 of internal freedom of trade in corn, at least in principle. Distribution was effected through thirty-three great fairs, headed by the famous Nizhni-Novgorod fair, by two hundred odd lesser ones, and over six thousand markets.

Trade was, however, still severely hampered (in addition to extremely low purchasing power) by the backwardness of communications, which remained still in the mid-nineteenth century largely governed by the waterways. These had indeed been extended by Peter the Great's initiation of canal building, linking the upper Volga with St. Petersburg, and by the expansion of his canal system under Catherine the Great, Paul and Alexander I. The first Russian steamboat had appeared as early as 1815 on the Neva, but there was no successful development of steam navigation until the fifties. The Russian navy by the time of the Crimean War was still almost entirely a sailing fleet, and in its few steam-propelled ships the screw had not, as in the British and French fleets, replaced the paddle-wheel.

Roads, where they existed, were mere tracks. Even the few state routes were little better. Chaussées were unknown until 1817, and undeveloped before 1840. Railways had only just begun, and Russia fought the Crimean War with only one line of importance, from St. Petersburg to Moscow, opened in 1851.[1]

That war revealed at humiliating cost the all-round weaknesses of the Russia of Nicholas I when pitted alone against the West. Russia must be modernized and freer scope given to those forces, already operating within her on a small scale, which would transform her economically into a nineteenth-century state on the Western level in material equipment and power. This involved the emancipation of the serfs

[1] The first railway was built some years earlier (1838). It ran from St. Petersburg to the imperial palace of Tsarskoe Selo, a distance of only eighteen miles.

(1861) and the other reforms of Alexander II (see pp. 68, 101-102, 126-131).

Between 1861 and 1917 a new Russia was emerging, and in this economic westernization the state played an essential rôle, above all in four fields—finance and currency, foreign investment in Russia, tariffs, and railways.

(1) The financial administration was reorganized, some publicity provided for the national budget, and the state bank reformed (1860), as the sole note-issuing bank and as the controller of credit. The foundation of private banks, previously unknown in Russia, and of new credit institutions was encouraged. Piecemeal reform of commercial law was undertaken. The first wave of company promotion took place in the sixties, and the rapid development of the stock exchange ushered in a new financial and commercial era.

Effective currency reform was not achieved until the end of the century. Between 1769 and 1839 Russia had lived on an inconvertible paper-money system. The paper rouble suffered enormous depreciation during the Napoleonic period, especially between 1806 and 1812, despite the efforts of Speransky at financial reform (*cf.* pp. 102 and 379 ff.). In 1839-41 a currency reform was effected, the essential of which was a convertible paper money based on the silver rouble. This, however, broke down and the collapse of the finances in the Crimean War was followed by the official abandonment of the metallic standard in 1858. Thereafter the control of the rouble and the struggle to attract gold and to maintain the foreign exchange rate were primary factors in state economic policy. At last, in 1897, the finance minister, Witte, succeeded in putting Russia on the gold standard. Thanks largely to this extremely important measure Russia's financial credit weathered the war with Japan and the 1905 Revolution with surprising success, and by 1914 a large war chest had been built up.

(2) Under Alexander II for the first time the policy of foreign capital imports on a large scale was deliberately adopted as an indispensable means of modernizing Russia. She became the largest borrowing country in Europe. Ini-

tially the flow of foreign money was directed to railways, but thereafter to all branches of industry and to many other concerns.

Witte, who from 1892 to 1903 was minister both of finance and of trade and communications, did his utmost to encourage foreign capital in his very energetic forwarding of industrial and transport development. In 1892 the total direct national debt stood at 5,300 million roubles, in 1914 at 8,850 million, when the interest on it accounted for a little over a fifth of the expenditure and the interest on the external portion of this debt for nearly fourteen per cent. Of this direct debt 48 per cent was held by foreigners, as compared with 30 per cent in 1875. In 1914 no less than 80 per cent of the external government debt was held in France.

In financing Russia France under the Second Empire had first taken the lead, then vied with England. After 1870 London and Berlin replaced Paris as the main centers for dealing with Russian government stock. The return to Paris came as a result of the crisis in 1887 between Russia and Germany and her ally Austria-Hungary over the Bulgarian question, when Bismarck gave official support to the campaign being waged in Germany against Russian credit (*cf.* p. 412). Within the next few years Russia was driven into the arms of the French money-market. Bismarck was aware of this danger and apparently intended his action to be only a temporary measure. In fact, however, the German market remained closed to Russian state securities until 1894. In conjunction with Russian anti-German legislation in the Baltic provinces and with heated tariff disputes, a far-reaching change began in Russo-German relations.

Between 1892 and 1914 fifteen government loans and railway bond issues were floated abroad (not including conversion loans); ten in Paris, only four in Berlin, and one in London. The long series of French loans began at the same time as the making of the Franco-Russian alliance (1891-93), and the export of French capital to Russia was a cardinal factor in international relations. Although it was German, not French, advances that helped to tide Russia through her war with Japan (1904-5), in 1906 the largest of all the Paris loans was issued, after the French government had made certain of Russian support at the Algeciras conference on Morocco. It aroused violent controversy, since it was rushed through in advance of the first meeting of the Duma notwithstanding the new fundamental laws. This loan "to strangle the revolution" was bitterly denounced by all groups in Russia from the liberals leftwards, and they coupled denunciation with threats of subsequent repudiation.

In addition to government loans, Russia borrowed abroad heavily for industrial and other development. Foreign capital flowed continuously into Russian companies and banks, until by 1914 about a third of the issued stock of Russian joint-stock companies (even apart from banks) was estimated to be foreign-held. Of these foreign investments (*i.e.*, apart from government loans) France again held a major share, about one-third. Great Britain and Germany were a close second and third, each supplying about one-fifth. Belgium, with her heavy investment in South Russian coal and iron companies, came fourth. French money went principally into mining and metallurgy; British into oil, gold and other mining concerns in Siberia and the Urals. German investment was more widely spread and was notably strong in the western fringes of the empire.

Foreign capital, particularly French and German, also figured largely in the financing of Russian banks. It is, however, disputed whether this amounted to a predominance of foreign influence. Only one important bank was in majority foreign in its administration. There was much rivalry and opposition between the banks classed as "foreign." Some of them in some fields worked in close connection with the economic interests of their nationals, but in other fields they did not. Armaments were keenly contested between French, British and Germans. Down to about 1900 foreign banking interests tended to organize industrial concerns controlled and run by them and their foreign experts, but after 1900 their general rôle was that of accoucheurs: in the main they wanted commissions and dividends, not in addition actual control of firms. Thus foreign "daughter concerns," with a few notable exceptions, played a minor rôle in Russian industry.

(3) Tariffs were the third means by which the modern expansion of Russian industry was assisted. Before the Crimean War Russia had lived behind a high protective wall, except for the greater part of Catherine the Great's reign and for a few years under Alexander I. After 1822 there was a return to a system of high tariffs and prohibitions. Some reaction against extreme protectionism began already before the Crimean War, but it was the resultant internal crisis which made effective the ideas of Bastiat and Cobden. There followed a twenty-year period of low tariffs, with an important free list. The Balkan crisis of 1876 occasioned a heavy scaling-up of duties, on revenue grounds. Thereafter, in company with Germany, France and most other European countries, Russia re-erected her tariff walls, mainly in order to protect industry.

This return to high protection caused serious reactions, not with England, previously the chief participant in Russia's foreign trade, but with Germany, who had displaced England since the middle of the century. Two bitter tariff struggles, in 1893-94 and 1903-4, did much to worsen relations between Russia and Germany, where the Prussian agricultural interest was in a position to demand measures against Russian corn imports.

(4) Industrial revolution in Russia, unlike Great Britain but like most parts of the Continent, was from the first very closely linked with the revolution in communications caused by steam-power. The high tariffs of Nicholas I's reign had not assisted, or been accompanied by, a large development of manufactures, except in some branches of textiles. They did assist, or were accompanied by, very rapid industrial development from the eighties onwards. This was largely due to the fact that in the intervening period of Alexander II a low tariff policy had been adopted, which encouraged the import

of Western technique and capital goods, above all in the form of railways.

Nicholas I had shared the aversion to railways felt by most of his advisers, largely on the ground that they would involve the dependence of Russia on foreign capital and equipment. When he died (1855) there were only 650 miles of railway in the whole of his vast empire, not much more than in diminutive Piedmont. When his successor Alexander II died (1881), there were over 14,000 miles in operation. During this first railway boom, in the sixties and early seventies, the lines were built by private companies, but with the financial guarantee of the state and according to a general state plan. Subsequently, the majority of the lines were bought back by the state.

There was a big slackening in the rate of construction after 1875 until the beginning of the Trans-Siberian in 1891 and the great impetus given to railway expansion by the economic policy of Witte. In fifteen years (1891-1905) nearly 20,000 miles of new line were opened, a figure that is probably about the same as the corresponding figure for the years 1921-39. By the time of the 1917 Revolution the total mileage had increased to about 52,000, with another 7,000 building.[1]

The great railway expansion after 1891 was closely bound up with the similar expansion of the metallurgical industry, which now, in contrast with the sixties and seventies, supplied a very large part of the railway equipment. After 1891 also the combination of strategic and economic needs led to the revolution of communications in Asia. This was centered on the Trans-Siberian (see p. 291), but in addition Tashkent by 1905 was joined to European Russia by direct line through Orenburg, and already twenty years earlier it had been linked with the Caspian (see map 2). On the other hand, the idea of joining the cotton fields of Turkestan with the wheatfields of Siberia remained only a surveyed project. It was left for the

[1] Including Finland and Poland: without them the total mileage worked was about 47,000.

Soviet régime to translate the Turk-Sib railway into actuality (opened in 1930), as also to extend on a large scale the bare minimum of a railway system in Asia inherited from the imperial régime.

The interaction of these four factors—railways, tariffs, foreign investment and state encouragement of Western capitalism—combined with the results of the emancipation of the serfs to effect a revolution in Russian economy, both in scale and in technique. Internal and external trade increased by leaps and bounds. A new commercial, financial and industrial class began to be formed, partly by the transformation of the old-style merchants and entrepreneurs, largely by the rise of a new, westernized bourgeoisie, which by 1914, in extreme cases, would be building palaces such as that which now houses the British embassy in Moscow, or buying contemporary French pictures such as now make the Moscow Museum of Modern Art one of the finest collections of such painting in the world. Urban communities grew apace, in which an industrial proletariat was being welded, including a small core of skilled workers largely divorced from the old ties with the villages. By 1917 town and country were to a large extent different worlds, and the pace was being set by the town (*cf.* p. 114).

The tempo and volume of this industrial revolution may be illustrated by the following approximate figures of production (in millions of tons):

	1860	1900	1913
Coal	.28	16	36
Pig-iron	.31	2.7	4.8
Steel	.0016	2.5	4.0
Oil	.027 (1870)	10.4	9.0
Raw cotton (consumption)	.05	.24	.40

Since the early nineties in most branches of heavy industry and in coal output the rate of increase was considerably higher than that in the countries of western Europe or the United States. On the other hand, actual output in industrial goods was still far smaller. Thus, for instance (1913):

	Pig-iron	Steel	Coal
	In million tons		
Russia	4.8	4.0	36
U.S.A.	30.9	31.3	509
United Kingdom	10.3	7.7	287
Germany	19.3	18.3	190*
France	5.2	4.7	40.8

* If brown coal is included, 277.

Again, comparisons in terms of consumption per head, of productivity per unit or per man were overwhelmingly to the disadvantage of Russia. In 1914 she was still a "backward" country relatively to the West, though she was "advanced" in comparison with the Russia of 1861.

In one particular respect she was very "advanced"; namely, in the degree to which her industry was concentrated in large concerns, and, at any rate by 1914, for the most part with very up-to-date machinery. By then probably rather over half those classified as industrial workers were employed in plants with over 500 hands, and nearly a quarter in plants with over 1,000 hands—proportions that were much higher than those for any other country. Already in the nineties seven giant works in the Ukraine employed two-thirds of those working in metallurgical plants. Similarly the geographical concentration of factory-workers was very marked; primarily in the industrial regions of Moscow, St. Petersburg, Riga, Warsaw and Lodz. Mining and metallurgy had its heaviest concentration in the southern Ukraine. Baku had almost all the oil-workers.

The growth in industry and mining was particularly striking in the twenty years following 1895, even despite the upheaval of the 1905 Revolution. Only the oil industry of Baku, which had been the scene of particularly savage conflicts in 1905-6, showed no expansion in the following decade. The oil industry had developed very rapidly, with international capital and experts and with a minimum of state interference, ever since Nobel, a Swedish-Russian industrialist, began his activities in Baku in the late seventies. Russia became the largest oil producer in the world until about 1900, when the western American fields came into large-scale production and quickly left her far behind.

The textile industry remained concentrated between Moscow and the Volga, in and around St. Petersburg, and in Poland. It was very well equipped technically, and by 1914 was drawing well over a third of its raw-cotton supplies from home sources, the coarser brands of Central Asian cotton. By the time of the 1905 Revolution it was employing over 700,000 hands, not far short of half the total of those classed as factory-workers. Almost alone of the modernized, large-scale industries, it still worked primarily for the domestic consumer. But the very low effective demand of the bulk of the population had not risen proportionately with the increase in the productive capacity of the modernized mills. Hence, still as in the past, the export of cheap cotton goods to the Asiatic border countries was an important element in the profits of the big cotton firms. These were good allies of tsarist imperialism in the Middle and Far East, just as were the sugar magnates, who had built up the beet-sugar industry to a position of primary importance in Little Russia; an industry which provided the best illustration in Russia of the interlocking of state regulation with producers' cartels.

The most spectacular rise in output and capacity was that in the heavy industry. This was due to the development from almost nothing of the very rich iron-ore deposits of Krivoi Rog and coal deposits of the Donets basin (see map 1), which began in 1869 with the Welshman, John Hughes. (He gave his name, in russianized form, to the town where his works were started, Yuzovka: it is now the great city of Stalino.) The new South Russian mining and heavy industry swept ahead of the old metallurgical centers of the Urals, and by 1913 the South, with Kharkov as its chief industrial capital, was producing between sixty and seventy per cent of Russia's coal, coke, iron ore, pig-iron and steel (for the present position, see p. 224).

This modern metallurgical industry worked above all for railway equipment and armaments. Consumers' needs, for instance in agricultural machinery or corrugated iron, were largely met—in so far as they were met by all—by foreign imports. Similarly, the output of artificial manures was diminutive. The electrical and chemical industries were very weak, and Russia was also almost entirely dependent on imports for machine tools, the finer steels and precision instruments.

By 1917, and to a lesser extent by 1905, the high degree of concentration of industrial workers in large concerns and in certain regions had assisted the growth of an industrial proletariat and of revolutionary propaganda among them. The fact that St. Petersburg and Moscow, the two capitals, were also the two largest single industrial centers made them inevitably the foci of unrest. The actual numbers of industrial, mining or urban workers were still relatively very small, but they were increasing proportionately more rapidly than the peasants, and it was this fact that fortified the Bolsheviks in their concentration on the towns, the mills, the mines and the railways.

In 1863 in European Russia (excluding Poland, Finland and the Caucasus) out of an estimated population of 61,000,000 perhaps rather over 6,000,000 were living in towns; in 1897, 12,000,000 out of 94,000,000. In 1863 there were only three towns with a population of over 100,000, in 1897 there were fifteen.[1] By then St. Petersburg and Moscow were over a million, and they doubled within the next twenty years. By 1914 there were perhaps three million factory-workers, nearly a million miners and about eight hundred thousand railwaymen. This industrial section of the population was certainly extremely small in comparison with the peasantry. None the less it supplied the 1905 and 1917 revolutions with a determined "vanguard of the proletariat."

The relations of the industrial workers with the great mass of the population, the peasantry, were diverse and fluctuating. On the one hand, many of the works were not in towns, but in country districts at convenient points on rail-

[1] The corresponding approximate figures for the whole empire were 8,000,000 out of 76,000,000 in the sixties; 16,750,000 out of 129,000,000 in 1897; four towns with over a hundred thousand as contrasted with nineteen in 1897. The only official census taken for the empire was that of 1897. *Cf.* p. 375 for the figures for the Soviet Union.

ways or rivers. Here, and to a large extent in the mines, the men continued to have close ties with the peasantry, from which they were drawn. The same still held good of many of the unskilled workers in the towns. Fluidity of labor was very marked in pre-revolutionary, as in Soviet, Russia, and non-agricultural (as well as agricultural) seasonal labor was still regular among many of the peasantry. This linking up of town with country could help to disrupt the routine of isolation and to spread socialist ideas in the villages. But it also had the result that a large proportion of the industrial or semi-industrial workers did not constitute an urbanized proletariat, but remained strongly imbued with a peasant psychology, very difficult to organize, and the raw material for anarchic, sporadic risings rather than for co-ordinated revolutionary action.

On the other hand, already by 1905 a considerable section of the town-dwellers, especially the skilled workers, were divorced from ties with the village. A second, or even a third, generation of factory hands had grown up who were filled with contempt for the past, with its patriarchal habits and superstitious subservience, who were alien to the peasants, and who had an increasingly keen appreciation of the nature of the clash between their interests and those of the employers. The war of 1914 taught the all-too-few skilled munition workers a new consciousness of their key position.

For skilled and unskilled alike conditions of work and wages were deplorably low, though they varied widely. Housing conditions until about 1900 were almost incredibly bad, except in a few factories. There was then perhaps some improvement, but overcrowding in the big cities went from bad to worse during the war years of 1914-17, and the Soviet régime was faced with a gigantic task. Despite great efforts to inaugurate a new era in housing, the immense growth of cities during the last twenty years has heavily handicapped the supply of adequate accommodation.

Hours of work and workshop conditions (especially "truck" and fines) were virtually unregulated by legislation until the eighties, when a beginning was made with factory inspection and other reforms. A general eleven-and-a-half-hour working day for all factories and work-shops was not laid down until 1897, and even then overtime provisions and deficient inspection almost nullified the act. Nor was there any widespread system of collective agreements on wages and hours which could make up for legislation.

Trade unions were until 1906 subject to criminal law, except when they were insidiously encouraged by the authorities in the form of "police socialism." Even after the 1905 Revolution, strikes continued to be legally prohibited. Trade unionism, very weak before 1905, made some headway thereafter, but the unions were very small and very poor. As one union complained, "the membership . . . resembles rather a crowd of wandering gypsies than a properly organized body." During the war of 1914 they almost expired, or were snuffed out by the government. Only with the March Revolution could they develop freely and on a large scale.

Their checkered past and previous weakness had very important results for the future. Unlike the West the Russian workers had no tradition of solid, independent, self-reliant unionism. It had to be built up at intense speed (on industrial, not craft, lines) in the conditions of a revolution and with divergent views as to its function and working. While there was general agreement with Lenin that the trade unions were "the transmission belt between the Communist party and the masses," there was a long struggle as to what this should mean in practice. It was ended in 1928. Since then the trade unions have played indeed a very important rôle, but one that is fundamentally different from that of their namesakes in the West.

The weakness of working-class organization before the 1917 Revolution was not compensated for by the strength of the co-operative movement. This had grown widely and very rapidly, and it proved indispensable as a distributing agency during the war of 1914; but it was for the most part in the hands of the middle class and the better-off peasantry. After 1917 the co-operatives, somewhat like the trade unions, developed on a very large scale and for the next ten years were a vital element in distribution, but they became more and more closely controlled by the Communist party and eventually operated as species of state trading institutions, preserving the name of co-operatives, but differing in kind from those in Western countries.

Before the 1905 Revolution political parties could hardly operate legally, and after it working-class political activity was again almost entirely driven underground. Russia had always been unable to develop strong, voluntary or local associations such as have contributed so much to the making of most Western countries. In the generation before 1917 the upper and middle class were beginning to make such associations more effective (*cf.* p. 69), but the great mass of the working class and the peasantry had no regular organizations through which they could express and train themselves, except to some extent the commune. This helps to account for two great contrasted features of the 1917 Revolution—its uncanalized, anarchical, hydra-headed character, and, on the other hand, the ultimate victory of a numerically very small party, the Bolsheviks. The victory was possible because theirs was the only organization which succeeded in combining strict discipline, decisive action and mass appeal.

A further reason for the success of the Bolsheviks was the fact that they and some of the industrial workers had been steeled by the 1905 Revolution. The main constitutional and political results of 1905 have been set out earlier (pp. 59 ff.). Here certain other points require to be emphasized.

"The year of liberties" began with "Bloody Sunday" (22 January 1905) in St. Petersburg, when during a big strike mass columns of petitioners to the tsar were shot down in hundreds by the troops. There followed an outburst of strikes and protests from very varied classes all over the country. Throughout the year, which brought defeat in the unpopular war with Japan and culminated in revolution in its last three months, the weapon of the strike was used on a scale quite new to Russia. In all nearly 3,000,000 workers came out on strike in 1905, a figure then far exceeding that for any other country in a single year.

Strikes had been growing in the years before 1905, and in 1903 the first general strike had taken place in South Russia, led by the railwaymen and the skilled metal workers. Economic demands still predominated, but general political demands were beginning to be heard. In 1905 economic demands, which in many cases had to be met for the time being at least by the grant of the eight-hour day and better wages and conditions, were dwarfed by the political struggle; for a constitution and a parliament, for the franchise, for freedom of press, meeting, association and religion; but not for a republic. Clashes with the police and troops were frequent; large-scale outbreaks occurred in a number of towns, and in December 1905 the armed uprising in Moscow.

The workers' movement was uncoordinated and very weakly organized even locally in the soviets, which sprang up for the nonce in part as strike committees, in part as political bodies (*cf.* p. 54). But it was serious enough in itself, even if it had not been encouraged and supplemented by what has been called "the revolt of the cultural societies," by mutinies in the navy and the army, and by peasant uprisings (*cf.* p. 123). These last were even more elemental than the workers' struggle and they were not combined with it.

The professional classes and intelligentsia were stirred by "Bloody Sunday" and the series of defeats in the war against Japan to organize opposition to the authorities on a growing and a more and more defiant scale. In this they were at one with the more progressive among the provincial and district councils (*zemstva*) and the municipal councils. To extract their political demands they were prepared to use the weapon of the political strike. The combination, though it was not coalescence, of middle class, working class and peasantry in the general strike of October extorted from Nicholas II the October Manifesto, granting in principle a constitution and a parliament.

This proved the first turning-point of the 1905 Revolution. The liberals and middle class were now content to confine their energies to trying to secure the realization of the promises of the manifesto; above all through the Duma, which the Constitutional Democrats, under the leadership of Milyukov (1870-1943), aimed at developing more or less on Western, parliamentary lines.

The industrial workers, though they responded in very large numbers to a second general strike in December, were exhausted, leaderless and without strike funds. The government disbanded the St. Petersburg soviet without resistance, but in Moscow it took a week's street fighting to suppress armed insurrection. This was the second and final turning-point of the 1905 Revolution. The peasantry surged again into widespread upheavals in the summer of 1906, but they were scattered and unsupported, and repression was unsparing. During the Revolution some of the army was unreliable but enough had remained loyal; various concessions in pay had been made to it, and it was but little affected by specifically political agitation.

The government not only won through, but was capable of making a counter-offensive in the period of reaction which followed 1907; yet it was shaken, and hampered by the results of the October Manifesto. Although the old traditional attitude to the tsar as "the little father" was still widespread, tsarism as a system of government was under challenge. The economic transformation of Russia during the previous half-century necessitated sweeping changes in the institutions and methods of government; yet most, though not all, of the bureaucracy clung to the old ways or buried its head in the sand. The authorities were not prepared to use the Duma and the *zemstva*, freedom of the press and association, in such a way as to win back to them the bulk of the liberal, professional section of the educated minority (*cf.* pp. 314-315).

The third, and much the smallest, section of the educated minority, the revolutionaries and the class-conscious among the industrial workers, were still further embittered against the authorities, while they deeply distrusted or were strongly antagonistic to the liberal section. They had indeed made some gains, but they had suffered much in the Revolution. They were becoming more imbued with Western, socialist ideas. They were far removed from the peasantry, but not so far as either of the other two sections of the educated minority. As the years 1910 to 1914 showed, when there was a great increase of strikes, and notably of sympathetic strikes, they were becoming both more conscious of their strength and more violently resentful of repression. A storm of protest, not from the workers only, followed the ghastly shootings in the far distant Lena goldfields, when a strike, which was in essentials purely economic, ended with a casualty list of over five hundred (1912).

The summer of 1914 saw continued strikes, especially in St. Petersburg, where barricades were beginning to appear. Then in August the outbreak of war rallied, for the time being, almost all the workers to the patriotic front. Thanks to the economic westernization that had transformed Russia since the Crimean War and to the fact that she had her western allies, the national spirit and the hardihood and courage of the Russian people had sufficient material and technical backing, despite much inefficiency and gross blundering, to stand the strain for two-and-a-half years of war on the all-inclusive, modern scale against Germany, Austria-Hungary and Turkey combined. Then the strain proved too great. The army had won great victories against the Austro-Hungarians and the Turks, but had suffered heavy defeats at the hands of the Germans. The lack of adequate political and administrative reforms and of any leadership from the government accentuated divisions, multiplied disorganization, and ultimately destroyed all confidence.

By the beginning of 1917 it was agreed on all hands that a crisis had been reached. "The consequence of this, in my opinion, will be revolution and a state of anarchy which no one will be able to control." The opinion was not that of one of the left or the liberal opposition, but of the stout-hearted, patriot conservative president of the Duma, expressed in his final audience when the tsar persisted in refusing to listen to any sane advice.

4. *The Soviet Revolution in Industry*

The Revolution of March 1917, in the midst of war, opened the sluice-gates of liberty: freedom to say and write anything and everything, to form committees on anything and everything, to work or not to work; soon also freedom to take the land, take the factories, go home, stop fighting. This new, intoxicating liberty became anarchy; authority was more and more repudiated unless it claimed to be exercised in the name of the "workers, peasants, soldiers and sailors," and frequently even when it did so claim.

From the first there was a "two-headed rule," the Provisional Government and the Petrograd Soviet (*cf.* pp. 54-55), radiating out in rivalry from the capital far away in its Baltic corner. Broadly speaking, the former stood for Western democracy of a liberal or moderate socialist coloring, the Soviet for a full swing to the left, to the unknown. But for the mass of the people both were almost equally the unknown. The appeal of the extremists, divided though they were, came to be far stronger than that of the moderates, because it encouraged direct and immediate action, especially in regard to peace and the land.

In July 1917 the Provisional Government was challenged by an unorganized uprising in Petrograd which was a portent of the currents sweeping leftward. These were accelerated in the following months by the fears aroused by the commander-in-chief at the front, General Kornilov, who was, in his own words, "combating implacably anarchy in the army" and demanding "without any delay" appropriate measures in the rear. Kerensky, the golden-tongued pro-Ally, socialist lawyer, since July the head of the Provisional Government, was determined to prevent a "military dictatorship," but quite unable to stem the tide running towards the Soviets. By the autumn Lenin judged the tide sufficiently strong for the Bolsheviks to make an end of "the bourgeois-democratic revolution" and inaugurate the Soviet Revolution. In November, after brief but fierce fighting, they overthrew the Provisional Government and assumed power in the name of the Soviets. Moscow followed suit almost immediately, and nearly all the main centers of Russia.

For the next six months "chaos and enthusiasm reigned," as Lenin summed up this period of the Revolution; "when the peace of Brest-Litovsk was forced upon us because we were powerless in all fields"; when the Bolshevik government poured out a flood of decrees—propaganda signposts and general directives rather than legislation, which were intended to give the uneducated masses political ideas and to be applied in concrete actuality as and how the workers and peasants decided for themselves. The extension of workers' control and committee management intensified the drop in production and the chaos in distribution. Admittedly, according to Lenin, the Bolsheviks expropriated more than they knew how to cope with; but how actually to run heavy industry and the railways (which had been nationalized), how to administer industry or to work the banks could not be neatly formulated in advance, but only painfully evolved by trial and error from the experience of the masses.

Inevitably the industrial and economic life of the country sagged precipitately. The war had strained it to the uttermost by March 1917, particularly in transport, though as regards munitions Allied supplies had helped to place Russia in a better position than previously. The effects of "living on capital" and other consequences of two-and-a-half years of war were telling cumulatively, and to these were now added the disorganizing and anarchic influences that were spreading apace after March.

After November the pace of economic collapse became dizzy and desperate. The German occupation of the Ukraine deprived the central provinces of much fuel and grain. The rich Don Cossack country became the first center for the White anti-Bolshevik forces, eventually led by General Denikin. With the encouragement of the Allies other White forces gathered in the Far North, in the East and in Siberia, eventually led by Admiral Kolchak (*cf.* p. 296). The victory of the Allies over Germany increased the weight of Allied intervention in support of the Whites. After three-and-a-half years of war with Germany and her allies Russia was engulfed in two to three years of savage civil war.

Soviet Russia was cut off from the outside world. The rouble was demonetized. Internal trade shrank to local dimensions, mainly of a barter character. Supplies for the towns, even of bare essentials, were precarious in the extreme. Agriculture was producing perhaps half as much as in 1914, and little was coming on to the town markets. Industry was almost at a standstill; much equipment was destroyed; more was terribly run down. Rail transport sank to its nadir early in 1920: river transport was in an even worse plight. It was a guerrilla struggle on all fronts, the economic and the political, as well as on the actual battlefields of the Civil War. And in 1921 the final calamity of the great famine, far worse than any since that of 1891, capped the ravages of war and revolution.

The Civil War was the period of "war communism" (1918-20). It was based upon the attempt to create a moneyless system of state barter. It had grown out of the terror, made necessary according to the Communist view by the acute danger from the counter-revolutionaries thanks to Allied support of them. It meant in practice dictatorial militarization wherever possible, forced requisitions from the peasantry, and concentration of such industry and transport as remained working and in Bolshevik hands on the overriding task of winning the Civil War. Everything—and there was little enough of anything—must go to the new Red Army. The mass of the peasantry proved to be more hostile to the Whites than to the Reds, and the Whites were finally crushed; but by the end of the Civil War the tension between town and country, between the inert peasant millions and the proletarian shock brigades, had reached breaking point. In March 1921 even the Kronstadt sailors, once the Red core of the Baltic fleet and Petrograd, by then much diluted by newly enrolled peasant lads, rebelled against the Communist "dictatorship of the proletariat." Immediately after, the long discussions within the Communist party on the transition from war to peace were clinched by the adoption of the New Economic Policy (*cf.* pp. 119-120).

Lenin stated the position with his usual frankness. The central fact is "the relationship between the working class and the peasantry . . . the struggle or the agreement between which will decide the fate of our whole revolution. . . . The interests of [the two] classes are different; the small farmer does not want what the worker wants. We know that only through an understanding with the peasantry can the socialist revolution in Russia be saved, until revolution has broken out in other countries. . . . We must satisfy the middle peasantry economically and return to the free market; otherwise, with the retardation of the international revolution, it is impossible to maintain the power of the proletariat in Russia."

"A whole series of special transitional measures" were therefore necessary, in the shape of the New Economic Policy. It meant a retreat, if only temporary, and a "second breathing space"; the treaty of Brest-Litovsk imposed by the Germans in March 1918 had been styled the first. The state retained "the commanding heights," *i.e.* the nationalized banks, heavy industry, transport and foreign trade; but the peasantry and the small middleman were given internal freedom of trade, and a considerable range of private initiative and independence was allowed in agriculture, small-scale industry, and distribution.

From the lowermost depths of 1920-21 Soviet Russia during the next seven to eight years struggled back to approximately the 1914 level of production in most branches, though quality was extremely poor. The overwhelming bulk of the industrial output was coming from the big socialized undertakings, which had been repaired and extended; but it had not yet been possible to undertake much new construction. This surprisingly rapid recovery was due to a variety of reasons, apart from the restoration of agriculture.

(1) It was above all due to the resilience and vitality of a tough, enduring people, accustomed in general to a very low standard of living, habituated to meeting great calamities

with a mixture of massive fatalism and outbursts of intense energy.

(2) It was assisted by the great variety of the very rich natural resources of the Soviet Union, which by 1922 included, except in the West, the same vast area as the Russian empire. These resources, in contrast with the ruined or much depreciated capital equipment, were unexhausted or scarcely tapped and could quickly be again harnessed, given a restoration of equipment, technical skill, and organization.

(3) The leadership of the Communist party infused a sufficiency of faith in a new order to be built up on a reconstructed and transformed economy through a new discipline and a new education, for men and women alike, which put the utmost emphasis on the conquest of the material world by the extension of the technical triumphs of Western twentieth-century science.

(4) There were just enough specialists available (almost all of them non-Communists) for the reconstruction of industry and transport and for the training of the Soviet specialists who were to replace them. Lenin had always preached the necessity of learning from "bourgeois civilization," of taking over its material achievements and scientific (and artistic) heritage and transforming them to the needs of socialist society. But the war and the civil war left them in a ruinous condition, and the whole revolutionary ethos, with its violent iconoclasm and pitiless animosity against anything "bourgeois," made the task of reconstruction tragically difficult, since it had to be done with the help of a suspect and outcast technical class.

(5) Foreign aid in various forms made an important contribution. Foreign specialists, mainly German and American, did much work of value. The political hostility of the West made heavy financial borrowing impossible, even had not the majority of the Communist party been emphatically against any return towards what had been denounced as the tsarist enslavement of Russia to Western finance capitalism. None the less, bitter necessity compelled the seeking of some foreign advances, mostly short-term credits. This was essential

in the re-equipment of industry and the restoration, on a small scale, of foreign trade. Actual concessions to foreign concerns were also resorted to, but they did not bulk heavily and eventually disappeared as they became more and more hedged about with restrictions.

(6) Slowly, with the pains of travail, amid the clash of rival groups, a central governmental apparatus was being built up which succeeded in working out and operating better the various controls instituted by the party and the growing bureaucracy. These controls, from 1924, aimed especially at a continuous price reduction and a planned increase of output. In that year the establishment of a new currency was accomplished, after astronomic inflation and the "scissors" crisis, caused by the price gap between manufactured goods and food products. Attempts to centralize both the direction of economic policy and the administrative operation of trade and industry were abandoned, and the latter was in the main decentralized. Committee management of factories fell from favor. Labor discipline began to improve. "Workers' control of industry" was gradually changed from an obstructive brake to a means of increasing production. Finally, the Union constitution, adopted in 1923, went a long way towards centralizing in Moscow the direction and pace of economic rehabilitation.

The restoration of production under the N.E.P. approximately to the 1914 level (and in some branches above it) was a remarkable achievement, belying the hostile prognostications of most outside observers. The N.E.P. had indeed provided the basis for at least a temporary accommodation between town and country and for an all-round revival. But this revival in many ways sharpened the antinomy inherent between socialized industry and uncontrolled, individualistic agriculture. At the same time, by 1927 reconstruction had reached a point from which it seemed possible to proceed to what had always been the gospel of Lenin—a gigantic program of electrification and industrial expansion.

The struggles for power within the party since the death of Lenin in 1924 and the acute divisions as to how the peasantry were to be treated and how industrial expansion was actually to be carried out led to the final crisis over the N.E.P. in 1927 (*cf.* pp. 52 and 119-120). It ended with the victory of Stalin over Trotsky and other opponents and the adoption in 1929 of the policy of the first five-year plan. The triple aim was to solve the divorce between workers and peasantry by collectivization of agriculture, to expand industry to the utmost, and to render the Union safe against external attack.

This was the key turning-point, which inaugurated the Second, Stalinist Revolution, second only in import to November 1917 and victory in the Civil War.[1]

Certain results of this Soviet revolution in industry can be seen from a bare table of output figures (unless otherwise stated, units are millions of tons): [2]

	1913	1929	1938	1940
Coal	29.1	40.1	132.9	164.6
Iron ore	9.0	8.0	26.5	..
Pig-iron	4.2	4.0	14.6	14.9
Steel	3.6	4.9	18.0	18.4
Oil	9.0	13.8	32.2	34.2
Sugar	1.3	1.3	2.5	..
Cotton textiles (millions of meters)	2,227	3,068	3,491	..
Woolen textiles (millions of meters)	103.0	100.6	114.0	..
Copper (thousands of tons)	33.2	35.5	103.2	..
Manganese ore	1.2	1.4	2.3	..
Cement	1.5	2.2	5.7	..
Electric power (billion kw.)	1.9	6.2	39.6	40.8
Chemicals (1926–27 roubles; in millions)	450	619	6,715	..
Agricultural machinery (1926–27 roubles; in millions)	55	196	1,617	..
Machines and metal industry (1926–27 roubles; in millions)	1,446	3,349	33,613	48.4

[1] For collectivization, the Soviet revolution in agriculture, see pp. 114-121.
[2] The figures for 1940 are approximate; those for 1938 preliminary. Those for 1913 differ from those given on pp. 351-352, which refer to the whole Russian empire, since the figures given here refer only to that portion of the empire which forms part of the U.S.S.R.

These figures give a fair indication of the immense industrial expansion under the three five-year plans, with the significant exception of the three classes of consumers' goods included, cottons, woolens and sugar. By 1937 the U.S.S.R. was the largest producer in the world of agricultural machinery, notably combine-harvesters.[1] She was second only to the United States in machine-building, tractors and lorries. Remember also that she was the largest world producer of wheat, rye, barley, oats, potatoes, flax and beet-sugar, and a close third to India in cotton. The carrying out of the gigantic output plans, although the goals set were not reached in very many cases, was all the more impressive in that the rest of the world in the early thirties was plunged in the most severe economic depression of modern times and in mass unemployment.

The years of the first five-year plan (1928-32) were grim beyond grim, harrowing and frantic in human energy and suffering, in resistance and repression. In the course of the second five-year plan (1933-37) conditions eased somewhat: there was more to eat, something to buy. In 1935 rationing of food and other goods, which had had to be introduced, could be abolished. Collectivization and the great program of new works were showing results. The new economic order was settling into shape, even though the political situation was tense with mass party purges and the sensational trials and executions of "Old Bolshevik" leaders and Red Army generals. The third five-year plan, from 1938, brought a tightening of the strain as more and more was sacrificed to defense measures. After September 1939 and the war with Finland nothing was spared in mobilizing all resources to confront whatever the Second World War might bring.

One glimpse, typical of much though not of all, may be taken of the sacrifices demanded, the toil imposed, of what planning the Soviet revolution in industry meant for the human beings "planned." "This was the Magnitogorsk of 1933. A quarter of a million souls—Communists, Kulaks,

[1] Pre-revolutionary Russia had not manufactured any of these, nor any aluminum, of which the U.S.S.R. was the third-largest producer in 1937.

foreigners, Tatars, convicted saboteurs and a mass of blue-eyed Russian peasants—building the biggest steel combinat in Europe in the middle of the barren Ural steppe. . . . Men froze, hungered and suffered, but the construction work went on with a disregard for individuals and a mass heroism seldom paralleled in history." [1]

The outstanding achievements that have been won by the sweat and blood, the enthusiasm and the anguish of the Soviet peoples have been due to many causes. Two primary reasons are the variety and magnitude of the natural resources of the U.S.S.R. and the imposed system of applying human resources to these natural resources, *i.e.* totalitarian, economic planning.

In the socialist Soviet state planning has come to occupy the central position. It means that the state draws up integrated output plans for the national economy; that it directs or controls almost all production, including agriculture, all transport and foreign trade, all banks and currency; that it decides all questions of investment and credit, and hence of reconstruction and new construction; that it controls and fixes wholesale prices and to a large extent retail prices.

Planning in the U.S.S.R. did not begin *ab initio* with the first five-year plan, nor on the other hand was it a fully worked-out mechanism by then. It has been the result of growth and experimentation both before and after its full-scale, official adoption in 1929. Large-scale industrialization and planning were for Lenin central features in communism. As early as 1920 an initial step had been taken in his electrification program, out of which next year the State Planning Commission was born. Under the conditions of the New Economic Policy this could only remain a very small and secondary advisory body, entirely subordinated to the Council of Labor and Defense. None the less it gradually extended its activities and began to draw up provisional outline plans on an annual basis. By 1927, when the question of unified planning had come to the front in the bitter party struggles

---
[1] John Scott, *Behind the Urals* (1942), an excellent account of Magnitogorsk by an American working there for five years.

over the future of the N.E.P., there was the experience of several years' tentative economic and regional planning to draw upon, and the State Planning Commission was toiling at a "Five-Year Plan for the Development of the National Economy." This was the basis for the five-year-plan as officially adopted in 1929.

Thereafter the machinery of planning has been greatly extended and constantly modified, but the State Planning Commission, working under the dominating control of the Politbureau, is the central hub. It has developed into an immense apparatus, both at the center and in the constituent republics, just as have the commissariats, upon which, together with the central and local party committees, the actual carrying out of the plan in the main depends.

The difficulty of combining sufficient, but not overgreat, rigidity with the requisite elasticity in detailed execution and control is admittedly very great. The centralized direction of industry, transport and agriculture has been repeatedly modified by new organs of administration and methods of direction. Thus, a very marked feature in the late thirties was the subdivision of the over-weighted commissariats and the introduction of a greater degree of decentralization. Even so, the prevalence of the bureaucratic spirit has been the object of ceaseless attack, in particular the disproportionately large administrative staffs in comparison with the numbers directly engaged in production.

Parallel with the work of preparation, co-ordination and administration, there has been continuous development in the machinery of control, in enforcing the instructions of the central authorities and in accounting for and economizing money and materials. In the early days the task of securing effective control over what had been socialized was devolved upon the Commissariat of Workers' and Peasants' Inspection. To this body were given the combined duties of keeping the government in touch with the rank and file of the workers, of combating opposition and sabotage, and of controlling the execution of the government's economic and labor instructions. Lenin attached extreme importance to the Commissariat, and in 1922 Stalin took charge of it for a time. In conjunction with the Central Control Commission of the Party, it was one of the chief means of his ultimate ascendancy. With the changed political conditions after the first five-year plan and the crisis of collectivization, a big reorganization was made and the Commission (since 1940 the Commissariat) of Soviet Control was set up. This was less closely identified with the party machinery and more purely concerned with financial and economic accountancy, for which purposes it was later given wide executive, as well as inspection, powers.

This outline of the growth of planning machinery may serve to bring out that Soviet planning is not a rigid mechanism or schedule, but a constantly adjusted effort to coordinate perspectives or estimates and operational programs, with constantly altered organs and methods. It has been to a large extent a gigantic experimentation in trial and error, though it is of course maintained that there is far less avoidable trial and error after productive commitments have been incurred than in non-socialist countries. Natural conditions, human mistakes or malpractices, political decisions and international reactions make it inevitable that the plans are subject to perpetual alteration in detail and also to major changes. For instance, even apart from the recasting of the third five-year plan as a result of the outbreak of war in September 1939, the great slump in agricultural prices caused by the world economic crisis that started in 1929 compelled the Soviet government to export far larger quantities of agricultural produce than allowed for in the first five-year plan, in order to meet its very large capital equipment imports.

Certain other features connected with the five-year plans help to show how the Soviet Union has been transformed in the last fifteen years.

The fundamental aim has been to end the backwardness of Russia, the low productivity of her labor and hence the low level of her consumption. The Soviet peoples have been continuously urged on to make up the leeway between the Union and the West. The slogan "to overtake and to surpass" the production of the foremost industrial states in the world has been dinned into their ears. The advances in production have been most impressive, as the figures already given indicate, and the rate of increase in most branches of industry has been out of all comparison with that in any other major country.

Nevertheless, the Soviet leaders have insistently pointed out that even in heavy industry, fuel and power, fields in which advance has been specially striking, the U.S.S.R. was well behind Germany and far out-distanced by the United States. The following table illustrates the relative Soviet position on the eve of the Second World War (*cf.* the table on pp. 351-352 for the relative position on the eve of the First World War, when Russia was larger than the U.S.S.R. and Germany included Alsace-Lorraine, though not Austria, which was however her ally):[1]

	Pig-iron	Steel	Coal	Electric Power
	In millions of tons			Millions of kilowatts
U.S.S.R.	14.9	18.4	164.6	39,600
U.S.A.	31.9	47.2	395	115,900
Great Britain	6.7	10.3	227	30,700
Germany	18.3	22.7	186[2]	55,200
France	6.0	6.1	45.5	19,300

Apart from such absolute figures, even stronger emphasis has been repeatedly laid by Soviet leaders on the lowness of Soviet productivity and *per capita* output in comparison with the West. By the time war came, very heavy leeway remained to be made good, and still more so in consumers' goods. There seems no doubt, too, that (apart from military equipment) the quality of goods produced, though it had improved, was still far lower than in the West.

The satisfaction of individual consumers' demands has

[1] The figures for electric power, which are given in millions of kilowatts, are for 1938. The other figures are for 1940, approximate, for U.S.S.R.; 1939 for U.S.A.; and 1938 for the other countries. Germany includes Austria. Actual production is of course not necessarily equivalent to productive capacity, a point of special importance in the U.S.A.

[2] Plus 198,000,000 tons of lignite.

been very much in the background, owing to the fact that in all three plans (though to a lesser extent in the second) exceptional emphasis was placed on capital goods. As a result the planned satisfaction of demand for consumers' goods has not yet emerged as a fundamental difficulty in Soviet planning, since on the whole consumers' demands have been limited to basic necessities. The first great essential has been to plan for a supply of these. Ever since 1928 the Soviet Union has been living under conditions equivalent or approximating to those of "war economy." Hence questions of taste and quality become of relatively little consequence, provided that a certain standard in nutrition and warmth can be maintained.

The profit incentive as a regulator of investment and production is, in contrast with the West, entirely absent. On the other hand, in reaction against the equalitarian conceptions and practices of the early years of the Revolution, the incentive to earn higher wages is explicitly emphasized as a most important factor in increasing and improving production. As a consequence, there has been a wide extension of piece rates, overtime rates, and all kinds of bonuses on outputs above a certain norm. The immense development since 1935 of the Stakhanovite movement and various other methods of increasing productivity of labor (in agriculture and transport as well as in industry) has been closely linked up with the money incentive, and there has grown up a very marked differentiation in reward between the directing, managerial and specialist staffs and the less skilled, and still more between them and the unskilled. However wide the differences in individual earnings, it remains true, however, that all earnings, with insignificant exceptions, are work incomes, and that the differences do not affect either the scale or the direction of investment and production.

One outstanding fact in the building of "socialism in one country" is that it has been carried on without recourse to long-term foreign loans. This is in complete contrast with the economic westernization of Russia between 1861 and 1914. The investment plan of the first five-year plan amounted to perhaps a quarter of the national income; a proportion which has been estimated to be two-and-a-half times greater than that of pre-1914 Russia and nearly twice that of pre-1914 Britain. The mobilization of such an enormous amount of internal capital was only possible through the harshest regimentation, much use of forced labor, and a considerable, in some cases a great, drop in an already low standard of living. The second five-year plan provided for a somewhat smaller proportion of capital investment, and living conditions eased noticeably; but the third five-year plan aimed even higher than the first, and with the outbreak of war the burden was yet further increased, until by 1940-41 approximately forty-five per cent of the national income, according to one calculation, was swallowed up in investment and defense.

On the other hand, the tempo of the Soviet revolution in industry was only possible with the assistance of imports from the West, both of goods and of technical skill. The first five-year plan provided for a very large expansion in foreign trade, above all in imports of agricultural machinery, engineering equipment and machine tools. They were financed by short-term foreign credits and by a forcing of exports, principally oil, grain, furs and timber. The second and third five-year plans relied on imports of capital construction and scarcity goods to a much smaller extent, and Soviet foreign trade declined heavily and almost continuously from its peak in 1931-32.

Foreign technical aid also was an indispensable element in the extraordinarily rapid expansion and transformation of Soviet industry. In addition to some training of Soviet technicians abroad, foreign specialists were enlisted in considerable numbers, especially Americans in the giant new construction works. There was, however, no return to the limited concessions policy of the N.E.P. period, and there was no financial or operational control by foreign firms of works equipped with their most up-to-date machinery.

At the same time, Soviet mastery of twentieth-century science was not to be dependent upon foreigners, but to be secured by the training of a new generation of scientists, technical experts, and skilled workers. In the past lack of specialist and skilled labor in Russia had been the greatest single obstacle to quality and high output and maintenance. The Soviet régime has made sustained efforts to make good this weakness by its enormously expanded educational system. Much has been done, though the weakness has been far from overcome. By 1940 the supply of "white-collar" specialists may perhaps have been adequate in numbers, if not in quality, but the demand for skilled and semi-skilled labor was still so large that a labor recruitment plan was put into operation which involved the training of 800,000 to 1,000,000 youths a year in industrial and constructional work.

The revolution in industry has not only done much to transform the technical level of labor; it has, designedly, involved a great transference from agriculture and great shifts in population. A comparison between the 1939 and 1926 censuses shows (*cf.* p. 354):

	1939	1926
Total population	170,500,000	147,000,000
Urban	55,900,000	26,300,000
	(32.8 %)	(17.9 %)
Rural	114,500,000	120,700,000
	(67.2 %)	(82.1 %)

Thus while the rural population decreased by six millions, the urban more than doubled. There were in 1939 eighty-one towns with over a hundred thousand inhabitants (compared with fifteen in the same area of the Russian empire forty years before), and these included nearly three-fifths of the urban population.[1] Some of the new up-growths were still only in the stage of camp-cities, and a very high proportion of those who were classed as urban were living under material and psychological conditions very different from the city populations of the Western world. None the less the changes in concentration and grouping that have occurred as a result

[1] A rather larger proportion than that in the United States, where there were (1940) ninety-two cities of 100,000 and over, compared with (1939) sixty-three in Great Britain and Northern Ireland, and sixty-one in Germany (including Austria).

of the five-year plans have already made new patterns in Soviet life, especially in the Volga-Urals region and Soviet Asia, where the non-Russian peoples have been propelled with uprooting rapidity into a new era of history. War with its all-devouring demands has cut across these patterns, but in certain respects it has but given them fuller shape, notably as regards industrialization in Soviet Asia and the eastward trend of population.

These last two demographic changes are largely a consequence of the altered location of industry, which has been increasingly marked in the last ten years. The vast sums expended by the government on geological research have been followed by the rapid development of the very great mineral wealth of the Urals, the Altai, the Baikal region and Kazakhstan (see map 2). The Urals and the Altai have returned, on a far larger scale, to their earlier mining and industrial importance in Russian history. The Kuznetsk basin, the great new coal and iron center in Central Siberia, was producing in 1929 7.5 per cent of Union coal, in 1940 approximately 15 per cent; in 1929 no pig-iron or steel, in 1940 round about 10 per cent of the Union output. For the first time Kazakhstan and, still more recently, Central Asia are being transformed by coal, copper and other metals, by oil, by textile, chemical and other industries. For the first time the Far East and the Far North have begun to be developed along new lines, not solely for gold, timber, or fish.

The altered location of industry has been powerfully influenced by defense considerations, especially since 1937, but it was primarily governed by the existence of great natural resources far away in the interior of the country. And, from the first, Soviet planning aimed at regional diversification of economy and at the cutting down of the immense cross-hauls that still so greatly impede much of Soviet industry, despite the very marked improvements in railway (and to a much lesser extent water) transport that have taken place since 1935.

The spectacular achievements to the east of the Volga did not mean a shift of industry that spelled any absolute decline in the old industrial districts. On the contrary, the five-year plans provided for a very large increase in their output. What has declined has been, in most branches, the relative share of the old centers in total Union production. Even so, that share remained very large. The Caucasus and the Ukraine were still, as before 1914, far the largest producers of oil and manganese, coal, iron and steel (*cf.* pp. 224 and 354). The essential importance of the Ukraine and the Moscow and Leningrad regions, *e.g.* for coal, iron ore and steel, textiles, engineering and machine industry, aluminum, cement and sugar-beet, has been tragically experienced by the loss or wrecking of so much western territory since June 1941.

On the industrial front, the terrible storms of the war have so far been weathered owing to the evacuation eastward of much plant and skilled labor, to Allied shipments of supplies, and above all to the heroism and stamina of the Red Army and the Soviet peoples. The combined effects of these three factors have enabled the newer, eastern industries to expand enormously. That they were in a position to do so was due to the policy pursued in the ten years before 1941, but they were not by then a substitute for the Ukraine, Moscow and Leningrad.

Another feature of the second and third five-year plans that has proved of the utmost importance during the war is the increasing tendency towards autarky. This has been lauded by Soviet leaders since 1932 as necessary on grounds of defense, but not with the express object of cutting off the U.S.S.R. from foreign countries. The result has been that the very heavy dependence of pre-1917 Russia upon the outside world for finished goods, much raw material (*e.g.* rubber, non-ferrous metals, colonial goods) and shipping had disappeared by 1940.

Along with the great expansion of industries already existent before 1917, there has been an even greater expansion in the output of what previously had not been produced at all or only in very small quantities. Ten new branches of industry of major importance have been built up with such ruthless energy that by 1940 they were supplying the bulk, in some cases the whole, of Soviet consumption: rubber (mainly synthetic), chemicals, artificial manures, agricultural machinery, lorries and automobiles, electrical equipment, precision instruments, machine tools, aluminum, non-ferrous metals. In addition, the Red Army was self-sufficient in aircraft, tanks, guns and munitions.

It is true that there were dangerous bottle-necks and that Soviet industry was still dependent in 1940 on certain vital imports, but for the most part in small amounts and to a lesser degree than the industry of any other country. It was specially significant that the concentration on machine tools and machinery, fostered by systematic encouragement of inventions, was diminishing dependence on foreign imports and technical assistance in the replacement or extension of high-grade equipment.

Finally, the overriding feature of Soviet planning and the revolution in industry has come to be, not merely the predominant emphasis given to heavy industry and capital goods as against consumers' goods, but the pre-occupation with defense needs. This was much less true of the first period of total planning. In 1933, according to official announcements, direct budget allocations to defense amounted to little more than four per cent (1.4 milliard roubles) of the total expenditure. The change by 1939 was staggering; over a quarter (almost forty-one milliards) of total expenditure was being spent on defense; in 1940 nearly one-third, fifty-seven billions. These figures are yet more weighty when it is remembered that the national budget is far more extensive than that of Western countries, including as it does the great bulk of capital investment; and further that a large proportion of that investment, which is not included under the budget heading of defense, was directly and indirectly being employed for military and naval requirements.

"Socialism in one country" was to be built up by total planning, but in a world of "capitalist encirclement," a world that after Hitler's advent to power in 1933 and his alliance with Italy and Japan was more and more threatening to the safety of the U.S.S.R. To be secure she must match power with power and shape her planning accordingly. The Soviet Union, like the Russian empire, covered one-sixth of the land surface of the globe, comprised, after China and India, the largest aggregation of people in any one state, and contained a richness and variety of resources unsurpassed by any other country. The First World War, the Revolution and the Civil War brought Russia very low, but it did not cripple her vitality. What grew out of the October Revolution laid the basis for the Second, Stalinist Revolution which in the last fifteen years has converted the Union into a great power, in many quarters only too tardily regarded as such, but proved in the last two years to be without question one of the deciding forces in the world. Just as for two centuries before 1917 Russia ranked as one of the great powers, so the Soviet Union has resumed her place, on a far stronger foundation though now so sorely beset.

5. *Russia and the Powers*

From 1700 to 1917 Russia had a hand in all the major European questions that divided the powers, except the Spanish Succession War and the partition of Africa. As often as not she was one of the decisive factors in them. History would have been unrecognizably different had Russia played no part in the Turkish, Polish and Baltic questions, in the Seven Years' War, in the struggle against Napoleon, in the 1848-9 revolutions, in the Far East, in the First World War. By the end of the eighteenth century Russia loomed ponderously, in size and numbers; "a kingdom, almost unknown in Europe during the last century and gradually aggrandized at the expense of all her neighbors, . . . has menaced for forty years the political balance of power. . . . This vast empire . . . embraces all varieties of climate, and comprehends every species of resource. . . . Solitary resistance is vain against an empire which can produce soldiers like grains of sand...."[1] Russian manpower, though sometimes exaggerated in the West, for the last two centuries has bulked more and more impressively. Look at the relative population figures of the principal states, even though they are but dubious estimates for the earlier years and are no guidance to density, economic potential, or organized power.[2]

In Millions

	1700 c.	1800 c.	1871 c.	1914 c.	1939 c.
Russia	13 (1725)	36	87	174	170
France	19	27.5	36	41	42
Austria	10	20	33	50	..
Prussia	2	9	41	67	72
Poland	11.5 (1760)	..	..	..	35
Italy	..	..	27	36	45
Great Britain and Ireland	7.5	16	32	46	47
United States	[260,000]	5	38.5	98	131
Japan	..	..	33	54	73

This table, for all its uncertainties and deficiencies, brings out two broad facts:

(i) Prior to about the end of the eighteenth century Russia did not have far the largest population of any European state. Behind the Great Northern War the darkness thickens. Such evidence as there is

[1] *The Danger of the Political Balance of Europe*, attributed to Gustavus III of Sweden (London, 1790). The original, in French, was published in the same year in Stockholm.

[2] Except in the case of the thirteen American colonies in 1700, the figures are for states, and the extent of the states (except Japan) differs at the different dates; thus, *e.g.*, conquest and acquisition enormously enlarged Russia between 1725 and 1871 and the U.S.A. between 1800 and 1871, and Prussia from 1871 is Germany. The 1939 figure for Russia is that of the Soviet census, covering a smaller area than the Russian Empire. France is the 1789 France except in 1871 and 1914 when it excludes Alsace-Lorraine. Austria in 1871 and 1914 means Austria-Hungary, in 1700 and 1800 the Austrian dominions excluding territory in Germany, the Low Countries and Italy. Prussia from 1871 is Germany; the figure for 1939 includes Austria, but not any of Czechoslovakia. The area of 1939 Poland was much smaller than that of pre-partition Poland. Eire is excluded in the British 1939 figure. The Japanese figures are for Japan proper, excluding her empire.

indicates that the population of Muscovy after the Time of Troubles (1604-13) increased steadily, whereas between 1570 and 1620 it had very likely dropped. But until the later seventeenth century she was almost certainly weaker in manpower than Poland-Lithuania. Only then did the defection of much of the Ukraine and the probable natural increase in Muscovy proper begin to turn the scale in her favor.

(ii) Since the French Revolution conquest, acquisition and natural increase have resulted in a phenomenal rise in the population of the Russian empire; on a scale surpassed (apart perhaps from India and China) only by the United States, where very large immigration has to be added to the above three factors. In mere numbers Russia already by 1871 was more than twice as big as any single European state. On the other hand, thanks to the attainment of German unity there was between 1800 and 1914 an even larger relative increase in the subjects of the Hohenzollerns than in those of the Romanovs.

Absolute numbers can mean little. Russian manpower was too often terribly offset by inability to utilize it, by lack of organization and modern training, equipment and communications, by very grave social and economic disharmonies. The new world born out of the industrial revolution and modern science told against Russia, as the Crimean War gave ample proof. The next two generations saw rapid and profound changes, not merely in the economic and military spheres. Yet still by 1914, in comparison with the all-round development of the West, the Russian numerical superiority was heavily counterbalanced by her general qualitative inferiority.

The full recognition of Russia as a great power dates from the Seven Years' War. For thirty years after the death of Peter the Great (1725) disputed successions and rival court camarillas gave ample opportunity for foreign diplomacy to mitigate the effectiveness of Russian action abroad. None the less Russia was the deciding power in the War of the Polish Succession (1733-5), when she defeated the French candidate for the throne and installed Augustus III of Saxony in Warsaw. In 1735 a Russian corps appeared for the first time on the Rhine; in 1747-8 for the second time: they did no fighting, but they were a portent.

Russia had not intervened earlier in the wars of the Austrian Succession (1740-42), despite her guarantee of the Pragmatic Sanction. French diplomacy was responsible. France had added to her long established policy of using Turkey, Poland and Sweden against the Habsburgs the policy of using them also against Russia, since 1726 in regular alliance with Austria. She scored one great success for herself and Turkey by the treaty of Belgrade (1739). She aimed at another by deflecting Russia from support of Maria Theresa through a palace revolution and embroilment with Sweden. France was successful to the extent that Elizabeth replaced the baby Ivan VI and his mother the regent, a strong Austrophil (1741), and that Sweden duly plunged into a war of revenge. But Sweden fared disastrously, and Elizabeth, after some indecision, came down definitively on the side of her foreign minister, Bestuzhev-Ryumin (1693-1768; chancellor, 1744-58). He held unwaveringly to alliance with Austria, and if possible England, against the dangerously growing strength of Frederick the Great (reigned 1740-86), at that time the ally of France.

The struggle was renewed in the Seven Years' War, but "the diplomatic revolution of 1756" had changed the alignment of the powers. Bourbon and Habsburg for the first time became allies against the Hohenzollern when they found he had won to his side Great Britain with Hanover. Bestuzhev, completely taken by surprise by this last move, was badly shaken, for he had but just made an agreement with England directed against Prussia. He did not budge, however, from his adherence to Vienna and his fears of Berlin. Nor did most of his Russian rivals differ fundamentally from him in this, although they strongly disagreed with his conduct of affairs and intrigued successfully against him.

The confusion of counsels in St. Petersburg lasted throughout the war (1756-62). The empress Elizabeth, a determined enemy of Frederick, was ailing and thought likely to die shortly. The heir-apparent, Peter, duke of Holstein, was a fanatical admirer of Frederick. Catherine, his wife, ambitious and utterly estranged by his repellent characteristics and his follies, yet leaned strongly towards Prussia. The intrigues of policy and personal rivalries were multiplied by veering calculations as to the death of the empress. A conference of ministers not only attempted to co-ordinate and direct strategy from St. Petersburg (a very necessary aim), but insisted on issuing detailed instructions which tied the hands and tore the hair of the four successive commanders-in-chief in the field, only one of whom possessed even second-rate military abilities. Co-operation with the Austrians was at best fluctuating, frequently non-existent. The alliance of Russia with France was as nominal as her hostility to Great Britain, where Pitt refused to give Frederick naval aid in the Baltic or to break off relations with St. Petersburg.

The senior Russian generals on the whole deserved Frederick's whole-hearted contempt of them, but he had good cause to rue disparagement of their soldiery. The depredations of the Cossacks and irregular cavalry made a terrible and permanent byword of the whole Russian army. In fact, however, the regular troops were, almost throughout, well-disciplined and did not live off the country by looting. The Russian armies were indeed even more tied to their magazines and winter quarters than the other armies of their day. East Prussia seems to have fared much better during its four years of Russian occupation than Frederick's other provinces, bled by his levies and requisitions.

The Russian armies were untrained for the tactical offensive, even had their generals dared to attempt it in the face of Frederick's genius; but their unbreakable steadfastness, even with fifty per cent losses, robbed Frederick of any fruits from Zorndorf (1758) and next year at Kunersdorf brought him to his knees. In 1760 they captured Kolberg and crossed the Oder to raid Berlin, laying it under contribution (a suspiciously light one) and doing considerable military damage. By the end of 1761 Frederick, all but deserted by the British now that Pitt had been forced to resign, was reduced to his long conducted, but fruitless negotiations with the Turks as "the sole barometer" of Prussian policy. He was almost at his last gasp.

So was the empress Elizabeth, and in January 1762 she died. "Thanks be to Heaven," Frederick wrote to his brother, "our back is free." The undammable weight of Russian numbers was at last removed. Whereas on the ocean flank of the far-flung struggle the death of Ferdinand VI of Spain had brought Charles III to the throne and the entry of Spain into the war against England (1761), the death of Elizabeth brought Peter III to the throne and, as all counted on, the immediate withdrawal of Russia from the war. The *coup d'état* six months later, by which Catherine the Great deposed her husband, had little effect on foreign affairs. The policy of peace with Prussia was in general popular and it remained Catherine's fixed aim, though she withdrew the corps that Peter had proffered Frederick.

Peace soon came between the other powers in 1763. Prussia was the victor in Europe at the expense of Austria and France; England overseas at the expense of France and Spain.

Whether Russia had any compensation for her losses has been questioned. The war had been very costly in men and money, and the internal strain very great. She made no territorial gains. Peter had at once jettisoned Elizabeth's design to retain East Prussia (or its coastline, the remainder to be exchanged with Poland for a portion of "the western lands"). The primary object of Russia had been to diminish the growth of Prussian power and shatter Frederick's territorial ambitions. Silesia remained his; and he himself stood out as Frederick the Great. But his astonishing performance against such odds can but suggest that, had not Russia been in the lists against him, he might have speedily imposed his will on a larger scale and at a far less cost: Prussia might have emerged in so dominating a position as to ruin Russian interests in Poland and the Baltic.

At least it is certain that the Russian armies, cumbrous and ill-led though they might be, made an impression on Prussia and Europe that was never forgotten. Henceforward there was always the Russian soldiery to reckon with; apparently inexhaustible in numbers, indomitable fighters, staunch to the last. Frederick knew that his country was worn to the bone and must have a long period of recuperation. For the rest of his life, come what may, he must have peace with Russia. Prussia must never face another two-front war. And until 1914 she never did. For a century and a half after the Seven Years' War Prussia (or Germany) never fought Russia, save once nominally and under compulsion in 1812.

Alliance with Prussia, sealed by treaty in 1764, was until 1780 a main line of Catherine's foreign policy. It was only partly under the direction of her foreign minister Panin (1718-83). His over-elaborate "Northern Accord" system never worked, and he himself was always regarded with suspicion by Catherine and with emulous opposition by her early favorites, the Orlovs. Yet Russian policy decisively swayed the fortunes of Poland, Turkey and Sweden (see pp. 198 ff., 258, 261 ff.). After 1780, when the emperor Joseph II paid the first of two famous visits to Russia, return was made to alliance with Austria against the Turks (see p. 228).

The high position of Russia in Europe was sharply illustrated by the Bavarian succession question and the War of American Independence. In the contest between Frederick the Great and other German princes against Joseph II over Bavaria (1778-9) Catherine emerged as a guarantor of the Teschen agreement. Her mediation in German politics (as distinct from German-Danish politics in Holstein) was a novelty and the foretaste of a long period of intervention in Germany by Romanov dynastic diplomacy that lasted until Olmütz in 1850.

In the closing stages of the War of Independence Catherine gave birth to the Armed Neutrality (1780), her "darling child." She arrayed Denmark, Sweden and Prussia (followed later by other powers) in defense of the widest interpretation of the rights of neutrals against the British enforcement of their conception of maritime rights. The British government at the moment was too beset to stand out against Catherine's demands, though it did not accept her principles. Subsequently Russia proved ready to modify them as suited her, but maritime rights continued a most contentious issue. When the emperor Paul, incensed with his allies, the Austrians, for their military obstinancy, the British for their seizure of Malta and treatment of shipping, broke with the second coalition against France and made common cause with Napoleon, he immediately resuscitated Catherine's Armed Neutrality (1800-01), which led to Nelson's action against Copenhagen and his destruction of the Danish fleet. Alexander frequently pressed England for "some change in its maritime code": during his period of alliance with Napoleon (1807-10) he proclaimed again the principles of 1780 and 1800, and they continued to be the basis of the Russian attitude on maritime rights.

A second rift between Russia and England appeared in Catherine's reign, which later was to become a dividing chasm. In her first Turkish war Catherine had been much beholden to England, who had enabled her Baltic fleet to make its dramatic appearance in the Aegean (1770; *cf.* p. 228). But in her second she found the younger Pitt, allied with Prussia and in support of Sweden, moving further and further against her in his efforts to maintain the *status quo* (*cf.* pp. 259-260). "The Ochakov affair" (1790-1), with which the Foxite Whigs in collusion with the Russian minister made such play, ended in the resounding victory of Catherine. She did not yield to Sweden or Prussia and kept what Pitt was clumsily trying to intimidate her into giving up, namely the Black Sea strip between the Bug and the Dniester with the fortress of Ochakov. Pitt was less swayed by fears for the safety of the Ottoman empire than by other considerations, and he had no popular support in standing against Russia; but none the less the eastern question in its modern form begins to take shape for England in 1791.

By that date the French Revolution was far unleashed. By

the next year Austria and Prussia were at war with France; by 1793 Great Britain. Catherine was anxious enough to stay the Revolution and urge on coalition against it, the more readily since Austria and Prussia would thereby have their hands full on the West. For her main energies were absorbed in making an end of Poland (see pp. 199-201). Thus Russia, too far distant and too otherwise engrossed, did not take more than a nominal part in the first coalition against France (1792-5).

Thereafter it was very different. Russia fought France in the second coalition (1798-9) in Holland and above all in northern Italy and Switzerland, where Suvorov (1730-1800) performed his last and most brilliant feats. She fought France in the third coalition (1805-7), in 1812, and in the final coalition that ended on the field of Waterloo. Twice she swerved to the side of France; first, momentarily in 1800-1 owing to the incalculable emperor Paul; a second time, after bloody defeats in 1807 when Alexander I was constrained to ally himself, very uneasily, with Napoleon, much as Austria was after Wagram (1809).

The fundamental reason for Russia's participation in the Napoleonic wars was the same as that for the participation of the other powers—fear of an over-mighty France giving the law to Europe. Russia, in the eyes at any rate of her government, was a great European power, inevitably bound up with the West; even though throughout the Napoleonic period her eastern interests were being vigorously extended in the Caucasus (see pp. 281 ff.) and on the Danube. Dynastic connections, notably with Baden and Oldenburg, and Alexander's predilection for Frederick William III of Prussia and his beautiful queen Louise reinforced the political and economic ties with the West.

Thus Alexander joined with England and Austria in the third coalition. He brought Sweden in, but failed to coerce or cajole Prussia to effective action before the crushing defeat of Austerlitz (December 1805) drove the emperor Francis to sign peace and Alexander to withdraw to his frontiers. St. Petersburg was a prey to rival counsels. Czartoryski and Alexander's other early friends lost influence; they complained that he insisted on "remaining absolutely passive and not moving until we were ourselves attacked."

Then the sudden plunge of Prussia into war brought action; but before Russian aid could approach Jena had been fought (October 1806) and Prussia overwhelmed. Berlin was occupied, Napoleon himself in Warsaw, only East Prussia remained. There, battling through mud and blood, he won Eylau and Friedland, and on the famous raft on the Niemen met "the Byzantine Greek" and concluded the peace of Tilsit (July 1807).

Something was saved of Prussia, under hard and ambiguous terms. The Polish question was resurrected by the creation of the grand-duchy of Warsaw. Alexander was to join the Continental System against England, if she did not yield. He might take Finland as the price of forcing Sweden into it. Napoleon and Alexander were to settle the Ottoman empire between them.

Peace with Napoleon was imposed upon Alexander by the heaviness of the Russian losses, the state of his reserves and the exhaustion of his country. There had been an almost complete crop failure in 1806. The wavering "ministry of all the talents" in England had refused to guarantee a new loan. Russian finances had begun to collapse, largely owing to unrestricted emissions of paper money. In the course of the next three years the paper rouble dropped to below a fifth of its nominal value, and Russia was faced with bankruptcy. She just staved off collapse, mainly owing to the effects of her break-away from the Continental System. Measures taken by Speransky helped, though his comprehensive scheme of financial reform was not adopted (*cf.* p. 102). Resort had to be made to the equivalent of requisitions from the landowners. In 1812 the wave of patriotism that swept the country brought the government large voluntary contributions. After 1812 the contribution of Russia to the downfall of Napoleon was paramount, but it was financed by British subsidies to the tune of seven million pounds.

The economic effects of Tilsit proved very severe. Alliance

with Napoleon involved adhesion to his Continental System, that is to say the rupture of Russia with England, her best customer and an indispensable supplier of colonial and other goods. British shipping and firms, which handled the bulk of Russian foreign trade, were banned, and neutral (which meant in the main American) shipping had to obtain certificates of non-enemy origin for their cargoes. In fact there was much illicit trading in these certificates and smuggling flourished fantastically, though prices ran to ruinous heights. Exports slumped disastrously, and the active trade balance, upon which Russia had largely depended, vanished. A commercial treaty favorable to France and efforts to develop trade with France brought no relief. One particular industry, it is true, profited from the prohibition on English imports: there was a rapid, though not sustained, expansion of cotton mills. Some other Russian interests made a good living. But the staples of Russian exports, flax and hemp and other naval stores, iron ore and tallow, were cut off from their regular market and, being too bulky for long-distance land transport, could in any case find no adequate alternatives in face of British sea power.

If the situation in England became very critical (*cf.* p. 257), it was almost as serious in Russia. The effects of the Continental System hit particularly the bigger landowners, the one class with some political influence. From the first they had chafed at Tilsit, galled by the humbling of their pride and by the blunders that had led to Austerlitz and Eylau and Friedland. The unpopularity of the French alliance reacted sharply against Alexander's own position; in some quarters he was regarded with something worse than hostility—with abhorrence. He had good cause to remember that he was sitting on the throne of a deposed—and murdered—monarch, his father Paul. On the last day of 1810 he issued edicts opening Russian ports to neutral shipping without certificates and imposing a new tariff aimed against French luxury goods. Russia had left the Continental System, just when Napoleon was pressing Alexander hard to make it a reality. The breach with England was over.

There were two other reasons for the failure of the alliance with Napoleon, Turkey and Poland. For Russia the *quid pro quo* for the breach with England was to be, not Finland, which needed conquering (1808-9; see pp. 259-260), but a free hand in the Principalities, which had already been occupied when war broke out with Turkey at the end of 1806. Napoleon had been successful in stirring the sultan against Russia, and he had no intention of giving Alexander a free hand in his renewal of Catherine the Great's expansionist policy (see pp. 228, 267). Two *coups d'état* in Constantinople added to the entanglements of diplomacy, and Alexander refused to abandon the Principalities and stop war with Turkey. Napoleon turned to schemes for a joint attack on England in the East, in India. This might well involve some partition of Turkey; but Napoleon did not desire it. When he and Alexander met again at Erfurt (October 1808) he succeeded in adjourning negotiations as to partition, but he had to yield on the Principalities. His revenge came four years later, when Alexander in face of the Grand Army had to abandon them hurriedly and content himself with Bessarabia only (June 1812).

The eastern question was not a direct reason for 1812, but it was an important contributory factor to Russo-French ill-will. The rivalry of France at Constantinople in the eighteenth century had created a gulf; under the First Empire it remained a gulf; under the Second it led to war. But certainly for the great Napoleon, probably for Napoleon III, a deeper cause of hostility lay in the Polish question.

Poland as a state had disappeared from the map in 1795 as a result of the third partition between Russia, Prussia and Austria. Twelve years later a nucleus reappeared under the name of the grand-duchy of Warsaw, which in the first instance included only what had been the Prussian share of the partitions. At Tilsit Napoleon was the victor; the grand-duchy could not fail to be the standard-bearer of Polish nationalism, and it became as well a military spearhead of the Napoleonic empire. Alexander genuinely desired a better future for the

Poles; but it must be his own doing. A French solution of the Polish question was fatal, for it opened vistas of a Polish reconquest of "the western lands" and a permanent French military threat on his western frontier (*cf.* p. 203).

In 1809, after Wagram, Alexander was the more perturbed by Napoleon's extension of the grand-duchy to include Austria's share of the third partition, and especially by Napoleon's refusal to pledge himself against the use of the name Poland and against any further enlargement of the grand-duchy. The tsar was spurred by this failure and piqued by Napoleon's preference for marriage with the daughter of the emperor Francis, Marie Louise, rather than with his sister Anna. He turned again towards Czartoryski and schemes for the restoration of Poland with himself as king. Connections with the Poles were multiplied, military measures pressed forward. In 1811, feeling that Napoleon was near a rupture, he cogitated forestalling him. If Alexander were sure of the 50,000 Polish troops of the grand-duchy, he could launch his campaign from the Oder. But he did not receive positive assurances from Warsaw. There he was too much distrusted, and, though the French had lost most of their popularity, the Poles believed that they could gain more from Napoleon. When Russia and France renewed the struggle, it began from the Niemen, not the Oder.

Before daybreak on June 24, 1812, the Grand Army, in all over half a million strong, began to cross the Niemen. Twelve weeks later Napoleon rode into Moscow. In the evening of December 14, behind a derelict remnant a few thousand weak, Ney repassed the Niemen, last over the last bridge. A month later the Russian vanguard crossed the river. On March 31, 1814, Alexander, at the head of the Allied troops, rode into Paris, never entered by any foreign army since the days of Joan of Arc.

1812 was "the War for the Fatherland." In its combination of dramatic scale and intensity and in its consequences it stands unequaled in Russian history between the Mongol invasions far back and the two death grapples of our own day. Now again it is the exemplar of patriot resistance to the last and of final triumph.[1]

Divergent estimates have come from Russians as to the main characteristics of 1812 and of the rôles of particular individuals. But there is now general agreement that it was "a people's war." The patriotic elements among all classes (except in St. Petersburg) were much more to the fore than the renegades or the faint-hearts or the lath and plaster talkers; and the peasants were Russians first, serfs second.

Among the government and the serf-owners there were fears that the French might appear as liberators. The Russian peasants did not regard them as such. Any army living to a large extent off the country arouses hostility, and the hostility of the Russian peasantry when aroused is merciless. Wherever the French penetrated peasant guerrillas played a notable part against them. In the western provinces, in cases where there were outbreaks of the peasants against their masters, the French aided in quelling them. Napoleon aimed at winning over the upper class and compelling Alexander to treat, not at overturning existing order by appeals to what must lead to chaos.

The long Russian retreat from the frontier to the old capital and beyond was not "according to plan," but imposed by divided counsels, by the numerical inferiority of the Russian field army and by failure to stop Napoleon, especially before Smolensk and before Moscow, on the field of Borodino, even more blood-soaked than that of Eylau. Popular clamor against foreign or semi-foreign generals forced Alexander to substitute for Barclay de Tolly as commander-in-chief Kutuzov, whom he could not abide. Nor could Kutuzov Alexander. In fact, the foreigners in Russia, particularly the Germans (among them Stein), were full of fight, and had every reason to urge the Russians on to expel Napoleon not only from Russia but from his conquered lands. Despite Kutuzov and Borodino, Moscow had to be abandoned. The

[1] Although it is superfluous, it is impossible not to say: read and re-read *War and Peace;* almost as great as a historical interpretation as it is as a work of art.

barest shadow of consolation that he could find was that it would be for the Grand Army "like a sponge which will suck it up."

Even as the French entered their haven—to find it half-deserted, "the queenless hive" of Tolstoy—Moscow began to burn. The initial fires were at least in part due to orders given by Rostopchin, the flamboyant, chameleon governor-general, who at one and the same time had sought to inflame the patriotism of the masses and recoiled in terror of their independent action. But the devastating spread of the fire was due to chance, carelessness and individual malice in a city largely built of wood and filled with an out-of-hand rabble and carousing, looting French soldiers. In five days three-quarters of the city was in ashes. Yet the material effects of the fire were far less serious for the French than the moral. Believing it to be due to deliberate Russian policy, they were aghast at the "decisiveness" of these "Scythians," which destroyed their expectations that Moscow would mean the end of yet another victorious campaign. The Russians, at the time, ascribed the burning of Moscow to "the modern Attila," with whom there could be no question of peace.

The retreat of the French was caused by the refusal of the Russian people, of Kutuzov, and of Alexander (despite the irresolute gloom of St. Petersburg) to accept a peace dictated by Napoleon from Moscow. Kutuzov (1745-1813), the crafty, enigmatic, one-eyed idol of the troops, summed up the national spirit of resistance to the invader. He was torn to the quick by his failure to save Moscow. He was inflexibly determined somehow to eject the French from Russia, but he must save his army the terrible losses suffered at Borodino (43,000 out of 110,000). Hence his much criticized delaying, "parallel" strategy during the French retreat. Twice, at Krasnoe and at the passage of the Berezina, the Russians failed to inflict a mortal blow. But Kutuzov sensed that, once the retreat was under way, the cumulative momentum of disorder in so composite an army, strung out along an already ravaged route, might cause its complete disintegration when the Cossacks, guerrillas, and winter destroyed cohesion. Russia might be freed without a major battle and therefore major casualties. Even so, the pursuit was costly enough for the Russians; for the time being Kutuzov lost two-thirds of his men, including sick and stragglers.

But for the French the retreat was a catastrophe. That year the great cold came six weeks earlier than for forty years past, and thereby ruined the reckoning of Napoleon's experts. The horses succumbed first, leaving guns and transport immobilized. Then the tightening grip of winter, lack of supplies and the harassing of the Russians broke morale, and the Grand Army dwindled and dwindled, in the end to mere bunches of crushed fugitives. The spell was broken for all Europe. Russia had destroyed the largest army that Napoleon ever put into the field.

Kutuzov and others highly placed wanted to stand on the frontier. Russia had been saved; she was fearfully exhausted; it was not her task to save Europe. Alexander thought it was; or at least his; and for the time being he probably had the bulk of Russian opinion with him. Later, his prolonged absences in the West, his immersion in its affairs, and above all his policy towards the Poles (see pp. 204 ff.) led to much criticism that Russian interests were being sacrificed to some vague entity called the concert of powers or to Alexander's "philanthropic and Christian utopias," as a Russian critic later complained.

At least there could be no complaint that Russia was not one of the powers. The downfall of Napoleon, the double restoration of the Bourbons in France, and the reconstruction of Europe were the work of the Grand Alliance headed by the four powers, Russia, Austria, Great Britain and Prussia. Never has the influence of Russia throughout Europe been greater than during the years 1813-15. The might of Russia weighed heavily on Metternich and Castlereagh, and at the Congress of Vienna the Polish-Saxon struggle almost brought them to blows with Alexander and Frederick William.

Napoleon's escape from Elba renewed the combined action of the four powers. Waterloo decided the fate of Napoleon for ever, that of France for fifteen years. To guard against any recrudescence of revolutionary or Napoleonic France the Quadruple Alliance (November 1815) was renewed for twenty years, and in it the four powers also agreed to continue their periodical meetings in order to maintain "the repose . . . and peace of Europe." This, together with the comprehensive nature of the final act of Vienna, was the original, diplomatic basis of the Concert of Europe, into which France was admitted in 1818, and of the conferences which met between 1818 and 1822 at Aix-la-Chapelle, Troppau, Laibach and Verona.

Alexander from the first viewed the Concert of Europe in a special light. For him it meant his own child, the Holy Alliance (September 1815). This is usually regarded as an unholy alliance of reaction against liberalism, constitutionalism and nationality. But in origin it was not intended to be an instrument of obscurantism or the *ancien régime*. Nor was it a sudden idea first embraced by Alexander in Paris in 1815. Many years earlier, when negotiating the third coalition, he had suggested to Pitt (1804) as a principal war aim the constitution of a new international order in Europe; the countries emancipated from the "tyrannical" Napoleon "should . . . be assured of liberties on a solid basis"; "a sort of new code of international law" might be laid down, to include a provision that no state should "begin a war without exhausting every means of mediation by a third power"; a league for the preservation of European peace might be formed, under the special guarantee of Russia and Great Britain.

In the intervening years these ideas became transmuted through the development of Alexander's religious views, which were deeply influenced by mysticism, Lutheran pietism, and the evangelism of the Bible Society (*cf.* p. 337). He became profoundly, if confusedly, convinced that society in the last resort rested upon a religious basis, that Europe was one whole, a Christian fraternity, and that public and international relations could only be satisfactorily conducted on the same moral principles as those applicable to private conduct.

Hence in the Holy Alliance sovereigns were "to take for

their sole guide the precepts of . . . Religion, namely the precepts of Justice, Christian Charity, and Peace, which, far from being applicable only to private concerns, must . . . guide all their steps, as being the only means of consolidating human institutions and remedying their imperfections." In consonance with this Alexander, or his agents, could and did appear for a time in a moderate liberal hue, in Poland, in France and elsewhere.

But the Holy Alliance also laid down that sovereigns "considering each other as fellow countrymen, . . . will, on all occasions and in all places, lend each other aid and assistance . . . to protect Religion, Peace and Justice." Already in 1818 at the conference of Aix-la-Chapelle Alexander tried to extend the Holy Alliance into a system of collective security. All depended on how peace, justice and the remedying of imperfections were defined. In 1820 a series of revolutions, in Spain, Naples and Piedmont, and a mutiny in one of Alexander's own guard regiments completed his transition to the reactionary camp represented at home by Arakcheyev and Photius,[1] abroad by Metternich. Peace and justice now meant only the joint guaranteeing of territories, thrones and the *status quo*. "Too strong to employ despotism, too weak to establish liberty," Alexander in his closing years was "imagining himself as the defender of civilization against anarchy, in the same way as he had saved it from the despotism of Napoleon" (Chateaubriand).

From 1820 the Holy Alliance became identified with the

[1] Arakcheyev (1769-1834) has given his name to the last period of Alexander's reign, as his specially trusted vizier priding himself on "being a real Russian unlettered squire" devoted "without adulation" to Alexander. He used his very great power to further cruel and systematic reaction and was specially identified with the disastrous and very unpopular "military colonies" upon which Alexander set such store. Both under Paul and Alexander Arakcheyev occupied a series of high military posts and had done much for army reorganization, notably in the artillery.

Archimandrite Photius (1792-1838), closely bound up with Arakcheyev, was the most insidious representative of the anti-foreign, ultra-conservative circles in the church which at the end of Alexander's life won the day for intolerance and reaction. The stirring obscurity of his apocalyptic eloquence was more than matched by the admired severity of his fanatical asceticism.

doctrine of coercive intervention against actual or threatened revolution. Castlereagh vigorously repudiated both the doctrine and its applications, and Canning demonstratively completed the withdrawal of Great Britain from the European concert. On the other hand, Russia soon became divided from the other continental powers as regards her application of the doctrine of intervention, and especially as regards the Greek revolt which began in 1821.

Russia was widely suspected of backing the revolt, the more so since Capodistrias, the Greek patriot, was Alexander's foreign minister. Alexander, however, did not squarely adopt the line that revolution of Christian subjects against a Moslem sovereign was quite different from revolution of Christian subjects against a Christian sovereign. He dismissed Capodistrias and refused to take independent action, popular though that would have been in Russia. Gradually, however, he became convinced of the futility of his long-drawn-out negotiations with the other powers, and he broke first with England, then with Austria. Shortly before his death (1825) he had decided on coercive action, if necessary alone, against the Turks, with whom the Greek question was by no means the only bone of contention.

Nicholas I immediately carried into effect his brother's intentions. He was prepared "to talk Greek" with Canning, provided that force was not ruled out. The result was Navarino (1827) in concert with the British and the French, followed by war with the Turks alone (1828-9). By the treaty of Adrianople he imposed his own settlement on the Turks, except as regards the Greek question. On that he was still ready to co-operate with England and France. But with Metternich he had remained throughout on the coldest terms. The divergence of Russia and Austria on the Near Eastern question had for the time being destroyed the Holy Alliance. Russia and Austria had rarely been further apart than in 1830 when revolution again shook Europe.

The result of the 1830 revolutions was to draw Russia, Austria and Prussia together into what was tantamount to a new edition of the Holy Alliance. Nicholas from the first breathed fire and slaughter against "l'infâme révolution de juillet." The revolution in Belgium immediately confirmed him in his detestation of France as the fountain-head of aggression and danger. He never ceased to revile and condemn Louis Philippe and his régime. But he had very little backing at home for his initial bellicose schemes in support of King William of Holland, whose son and heir was married to his sister Anna. In November 1830 the Polish revolt broke out, and therewith any chances of successful Russian intervention in the West were destroyed. England and France decided the issue of Belgium, and Nicholas was reduced to a long, twisting, diplomatic rearguard action.

Poland antagonized Nicholas and Russia the more against France and England, where sympathy for the Polish cause was vociferous. In contrast, Poland united the three eastern powers. Austria and, in particular, Prussia took almost all the desired steps to assist Russia in defeating the Poles, and the three powers bound themselves (1833) to closely concerted action on Polish affairs for the future. Cracow, it was agreed (1835), must be suppressed, and in 1846 it was annexed to Austria (*cf.* p. 204).

Disturbances in Germany and risings in Italy, where the intervention of France challenged that of Austria, drove Metternich closer to Nicholas. At Münchengrätz and four other meetings (1833-5) the three eastern powers bound themselves to mutual aid in support of legitimacy and the treaty settlement of 1815. In addition, Nicholas and Metternich came to an agreement couched in very general terms as to a common line of policy in regard to the Ottoman empire. Metternich, who had been kept in the dark by the Russians during the first Mehemet Ali crisis (1832-3; see pp. 269-270), congratulated himself that now their hands were well tied. Nicholas was equally well-pleased, for he thought that the Austrians would follow him on Turkey; Austria and Prussia would stand on guard facing west, with himself in reserve to them, while he stood on guard facing south.

For fifteen years after Münchengrätz (1833) Nicholas stood out as the leader of the new version of the Holy Alliance against liberalism, nationalism and socialism. Subsequently, Russian critics inveighed against his whole foreign policy on the ground that Russia had no real links with Austria or Prussia and that her true interest was to settle issues with Turkey for herself. Nicholas and his foreign office, on the contrary, regarded ideological interests as a fundamental basis of policy. If Russia pursued a policy of isolation, "the rampart now [1838] formed by Austria and Prussia against revolutionary doctrines would collapse": they would sweep from the Seine across the Rhine to the Danube and the Oder: "Russia, as in 1812, would be obliged to grapple with France in a hand to hand struggle. The true and permanent interest of Russia is to maintain between us and France this moral barrier, formed by friendly powers and monarchies, solidly based on principles analogous to our own . . ."

This conception of conservative monarchical solidarity was a dominant line in Russian foreign policy throughout the period from the Congress of Vienna to the Crimean War. Thereafter it was never again dominant. Alexander II hankered after it and revived it after 1870 for some years. Then it was overborne, though not extinguished, by the force of the new nationalisms and rivalry with Austria-Hungary in the Balkans.

In 1848 the rampart of Münchengrätz collapsed with a crash. Austria, Germany and Italy followed France into revolution. Nicholas was resolved to do what he could to rebuild the rampart, to restore the German lands to their previous position, with Austria controlling the Confederation, to maintain as far as possible the 1815 settlement of Europe. Poland must be held down at all costs, Russia sealed off from infection from the West. But internal conditions made any immediate active intervention difficult, and opinion in Russia was in general very averse to pulling Austrian or Prussian chestnuts out of the fire. The extreme severity of the police-censorship rule of Nicholas's closing years so alienated Russia from him that his death, in the midst of the Crimean War (1855), was greeted with undisguised relief.

The three enemies to be fought were constitutionalism,

nationalism and socialism. The French Republic was naturally odious in the eyes of Nicholas, but not more so than the bourgeois monarchy of Louis Philippe; and, unlike Nesselrode, he looked with favor upon Louis Napoleon, until "the savior of society" became also Emperor of the French (1852) and the restorer of the French guardianship of Catholic rights in the Levant. In any case France was far away, but revolution near at hand in central Europe.

Nationalism in Poland was the tsar's first concern. Russian Poland was held down by additional troops and police. A rising in Prussian Poland was quashed. The Polish question proved again the strongest tie between St. Petersburg and Berlin. Nationalism in Hungary was the second concern of Nicholas, not merely because it was a challenge to Habsburg rule: with Kossuth there were over a thousand Polish refugees. "We cannot allow the formation on the frontiers of Poland of an independent Polish Hungary" (Nesselrode). The young emperor Francis Joseph appealed for help: a Russian army crossed the Carpathians, and saved the Habsburgs (1849).

The intervention in Hungary branded Russia with still darker colors in the eyes of the West and led to a tussle at Constantinople over the extradition of five thousand refugees who had escaped from Hungary; a tussle in which Palmerston and Louis Napoleon joined in successful defense of the Porte. The intervention gave birth to anti-Russian feelings among the Magyars, which, reinforced by other grounds of antipathy, was to count for much in later years. Nor, on the other hand, did intervention make for amicable relations with Austria. The two armies got on badly together: the weak sides of the Russian military machine were clearly shown up: Haynau's excesses wounded Nicholas in his touchiest spot, his honor. He was to be cruelly disabused of his belief in Austria's gratitude.

Nationalism in Germany, in the third place, had to be combated, especially in "the odious complication" of the Schleswig-Holstein question. Denmark with her key position in the Baltic could not be ignored. Nicholas was determined not to watch as a mere spectator any destruction of Denmark by the hated Confederation or by Prussia. He was far from successful in the shifts and turns of his diplomacy, but in the end his threats of intervention helped to swing Prussia to the armistice of July 1849, followed a year later by peace. The North Sea-Baltic aspirations of Prussia or Germany were dissipated, for a time.

For Nicholas the intransigence of Prussia against Denmark was only one degree less reprehensible than what he regarded as the deplorable truckling of Frederick William IV to revolution and constitution-mongering in his own kingdom and in the German lands. He promised Frederick William his help, just as he was helping Francis Joseph in Hungary, but only on condition that he stopped war with Denmark, broke with Frankfurt and acted firmly so as "to re-establish in your monarchy a state of things founded on the principles of order and conservatism." That meant a return to Münchengrätz and the Confederation under Austrian dominance. Thanks primarily to events and personalities in Germany and Austria, in part to Russian diplomatic and military pressure, the policy of Nicholas was to all appearances successful when in 1850 Prussia "capitulated" to Austria at Olmütz.

In fact, however, there was no real return to Münchengrätz. The challenge of Prussia to Austria was not laid aside, and within four years of Olmütz the Crimean War revealed the weakness of Nicholas's version of the Holy Alliance. There were, indeed, important forces linking together the three powers in the maintenance of their social structure and system of government, but these forces only operated powerfully enough to counteract other forces pulling them apart when revolution, threatened or actual, inspired sufficient fear. Once the Austrian government had weathered the storms of 1848, the pull of its eastern interests were certain to have more weight against Russia. Nicholas paid the penalty in the Crimean War.

The Crimean War began for three main reasons: Turkish national feeling and suspicions of Russian designs; the requirement by the Russians of guarantees that the Turks would carry out their undertakings; the belief of the Turks, encouraged by the masterful British ambassador Stratford Canning, that in the last resort Great Britain, if not also France, would come to their aid in arms. The dispute over the Holy Places was originally a contest between two Christian powers, Russia and France, in which the Moslem possessor of Palestine under heavy chivying made incompatible promises to each separately. It was, as Stratford Canning urged, capable of adjustment, and it would have been settled but for further Russian requirements which seemed (with considerable reason) to most of the Turkish government to amount to a recognition of Russian claims to intervene on behalf of all the Orthodox subjects of the sultan.

The requirements were not met, and feelings against Russia were still more inflamed when she retaliated by occupying the Principalities in July 1853. Thenceforward it was almost certain that the Turks would not give in without fighting, whatever the outcome of the negotiations between the powers. Late in the autumn the fighting started, and the miscalled "massacre of Sinope," in which a Turkish fleet in the Black Sea was destroyed, led to the final collapse of the pacific half-measures of Aberdeen, the British prime minister, and the entry of Great Britain and France into the war (March 1854).

The British attitude to Russia was the result of half a century of clash of interest and clash of outlook. Pitt, as has been seen, in 1791 first voiced, though ineffectually, the dangers to British interests of Russian southward expansion. Experience in the Napoleonic wars and the continued advance of the Russians at the expense of Turkey and Persia bred in government and military circles the belief that Russia was a danger to the Middle East and the overland routes to India and that therefore the maintenance of at least a reasonably strong Turkey was essential.

Palmerston, who became foreign secretary in 1830, thoroughly agreed; and he did not hide the fact. Throughout the thirties Anglo-Russian relations could not be worse, and every incident was swollen disproportionately. Persia again came to the fore, and for the first time Russian instigation in Afghanistan was at work. Then a Russian setback in Central Asia and the changed Russian policy in the second Mehemet Ali crisis (see p. 270) eased matters. Fears as to the routes to India and the Middle East receded into the background.

In the thirties Russian commercial expansion in Turkey and Persia caused much concern. Palmerston's successful commercial treaty with Turkey in 1838 redressed the balance, and by the time of the Crimean War the Ottoman empire was a more important market for England than Russia. All the more reason to support her; if left to the mercy of the Muscovite bear his squeeze would eliminate British trade. Turkey was regarded by many as attempting to go forward on the path of reform, whereas Russia not only shut herself up behind a towering tariff wall, but figured as the fountain-head of brutal despotism.

Still more after 1848 public opinion tended to look upon Russia as an obscurantist, slave-owning autocracy, ruling with the knout and the Cossacks, stocking Siberia with innocent deportees, the persecutor of Poles and Circassians, the enemy of freedom throughout Europe, standing in all social, political and religious matters at the opposite extreme to England. In the Crimean War England was fighting much less for the Turk than against the tsar pictured as the gendarme and hangman of Europe. Left to himself he would swallow Turkey, or, at the least, partition her greatly to his own advantage. The substitution of tsarist despotism for Ottoman rule would be no improvement, and Russia in command of the Straits and Constantinople would mean the yet greater menace of the bully and the tyrant.

Such a stereotype, though it was based on much that was exaggerated, ignorant and ignobly bellicose, was far from being merely spurious. It did correspond, in a very rough and ready manner, to much of the all too dark sides of tsarist Russia. England and Russia were poles apart and stood for totally different world conceptions. And Nicholas himself gave cause for the belief that he wanted to make an end of Turkey.

The policy of Nicholas towards the Slavs and the Straits has been sketched in previous chapters (pp. 229 ff., 268 ff.), where it was pointed out that he spoke with two voices. During the first half of his reign he followed on the whole the policy of maintaining Turkey, but weak and with his own influence dominant in Constantinople. He was successful in this until after the crisis of 1839-40. Thereafter British influence grew apace, thanks to the commanding character of Stratford Canning, who shared with Palmerston the distinction of being Nicholas's chief bugbear.

In consequence, the tsar swung the more towards those influential Russian circles which had always believed that the days of the Ottoman empire were numbered and that it was for Russia to reap her reward before she was out-distanced by others. Nicholas, in opposition to England, was not interested in trying to revive a decomposing Turkey: he looked upon her with the eyes of a part heir, not those of a doctor. When he broached this most delicate of questions with Austria, England or France, he took as his standpoint:— "the sick man" is dying rapidly; we must agree in advance as to what shall be done, especially what shall *not* be done. In 1844 he visited England and thought that his views had been accepted by Aberdeen, then foreign secretary. In December, 1852, Aberdeen became prime minister, much to the satisfaction of Nicholas, who at once renewed his proposals. They were doomed to failure: the object of England was to concert to prevent the collapse of Turkey, that of Russia to concert what should follow collapse. Hence Palmerston, for one, drew the conclusion that Nicholas was actively working for collapse.

This was not strictly true of Nicholas (and not at all of Nesselrode), but it was true of many of the Russian diplomats and agents in the Balkans. Their activities especially alarmed Vienna, which for a hundred years past had always feared lest the Principalities and Serbia fall completely under Russian sway. When at last Francis Joseph came out into the open in his long correspondence with Nicholas, it was to require (January 1854) the cessation of incitement of the Balkan Christians, no changes to be made in the political situation in European Turkey, and the evacuation of the Principalities.

The divergence between Russia and Austria became a direct contest, the wounds of which were never healed. Buol, the foreign minister, strove to extend Austrian interests against Russia by every possible means. There was no actual fighting and the Russians exaggerated the strength of the war party in Austria; but it must not be forgotten that for them the Crimean War had four fronts, the Crimea and southern littoral, the Caucasus, the Baltic, and the Austrian frontier: on this last a large proportion of the Russian forces (until the final stages of the war) were kept immobilized. Nor must it be forgotten that it was an Austrian ultimatum that brought Russia to the peace conference of Paris (1856; see p. 271). Within the next half century Russia and Austria were three times again very near to war; the fourth time, in 1914, both fell into the abyss. On each occasion the future of the Balkans was at stake.

The Crimean War caused the breakdown of Nicholas's policy both at home and abroad. For the next twenty years the major issues were internal. Russia ceased to play a leading rôle in the affairs of Europe. She could not fail to be important, but the great events, Italian and German unity, took place with Russia in the background.

Both remade the 1815 map of Europe, yet without an European conference. Russians were unpleasantly struck with the contrast in their own case. Twice, in 1856 and 1878, Russia was compelled to lay the eastern question before the great powers, whether belligerents or not; and in 1878 none save she herself had been one. During the crisis of 1876-78 Ignatyev and the panslavs had done their best to force a Russian solution on Turkey and face the West with an accomplished fact (see pp. 234 ff., 272 ff.). They failed. Alexander II and his foreign minister Gorchakov were not prepared to defy Europe at the almost certain expense of war with Great Britain and Austria-Hungary. Thus the eastern question was settled again by the powers, not by Russia alone. But the congress met at Berlin, not Paris as twenty years before. Prussia had become Germany, and Bismarck was the central figure in Europe in the stead of Napoleon III.

This change was to transform the eastern question during the following generation. A second fundamental change was also occurring. The development of nationalism and other Western influences upon the Balkan Christians had gone so far that at Berlin Roumania, Serbia and Montenegro were recognized as independent states. Bulgaria, though cut down and divided, was given a special status which was soon overturned by the Bulgars: from 1887 she was in effect independent of the sultan, though not formally so until 1908.

The independence of the Balkan states owed more to Russia than to any other power. Yet Russia did not reap the fruits she expected. For this there were various reasons. The Crimean War and the stand of Disraeli and Andrássy against her in 1878 decided that the Balkans should not be a Russian preserve. Russia was tsarist Russia and in that capacity unpopular in the Balkans (*cf.* p. 235). The pull of the western world was very strong in Roumania and Greece, considerable in Serbia, marked in Bulgaria after 1879 and especially 1886. The new states did not wish to be appendages of Russia or Austria-Hungary or any of the powers; they wanted "the Balkans for the Balkan peoples." But their weakness compelled them to align themselves now with one power, now with another.

On the other hand, the Balkans did not become the powder-barrel of Europe merely because of the intrigues of the great powers. The claim of "the Balkans for the Balkan peoples" was neither a watchword that spelled peace and prosperity as opposed to perpetual interference by the powers, nor a slogan that was clear in meaning. Mutual animosities were intense. Each had their *irredenta* and claims and counterclaims against each other. Macedonia and the beginnings of Albanian nationalism added to competing rivalries. And, what did the Balkans mean? Did they include

Constantinople? Did they include Bosnia and Herzegovina? Dalmatia, Croatia, Slovenia, southern Hungary? Transylvania, Bessarabia? The Ægean isles, Smyrna and much in Anatolia? All the lands inhabited by the Balkan peoples? If so, that meant not merely the continued and complete disruption of the Ottoman empire—serious enough in itself—, but the revolutionary novelty of the disruption of what had been since 1867 the Dual Monarchy, Austria-Hungary.

Within thirty years of 1878 both these great issues had ripened. For Austria-Hungary Serbia was vital, because the growth of Jugoslav feelings and claims, more than any of the other nationality problems within the Dual Monarchy, threatened its continued existence. In 1878 Austria-Hungary, with the prior agreement of Russia, had taken over from Turkey the administration of Bosnia-Herzegovina, a Slav land, mixed Moslem, Orthodox and Catholic, the magnet of Serbian aspirations. In 1908 she suddenly annexed it, and thereby intentionally dashed pan-Serbian hopes to the ground.

Serbian nationalism blazed out irrepressibly. The connections of Russia with Serbia had by now again become very close (see p. 236), and public opinion was loud in support of her small Slav brother. But Russia was in a very weak position to secure some compensation for Serbia. Izvolsky, the foreign minister, had badly misjudged the situation and had just bartered, in vain, Bosnia-Herzegovina for the Straits (see pp. 275-276). Secondly, Russia could only use the arms of diplomacy, for she had not yet recovered from the effects of the war with Japan and the 1905 Revolution. The military were agreed that Russia could not fight, and this was made quite clear in a secret session of the Duma.

Germany, knowing this, closed the crisis by requiring of Russia abandonment of Serbia (March, 1909). The German note was not technically an ultimatum, but its drafter, Kiderlen Wächter, almost certainly intended it to have that effect and quite certainly "to press Izvolsky to the wall." The humiliation by Germany was bitterly resented in Russia. Yet even without the German "ultimatum" she was bound to suffer rebuff, since Austria-Hungary was determined to have her way with Serbia, and Russia was too weak to prevent her. Henceforward Russia and Austria-Hungary engaged in what was to prove a mortal duel in the Balkans.

Russia set to work to encourage a Balkan league under her ægis, directed in the first place against Turkey, but ultimately against Austria-Hungary. It won surprisingly rapid successes against the Turks in the first Balkan war (1912-13). But the allies (Serbia, Montenegro, Bulgaria and Greece) could not be controlled by the tsar as arbiter. They fell out among themselves over the division of the booty, especially in the *comitadji* battleground of Macedonia. Russia could not prevent the second Balkan war (1913) of Serbia and Greece, joined by Roumania, against Bulgaria; and the Turks seized their chance to retake Adrianople. The Bulgars lost still more heavily; Macedonia was divided between Serbia and Greece; Roumania seized the southern Dobrudja. In the western Balkans a new, independent Albania was set up by the powers, and the efforts of Serbia to secure access to the Adriatic, which were favored by Russia but resolutely opposed by Austria-Hungary, were unsuccessful.

The Balkan wars had four main consequences:—

(i) Turkey, more than ever suspicious of Russia, moved nearer and nearer to the alliance with Germany which she concluded in August, 1914 (*cf.* p. 275).

(ii) Russia lost her hold in Bulgaria, who sought revenge against Serbia and Greece through concert with Austria-Hungary. She took it in 1915 when she fell upon the rear of Serbia.

(iii) Roumania was now at enmity with Bulgaria and was more and more alive to the claims of her kinsmen in Transylvania to liberation from the Magyar yoke. The divergences between Germany and Austria-Hungary on policy towards Roumania gave Russian diplomacy an opportunity which she used skillfully. Roumania turned her eyes from her *irredenta* in Bessarabia to her much more numerous *irredenta* in Hungary. When European war broke out in August 1914, the Hohenzollern king Charles, though allied ever since

1883 with the central powers, could do nothing but declare neutrality. Two years later Roumania entered the war on the side of Russia and her allies.

(iv) Serbia and Montenegro continued to be even more closely tied with Russia in self-defense against Austria-Hungary. In Russian eyes, "our fundamental task is to guarantee the political and economic emancipation of Serbia" (Sazonov).

The fundamental reason for the beginning of war in August 1914 was the inability or refusal of the Austrians and Magyars to solve their nationality problems, above all, the Jugoslav question. The internal structure of the Dual Monarchy was precarious in the extreme and its continued existence in doubt when at long last Francis Joseph should die (b. 1830, reigned 1848-1916). The Ballplatz and the Wilhelmstrasse did not always work hand in hand in 1912-14, but the two general staffs were in agreement as to automatic mutual support, and the emperor William II had made his attitude on Serbia clear to Vienna: "The Slavs were not born to rule but to serve. This they must be taught. . . . I stand behind you and am ready to draw the sword when your action makes it necessary" (1913).

These were typically rash words; nevertheless, since Germany considered the safety of her one secure ally as essential to her, she was bound *in the last resort* to support her in arms. Vienna and Buda-Pest regarded Serbia, the Piedmont of the Jugoslav movement, as fatal to the safety of the Dual Monarchy, though they differed as to the exact means of rendering her innocuous. The reckoning against her was precipitated in July, 1914, by the murder of the heir-apparent, the archduke Francis Ferdinand, in Sarajevo, the capital of Bosnia, by an Austrian Serb in complicity with a secret society across the border in Serbia.

Russia, where public feeling influenced by the bitter memories of 1909 was boiling, would not stand by and watch the crushing of Serbia, which she rightly thought Austria-Hungary was determined upon. Alone, Austria-Hungary was no match for Russia and Serbia. Therefore Germany must act at once; and so too must France; she could not desert her ally Russia in such a struggle for life. Great Britain was questionable as regards immediate action, partly owing to the uncertain character of her entente with France, partly to the imminence of civil war in Ireland; but the German violation of Belgian neutrality turned the scale decisively in favor of immediate declaration of war.

How was it that Germany was thus alienated from Russia and bound to Austria-Hungary, France similarly to Russia? And that Russia had the aid of her old enemy England?

For forty-four years Russia had been moving farther and farther from Germany. But the movement was unsteady and not continuous. Although the defeats of France in 1870 and of Austria in 1866 had been too sudden and complete for the liking of Russia, she was only too pleased that the traitor of the Crimean War should be humbled and weakened, and in 1870 she gave notice that her neutrality was conditional on Austria-Hungary not supporting France.

Her support of Prussia was in addition based on a long tradition of friendly relations, once severed in the Seven Years' War, since then rarely strained by very serious rifts. And between 1854 and 1870 Prussia, as far as she could, had been Russia's one steady friend. The Polish question, as 1863 again demonstrated, forged common bonds. Friendship was also cemented by close dynastic ties since the reign of Alexander I. The importance of personal family links (with other German houses also, though not the Habsburgs) gave much ground for the criticism that the foreign policy of St. Petersburg was dynastic rather than Russian, additionally since the diplomatic service was so largely staffed by non-Russians (*cf.* p. 331).

This accusation had much less substance in it after 1870, when Prussia became so formidable as Germany and Bismarck bestrode the stage. The traditional connections with monarchical and conservative Prussia were wearing thin by the close of Alexander II's reign; under Alexander III they wore very thin; under Nicholas II they counted for more, but they were never ascendant.

An attempt to revive the old conservative alliance of the

three eastern powers in 1873 broke down five years later when Russia and Austria-Hungary fell out again over the Balkans. It was more significant that she fell out also with the new Germany and "the honest broker" of the Berlin congress. Russia had hoped for definite support from Germany if necessary against Austria-Hungary; but Bismarck, though he did his best to encourage amicable partition of the Balkans between the two, would not "opt" for either.

The outbreak of injured nationalism in Russia, which followed the imposition of the treaty of Berlin in place of her victorious treaty of San Stefano, went to extreme lengths against Germany and Bismarck, accused now of being responsible for Russia's defeat (*cf.* p. 234). "The war of the two chancellors" (himself and Gorchakov) and the chaotic conditions within Russia, which seemed to make her actions unpredictable, convinced Bismarck that a renewal of good relations with the Russian government was so uncertain that he must insure himself and Austria-Hungary. In October, 1879, the Austro-German alliance was signed, in defense against a Russian attack on either or Russian support of a French attack on Germany. This alliance, rather than the Triple Alliance between Germany, Austria-Hungary and Italy (first concluded in 1882), was the keystone of the union between the two central powers, and it was to run unchanged right down to 1914. Unlike the Triple Alliance, the exact terms of which were never revealed until 1919, the Austro-German alliance was officially communicated to Russia, Great Britain and Italy in 1887 and published to the world in the following year.

The isolation of Russia after the congress of Berlin was not desired by Bismarck, who feared she might drift into the arms of France. In Russia important circles were anxious to reknit relations with Germany, and the internal crisis that culminated in the assassination of Alexander II helped to diminish the force of panslav nationalism. Hence in 1881 the league of the three emperors was reconstituted. It seemed again that Bismarck's favorite idea of an accommodation between Russia and Austria-Hungary might bear fruit; the eastern Balkans and the Straits for the former; the western Balkans for the latter. Actually their mutual rivalries again proved far too deep and intertwined for any such apparently straightforward solution. Within five years the Bulgarian crisis shattered the league.

In 1885 the principality of Bulgaria, without agreement with Russia, took action on her own to incorporate her kinsfolk in the province of Eastern Rumelia, left by the 1878 treaty of Berlin under the sultan but with a special, autonomous régime. This step led to a fight for the continuance of the Russian dominance in Bulgaria. Alexander III (1881-94) was won over to the panslav policy of counter-revolution in Bulgaria, "the restoration of order" as he styled it. The pertinacity of the Bulgars and their support by Great Britain, Austria-Hungary and Italy caused an international crisis, which was further complicated by the simultaneous Boulanger crisis in Franco-German relations (1886-7). The blunders of the Russians gave the victory to the Anglo-Austro-Italian combination for the defense of Bulgaria and Turkey. Alexander III for the rest of his reign remained at daggers drawn with the new prince of Bulgaria (after 1908 king), the Austrian candidate, Ferdinand of Coburg, richly deserving his well-known epithet "foxy."

The Bulgarian crisis had other important consequences:—
1. Bismarck's attempt to prevent his two allies falling out again over the Balkans had failed. Although there was one further period (1897-1906) when the two governments worked amicably together, this was an interlude that did nothing to remove the fundamental grounds of hostility.
2. The Austro-Hungarian foreign minister was right in his judgment that at the height of the crisis it was not so much Bulgaria and the Straits that were "the chief causes of the hostile intentions entertained by Russia . . . but the predominant position of Germany and the Austro-German alliance." It had come very near to war: since 1876 Russia had become increasingly conscious that the old rivalries in the Balkans had

taken the new form of a struggle of the German against the Slav; in this she needed new allies.

3. Hence Russia began to turn to France. Katkov, then at the height of his influence in the press, and in personal touch with the tsar, was diatribing against the league of the three emperors: Russia should reserve her freedom of action; "our pilgrimages to Bismarck resemble rather too much our old journeys to the Golden Horde"; there should be close relations, if not actually an alliance, with France. Katkov died in the middle of the crisis (August 1887), but the links with France were not snapped and Bismarck's approval of financial measures against Russian credit had very serious consequences in strengthening them (see p. 347). The violence of Katkov's anti-Germanism went too far, and Alexander III broke with him. A minute of his is typical. "Katkov forgets himself and plays the rôle of the dictator, forgetting that foreign policy depends upon me . . ." Giers, foreign minister from 1882 to 1895, always a moderating influence, regained his lost ground, and the reinsurance treaty was made with Germany (June, 1887).

4. The overtures to this end that came from Russia were welcomed by Bismarck, for, though the league of the three emperors was dead, he had no intention of abandoning Russia to isolation and probable linking up with France. The reinsurance treaty was a success for Giers and the moderates, but it was scarcely a victory. It depended almost solely upon the tsar, and it had to be kept strictly secret for the worst of reasons; if it leaked out, it would be greeted with intense unpopularity in Russia. The treaty "reinsured" Germany in the sense that Russia, as in 1881, bound herself to benevolent neutrality in case of a Franco-German war, though now only if Germany were not the attacking party. A similar provision governed the case of an Austro-Russian war. In addition, the treaty committed Germany to new obligations, though not to

new lines of policy, in promising diplomatic support to Russia on Bulgaria and the Straits. This has justly been one of the most criticized points of Bismarck's diplomacy. He was so uncertain of the Russian government's ability or will to curb bellicose nationalism at home that in the greatest secrecy he encouraged England and Italy to combine with Austria-Hungary to prevent the realization of those Russian aims in Bulgaria and at the Straits, which in the reinsurance treaty he had undertaken to support diplomatically.

5. The long-standing Russian antagonism to England, already fanned by the Pendjeh crisis on the Afghan frontier (1885), was further increased by Salisbury's policy of the Mediterranean agreements (1887) directed against Russia in the Balkans. This concert with two of the Triple Alliance powers caused Russia to fear "the more or less probable adhesion of Great Britain to the political aims which that alliance pursues" (Giers, 1891).

This fear was very influential in bringing Russia to make definite alliance in 1893 with France. In 1890 Bismarck, who set the utmost store on maintaining a line with St. Petersburg, was dismissed by the young emperor William II (1888-1918), and despite Russian desires nothing was put in the place of the reinsurance treaty which was due to expire in that year. Alexander III was slowly driven to the reluctant conclusion that the Marseillaise must be played and the health of the Third Republic drunk.

The alliance with France was made in order to counterbalance the Triple Alliance, but it was the reverse of true that henceforward Europe was neatly aligned into two hostile camps. Since Russian energies were being more and more directed to the Far East and the Middle East and the central powers were not immediately menacing in Europe, the Franco-Russian alliance in fact for its first dozen years was pointed against the common enemy England, not the common enemy Germany, still less against Austria-Hungary, with whom France had no quarrels, or Italy, with whom Russia had none.

For those dozen years (1893-1905), apart from two serious tariff controversies, official relations between Russia and Germany were almost uniformly good, and agreements with Austria-Hungary in 1897 and 1903 for a common line in Macedonia and the Balkans worked none too badly. Russia, Germany and France combined in 1895 to tear up Japan's treaty of Shimonoseki (see p. 291), and Russia received frequent encouragement from Germany to plunge ahead in the Far East. The victory of the Far Eastern extremists in St. Petersburg in 1903 was also a victory for a Germanophil orientation, of which most of them were open adherents. War with Japan drew official Russia still nearer to Germany.

In October, 1904, Nicholas II, nervous over the Anglo-French entente announced in the previous April and additionally roused against the English by the Dogger Bank incident (see p. 426), welcomed suggestions from the Kaiser for a combination, in conjunction with France, against England. Negotiations between the two foreign offices during that winter did not bear fruit, but in July, 1905, when Nicholas, faced both with revolution and with full defeat by the Japanese, was plunged in the extremes of isolated dejection, he met the Kaiser in his yacht off the coast of Finland and sanctioned the dramatic signature of the treaty of Björkö.

By it each country was to support the other in arms in Europe if either was attacked by any European power, and Russia was to take the necessary steps to secure the adhesion of her ally France to the new alliance. Nicholas's foreign minister, Lamsdorff (1901-6), who had not been consulted, was aghast at the treaty, though he wanted good relations with Germany: it meant the abandonment of the Franco-Russian alliance and of any French hopes of regaining Alsace-Lorraine; at a moment when the Morocco crisis was straining Franco-German relations to the limit it would be quite impossible for French public opinion to swallow a combination with Germany; the only result would be to fling France into the arms of England and leave Russia alone, in dependence on Germany. The tsar insisted on France being approached. The French government could but refuse; and could but be disturbed as to the solidity of the alliance with Russia, even though the tsar was persuaded to back down from the treaty of Björkö, and it was abandoned. Within two years of this Russia, so far from making alliance with Germany against England, had brought into being the Triple Entente by reaching agreement with England (1907).

Even thereafter and despite the Bosnian crises of 1908-9, governmental policy was not irrevocably aligned against German, though public opinion was increasingly hostile. The desire for good, even for close, relations was strong in court and other conservative quarters, where the feeling had weight that Germany stood for a social and political order much more consonant with the interests of tsarism than France or England. If the German economic penetration of Russia aroused animus, the fact remained that Germany was far and away Russia's best customer: she took nearly a third of Russian exports (and supplied an even larger proportion, forty-four per cent of her imports). Sazonov, the new foreign minister (1910-16), was pacific and had none of the personal ambition or unpaid scores of his predecessor Izvolsky.

In 1910-11 Sazonov tried to improve relations, with some momentary success, by agreeing to abandon opposition to the Baghdad railway and making concessions in Persia, but the Agadir crisis over Morocco (1911) and the unabated Anglo-German naval rivalry augured ill, and Turkey and the Balkans worse. The triple combination of German naval, military and big business interests antagonized in their different ways at one and the same time both Russia and France and Great Britain, and they were drawn yet closer together by the provocative methods of German diplomacy, the pan-german section of the German press, and the erratic rodomontades of the Kaiser.

The menace of Germanism was felt the more acutely by Russia now that there was added to German might in Europe the expansion of German power in Turkey. The Baghdad railway had aroused great apprehension and Marschall von

Bieberstein, the exceedingly able German ambassador at Constantinople (1897-1912), appeared as another Stratford Canning. Public opinion in Russia was by now very widely conscious of the clash between German and Slav (*cf.* pp. 237, 332); it was still further stirred by the new fear of a virtual German domination at Constantinople and the Straits, perhaps to become the equivalent of the British position in Cairo. When in 1913 the Turks called in a German military mission to remodel their army and placed General Liman von Sanders at the head of an army corps in Constantinople itself, well-grounded Russian suspicions led to a sharp struggle with Berlin. But the Russians received no material satisfaction and gloomily forecast that "a lasting disturbance in the relations between Germany and Russia had arisen" (*cf.* p. 275).

The influence of moderate counsels was weakened, and Sazonov inclined more and more to the general view of the high command that Germany and Austria-Hungary were bent on taking every advantage of Russia and would not stop at war to gain their ends. In the eyes of Russia the two countries were one. Her mobilization plans were based on the eventuality of simultaneous war against both. When in June, 1914, the archduke Francis Ferdinand was murdered and Austria-Hungary four weeks later declared war on Serbia, Russia did not doubt (and she was right) that Germany was standing behind her ally. She responded accordingly with general mobilization. By August 6 she was at war with both the central powers and at her side in arms stood France and the British Empire.

Russia had France as her ally because of mutual fear of Germany, because of the hope of Alsace-Lorraine, because there was no other such ally. England had a great navy, but a very small army. France required an ally with a great army. For Russia alliance with republican France was rendered less difficult owing to the subsidence of three issues which had separated the two countries almost continuously for a hundred and fifty years before 1870. The French support of Sweden against Russia was in the main an eighteenth-century memory, though it had been revived in the Crimean War (see p. 260). French thwarting of Russia in Turkey and championship of the Polish cause were even more conspicuous than ever under the Second Empire, but during the Third Republic they ceased to be dividing lines.

The Crimean War in itself did not make any deep breach. Both governments were at once anxious for good relations, soon even for an entente. Russia welcomed French money to build her railways and especially Napoleon's designs against Austria. But Poland ruined the entente between the two emperors. As was to be expected the Polish revolt of 1863 was loudly applauded by French opinion of all shades. Napoleon III made matters much worse by a diplomatic campaign against Russia, elaborate in scope, but misty or confused in particulars. England joined in it, more cautiously. Austria was inveigled. In the end the Poles were in no wise profited, while Russian opinion was even more passionately stirred against the West than in 1830 (*cf.* pp. 207 ff.).

Napoleon's one chance of recovering ground lay in the Near East. His influence was predominant in Constantinople, but it was not used to give Russia some modicum of satisfaction. French support of Roumanian nationalism was a barrier. Neither in the Cretan question (1867-8) nor in that of the abrogation of the Black Sea clauses of the treaty of Paris did French diplomacy satisfy St. Petersburg. Alexander II was on very close terms with his trusted uncle, king William of Prussia. When 1870 came there was no hope of any kind of support for France from Russia.

The downfall of France, completely upsetting the balance of power in Europe, was after a time followed, very slowly, by the drawing together, finally the alliance, of the two countries. At first France was too weak and too unstable to be reckoned with. Russia was anxious for a stronger, and a monarchical, France, and Gorchakov intervened over-ostentatiously against Germany to extinguish "the war scare of 1875." But as the Republic took shape, its political principles and its harboring of Russian political refugees kept it at arm's length from tsarist Russia.

On the other hand, the very weakness of France and new

developments led to a changed outlook on foreign relations. In the first place the traditional policy of the support of Turkey against Russia was dropped. France remained financially and economically of great consequence in Turkey, but she had lost her political position in Constantinople and did not attempt to regain it at the expense of Russia. Secondly, the French colonial expansion of the eighties and nineties clashed with British expansion in Africa, in southeast Asia, and in the Pacific. After 1878, Anglo-Russian hostility increased in the Near and Middle East and was extended to the Far East. Opposition to England was common ground upon which Russia and France could co-operate. Their mutual interests nowhere conflicted. In the third place, gradually the Polish question ceased to be the stumbling block it had been in the past. Poland retained the sympathy of France, especially of the left, but feelings became toned down. Bitter experience had shown how difficult it was to help the Poles in practice even when France was strong and Russia relatively weak and Prussia had not become Germany. Fortunately for the Third Republic, between 1870 and 1914 there was no revolt in Poland and no international raising of the Polish question.

In the eighties, Russia moved much nearer to France. Panslav nationalism began to join hands with the new groups that were making rapid headway in France with their eyes on "the blue line of the Vosges" and their thoughts turning to Russia as their helpmate. Already in 1882 when the irrepressible general Skobelev, an ardent nationalist and the popular hero of Russia, visited Paris, he was greeted in French newspapers as the apostle of the inevitable struggle between Teuton and Slav—"the enemy is Germany"—and of alliance between France and the Slavs. The inflammatory Déroulède, at the head of his *Ligue des Patriotes,* and closely linked with Boulanger, played up to Russian nationalist feeling and maintained close relations particularly with Katkov during the Bulgarian crisis (1886-7).

Hostility to Germany and to England was the common ground for this rapprochement. As has been already seen,

Katkov was heading the anti-German campaign in Russia and giving to it a pro-French orientation, and he was in touch with French financial circles who were active to renew the close links of Russia with the Paris money market that had subsisted under the Second Empire. Official overtures even came during the Boulanger crises from the French government. Alexander III wanted the French to be strong: "nous avons besoin de vous and vous avez besoin de nous." But Boulangism and the principles and practice of the Third Republic disgusted him. Katkov overshot the mark. Giers succeeded in renewing links with Berlin.

Nevertheless, five years later there was no treaty with Germany, and there was alliance with France. The reasons for it have already been indicated. Unlike the Triple Alliance and the Austro-German alliance, which were never supplemented by detailed military agreements, that between Russia and France was not formally a treaty and the heart of it was from the first a military convention, revised and extended in 1900-1 and between 1906 and 1914.

The essentials were:— (i) Russia and France would fight together if either were attacked by Germany, or by Austria-Hungary or Italy supported by Germany. (ii) The two general staffs were to meet annually to concert joint measures. (iii) The two governments "will take counsel together" on every question likely to jeopardize the general peace, and in the event of being threatened by aggression "undertake to reach an understanding" on the necessary measures. (iv) The object of the alliance, originally defined as the maintenance of peace, was extended in 1899 to include the maintenance "of the equilibrium between the European powers." (v) The terms (though not the fact of the existence) of the alliance were to be kept strictly secret; and they were.

The diplomatic terms of the alliance were vague and led to divergence of interpretation. The French, down to 1912, were very cautious as to the *casus foederis* arising out of the Balkans, and the Russians were similarly cautious as to Morocco. Thus during the 1908-9 Bosnian crisis the French did not consider that "the vital interests of France and Russia are menaced," and Izvolsky complained bitterly that "France has gone over bag and baggage to Austria." The annual general staff conferences provided for in the original military convention were not held (except in 1900 and 1901) until 1906 onwards. The Russian military resented the peremptory attitude of the French, who treated them like inferiors, and there was much wrangling and shuffling. Nevertheless, the core of the alliance came to lie in the joint military plans, which were duly put into effect in August 1914. The contrast between the Franco-Russian alliance and the Soviet-French alliance of 1935, which was never implemented by staff discussions, could not be more striking.

Public opinion was variable. In Russia the alliance was in general popular, but many conservative circles disliked and feared French parliamentarism and socialism. Russian interests nowhere clashed with French, and the French financing of Russia which accompanied the alliance created very strong ties (see pp. 347-348). French culture had always played a great rôle in Russia; whereas German cultural influences were offset by the rising tide of anti-German feelings, the mass of Russians knowing little or nothing of the French had no antipathy against them.

In France, alliance with tsarist autocracy was always unpopular with the left, and very pronouncedly during the 1905 Revolution. The Russian money expended on the press could buy support, but could not buy out opposition. On the other hand, the small French investor was at least favorably impressed by the fact that the tsarist government always paid the dividends due on its mounting loans. Above all, what other alternative to Russia was there to make good the inferiority of French manpower in comparison with German?

The alliance, though in origin directed against the Triple Alliance, was for its first dozen years mainly a diplomatic combination against England; in Egypt, Siam, China, the Persian Gulf. During the Boer war, after the blow to France at Fashoda (1898) and when Russia and England were more than ever at loggerheads in the Far East, Delcassé (foreign minister from 1898 to 1905) revivified and extended the alliance, explicitly aiming it at England. An additional military convention was signed (1900) providing for common military action if war was imposed on either by England: Russia would act against India with three hundred thousand men when the Tashkent railway was completed. Russia did not lack the will, but the Tashkent railway was not yet even begun, and it was not finished until 1905.

By then conditions had completely changed, and the anti-English provisions were discarded. England, though the ally of Japan (1902), had made the entente with France (1904); Russia was at war with Japan and in the grip of Revolution. Delcassé went to the limit of neutrality, and beyond, in helping Russia during the war, but there was no question whatever of French intervention, which would have brought England into the war under her (public, not secret) alliance with Japan. He was anxious both to develop the entente with England, and somehow to bring her and Russia together.

On the Russian side the Revolution yet further weakened the government and made it desperately in need of French financial assistance (see p. 347). For the next few years the internal situation and army reorganization rendered the alliance extremely dubious as an effective instrument. The plans for Russian military co-operation were whittled down; the pessimism and new defensive strategy of the Russian high command would have left France to bear all the early brunt in the event of a war with Germany. On the other hand, politically the alliance was strengthened in 1907 by the Anglo-Russian agreement. The Triple Entente had come into being, even if it were but a delicate infant.

The final turning point in the history of the Franco-Russian alliance came in 1912. Russia was sufficiently recovered to pull her weight, which she did only too heavily. The French had always been insistent on the earliest possible large-scale action of Russia against Germany, as opposed to Austria-Hungary, if it came to war. The Russians now (1912) returned to their original engagement to concentrate 800,000 men against Germany, and they undertook to begin an offensive against her after the fifteenth day of mobilization; an undertaking that they honored to the full in August, 1914, thereby perhaps saving the battle of the Marne, but at the price of the disaster of Tannenberg. Russian strategic railways were pressed on, though not without much disputation on both sides. Delcassé, back in power as minister of marine since 1911 and ambassador in St. Petersburg in 1913, was again extremely active, making a naval agreement with Russia and another with Great Britain (1912), and concluding a big five-year loan program, in which strategic railways to the western frontier were to have the lion's share. In France the three-year military service law was passed, in the face of much opposition. Poincaré, first as prime minister (1912), then (from 1913) as president, lent his great weight to the solidifying of the alliance.

By 1914, Russian governing circles, far more than those in Great Britain or France, felt that a trial of strength with the central powers was near at hand. If war came, in all countries almost everyone thought in terms of a brief war. For a hundred years all wars (except civil and some colonial and South American wars) had been short. Two years was the extreme maximum. The four years of holocaust that actually occurred was outside men's vision. The economic capacity of Russia for war was far greater than twenty years previously. For this she was largely indebted to French capital exports. None the less, though the general effects of French investment in Russia were very great, French financial power was not a decisive factor in Russian diplomacy, except in 1906 at the Algeciras conference on Morocco, and it is not true that the creditor set the pace for the debtor. The reverse was much nearer the truth.

Russia had pursued her own course, often with little, sometimes with no regard for France. Despite the indignant protests of Poincaré in 1912, when he discovered that he had been kept in the dark as to the Balkan league, he continued to be perturbed by independent action by his ally. Yet it was Poincaré who recognized that France could no longer argue that "the maintenance of the general peace" or "the equilibrium between the European powers" was not directly affected by Balkan affairs. From 1912 France admitted that the *casus foederis* must arise not merely in case of attack on the actual territory of Russia, but also on those of her interests which she considered vital; and there was now no doubt that she so considered Serbia and the Straits.

In fact, the situation had radically changed since the days of Bismarck and the early years of the Franco-Russian alliance. Since Germany had committed herself so deeply to Austria-Hungary, France could only do likewise to Russia. She could not afford to stand aside and see Russia defeated by the superior combination of the central powers. In that case she would stand alone exposed to Germany. Since the Balkans, not Franco-German or Anglo-German relations, were the immediate origin of war, Russia in the last resort was the deciding partner in the alliance. The issue in July, 1914, extremely complicated in detail, was not in doubt once Russia decided that her vital interests compelled her to fight. So must France.

Great Britain followed suit, and once again as a hundred years before, and now today, was joined with Russia in comradeship of arms to save themselves and Europe from dictation.

In the intervening century England and Russia had stood for different systems in the world and the interests of the two empires had clashed in Asia and the Levant. Yet they had actually fought each other only once in the whole course of their history, in the Crimean War.

In the fifty years between then and 1907 the hostility of the two countries was founded on the same basis as that during the preceding half-century; but rivalry in the Far East was added and the Russian conquest of Central Asia brought "the threat to India" into far greater and more continuous prominence than previously.

While during the first half of the nineteenth century the British had extended their dominion in India to the Himalayas and the Indus and beyond, the Russians had been pegged down by the task of subjugating the Caucasian mountaineers (see pp. 284 ff.), the equivalent for Russia of the

Pathans and the Northwest frontier. When this conquest was completed, they turned to the east of the Caspian and in twenty years (1864-85) overran the independent oases of Central Asia and subdued the nomads. Frontiers in the European sense did not exist, but by 1880 there did exist the new fact of the contiguity of Russian power with Persian weakness and Afghan instability.

The British were quick to take alarm: for the first time since Napoleon their ascendancy in southern Asia was in danger of being challenged by another European power. To the Russians it seemed that they were but following the example of the British in India, and that, if they combined economic advantages for themselves with their civilizing mission, the British were the last people who could object. They rightly denied that their conquest of Central Asia was planned as a step toward the invasion of India. Once the Russians had expanded down the Volga, across the Urals, across Siberia, the impact of settled, organized power on nomad or oasis life was bound to be overwhelming, when the one had the armory of Western technique at its command and the other had nothing but ramshackle khanates, distance, or the desert.

It was, however, true that Central Asia gave the Russians "a basis of operations which, if need be, can be offensive" (Giers, 1883). As has been seen, in 1900, in concert with the French, they were prepared to make it such. Once at least, at a moment of expected war with England (1878), an expedition was on the move in Turkestan, and the British were justified in holding that the second Afghan war which followed was partly due to Russian instigation. They were also justified in their view that the Trans-Caspian railway, built (1881-8) along the northern frontier of Persia, had strategic objects, and in their repeated complaints that the St. Petersburg authorities could not or would not control their subordinates on the distant confines of the empire. The Russian foreign office in particular had little effective say in Central Asia, where the real rulers were the ministry of war and the governors-general, and where the Russians were constantly at logger-heads with each other, a fact which was one main reason for the protractedness of the dispute with England over the Pamirs (1891-95).

The British fears for India proved to be much exaggerated. The Suez Canal (1869) and the extension of railways in India had greatly improved their position. But the memory of the Indian Mutiny was green, and the danger of Russian stirring of the Afghans and resultant ignition or explosion of revolt in India could not be discounted.

"The threat to India" powerfully reinforced the old, popular hostility to Russia as a barbarous, yet wily and far-scheming, despotism. British opinion took little heed of Alexander II's reforms: Russia was still in the main summed up as reactionary police government, oppressing Poles and Jews and instigating panslavism and perpetual aggression in new parts of Asia. Similarly, Russian opinion was given a lurid picture of British oppression of the Indian millions, "sick to death . . . waiting for a physician from the North," and of the faithlessness and insatiable appetite of the British (Cyprus, 1878; Egypt, 1881), especially if possible at Russian expense.

Three times Russia and England stood very near to war: in 1878 when a Russian army was at the gates of Constantinople and a British fleet riding off the Golden Horn (*cf.* p. 272); in 1885 when the delimitation of the Russo-Afghan frontier led to the Pendjeh crisis, a fight between the Russians and Afghans that embroiled the British; in 1904 when the Baltic fleet, outward bound for the disaster of Tsushima, cannonaded the Hull fishing fleet off the Dogger Bank in the North Sea, suspecting a night attack by Japanese torpedo boats. The bulk of opinion in both countries would probably have acclaimed war on the first two occasions; in England, but not in Russia, in 1904.

War was averted in 1878 by the divisions among the Russians, which enabled Shuvalov, the skillful Russian ambassador in London, and the moderates to steer for diplomatic retreat from the treaty of San Stefano to the treaty of Berlin; in 1885 by the patience and reasonableness of Gladstone and Salisbury (though even Gladstone rushed through a vote of credit for eleven million pounds) and by the fact that the Russian military did not in fact at that time have designs on Herat or Afghanistan; in 1904 by the restraint of the Balfour government and by the patent fact that, however furiously Nicholas II might inveigh against "the insolent conduct of England" and "our filthy enemies," he could not afford to drive them into his alarmingly unsuccessful war with Japan.

Russian foreign policy in its opposition to British was much strengthened by the similar opposition of French policy. Already in 1887 Russian and French diplomacy made common cause against the British plans for Egypt. The Franco-Russian alliance, as has been seen, in its first period (1893-1904) functioned primarily against Great Britain. One result for the time being was the change in the balance of power in the Mediterranean.

By then Russia had created a Black Sea fleet, and from 1894 a small Russian squadron reappeared in the Mediterranean. The French navy was second in strength to the British, and, even if it were not combined with the Russian fleet sallying through the Straits, challenged superiority in the Mediterranean. The weakness of British sea-power was a major issue for government and public alike. Only with the return of the Salisbury government to power in 1895 did large naval programs slowly re-establish naval supremacy. Even so, the nineties marked two important changes in the British attitude towards Russia and Turkey.

The Armenian massacres (1895-6) gave the *coup de grâce* to the strength of British Turcophil opinion, which had for twenty years been powerfully countered by Gladstonian liberalism. Now the Turk became "the unspeakable Turk" and the sultan "Abdul Hamid the Damned." Their conduct was the worse in that they spent their money on fortifying the Dardanelles but not the Bosphorus, and seemed prepared to accept Russian ascendancy in Constantinople. Salisbury, always very conscious of public opinion in foreign affairs, abandoned the threadbare principle of the integrity of the Ottoman empire and broached partition. He was the more inclined to this by the fact that one keystone of British policy towards Russia, the protection of Constantinople against her, had become impracticable, or at best extremely questionable. His naval experts in the end convinced him that "there is no practical way, as long as France supports Russia by force of arms, of preventing the latter from using the Straits unless opposed by the Turks [which was thought highly improbable] . . . the time . . . for jealously guarding the inviolability of the Dardanelles is passing away"; in Egypt and Alexandria, not at the Straits, "the last stand will have to be made" (1896). Thereafter, though the conditions changed, the naval experts did not return to the old doctrine of the necessity of barring Russia at Constantinople and the Straits. When the entente with Russia was made in 1907 and Izvolsky in the following year raised the question of the Straits with Grey (*cf.* p. 275), the difficulties in England lay not with the admiralty, but in the unpreparedness of public opinion for a sudden *volte face*.

Salisbury in 1897 gave vent in the House of Lords to his much quoted phrase: "the parting of the ways was in 1853, when the Emperor Nicholas's proposals were rejected . . . we put our money on the wrong horse." But the difficulties in the path of his policy of practical co-operation as applied to Russia were insurmountable owing to the suspicions of the Russian government in the Near East and its aims in the Middle and Far East. A few months before Salisbury's admission the Russian government had secretly decided to seize the Black Sea entrance to the Bosphorus *"for ever,"* [1] if the crisis over the Armenian massacres led to a joint fleet demonstration of the powers through the Dardanelles.

As the nineties wore on, it was less on the Near East than on Persia, and above all the Far East, that Anglo-Russian rivalry became concentrated (*cf.* pp. 290 ff.). The advance of Russia in the Far East was accompanied by a doubling of her Pacific squadron, and that of the French (1895). When Salisbury offered to Russia (1898) an understanding based on "a partition of preponderance," but "no partition of territory," in either China or Turkey, the answer was the occupation of

[1] Underlined by the tsar in pencil.

Port Arthur and an apparently very alarming new naval program, to which the British government replied with supplementary estimates and the outspoken threat to build ship for ship against Russia and France combined.

After 1900 the Russian occupation of Manchuria and continued opposition to the policy of "the open door" in China drove Great Britain to a revolutionary reversal in her traditional policy of binding herself by no alliances, except in actual war. In 1902 she concluded alliance with Japan. The treaty was public. Henceforward Russia knew that, if war came with Japan, Great Britain would aid Japan with benevolent neutrality and join with her in arms should a third power (France) enter the war.

At this same time Russian imperialism in Persia reached its high-water-mark of success. Since 1878 Russian interests and influence in Persia had been more and more actively promoted at the expense of British imperialism. The Loan and Discount Bank (a close parallel to Witte's Russo-Chinese Bank; *cf.* p. 291), the Persian Cossack Brigade (officered by Russians and Persia's one reliable body of troops), the multiplication of consulates, a new shipping line to the Persian gulf—these and other less up-to-date means of penetration made Russia dominant in northern Persia and, in British eyes, a serious danger in the south and the Gulf.

In Afghanistan, where the British regarded their own exclusive influence to be essential, Russia was working for what even Lamsdorff, the cautious and pacific foreign minister, admitted to be "a certain freedom of action." The Russian extremist press demanded "a free exit for Russia to the Indian Ocean" and "no division of spheres in Persia, which, together with the waters that bathe its shores, must remain the object of Russian material and moral protection." Even as late as 1904 the government continued to hold to its policy of no division of Persia into spheres of influence and of activity in the Gulf and along the eastern frontier of Persia.

Meanwhile among Persians themselves a modern, nationalist and constitutionalist movement had grown rapidly, which was directed both against the arbitrary and ruinously expensive despotism of the shah and against Western imperialism. The electric effect of the victory of an Asiatic state over an European in the Russo-Japanese war and the repercussions of the 1905 Revolution in Russia resulted in a revolution in Persia (1906) and a prolonged struggle of the newly created national assembly against the shah and reaction, backed by tsarist Russia. Great Britain and Russia still faced each other, but under fundamentally changed conditions.

The Russo-Japanese war and the 1905 Revolution caused a radical reversal of Russian policy. In 1907 the entente with England was concluded.

This rapid change in the long-continued hostility between the two governments was due, on the Russian side, primarily to the reaction against absorption in Asia and the feeling that it was essential to clear up differences with Great Britain in order to keep free for developments in Europe. Izvolsky, the new foreign minister (1906-10), whose gaze had always been westward, held strongly that "we must put our interests in Asia on a reasonable footing, otherwise we shall simply become an Asiatic state, which would be the greatest disaster." Hence he was the prime mover in the agreement with England. He had a hard fight against his own subordinates in Persia and against the general staff, who got their way on some points, but he had useful support from the minister of finance, Kokovtsev, an upright and genuinely conciliatory man, though without any driving force (later, 1911-14, prime minister).

On the British side, anxieties on the side of Germany probably had the most weight. The success of the entente with her old enemy France suggested a similar accommodation with her other old enemy, and French diplomacy did what it could to smooth the path. Like the agreement of 1904 with France, but unlike the Franco-Russian alliance or the Triple Alliance, the 1907 agreement was public and took the form of a settlement of disputes in certain regions, not of an alliance or the proclamation of a joint policy. Unlike the entente with France, it was not followed by any military or naval plans.

The agreement covered Tibet, Afghanistan and Persia only, not the Baghdad railway or the Straits. But Izvolsky was right in his judgment that, if Asiatic difficulties could be smoothed out, the British government would be ready to consider concessions on the Straits. In Afghanistan, the Russians accepted the British claim to predominance. This was the most important result of the agreement: the removal of "the threat to India" was an essential for any real entente. Persia was divided between a Russian and a British sphere of influence, with a neutral zone between. The oil fields were not at that time realized to be of the importance five years later attached to them, and they neither then nor later caused difficulties with Russia.

The Persian agreement was heavily criticized in various quarters in England. In Persia itself it was regarded as a partition treaty and hence was anathema to most Persians. In the following ten years, despite restraining British efforts, the Russians did all they could to destroy the nationalist-constitutionalist movement and behaved more and more openly, in the tsar's own words, as "the masters of northern Persia." It may be doubted whether agreement with Russia could have been reached on any better terms, and Russia was in any case well placed for influence in northern Persia. The truth was that fear of Germany impelled Grey to truckle to tsarist imperialism.

The fact that Russia was tsarist Russia made the entente less of a reality than that with France. British opinion in general had welcomed the 1905 Revolution and hoped that the Duma would inaugurate a new era of relative freedom and toleration under a form of constitutional monarchy. Hopes had been dashed by the reaction that followed 1907, and there was still much scathing criticism of tsarism, not least of its doings in Persia. Alliance with tsarist Russia would have been impossible; entente was difficult enough. Salisbury on one occasion criticized Palmerston's policy as having been "guided by common sympathies [i.e. political proclivities] instead of by common interests." If the distinction be allowed, the British Liberal government, often against the grain, followed Salisbury rather than Palmerston. And the Russian government did likewise. A common fear drove both to combine, loosely, against the overmight of Germany.

Yet it cannot be said that the Anglo-Russian entente was merely diplomatic. Relations between the two countries were in some ways deeply changed compared to fifty years before. The new liberal movement, and some of the left, were much influenced by British political and social thought and practice. The old phobia of empire-grabbing England as the inevitable foe of Russia and the Slavs had rapidly lost strength with changing political conditions and wider interchange between the two countries. Englishmen in Russia in general had always liked, and been liked by, Russians, and they made a totally different impression from Germans. For thirty years past a series of informed and sympathetic studies of past and present Russia had made her much better known to England. Religious connections were fruitful in better understanding. Russian literature had come fully into its own in the West; Dostoevsky and Chekhov had been added, with profound effects, to Tolstoy and Turgenev. Russian opera and ballet had just burst upon the Western world. England was realizing that the dark evils of tsarism did not sum up the whole of Russia and that she had great achievements to her credit. England believed that a great and gifted people, as yet shackled by an outworn form of government, had begun its struggle to make a new world of Russia, moving forward whether with explosive force or at a slower pace towards a future different from her past.

Another struggle intervened. Once again, as a hundred years before, Russia and England were joined in comradeship of arms to save themselves and the world from dictation. By the time three hostile empires crashed, the Russians had exploded. The new Europe was shaped without and in despite of Russia. In her place, after three years of civil war and contest with her former allies, the new revolutionary republic of the soviets emerged, uncrushed but almost spent.

The October Revolution proved not to be the father of world revolution, but its spell was potent and kept the Soviet

Union in isolation. Yet she grew stronger; then entered more closely into multiple relations; then rose to rank among the great powers, but still so sharply dividing opinion in every country that neither she nor they could count upon the network of treaties and combinations woven round the world.

When the Nazi revolution had conquered Germany and forged the Axis, three powers were arrayed against four; but the four were not united. The Soviet Union remained so suspect that she was not certain whether she might not in effect be left to the Axis wolves. She parleyed with the wolves. The war cloud burst. Poland was struck down. The Low Countries, Norway, were overrun. France was crushed. Britain fought on, alone, in desperate but unfaltering defiance. Greece fell. The Balkans were lost. Then, massing in the east, the Red Army, many millions strong and mightily equipped but uncertain yet in quality, drew Hitler to nemesis.

For the second time within a generation Russia and Britain are plunged together in death grapple with Germany. On the greatest of all the battle fronts, from the Arctic to the Euxine, the destiny of our time hung in the balance. But at the darkest hour, when Moscow might have fallen, the Red Army did not doubt that they were the heirs to the future and of the past, the past of the Russian people. "The land of our forefathers has swallowed not a few hordes of invaders striving to conquer it. In the west, empires rose up and perished. The great were debased. The rich were made poor. Our native land grew and strengthened and nothing can shake it. Our land will swallow the German hordes. Thus it was. Thus it will be" (Alexis Tolstoy, November, 1941).

CHRONOLOGICAL TABLE

Dates, as elsewhere in this book, are given in the new style, *i.e.* according to our calendar.

860	*Period of Kiev Russia to 1240.*
	First Varangian expedition against Constantinople.
862	Traditional date of summoning of *Rurik*, the Varangian, to rule in Novgorod.
907?	Expedition of *Oleg* against Constantinople.
911	Treaty of Oleg with Byzantine empire.
944? 941	Expeditions of *Igor* against Constantinople.
945	Treaty of Igor with Byzantine empire.
957	Visit of *Olga* (Christian), mother of Svyatoslav, to Constantinople.
957?-72	*Svyatoslav,* grand-prince of Kiev Russia.
961	Ecclesiastical mission from Otto the Great to Kiev.
965 c.	Campaigns of Svyatoslav to the Volga and Caspian: disruption of the Khazars.
969-71	Campaigns of Svyatoslav against Bulgaria and the Byzantine empire.
972	Death of Svyatoslav at the hands of the Pechenegs.
978 c.-1015	*Vladimir,* grand-prince of Kiev Russia.
988	Baptism of Vladimir and "conversion" of Russia.
1019-54	*Yaroslav the Wise,* grand-prince of Kiev Russia.
1025-36 c.	Foundation of Yaroslavl.
1037?	Santa Sofia, Kiev, begun.
1045-57	Building of Santa Sofia, Novgorod.
1051 c.	Foundation of the Monastery of the Caves at Kiev.
1067	First serious raids of the Polovtsy.
1113-25	*Vladimir Monomakh,* grand-prince of Kiev Russia.
1147	First written mention of Moscow.
1157-74	*Andrew Bogolyubsky,* prince of Vladimir-Suzdal.
1158	Beginning of Uspensky cathedral in Vladimir.
1169	Sack of Kiev by Andrew Bogolyubsky.
1176-1212	*Vsevolod III,* Great-Nest, grand-prince of Vladimir-Suzdal.
1188 c.	Beginning of German conquest of Livonia and Estonia; Knights of the Sword (from 1202); Teutonic Knights from 1230 in E. Prussia.
1193-7	Building of St. Dmitri, Vladimir.
1204	Capture of Constantinople by the Fourth Crusade; beginning of the Latin empire (till 1261).

1221	Foundation of Nizhni-Novgorod (Gorki).
1223	First Mongol invasion; defeat of the Russians and Polovtsy on the Kalka.
1227	Death of Genghis Khan.
1237-42	Mongol conquest of Russia and invasion of Poland and Hungary.
	Mongol Period, 1240-1480.
1240	Victory of Alexander Nevsky over the Swedes.
	Batu (shamanist), khan, till 1255.
1242	Victory of Alexander Nevsky over the German Order.
1249 ff.	Swedish conquest and conversion of Finland.
1252-63	*Alexander Nevsky, grand-prince of Vladimir.*
1253 c.	Founding of the first Sarai as capital of the Golden Horde.
1261	End of Latin empire and restoration of Byzantine empire at Constantinople under the Palæologi.
	Berke (Moslem), khan, 1257-66.
	Sartak (Nestorian), khan, 1256.
1266 c.	First Tatar grants to Genoese in Crimea.
1300	Metropolitan of Kiev settles at Vladimir.
	Tokhta (not Moslem), khan, 1290-1312.
	Tula-Buga (? Moslem), khan, 1287-90.
	Predominance of Nogai, until 1299.
	Tuda-Mangu (Moslem), khan, 1280-87.
	Mangu-Timur (? Moslem), khan, 1266-80.
1304-27	Dominance of Tver (Kalinin) in rivalry for grand-princedom.
1326	Final establishment of metropolitan in Moscow.
	Ivan Kalita, 1325-41.*
	Yuri Danilovich, 1318-22.†
	Gedimin, grand-duke of Lithuania, 1316-41.
	Uzbek ‡ (Moslem), khan, 1312-40.
1337	Foundation of Troitsko-Sergievsky monastery; St. Sergius.
1348	Pskov secures independence of Novgorod.
	Olgerd, grand-duke of Lithuania, 1345-77.
	Simon the Proud, 1341-53.
	Djanibek, khan, 1340-57.
1354-68	Metropolitan Alexis.
	Ivan Ivanovich, 1353-59.

* Prince of Moscow from 1325; grand-prince from 1328. The grand-princedom thereafter (except 1359-62) remained with Moscow and the direct descendants of Ivan Kalita until 1598.

† Prince of Moscow from 1303; the first such to be recognized as grand-prince, in 1318.

‡ All the succeeding khans were Moslems.

1362	Defeat of the Tatars by Olgerd.
	Dmitry Donskoy, 1359-89. §
	Berdibek, khan, 1357-9.
1367-8	First stone fortifications of the Moscow Kremlin.
1368, 1370, 1372	Attacks on Moscow by Olgerd of Lithuania.
1375	Final defeat of Tver (Kalinin) by Dmitry Donskoy.
	Jagellon, grand-duke of Lithuania from 1377; from 1386 king of Poland.
1378	Defeat of the Tatars on the Vozha.
1380	Victory of Dmitry Donskoy over the Tatars (Mamai) at Kulikovo.
1382	Moscow burnt by Tokhtamysh.
	Tokhtamysh, khan, 1380-95.
1385-6	First "union" of Lithuania with Poland; Jagellon accepts Catholicism and becomes King Ladislas I.
	Vitovt, grand-duke of Lithuania, 1392-1430.
	Vasily I, 1389-1425.
1393	Incorporation of Nizhni-Novgorod (Gorki) in grand-princedom of Moscow.
1395	Defeat of the Golden Horde (Tokhtamysh) by Timur the Lame (Tamerlane).
1397	Foundation of Byelozero monastery.
1399	Defeat of Vitovt by the Tatars on the Vorskla.
1404	Capture of Smolensk by Vitovt.
1406-8	Campaigns of Vitovt against Moscow.
1408	Siege of Moscow by the Golden Horde (Edigei).
1410	Victory of Poland-Lithuania over the Teutonic Knights at Grünwald (Tannenberg).
	Vasily II, the Blind, 1425-62.
1430-66 c.	Growing disintegration of the Golden Horde; formation of the khanates of the Crimean Tatars, Kazan Tatars and Astrakhan.
1432-50	Civil war for the grand-princedom of Moscow.
1436	Foundation of Solovetsky monastery.
1439	Council of Florence; reunion of eastern and western churches.
1441	Metropolitan Isidore deposed for acceptance of Council of Florence.
1453	Capture of Constantinople by the Ottomans.
1463	Incorporation of Yaroslavl in Muscovy.
	Ivan III, the Great, 1462-1505.
1471	Campaign of Ivan III against Novgorod and its reduction.

§ Prince of Moscow from 1359; grand-prince from 1362.

1472	Marriage of Ivan III with Zoe (Sophia) Palæologus. Unsuccessful campaign of the Golden Horde against Moscow.
1474-1507	Alliance of Ivan III with the Crimean Tatars.
1478	Incorporation of Novgorod in Muscovy.
1480	Unsuccessful campaign of the Golden Horde against Ivan III: end of Muscovite dependency.
1482	Crimean Tatars raid Lithuania and sack Kiev.
1485-1516	Building of the new Kremlin in Moscow.
1485	Incorporation of Tver (Kalinin) in Muscovy.
1489	Incorporation of Vyatka (Kirov) in Muscovy.
1494	End of the Hanse in Novgorod.
1497	Code of Ivan III.
1500-3	War with Lithuania and the Livonian Order; Ivan III regains upper Oka and Chernigov.
1501	Defeat of the Livonian Order by Ivan III.
1502	Destruction of the Golden Horde by the Crimean Tatars.
1503	Church council: victory of "the Josephines" over the "no property" group.
1507-8	War with Lithuania.
	Vasily III, 1505-33.
1510	Incorporation of Pskov in Muscovy.
1512-22	War with Lithuania; capture of Smolensk by Muscovy (1514).
1521	Siege of Moscow by the Crimean and Kazan Tatars.
	Ivan IV, the Terrible, 1533-84.
1533-39	Regency of Elena Glinskaya, mother of Ivan the Terrible.
1547	Ivan the Terrible assumes power; his coronation as tsar.
1547-56	Internal reforms; code of 1550; military service from land regularized.
1551	Reforms of church council (*Stoglav*).
1552	Capture of Kazan.
1553	Opening of White Sea route by Chancellor.
1554	War with Sweden.
1556	Capture of Astrakhan.
1558-83	The Livonian War against Poland, from 1561 also against Sweden.
1564	First book printed in Moscow.
1565-72	Ivan the Terrible's reign of terror; the *oprichnina*.
1569	Union of Lublin between Poland and Lithuania.
1571	Crimean Tatars burn Moscow.
1571-1600	Fortification and expansion of southern frontier in wooded steppe, and along Volga; beginning of the Don, Zaporozhian and Ural Cossacks.
1581	Yermak and the beginning of the conquest of Siberia.

1582	Truce with Poland.
1583	Truce with Sweden.
1585	Foundation of Arkhangel.
	Feodor Ivanovich, 1584-98.
1587-98	Boris Godunov as "Lord Protector."
1589	Creation of Moscow Patriarchate.
1590-3	War with Sweden (treaty of Tyavzino, 1595).
1596	Union of Brest-Litovsk; creation of Uniat church in Poland.
1598	End of conquest of W. Siberia. Election of Boris Godunov as tsar by assembly of the land.
	Boris Godunov, 1598-1605.
1601-3	Famine.
1604	Beginning of civil wars.
	"Time of Troubles," 1604-13.
1605-6	*First False Dmitri* as tsar, with Polish help.
1606-7	Revolt of Bolotnikov.
1606-10	*Shuisky* as tsar.
1607-10	*Second False Dmitri* as rival tsar with Cossack support and intensification of Polish intervention; revolts in middle Volga.
1610	Poles in Moscow; *Vladislav* chosen tsar; Shuisky overthrown.
1611	Swedes in occupation of Novgorod. Poles capture Smolensk.
1611-12	Organization of national resistance under Minin and Pozharsky; reconquest of Moscow from the Poles.
1613	Election of Michael Romanov as tsar by assembly of the land.
	Michael Romanov, 1613-45.
1618	Truce of Deulino with Poland; Smolensk retained by Poland. Peace of Stolbovo with Sweden; loss of any outlet to the Baltic.
1619-33	Patriarch Filaret.
1632-34	War with Poland; failure to regain Smolensk; treaty of Polyanovo.
1636-52	Fortification and expansion of southern frontier; Byelgorod defence line.
1645 ff.	Migration of Ukrainians into Slobodskaya Ukraine; foundation of Kharkov (1656).
	Alexis Mikhailovich, 1645-76.
1648-9	Risings in Moscow and other towns; assembly of the land; the code of tsar Alexis.
1649	Abolition of English trading privileges.

1650	Risings in Novgorod and Pskov.
1652	Nikon becomes Patriarch.
1653	Last full meeting of the assembly of the land.
1654	Church Council adopts Nikon's reforms; beginning of the Schism.
1648-59	Bohdan Khmelnitsky, Hetman of the Ukraine; struggle against the Poles.
1654	"Treaty" of Pereyaslavl; "union" of the Ukraine with Muscovy.
1654-67	War with Poland over the Ukraine; truce of Andrusevo.
1654-81	"Time of ruin" in the Ukraine.
1656-58	War with Sweden; truce of Valiesari (peace of Kardis, 1661).
1662	"Copper riots" in Moscow.
1666	Church council deposes Patriarch Nikon.
1667	New trade regulations.
	Truce of Andrusevo with Poland; cession to Muscovy of Kiev, Little Russia and Smolensk.
	Church council confirms measures against Old Believers and sectarians.
1667-76	Revolt of Solovetsky monastery against church reforms.
1670-1	Revolt of Stenka Razin; beginning of curtailment of autonomy of the Don Cossacks.
1676-81	War with Turkey and the Crimea; treaty of Bakchi-Serai.
	Feodor Alexeyevich, 1676-82.
1682	Abolition of the code of precedence.
	Sophia proclaimed regent with Peter and Ivan V as joint tsars.
	Peter I, the Great, 1682-1725.
	Ivan V, 1682-96.
1686	"Permanent peace" with Poland.
1687, 1689	Campaigns against the Crimea.
1689	Fall of the regent Sophia and Golitsyn.
	Treaty of Nerchinsk with China.
1694	Peter takes over the government.
1695-1700	War with Turkey.
1696	Capture of Azov from the Turks.
1697-8	Peter's first visit to the West.
1698	Revolt of the *streltsy* crushed.
1700-21	Great Northern War against Sweden; treaty of Nystad.
1700	Suspension of Patriarchate.
	Reform of the calendar.
1700	Charles XII's victory at Narva.
1701-4	Conquest of Ingria.
1703	Foundation of St. Petersburg.

1705-6	Astrakhan revolt.
1705-11	Bashkir revolt.
1707-8	Revolt of Bulavin on the Don.
1709	Poltava.
	Little Russia loses its autonomous position.
1710	Conquest of Livonia, Estonia and Viborg.
1711	Institution of the Senate.
	War with Turkey; disaster on the Pruth.
1713	Treaty of Utrecht; end of War of the Spanish Succession.
1713-14	Conquest of Finland.
1714	Edict on primogeniture.
1718	Institution of poll tax and "colleges."
	Tsarevich Alexis condemned to death and killed.
	Death of Charles XII.
1721	Abolition of Patriarchate and creation of Holy Synod.
	Treaty of Nystad with Sweden; acquisition of Livonia, Estonia, Ingria and Karelia.
	Adoption of title of emperor.
1722	"Table of ranks."
	Peter's succession edict.
1722-3	War with Persia.
1725	Foundation of Academy of Sciences.
	Catherine I, 1725-27.
	Peter II, 1727-30.
	Anna, 1730-40.
1730	Struggle over terms of succession of Anna.
	Abolition of Peter's primogeniture law.
1730-40	Ascendancy of Biron.
1733-5	War of the Polish Succession.
1735-9	War with Turkey; treaty of Belgrade.
1740	Fall of Biron.
	Ivan VI, 1740-41.
1741	Deposition of Ivan VI and his mother, the regent.
	Elizabeth, 1741-62.
1741-3	War with Sweden; treaty of Åbo.
1754	Abolition of internal tolls.
1755	Foundation of Moscow university.
1756-63	Seven Years' War.
1762	*Peter III, 1762.*
	Peace and alliance with Prussia.
	Edict freeing the nobility and gentry from service.
	Deposition and murder of Peter III.
	Catherine II, the Great, 1762-96.
1764	Shooting of Ivan VI.
	Final secularization of church lands.

1767-8	The Legislative Commission.
1768-72	Armed resistance of Confederation of Bar to Russian demands on Poland.
1768-74	War with Turkey; treaty of Kuchuk-Kainardji.
1772	First Partition of Poland.
1773-5	Revolt of Pugachov.
1774	Treaty of Kuchuk-Kainardji with Turkey; acquisition of Black Sea steppes.
1775	Liquidation of the Zaporozhian Cossacks. Local government reforms.
1780	Renewal of alliance with Austria. First Armed Neutrality against England.
1781-6	Full absorption of Little Russia in the empire.
1782	Catherine's "Greek Project."
1783	Incorporation of the Crimea.
1785	Charter constituting the nobility and gentry an estate.
1787-92	War with Turkey; treaty of Jassy.
1788-90	War with Sweden; treaty of Verela.
1789	Beginning of the French Revolution.
1793	Second Partition of Poland.
1795	Third Partition of Poland.
	Paul, 1796-1801.
1797	Law on the succession to the throne.
1799	Second Coalition against France; Suvorov's campaigns in N. Italy and Switzerland.
1800-1	Alliance of Paul with Napoleon; second Armed Neutrality against England.
1801	Deposition and murder of Paul.
	Alexander I, 1801-25.
1801-4	Internal reforms.
1801-29	Acquisition of E. Georgia (1801) and conquest of Transcaucasia: 1785-1864 conquest of the Caucasian mountaineers.
1805	Third Coalition against France; Austerlitz.
1806	Jena.
1806-12	War with Turkey; treaty of Bucarest.
1806-13	War with Persia; treaty of Gulistan.
1807	Eylau and Friedland.
July	Peace of Tilsit with Napoleon; break with England; setting up of Grand Duchy of Warsaw.
1807-11	Reforms of Speransky.
1808-9	War with Sweden; treaty of Frederikshamn; acquisition of Finland.
1810 Dec.	Abandonment by Russia of Continental System.

1812 June	Treaty of Bucarest with Turkey; acquisition of Bessarabia.
June-Dec.	The War for the Fatherland; Borodino, burning of Moscow.
1813-15	Grand Alliance against Napoleon.
1814-15	Congress of Vienna.
1815	Constitution of "Congress Kingdom" of Poland.
1815-25	Ascendancy of Arakcheyev.
1821	Outbreak of Greek revolt.
1822	Return to high protective tariff.
1825	*Nicholas I, 1825-55.*
Dec.	The Decembrist rising.
1826-8	War with Persia; treaty of Turkmanchai.
1827	Navarino.
1828-9	War with Turkey; treaty of Adrianople.
1830	Revolution in France and Belgium.
1830-1	Polish rebellion.
1832	Final settlement of Greek independence.
1832-3	First Mehemet Ali crisis; treaty of Unkiar-Skelessi.
1833	Code of Laws.
	Münchengrätz agreement between Russia, Austria and Prussia.
1839-41	Second Mehemet Ali crisis; London Convention on the Straits.
1846	Annexation of Cracow by Austria.
1848-9	Revolution in France, Austria, Germany and Italy.
1849	Intervention in Hungary.
1853-6	Crimean War.
1855	*Alexander II, 1855-81.*
1856	Congress of Paris.
1857	Moderate protective tariff.
1858-60	Acquisition from China of Amur and Maritime provinces.
1859	Surrender of Shamil; conquest of Caucasus completed (except Circassians, 1864).
1860-73	First railway boom.
1861	Emancipation of the serfs.
1863	Polish rebellion.
1863-4	Law and education reforms.
1864	Local government reforms (*zemstva*).
1864-85	Conquest of Central Asia.
1865	Press Censorship reforms.
1867	Sale of Alaska to U.S.A.
1870	Municipalities reform.
1871	London Convention on the Straits.
1874	Compulsory military service.
1877	Beginning of return to high protection.

1877-8	War with Turkey; treaty of San Stefano; congress of Berlin.
1881	Assassination of Alexander II.
	Alexander III, 1881-94.
1885	Pendjeh crisis.
1885-7	Bulgarian crisis.
1891	Beginning of the Trans-Siberian railway. Famine.
1891-3	Making of the Franco-Russian alliance.
1892-1903	Witte minister of communications, finance and commerce.
1894	*Nicholas II, 1894-1917.*
1896	Russo-Chinese treaty and concession for Chinese-Eastern railway.
1896-7	Armenian massacres.
1897	Witte's monetary reforms; adoption of gold standard.
1898	Occupation of Port Arthur.
1900	"Boxer" rebellion; Russian occupation of Manchuria.
1904-5	Russo-Japanese War; treaty of Portsmouth (Sept. 1905).
1905	The 1905 Revolution; October Manifesto; Moscow rising (Dec.).
1906	First Duma.
1906-11	Stolypin prime minister: agrarian legislation.
1907	Anglo-Russian entente.
1908-9	Bosnia-Herzegovina crisis.
1912-13	Balkan wars.
1914 Aug.	Outbreak of First World War.
1917 Mar.	*March Revolution.*
	Revolution; abdication of Nicholas II; Provisional Government.
	October Revolution.
Nov.	The Bolshevik Revolution (according to the calendar then in use, October).
1918 Mar.	Treaty of Brest-Litovsk with Germany and her allies.
Nov.	Victory of the Allies over Germany.
1918-20	Civil War; German and Allied intervention; Soviet-Polish War (1920).
1919	Foundation of Communist International (dissolved May 1943).
1921	Adoption of the New Economic Policy.
1921-2	Famine.
1922	Soviet-German treaty of Rapallo.
1923	Failure of Communist risings in Germany. U.S.S.R. constitution adopted.
1924	Death of Lenin.

1926		Locarno treaties; admission of Germany to League of Nations.
1927		Anti-Communist drive in China.
		Victory of Stalin and expulsion of Trotsky and others from Communist party.
1928		Beginning of first five-year plan and collectivization of agriculture.
1929		Beginning of world economic crisis.
1931		Japanese seizure of Manchuria.
1933	Jan.	Beginning of second five-year plan.
	Jan.-Mar.	Nazi revolution in Germany.
1933	Nov.	Recognition of U.S.S.R. by U.S.A.
1934	Sept.	Admission of U.S.S.R. into League of Nations.
1935	Mar.	Announcement of German re-armament.
	May	Signature of Soviet-French and Soviet-Czechoslovak treaties of alliance.
1935-6		Abyssinian crisis and war.
1936	Mar.	German reoccupation of the Rhineland.
	July	Montreux Convention on the Straits.
	Nov.	Anti-Comintern pact between Germany and Japan.
	Dec.	Adoption of new U.S.S.R. constitution.
1936-8		Moscow trials.
1936-9		Spanish Civil War.
1937		Beginning of Sino-Japanese War.
1938	Jan.	Beginning of third five-year plan.
	Mar.	"Vienna."
	Sept.	"Munich."
1939	Mar.	"Prague."
	Aug.	Soviet-German Treaty.
	Sept.	Germany invades Poland; Outbreak of Second World War.
	Sept.	Soviet occupation of E. Poland, followed by incorporation in U.S.S.R.
	Sept.-Oct.	Soviet treaties securing bases in Estonia, Latvia and Lithuania.
1939-40	Dec.-Mar.	Soviet-Finnish War; expulsion of U.S.S.R. from League of Nations.
1940	June	Collapse of France.
	June-July	Incorporation in U.S.S.R. of Lithuania, Latvia, Estonia, Bessarabia and N. Bukovina.
1941	April	Soviet-Japanese Neutrality Pact.
	June	Germany invades U.S.S.R.; followed by Finland, Roumania, Hungary and Italy.

NOTE ON BOOKS

THE following list of suggestions is intended for those who do not know Russian. For those who do, apart from the Russian originals of books mentioned below and from books mentioned in the Reference Notes, two very useful, comprehensive manuals, with good bibliographies and maps, are: *Istoriya S.S.S.R.*, vol. 1, *s drevnyeishikh vremen do kontsa XVIII v.* (ed. by V. I. Lebedev, B. D. Grekov, and S. V. Bakhrushin; Moscow, 1939),[1] and P. I. Lyashchenko, *Istoriya narodnogo khozyaistva S.S.S.R.* (vol. 1, Moscow, 1939; especially full on 1750-1917).

All the books mentioned below, as also those which have been referred to in the footnotes to this book, were published in the United States, unless otherwise stated.

Those books marked with an asterisk are suggested as specially, though not only, suitable for introductory purposes.

1. GEOGRAPHY, ETC.

P. Cameina d'Almeida, *Etats de la Baltique: Russie* (Paris, 1932; vol. 5 of *Géographie universelle*, ed. by P. Vidal de la Blache and L. Gallois; covers the whole of the U.S.S.R.; admirable descriptive geography, with excellent illustrations and useful historical and economic references); J. S. S. Gregory and D. W. Shave, **The U.S.S.R.: a Geographical Survey* (London, 1944). M. Slonim, *Les onze républiques soviétiques* (Paris, 1937; outline of economic and historical geography). L. Niederle, **La race slave* (Paris, 2nd ed., 1916; brief outline by the great Czech Slavic scholar).

2. OUTLINE HISTORIES

R. Beazley, N. Forbes, and G. A. Birkett, **Russia from the Varangians to the Bolsheviks* (Oxford, 1918); Sir Bernard Pares, *A History of Russia* (3rd ed., 1943); S. F. Platonov, **History of Russia* (1929; somewhat abridged version of the last Russian ed.

---

[1] The second volume, covering 1801 to 1937, was published in Moscow in 1941, but I have not seen a copy.

(1916); goes down to 1881; by a great Russian scholar); S. R. Tompkins, *Russia through the Ages; from the Scythians to the Soviets* (1940); G. Vernadsky, **A History of Russia* (3rd ed., 1944). Pares, Tompkins, and Vernadsky cover the Soviet period.

3. LONGER COMPREHENSIVE HISTORIES

V. O. Klyuchevsky, *A History of Russia* (5 vols., London, 1911-31; a great work of one of the great historians of any country; originally published in Russian 1904-21; very brief on the nineteenth century; the translation is bad); P. Milyukov, C. Seignobos, and L. Eisenmann, *Histoire de Russie* (3 vols., Paris, 1932-33; vol. 1 up to 1725, vol. 2, 1725-1855, vol. 3, 1855-1932; by various Russian *émigrés* scholars, mainly P. Milyukov and A. Kizivetter; good on internal affairs up to 1916, but very inadequate on foreign relations); M. N. Pokrovsky, *History of Russia from the Earliest Times to the Rise of Commercial Capitalism* (1931; goes down to 1725) and *Brief History of Russia* (2 vols., 1933; mainly the nineteenth century and the 1905 Revolution; Pokrovsky, a posthumously excommunicated Marxist, must be used with great caution); K. Stählin, *Geschichte Russlands von den Anfängen bis zur Gegenwart* (4 vols., Berlin, 1923-39; goes down to 1917; vols. 2 and 3 covering Peter the Great to the Crimean war are specially useful).

4. SOCIAL AND ECONOMIC HISTORY

Besides Klyuchevsky and Pokrovsky in §3: J. Kulischer, *Russische Wirtschaftsgeschichte* (vol. 1, Jena, 1925; goes down to the end of the seventeenth century); James Mavor, *An Economic History of Russia* (2 vols., 2nd ed., 1925; good outline up to Peter the Great; then a detailed history of social and revolutionary movements as well as of economic development from Peter to 1907); P. Milyukov, *Essais sur l'histoire de la civilisation russe* (Paris, 1901; illuminating studies in demographic, economic, financial, and administrative history); D. S. Mirsky. **Russia; a Social History* (London, 1931; republished 1943; oversweeping, but stimulating; semi-Marxist); G. T. Robinson, *Rural Russia under the Old Régime* (London, 1923; detailed analysis, mainly covering 1850-1916).

5. RELIGIOUS HISTORY

Besides Klyuchevsky in §3, Leroy Beaulieu, vol. 3, in §8, and Masaryk and Maynard in §9: F. C. Conybeare, *Russian Dissenters* (1921); W. H. Frere, *Some Links in the Chain of Russian Church History* (London, 1918); P. Milyukov, *Outlines of Russian Culture*, vol. 1, *Religion and the Church* (ed. by M. Karpovich; 1942).

On religion in the U.S.S.R., besides Milyukov above and Maynard in §10: W. C. Emhardt, *Religion in Soviet Russia* (1929; covers 1917 to 1928; by an American Episcopalian); J. F. Hecker, *Religion and Communism* (London, 1933; Communist standpoint; covers both pre-1917 and post-1917 Russia); M. Spinka, *The Church and the Russia Revolution* (1927; covers 1917 to 1926; by an American Protestant: see also his more general, and much more hostile study, *Christianity confronts Communism*, 1936); N. S. Timasheff, *Religion in Soviet Russia, 1917-42* (1943; strongly anti-Marxist; mainly on the last dozen years).

6. LITERATURE AND THE OTHER ARTS

Maurice Baring, *An Outline of Russian Literature* (Home University Library, 1914) and *Landmarks in Russian Literature* (1910; both are exceptional); Janko Lavrin, *An Introduction to the Russian Novel* (1942; good, brief outline); E. J. Simmons, *An Outline of Modern Russian Literature 1880-1940* (1944); D. S. Mirsky, *Modern Russian Literature* (World's Manuals series, 1925; from Pushkin to Mayakovsky; incisive, brief outline) and *A History of Russian Literature from the Earliest Times to the Death of Dostoevsky* (1927) and *Contemporary Russian Literature, 1881-1925* (1926); P. Milyukov, *Outlines of Russian Culture*, vol. 2, *Literature* (ed. by M. Karpovich; 1942); G. Struve, *Twenty-five Years of Soviet Russian Literature* (London, 1944).

D. R. Buxton, *Medieval Russian Architecture* . . . (Cambridge, 1934; excellent photographs; includes Transcaucasia); N. P. Kondakov, *The Russian Icon* (Oxford, 1927; the authoritative work by the greatest master of the subject; excellent reproductions); P. Milyukov, *Outlines of Russian Culture*, vol. 3, *Architecture, Painting, Music* (ed. by M. Karpovich, 1942); L. Réau, *L'art russe des origines à Pierre le Grand* (Paris, 1921), and *L'art russe de Pierre le Grand à nos jours*

(Paris, 1922; these two books form a comprehensive survey of architecture, painting, and sculpture).

M. D. Calvocoressi and G. Abraham, *Masters of Russian Music* (1936; from Glinka to Scriabin). M. D. Calvocoressi, *Russian Music (London, 1944; Pelican series); G. Abraham, *Eight Soviet Composers* (London, 1943). See also Milyukov, vol. 3, above.

R. Fülöp-Miller and J. Gregor, *The Russian Theatre: its Character and History* (1930; numerous excellent illustrations, prefixed by a sketch of the growth and ideas of the theater and ballet); Joseph Macleod, *The New Soviet Theatre* (London, 1943).

7. CERTAIN REGIONS

W. E. D. Allen, *The Ukraine* (Cambridge, 1940; detached); D. Doroshenko, *History of the Ukraine* (Edmonton, 1939; Ukrainian nationalist standpoint); M. Hrushevsky, *A History of Ukraine* (1941; abridged version of the monumental work by the great Ukrainian nationalist historian).

R. Grousset, *L'empire des steppes* (Paris, 1939; the nomad peoples from Attila to the eighteenth century); A. S. Krausse, *Russia in Asia, 1558-1899* (1899); F. H. Skrine and E. D. Ross, *The Heart of Asia* (London, 1899; Central Asia from the earliest times to the end of the nineteenth century); C. Stéber, *L'Asie centrale soviétique et le Kazakhstan* (Paris, 1939; mainly geographical and economic); V. A. Yakhontoff, *Russia and the Soviet Union in the Far East* (1932).

There are a number of first-class historical articles on the Moslems in Russia, many of them by Barthold, in the *Encyclopaedia of Islam* (1908-38).

8. CERTAIN PERIODS

In addition to the treatment in the books mentioned above in §§3 and 4, the following are particularly useful:

For pre-Varangian history and the general Slav background:

G. Vernadsky, *Ancient Russia* (1943; comprehensive study from prehistoric times to the ninth century A.D.; specially important for the steppe peoples); E. H. Minns, *Scythians and Greeks* (1913); M. I. Rostovtsev, *Iranians and Greeks in South Russia* (1922); L. Niederle, *Manuel de l'Antiquité slave* (Paris, 2 vols.,

1923-26; authoritative survey of the main problems concerning the history and civilization of the Slav peoples up to the tenth century).

For the Varangian question:

V. Thomsen, *The Relations between Ancient Russia and Scandinavia and the Origin of the Russian State* (London, 1877; still the best treatment of the problem available in English; see also in Niederle, vol. 1, above); N. K. Chadwick, *The Beginnings of Russian History* (London, 1946).

For the period 1240-1480:

B. Grekov and A. Yakubovsky, **La Horde d'Or* (Paris, 1939; translated from the Russian); A. Eck, *Le moyen age russe* (Paris, 1933; detailed study of "feudalism" and serfdom).

For the fifteenth to the eighteenth centuries:

M. Dyakanov, *Skizzen zur Gesellschafts- und Staatsordnung des alten Russlands* (Breslau, 1931; last Russian ed. 1926; a masterly work covering both Kiev Russia and Muscovy up to the end of the seventeenth century; the translation has been sharply criticized by German scholars); A. Brückner, *Die Europäisierung Russlands* (Gotha, 1888; in the seventeenth and eighteenth centuries); I. Lubimenko, *Les relations commerciales et politiques de l'Angleterre avec la Russie avant Pierre le Grand* (Paris, 1933); D. Gerhard, *England und der Aufstieg Russlands* (Berlin, 1933; Anglo-Russian economic and foreign relations in the eighteenth century).

For the nineteenth century:

M. Karpovich, **Imperial Russia, 1801-1917* (Berkshire Studies; 1932; a very succinct outline); A. Kornilov, *Modern Russian History* (2 vols.; published in Russia, 1912-14; covers 1796-1881; liberal standpoint; specially useful on Alexander II's reforms; very badly translated); Grand Duke Nicolas Mikhailovich, *Le Tsar Alexandre I* (Paris, 1931; shortened version of a work originally published in 1912); T. Schiemann, *Geschichte Russlands unter Kaiser Nikolaus I* (4 vols., Berlin, 1904-19; covers also the reign of Alexander I; particularly valuable on foreign affairs).

Two outstanding analyses of Russia in the fifty years before 1914, with much historical background, are:

A. Leroy-Beaulieu, *L'empire des Tsars et les Russes* (3 vols., Paris, 1881-89; also in [incomplete] English translation), and Harold Williams, **Russia of the Russians* (1914).

9. REVOLUTIONARY MOVEMENTS AND THE BACKGROUND OF THE REVOLUTION

N. Berdyaev, *The Origin of Russian Communism* (1937; penetrating study of the intellectual and spiritual background and nature of Russian Communism); M. T. Florinsky, *The End of the Russian Empire* (1931; analysis of Russia during the War); N. N. Golovine, *The Russian Army during the World War* (1931; by an eminent Russian general); Lenin, *The State and Revolution* (1919; written late summer 1917), and vols. 1-5, 11 and 12 of his *Selected Works* (1936-39; covering 1894-1916); T. G. Masaryk, *The Spirit of Russia* (2 vols., 1919; first published in German, 1913; weighty analysis of the main trends of social, religious, and revolutionary thought in nineteenth-century Russia, with much historical background); James Mavor, vol. 2, see above §4; Sir John Maynard, *Russia in Flux* (London, 1941; analysis of the century to 1917; excellent interweaving of Russian literature); M. N. Pokrovsky, see above §3; Sir Bernard Pares, *The Fall of the Russian Monarchy* (1939; detailed treatment of Nicholas II, the court, the ministers, and the War of 1914).

10. THE REVOLUTION AND THE SOVIET UNION

For literature and the other arts see §6; for religion §5.

N. de Basily, *Russia under Soviet Rule* (London, 1938; informative analysis by a hostile émigré); A. Baykov, *The Development of the Soviet Economic System* (London, 1946; thorough and valuable); F. Borkenau, *The Communist International* (1938). W. H. Chamberlin, *The Russian Revolution, 1917-21* (2 vols., 1935), *Soviet Russia* (1930; covers 1922-28), and *Russia's Iron Age* (1935; covers 1929-34; increasingly antipathetic); J. G. Crowther, *Soviet Science* (London, 1936; abridged in Pelican series, 1942; account of the main scientific institutions and their work); D. J. Dallin, *Soviet Russia's Foreign Policy, 1939-42* (1942; useful for reproduction of official reports and press material, but dubious in interpretation); M. Dobb, *Soviet Planning and Labour in Peace and War* (London, 1942) and *Soviet Economy and the War* (London, 1941; both are brief but essential accounts of the fundamentals of Soviet planning, finance, economics, and labor; favorable to Communism); Louis Fischer, *The Soviets in World Affairs* (2 vols., 1930; the most valuable account as yet of Soviet foreign policy; covers 1917 to 1929); M. T. Florinsky, *Towards an Understanding of the U.S.S.R.* (1939; short, critical analysis of Soviet institutions); S. N. Harper, *The Government of the Soviet Union* (1937; compact, general survey); *History of the Civil War in the U.S.S.R.*, vol. 1 (1937; introductory volume going down to early October 1917; the second volume (1942) has not yet been translated; official Communist Party publication by various authors); *History of the Communist Party of the Soviet Union (Bolsheviks)* (1938; the latest official history issued by the Party); C. B. Hoover, *The Economic Life of Soviet Russia* (1931; one of the best studies of conditions and developments down to 1930); Beatrice King, *Changing Man; the Education System of the U.S.S.R.* (London, 1936; well informed at first hand; a strong admirer); H. Kohn, *Nationalism in the Soviet Union* (London, 1933; Soviet nationalities policy); Lenin, vols. 6-12 of his *Selected Works* (1936-39); Sir John Maynard, *The Russian Peasant and Other Studies* (1942; despite the title covers also most other aspects of Soviet life and institutions; independent, very informative and very understanding); D. S. Mirsky, *Lenin* (1931; brief biography); Sir Bernard Pares, *Russia* (1941; study of Russia and the Russians in the last forty years); A Rosenberg, *A History of Bolshevism* (1934; history of the Party, and the Comintern, down to 1932, by a German ex-Communist); Stalin, *Leninism* (vol. 1, 1928; vol. 2, 1933; another, different edition, 1940; comprising articles and speeches 1924-38) and *Marxism and the National and Colonial Question* (1936; articles and speeches on the subject); T. A. Taracouzio, *War and Peace in Soviet Diplomacy* (1940; the only attempt at a critical analysis of Soviet foreign policy covering so much ground, *viz.* 1917 to 1939); L. Trotsky, *The History of the Russian Revolution* (3 vols., 1932-33; covers the background and the whole of 1917, but not later; a very remarkable work; written in exile; to be used with caution) and *The Real Situation in Russia* (1928) and *The Revolution Betrayed* (1937; the two most important of his attacks on the Stalinist policy); Sidney and Beatrice Webb, *Soviet Communism: a New Civilization* (2 vols., 1st ed., 1935, latest ed., 1941, with additional appendices; a massive and very well arranged repository and interpretation); D. F. White, *The Growth of the Red Army* (1944; much detailed information based on Soviet military books and press); A. Yugow, *Russia's Economic Front for War and Peace* (1943; an appraisal of their five-year plans; useful figures).

11. BIBLIOGRAPHICAL, ETC.

P. Grierson, *Books on Soviet Russia, 1917-1942* (London, 1943; excellent annotated guide to books and pamphlets published in England; also includes a number published elsewhere, but not in Russian); R. J. Kerner, *Slavic Europe* (Harvard, 1918; large-scale bibliography of books in West European languages covering the history, literature, etc., of all the Slav peoples); W. L. Langer and H. F. Armstrong, *Foreign Affairs Bibliography . . . 1919-32* (1933), and continuation covering 1932-42 (1945), edited by R. G. Woolbert (both are annotated and include books in Russian as well as in other languages); A. G. Mazour, *An Outline of Modern Russian Historiography* (1939; brief survey since 1700).

INDEX

Aberdeen, prime minister, 402, 404
Academy of Fine Arts, 333
Academy of Sciences, 326, 331
Adrian, patriarch, 323
Adrianople, 271, 408
 treaty of, 266, 397
Ægean, Balkans and, 407
Afghanistan, 414, 426-432
Agriculture, 16-17, 114-160
Åland Islands, 253, 259-261
Alaska, 26, 288
Albania, 406-408
Albertus Magnus, 321
Alexander I, 78, 391
 Black Sea policy, 263
 canal program, 345
 censorship under, 109
 church and, 184
 domestic government and, 63-64, 98, 100-104
 Finnish affairs, 246, 259
 German influence on, 331
 maritime policy, 386
 minorities and, 105-106
 moral philosophy, 337-338
 Napoleonic policies, 387-391
 Ottoman policy, 228-229, 267
 panslavism and, 228-231
 parliamentarism, 70, 99
 post-Napoleonic policy, 394-397
 Polish policy, 202-211
 serfs and, 137-139
 territorial acquisitions, 2
 trade policy, 266-267, 349
 universities and, 326
Alexander II, 78, 426
 agrarian reforms, 126
 assassination, 313, 411
 Black Sea-Straits program, 272-273
 censorship, 109-110
 economic advances, 345-346
 education and, 327, 328
 foreign capital welcomed, 346-348
 government reforms, 68-69
 French policy, 418
 local government and, 70
 panslavism and, 230-232, 234-236
 Prussian policy, 410-411
 railway policy, 350
 serf emancipation and, 131
 social reforms, 312
 tariff policy, 349-350
 Turkish policy, 405-406
Alexander III, Bulgarian policy, 412
 education and, 328
 French policy, 414-416, 420
 German policy, 413-414
 local government and, 69
 panslavism and, 235-237
 peasant policy, 127-131
 press and, 110-111
 Prussian policy, 410-412
 russification policy, 106
 Straits policy, 273-275
Alexander Nevsky, 58, 247
Alexis, tsar, 107, 179, 192, 196, 319
 Baltic policy, 251
 Ukrainians and, 216
Alexis, metropolitan, 174-175
Alexis, son of Peter the Great, 95, 184
Alphabet, 168-169
Alsace-Lorraine, 417
Altai, 376
American Revolution, 385-386
Amur region, 3, 22, 26, 239, 288-302
Anatolia, Balkans and, 407
Andrássy, 406
Andrew (Bogolyubsky), 28
Anglo-French entente, 415-416
Anglo-Japanese alliance, 293, 422, 429

Anna, tsarina, 76, 133, 330
Anti-Semitism, 111, 202, 236
Arakcheyev, 396
Architecture, 170-171, 316
Arkhangel, 19, 240
Armed Neutrality, 385-386
Armenia, 2, 280-287, 427
Army, Lithuanians and Poles in, 202
  Peter the Great and, 96
  serfs in, 133, 151
  (*see also* Red Army)
Artel, 116, 230-231, 344
Asia, industrial development, 376-377
  railroads in, 111-112, 350-351
Assembly of the Land, 71-73, 91
Astrakhan, 3, 31
  khanate, 31
  revolt, 252-253
Augustus II, 197, 251-252
Augustus III, 197, 382
Austerlitz, 387, 389
Austria, Black Sea-Straits policy, 230, 263-279
  Hitler takes, 188-189
  panslavism and, 227-238
  Poland and, 198-211
  Russian policies, 382-433
  Ukrainians in, 212, 221-225
Austria-Hungary, Balkan nationalism and, 407
  Bulgarian question, 347
  Crimean War policy, 405
  Russian policies, 397-433
  Straits policy, 271-277
  in World War I, 409-410
Austrian Succession, War of the, 382
Austro-German Alliance, 411
Autarchy, 377
Autocracy, 59-113
Autonomies, 105-106
Avvakum, 181
Azerbaidzhan, 2, 281
Azev, 102-103
Azov, 42-43, 262-263

Bacon, Francis, 321
Baghdad railway, 416-417
Baikal region, 22, 376
Baku, 280, 285-287
Bakunin, 135, 310

Balfour, Russian policy, 427
Balkans, nationalism in, 406-410
  panslavism and, 228-238
Balkan Wars, 275, 408-410
  panslavism and, 233-238
Baltic Sea, Russian power on, 238-261
Baptists, 162, 183
Barclay de Tolly, 392
Bashkirs, 8, 32, 154-155, 253
Bathory, Stephen, 195
Batu, khan, 28
Batum, 277, 283, 285-286
Belgium, 207, 348, 398, 433
Belgrade, Slav conference, 237
Bentham, J., 338
Berlin, 383-384, 388
  Congress of, 234, 273, 406-407
Bernadotte, 260
Bessarabia, 105, 407-409
  acquisition, 2, 38-39, 263
  cession of, 272
  colonization in, 38
  panslavism and, 227-238
  Ukrainians in, 214
Bestuzhev-Ryumin, 382
Bialystok, 201
Bible Society, 337, 395
Bibliography, 447-453
Bieberstein, Marschall von, 416-417
Biron, 330
Bismarck, 234-236, 347, 406-414
Björkö, treaty of, 415-416
Black George, 228
Black Sea, Russian policy, 239, 261-287
Blanc, Louis, 340
Bogolyubsky, Andrew, 28
Bolotnikov, 152-154, 161
Bolsheviks (*see* Communist Party)
Books, 109
Boris Godunov, 73-74, 317
Borodin, 169, 307
Borodino, 392-393
Bosnia, 233-238, 275, 407
Bosphorus, 266-279
Boulanger, 419-420
Boundaries, 1-4
Boxer Rebellion, 292-293
Brest-Litovsk, Treaty of, 53, 56, 221-223, 240, 362, 364

456

Union of, 175, 214
Buckle, 340
Bukovina, 214
Bulavin, 43, 152-161, 252-253
Bulgaria, 225-226, 347, 412
   Balkan War losses, 408
   independence, 406
   panslavism and, 227-238
Bulgars, colonies of, 38
   Volga tribe, 15, 26a, 121
Buol, Austrian minister, 405
Bureaucracy, Catherine the Great and, 98
   Peter the Great and, 97-98
   rôle of, 100-105
   rule of, 61, 63-67
   slavophils and, 231
Buryats, 22, 295
Business, state enterprise, 106-113
Byelinski, 231, 310-311
Byelozero monastery, 19
Byron, 331
Byzantium, influence of, 16, 78-84, 164-171, 227

Canning, George, 397-398
Canning, Stratford, 402, 404
Capital, Marx, 110
Capodistrias, 397
Caspian Sea policies, 279-287
Castlereagh, 394, 397
Catherine the Great, 58
   Balkan policy, 228-229
   Black Sea policy, 239, 263-264
   bureaucracy and, 98
   canal program, 345
   Caucasus policy, 281-283
   censorship under, 109
   church and, 184
   courts and, 102
   cultural interests, 334-337
   education and, 327
   foreign policy, 385-387
   German ancestry, 78
   German influence on, 331
   Greek project, 264
   industrial enterprises, 108
   industry and serfdom under, 343-344
   land grants, 137
   Legislative Commission, 70-71
   local government and, 67
   nobility and, 133-136
   Ottoman policy, 35, 267
   panslavism and, 227-230
   Polish policy, 198-211
   Pugachov and, 158
   religious tolerance, 155
   russification policy, 105
   senate and, 99
   in Seven Years' War, 383, 385-386
   Swedish policy, 258-259
   tariff policy, 349
   territorial acquisitions, 2, 239
   Ukraine under, 38
Caucasus region, acquired, 3
   Civil War in, 286-287
   collectivization and, 118
   India and, 425
   Russian policy, 279-287
   soviet development, 377
Censorship, 109
Central Asia, acquisition, 2
   India and, 425
   revolution and intervention, 287
Chancellor, Richard, 20
Charles I, of Roumania, 408
Charles III, of Spain, 384
Charles XII, 197-198, 218, 252-254, 258
Chekhov, A., 123, 308
Cherry Orchard, Chekhov, 123
Chiang Kai-shek, 299-301
China, 22, 288-302
Chinese Communist Party, 298
Chinese Eastern Railway, 291-302
Chinese Revolution (1911), 295
Chronology, 435-445
Church, 161-180
   state and, 168, 175-180, 183
   (*see also* Orthodox Church, Roman Catholic Church, Uniat Church)
Chuvash, 26a, 154
Circassians, 282-284, 403
Civil War, 51-52, 239-247, 286-287, 296, 362-364
Clergy, classes of, 167
Coal industry, 11, 351-353
Collective farms, 115-121, **223-225**

457

"Colleges," 98
Colonization, 38-48
Commune (*see* Mir)
Communism, Russian character, 303-306
Communist International, 297-300
Communist Party, 303-306
   Baltic affairs, 239-245
   Caucasian policy, 286-287
   church, and, 186
   Cossacks and, 44-45
   finance policy, 365-366
   foundation, 50
   industrial programs, 362-379
   Pacific policy, 295-302
   panslavism and, 225-226
   peasant policies, 114-121
   planning program, 371
   power of, 66, 361-379
   religion and, 161-164
   state and, 51-58
   status of, 303-306
   Straits policy, 276-279
   Ukraine and, 221
Comte, 340
Concert of Europe, 395
Constantine, grand duke, 206
Constantinople, 265-279, 407
   Ottomans capture, 31, 81, 176
Constitutional Democrats, 359
Constitution of 1936, 56-58
Continental System, 257, 342, 388-390
Co-operative movement, 356-357
Copenhagen, 252
Copper industry, 10
Cordon sanitaire, 188, 241-244
Corneille, 334
Cotton industry, 342-360
Cossacks, 32
   Bolsheviks and, 44-45
   colonization and, 23, 41-43
   Don, 33-34, 41-45
   origin, 10
   peasant revolts and, 152-153
   Persians and, 280, 429
   Poles and, 215-216
   in Seven Years' War, 383
   in Siberia, 45-46
   Ukraine and, 215-225

   Ural, 42
   Zaporozhian, 33-34, 38, 41-42, 153, 215-219
Council of Magnates, 91-94
Courland, Germans in, 330
Cracow, 204, 398
Croatia, 228, 407
Crimea, 31-35, 263
Crimean War, 228, 230, 271, 401-405
   Baltic consequences, 260-261
   Franco-Russian relations and, 417-418
   industry and, 344
   in Kamchatka, 289
   Poland and, 208
   serfdom and, 131
   slavophils and, 231-232
Culture, 307-314
Currency, 346
Cyril, St., 164, 168
Czartoryski, 202-203, 387, 391
Czechoslovakia, 189, 214, 226-227
Czechs, panslavism and, 237
   in Siberia, 47

D'Alembert, 335
Dalmatia, 407
Danzig, 200, 204
Darwin, 340
Decembrist revolt, 77-78, 103, 339
Delcassé, T., 421-423
Denikin, 188, 222, 277, 286-287, 362
Denmark, 246-260, 385-386, 401
Déroulède, 419
Descartes, 321
Diderot, 136, 335-336
Disraeli, 406
Dmitry, False, 158
Dmowski, 210
Dnieperstroi, 224
Dobrudja, 408
Dogger Bank incident, 415, 426
Donets basin, 11, 219, 353
Donskoy, Dmitri, 30
Dostoevsky, 308, 311
Duma, 59-67, 100, 123-125, 358-360

East Prussia, 194, 383-385

Economics, historical, 10-11, 16-18
  state initiative, 106-113
  westernization, 341-360
Education, 319-331
Egypt, 268-271, 427
1848 Revolutions, 399
1830 Revolutions, 399
Elections, 56-57
Elizabeth, queen of England, 249, 334-335
Elizabeth, tsarina, 99, 155, 197-198, 333, 382-385
Encirclement, industry and, 378-379
Encyclopædists, 334-336
Engels, F., 303-304
England, 255-257, 382-433
  Baltic policy, 241
  Caucasian policy, 283, 286
  Chinese policy, 288-302
  financial relations, 347-349
  Finland and, 245
  Franco-Russian alliance against, 422
  Nazis and, 188-189
  Pacific policy, 288-302
  panslavism and, 229-238
  Peter visits, 325
  Poland and, 211
  trade with, 20, 248
  Ukraine and, 222
  in World War II, 243-244, 433
Enver Pasha, 287
Erzerum, 276
Estonia, acquisition, 105
  Germans in, 247, 249, 330
  independence, 2
  Peter conquers, 253
  relations with, 238-261
  Serf emancipation in, 138
  Swedes and, 250
Estonians, 239
Estonian S. S. R., 2, 239-245
Ethnology, 8-10
Europe, Peter the Great and, 308
  relations with, 303-433
Eylau, 388-389

Far East, world politics in, 414-416
Far North, industrialization, 11
Fascists, 278-279, 379

Fashoda, 421
February Revolution (see March Revolution)
Fénelon, 334
Feodor, tsar, 73
Ferdinand, king of Bulgaria, 412
Ferdinand VI, 384
Feudalism, 86-90
Feuerbach, 332
Finance, 346-349, 373-374
Finland, acquisition, 105, 246
  government of, 105-106
  independence, 2, 241
  Napoleon and, 388
  relations with, 238-261
  russification in, 236
  Swedish-Russian struggles over, 247, 253, 258-260
  territory lost to U. S. S. R., 2, 239
  war with U. S. S. R., 244-245, 368
Finns, 239
Fioravente, Aristotele da, 316
Five-year plans, 368-379
Florence, council of, 175-176
Forestry, early, 10
Forests, conifer zone, 18
  mixed, 13-18
  types, 11-13
Forest zone, 11-13
  map, 14
Fourier, 340
France, Baltic policy, 241
  Black Sea-Straits policy, 263-279
  Chinese policy, 290-302
  1830 revolution, 207
  financial relations, 347-349
  Finland and, 245
  influence of, 329-340
  Nazis and, 188-189
  Pacific policy, 290-302
  Peter the Great and, 325
  Poland and, 197, 201-211
  Russian policies, 382-433
  Sweden and, 258
  Ukraine and, 222
  U. S. S. R. alliance, 226-227
  in World War II, 243-244, 302, 433
Francis, Austrian emperor, 387
Francis Ferdinand, 409, 417

459

Francis Joseph, 271, 400, 401, 405
Franco-Russian Alliance, 420-421
Frederick the Great, 197-211, 382-385
Frederick William III, 387-388, 394, 401
French Revolution, 338, 386-389
Friedland, 388-389
Frontier, 1-48
  government of, 35-37
  types of, 1-11
Fur trade, 19, 22-26

Galicia, 2, 191-193, 204-205, 212-215, 221-222
Galileo, 321
Genghis Khan, 28, 73
George I, 255-257
Georgia, 2, 105, 280-287
Germans, 78, 231, 318-319
  Baltic, 105-106, 249-261, 325, 330
  colonies of, 38-39
  influence of, 325, 329-332
  knightly orders, 194-195, 247
  in Poland, 188
  peasant revolts and, 156-157
  in the Ukraine, 221-225
  Volga, 33, 38-39
Germany, Balkan policy, 407-409
  Baltic policy, 240, 242-261
  Chinese policy, 291-292
  financial relations, 347-348, 413
  imperial consolidation, 405-406
  Nazi, 187-189
  Pacific policy, 291-302
  panslavism and, 237-238
  Peter's interests in, 254
  Polish policy, 400
  Straits diplomacy and, 278-279
  tariff contests with, 349
  in World War II, 244-245, 302, 433
  (*see also* Prussia)
Giers, 413, 420
Gladstone, 272, 426-429
Godunov, Boris, 73-74, 317
Goethe, 331
Gogol, 12, 109
Golden Horde, 18, 28-30, 73, 79, 82-84, 87, 171-175
Gold mining, 10
Golitsyn, Prince, 323

Gorchakov, 230, 233-236, 272, 405-406, 411-412, 418
Gorki, 32
  fair, 345
Gorky, Maxim, 307-308
Government, local, 67-73
Grain trade, 266-279
Grand Alliance, 394-395
Great Northern War, 246, 252-255
Great Russians, 211-212
Greece, 397-433
  panslavism and, 228-238
Greeks, colonies of, 38
Greek scholarship, 320-323
Grey, 428, 431
Grimm, 335
Grünwald, battle, 194
Gustavus III, 258-259
Gustavus Adolphus, 251

Handicrafts, 344
Hanseatic League, 18, 248
Haynau, 400
Hegel, 331-332
Herzegovina, 233-238, 272, 407
Herzen, 134, 231, 309
Hitler, A., 188-189, 302, 378
Hobbes, T., 110
Hoffmann, 331
Holy Alliance, 395-397
Hong Kong, 288
Hughes, John, 353
Hungary, 164, 193, 227-238, 400-401, 407
  Ukrainians in, 214, 221-225

Ignatyev, 234-237, 272-273, 289, 405-406
Illiteracy, 328-329
Ilya (Muromets), 30
Incentives, 373
India, 421-422, 424-428
Industrial Revolution, 349-360
  soviet, 361-379
Industry, development of, 341-360
  encirclement and, 378-379
  output figures, 367, 372
  planning, 368-379
  reconstruction of, 364-365
  serfdom and, 131

Ingria, 246, 250-252
Inner Mongolia, 295
Intervention, 51-52
  industry and, 362-364
Iran (see Persia)
Iron industry, 10-11, 342-360
Isidore, metropolitan, 175
Islam, 155-156, 161-162, 171, 281-287
Italy, 267, 278-279, 405
Ivan the Great, 177, 316
  Baltic policy, 248-249
  feudalism and, 86-88
  Hanseatic League and, 248
  Polish-Lithuanian policy, 192, 194-196
  Mongol influence, 83-84
  "removals" and "selections," 87-89
  serfdom and, 141-142
  Tatars and, 31
  tsarism and, 78-79
Ivan the Terrible, 58, 316-318
  aristocracy and, 91-93
  Baltic policy, 20, 195, 249-250
  Byzantium and, 81-82
  church and, 177
  feudalism and, 86-88, 90
  Lithuania and, 194
  local government and, 67
  Poland and, 194-195
  "removal" policy, 87-89
  representative assembly under, 72
  serfdom and, 142
  state philosophy, 59
  Tatars and, 31, 35
  tsarism and, 78
Ivan V, 75
Ivan VI, 382
Ivangorod, 249
Izvolsky, 236-238, 416
  Balkan policy, 407-408
  Baltic policy, 261
  British policy, 430-431
  French policy, 421
  Straits policy, 274-276, 428

Jagellon dynasty, 194-195
Japan, 288-301, 379
  westernization, 61
  in World War II, 302
Jena, 388

Jews, 188, 202, 204, 304
Joachim, patriarch, 322-323
Joffe, physicist, 307
John (Sobieski), 197
Joseph II, 385
Joseph, abbot, 177
Jugoslavia, 226-238
Jugoslavs, Austria and, 407

Kalinin (Tver), 87
Kalmuks, 22, 32
Kama region, 15
Kamchatka, 288-289
Karageorgevich, 228
Karageorgevich dynasty, 236
Karamzin, 339
Karelia, 240, 244-245
Karelian-Finnish S. S. R., 245
Kars, 272, 277, 283, 286-287
Katkov, 110-111, 413, 419-420
Kazakhs, 22, 32, 118
Kazakhstan, 2, 11, 45-46, 376
Kazan, 3, 31
Kemal, Mustapha, 162, 277-278
Kepler, 321
Kerensky, A., 55, 65-66, 361-362
Kharkov, 353
Khazars, 26a
Khmelnitsky, Bohdan, 196, 213, 216-217, 224
Kholm, 210
Kiaochow, 292
Kiel Canal, 240
Kiev, 3, 28, 166-167, 196, 251
  Lithuanian control, 172, 193
  origin, 15
  Polish rule, 172
Kiev academy, 320
Kiev Russia, 16-18, 26a-27, 164-166, 169-171, 195
Kirghizia, 2
Kirov, Sergei, 241
Knoop, Ludwig, 343
Kokovtsev, 430
Kolberg, 383
Kolchak, Admiral, 47, 188, 296, 362
Komsomolsk, 48
Korea, 291-295
Kornilov, 361-362
Kościuszko, T., 200

Kossuth, 400
Krasiński, 210
Kremlin, 316
Krivoi Rog, 11, 39, 219, 353
Kronstadt, 254, 363
Kropotkin, 134, 311
Kuchuk-Kainardji, treaty of, 228, 265
Kuchum, khan, 21-22
Kuibishev, 32
Kulaks, 118-122, 125
Kulikovo, 30, 174
Kunersdorf, 383
Kuomintang, 298-301
Kurbsky, Prince, 91
Kursk, 36
Kutuzov, 58, 263, 392-395
Kuznetsk basin, 11, 376
Kwangchow, 292

Labor, free, 130
Labor movement, 354-360
La Fontaine, 334
La Harpe, 337
Lamsdorff, 415, 429
Land, 114-160
   distribution of, 148-149
   ownership, 89-90, 127-129, 148-151, 209-210
Languages, 8-9
Latin scholarship, 320-322
Latvia, 2, 105, 138, 238-261
Latvian S. S. R., 2, 239-245
Lausanne, treaty of, 277-279
League of the Militant Godless, 163-164
League of Nations, 245
Lena, 22, 360
Lenin, V. I., career, 51-53
   Chinese policy, 297
   death, 366-367
   doctrine on state, 49-50
   industrial programs, 362-379
   1905 activity, 54
   New Economic Policy, 364-367
   planning policy, 369-371
   religion and, 161-164
   soviets and, 55
   world influence, 303-306

Leningrad, in Civil War, 240
   siege of, 241
   (*see also* St. Petersburg)
Lermontov, 58, 109, 308
Lesczinski, Stanislas, 197
Leslie, Alexander, 317
Letts, 239
Leviathan, Hobbes, 110
Libau, 244
Literature, 169-170, 307-308, 331, 333-335, 432
Lithuania, 2, 18, 87, 105, 172, 192-198, 242-261
   Polish relations, 188-197
   Ukraine and, 211-225
   wars with, 246-260
Lithuanian Corps, 202, 207
Lithuanians, 239
   in Poland, 188, 191
Lithuanian S. S. R., 2, 239-245
Litvinov, M., 242, 279
Livonia, 194, 247-253, 330
Livonian Order, 195, 249
Livonian War, 250, 317
Loan and Discount Bank, 429
Lobachevsky, 306
Lomonosov, 335
London convention, 270-271
Louise, queen of Prussia, 387-388
Louis Philippe, 397-398, 400
Lübeck, 249
Lublin, union of, 191, 194, 216
Lull, Raymond, 321
Lumbering, 10
Lunacharsky, 162
Lvov, 191

Macedonia, 406-408, 415
Magnitogorsk, 48, 368-369
Makhno, 222
Malta, 386
Mamai, khan, 30
Manchukuo, 301-302
Manchuria, 47, 112, 290-302
Mangazeya, 22
Mannerheim, 240, 244-245
Maps, 4, 6, 14, 26a, 190
March Revolution, 55-56, 62-63, 361-362
Mari, 154

Maria Theresa, 382
Marselis family, 318
Marketing, 117, 345-360
Marx, K., 50, 110, 303-304, 332, 340
Masonry, 337
Mathematics, 321-322
Mazepa, 218, 253
Mehemet Ali, 269-271, 398, 403
Memel, 242
Mendeleyev, 306
Mensheviks, 50
Metallurgy, 376
Methodius, St., 164, 168
Metternich, 394, 397-398
Michael, grand duke, 65
Michael (Romanov), 74, 179, 196, 250
Mickiewicz, 210
Mill, J. S., 340
Milyukov, 359
Minin, 195-196
Mining, 10-11, 138, 376
Mir, 116, 124, 128-129, 147-151, 230-231
Mogila, Peter, 320
Mohammedanism (*see* Islam)
Moldavia, 227-238, 263, 404-405
Moldavians, 38
Molière, 334
Molotov, V. M., 58, 243
Monasteries, 19, 40, 167, 172-173, 177-180
Mongolian People's Republic, 301-302
Mongols, 15, 28-30, 164-166, 171-175
Monks, 171-175
Montenegrins, panslavism and, 227-238
Montenegro, 406, 409
Montesquieu, 133, 334
Montreux convention, 278-279
Moore, Sir John, 259
Mordva, 15, 154
Moscow, 17-19
 Napoleon in, 393-394
 in 1905 Revolution, 54-55, 358-359
 Polish capture, 195
Münchengrätz, 398-399
Munich agreement, 189, 214, 226
Muravyov-Amursky, 26, 288-291
Murmansk, 240
Muromets, Ilya, 30

Muscovy, 33-35, 194-195, 248-251
 taxation in, 148-151
 territory, 2-3
 trade, 20
Music, 307
Musorgsky, 307

Nadir Shah, 281
Napoleon I, 203-211, 228, 257-260, 338-339, 386-393
 Russian campaign, 391-394
Napoleon III, 207, 400, 418-419
Narva, 249, 252-253
National defense, industrial plans and, 377-379
Nationalities, 8-9, 219-225
 soviet policy, 57-58
Naval stores trade, 256-257
Navarino, 397
Nazis, 278-279, 378
Nelson, Horatio, 386
Neoslavism, 236-238
Nesselrode, 229, 331, 400
 Pacific policy, 289
 Straits policy, 268, 270, 404
Netherlands, 20, 248-249, 325, 387, 433
Nevsky, Alexander, 58
New Economic Policy, 52-53, 364-368, 374
 agriculture and, 119-120
 planning under, 369-370
 in the Ukraine, 223-225
Ney, Marshal, 390
Nicholas I, anti-foreignism, 339
 censorship, 109-110
 church and, 184
 codification of laws, 71
 Decembrists and, 78
 education and, 327-328
 foreign policies, 397-405
 German influence on, 330-331
 industry under, 344
 Ottoman policy, 265-271
 panslavism and, 229-231
 peasant policy, 126-127
 police and, 103-104
 Polish policy, 204-211
 railway policy, 350
 russification policy, 106

serfdom and, 131-133
Straits policy, 404
tariff policy, 349
Nicholas II, 64-65, 78, 358-359
  church and, 185-186
  education and, 328-329
  English policy, 427
  foreign policy, 415-417
  Pacific policy, 290-302
  panslavism and, 235-238
  Polish policy, 210-211
  Prussian policy, 410-411
  russification policy, 106
  state philosophy, 59, 111
Nicholas, grand duke, 210, 238
Nietzsche, 340
Nihilists, 310
Nikon, 168, 178-180
1905 Revolution, 59-67, 357-360
  agriculture and, 121-131
  Balkan consequences, 407-408
  in Caucasia, 285-286
  education and, 328
  foreign influences and, 340
  foreign policy and, 422
  Georgia in, 284
  industry and, 352-353
  panslavism and, 235-237
  Persian consequences, 430
  Poland and, 210-211
  Russo-Japanese War and, 294-295
  senate and, 100
  soviets in, 54-55
  Ukraine and, 220-221
1917 Revolution, 361-362
  Caucasus and, 285-287
  in Central Asia, 287
  effect in China, 297-302
  world effect, 303-306
  (*see also* March Revolution, October Revolution)
Nizhni Novgorod (*see* Gorki)
Nobel, 352-353
Nobility, 136
  estate, 68, 77
  tsars and, 133-134
Nobles Land Bank, 131
Nogai horde, 31-32
Novgorod, 15, 18-20, 87, 195, 244-248, 250

Novikov, Mason, 337-338
Novosibirsk, 48
Nystad, peace of, 254

Ochakov affair, 386
October Manifesto, 59-60, 358-359
October Revolution, 48-58, 66-67
  panslavism and, 225
  peasants and, 114
  world politics and, 432-433
Odessa, founded, 38
Oil industry, 352-353, 377
Oka region, settlement of, 15
Olaf, 164
Old Believers, 156, 180-185, 322-324
Olga, Christian princess, 165
Olmütz, 401
Oprichnina, 93, 142
Ordin-Nashchokin, 251, 323
Orel, 36
Orenburg, 350
Orlov family, 385
Orthodox Church, Byzantine influence, 79-84
  history of, 161-186
  panslavism and, 227-238
  Peter the Great and, 322-324
  in Poland, 198-211
  Revolution and, 161-164
  schism, 40, 178-186
  in Siberia, 24
Osterman, 331
Ottoman Empire, 31, 35, 261-279, 385-433
  alliance with, 268
  Balkan nationalism and, 407
  Caucasus and, 279-285
  panslavism and, 227-238
  Polish alliance, 199
  Ukrainians and, 214-216
  Young Turk revolution, 236-237
  (*see also* Turkish Republic)
Outer Mongolia, 295-302

Pacific Ocean, Russian policy, 239, 287-302
Painting, 171
Palmerston, 260, 265, 270, 400, 402-405
Pamirs, dispute over, 426
Pangermanism, 416

464

Panin, 258, 385
Panslavism, 225-238, 406-433
 Straits diplomacy and, 272-279
Parkman, Francis, 12
Passports, 129
Paul, Armed Neutrality policy, 386
 canal program, 345
 censorship under, 109
 French alliance, 387
 fundamental law, 78
 land grants and, 137
 minorities and, 105
 Ottoman policy, 267
 Polish policy, 202-203
Pavlov, 306
Pearl Harbor, 302
Peasant revolts, 122-123, 132, 152-161
Peasantry, 313-315
 classes among, 128, 140
 free, 142-143
 in the New Economic Policy, 364-365
 Polish, 209
 revolution and, 114-131
Peasants' Land Bank, 124
Peasants' Union, 123
Pechenegs, 27
Pendjeh crisis, 414, 426
Persia, 112, 279-287, 428-431
Peter the Great, 2, 58, 308, 314-317, 324-326
 accession, 75
 army and, 133
 Baltic policy, 20, 239-240, 250-256
 Black Sea program, 262-263
 canal program, 345
 church and, 178-179, 182-184, 322-324
 Cossacks and, 43
 courts and, 102
 education and, 325-326
 feudalism and, 90
 Finland and, 246
 foreign interests, 318-319
 French influence, 333-334
 German family connections, 330
 industrial projects, 10-11, 106-113
 innovations, 94-99
 Mazepa and, 218
 mir and, 151

 nobility and, 134
 Pacific policy, 288
 panslavism and, 227-229
 Persian policy, 280
 Polish policy, 197-198
 serfdom and, 151
 Siberian policy, 24, 45
 state under, 106-108
 Swedish wars, 197-198
 Tatars and, 34
 taxation under, 133-134, 144-145, 151
Peter III, 78, 134, 157-160, 330, 383, 385-386
Petlyura, 222
Petrograd (*see* Leningrad, St. Petersburg)
Petrograd Soviet, 361-362
Philaret, patriarch, 179
Philip, metropolitan, 177
Philosophy, 307-314
Photius, 396
Pilsudski, 187-188, 211
Pitt, 383-386, 395, 402
Pobedonostsev, 185
Poincaré, 423
Poland, 2, 33-35, 105-106, 186-199, 246-260, 263-264, 385-433
 Christianized, 164
 church in, 185, 198
 "Congress," 204-211
 Cossacks and, 215-216
 cultural influence, 319-320
 "deluge," 196-198, 251
 1830 revolt, 207
 1848 movements in, 208
 1863 revolt, 207, 418
 France and, 197, 388-389
 Lithuania and, 188-197
 map, 190
 Nazis and, 188-189
 panslavism and, 225-238
 partitions of, 189, 198-211, 243
 russification in, 236
 Ukraine and, 37, 211-225
 in World War II, 2, 226-227, 433
Police, 102-106
Polish-Soviet War of 1920, 187, 189
Polish Succession, War of, 197-198, 382

Poll tax, 133, 144-145
Polotsk, 15, 247, 250
Polovtsy, 20
Poltava, 218, 253
Poniatowski, Stanislas, 198
Population, distribution of, 354-356, 375
  great powers, 380
  growth of, 379-381
Port Arthur, 288, 291-297, 428
Portsmouth, treaty of, 294-295
Posen, 200, 204
Potemkin, 38
Pozharsky, 195-196
Pragmatic Sanction, 382
Prague, Slav conference, 237
Precedence, code of, 90-91
Printing, 109, 180, 321-322
Prokopovich, Feofan, 324
Protestants, 183
Proudhon, 340
Provisional government, 361-362
Prussia, 197-211, 251-260, 263-264, 382-433
  (see also Germany)
Pskov, 195, 247-251
Publications, 109
Pugachov, 8, 32, 132, 152-161
Pushkin, A., 58, 109, 135, 138, 139, 152, 307-308

Quadruple Alliance, 395
Quakers, 337

Racine, 334
Radishchev, 136, 338
Railways, 111-112, 284-286, 345, 350-351
Rasputin, 64, 186
Razin, Stenka, 32, 43, 152-161
Red Army, 55-58
  Finnish experience, 244-245
  Ukrainians in, 224-225
Reinsurance treaty, 413-414
Religion, 161-186, 315-318
"Removals," 87-88
Revel, 244, 247, 250
Revolts, townsmen's, 154
  (see also Peasant revolts)
Revolutionary movements, 354-360

Richelieu, Duc de, 338
Riga, 20, 199, 242, 247, 252, 256-257
Rimsky-Korsakov, 307
Roads, 345
Roman Catholic Church, 161-162, 171-172, 202, 227-238
Romanov dynasty, 73-78, 330
Roosevelt, Theodore, 294
Rosicrucians, 337
Rostopchin, 393
Roumania, 214, 227-238, 263, 406, 408-409
Rousseau, 334
Rublyov, painter, 171
Rurik, 73, 87
Russian-American Company, 26
Russian Social-Democratic Workers' Party, 50
Russian S. F. S. R., territory, 2-3
Russification, 105-106, 206-211, 219, 235-236
Russo-Chinese Bank, 112, 292
Russo-Japanese War, 59-61, 112, 294-296
  Balkan consequences, 407-408
  panslavism and, 235-236
  Persian consequences, 430
  Straits diplomacy and, 274-275
Ruthenians (see Ukrainians)

Saint-Martin, 337
St. Petersburg, 3, 17, 20, 108, 255-256
  naval base, 252-255
  in 1905 Revolution, 54, 358-359
  Slav conference, 237
  (see also Leningrad)
Saint-Simon, 340
Sakhalin, 289-302
Salisbury, 426-432
Salt industry, 19
Samara (see Kuibishev)
Sand, George, 340
Sanders, Liman von, 275, 417
San Stefano, treaty of, 234-236, 273-274
Sarai, 82
Sarajevo, 409
Saratov, 32-33
Saxony, 252
Sazonov, 238, 267, 409, 416-417

Scandinavia, Christianized, 164
Schelling, 331
Schiller, 331
Schism, 40, 178-186
Schools, 320-321
Science, 306-307
Scots, influence, 317-318
Scott, Michael, 321
Scott, Sir W., 331
Sebastopol, 271
Sedan, Black Sea and, 271-272
"Selection," 87-89
Senate, 98-101
Serbia, 404-409
Serbs, 228-238
Serfdom, 19-20, 40-41, 72, 121-161
Serfs, emancipation, 59, 111, 126-128, 138-341
  mine, 138
  property status, 137
Sergius of Radonezh, 174
Seven Years' War, 197, 381-384
Shamil, 283
Shimonoseki, treaty of, 291, 415
Shuisky, tsar, 74
Shuvalov, 426
Siberia, 21, 45-48, 288-302
Sigismund III, 74, 195
Silesia, 384
Silver mining, 10
Simbirsk, 36
Sinkiang, 295
Sino-Japanese War, 291
Skobelev, 419
Slav conferences, 237
Slavery, 143
Slavonic Benevolent Committees, 231
Slavonic Church, 168-169
Slavonic Ethnographic Exhibition, 231
Slavophil movement, 230-238
Slavs, relations with, 186-238
  in World War II, 226-227
Slobodskaya Ukraine (see Ukraine, Ukrainians)
Slovaks, 228
Słowacki, 210
Slovenia, 407
Smith, Adam, 338
Smolensk, 3, 15, 193, 195-196, 251, 392
Smyrna, 407

Sobieski, John, 197
Socialism, 368-379
Social-Revolutionary Party, 50-52, 313
Sofia, Slav conference, 237
Solovetsky monastery, 19
Sophia, regent, 322-323
Sorsky, Nil, 177
Soviet Asia, map, 6
Soviet Control, Commissariat of, 371
Soviets, 54-57
Spain, in Seven Years' War, 384
Spencer, H., 340
Speransky, 70-71, 102, 388
Spinoza, B., 110
Staël, Mme. de, 206
Stakhanovite movement, 373
Stalin, J. V., 332-333, 371
  agricultural views, 120
  career, 51-58, 285
  Chinese influence, 299-301
  foreign policy, 189
  state theory, 49
  Trotsky contest, 367-368
Stalingrad, 32, 33
Stalino (Yuzovka), 353
Stalinsk, 48
Stanislas (Poniatowski), 198
Stanovoi mountains, 22
State, business enterprise, 106-113
  church and, 168, 175-180, 183
  soviet, 48-58
  tsarist, 106-113
State Planning Commission, 369-379
Steel industry, 342-360
Stephen (Bathory), 195
Stephen of Perm, 174-175
Stephen, St., 165
Steppe lands, 26-39
  map, 26a
  types, 12-13
Steppe zone, 11-13
  map, 14
Stolypin, 60-61, 100, 123-124, 274
Straits, Anglo-Russian rivalry, 428, 431
  panslavism and, 234-238
  Russian policy on, 261-279
Straits Convention of 1841, 270-271
Streltsy, 75-76
  Peter and, 322-323

Strikes, 357-360
  from 1910 to 1914, 359-360
Stroganov family, 19, 21
Suez Canal, 426
Suffrage, 56-57
  clergy, 163
Sugar industry, 353
Sun Yat-sen, 297-299
Suvorov, 58, 200, 263
  Italian campaign, 387
  Turkish campaign, 228
Svyatoslav, 27
Sweden, 192, 385-386
  in Armed Neutrality, 385-386
  Black Sea policy, 263-264
  England and, 259
  Finland and, 244-249
  French-Russian struggle in, 258
  wars with, 20, 195-198, 246-260
Sword, Knights of the, 247
Synod, 184

Table of Ranks, 97-98
Tadzhikistan, 2
Tale of the Host of Igor, 169
Tallinn, 244, 247, 250
Tambov, 36
Tamerlane, 30-31
Tannenberg, battle, 194, 249, 423
Tariffs, protective, 349
Tashkent, 350, 422
Tatars, 3, 30-31, 78-84, 87, 154-155
  Caucasian, 284-285
  Crimean, 33-35, 155
  Kazan, 154-155
  Siberian, 21-22, 31
Taxation, agricultural, 117
  serfdom and, 143-144, 150-151
Tchaikovsky, 307
Tea, 22
Technicians, 365-366, 374-375
Telegraphs, 111-112
Telephones, 111-112
Terek region, 280-281
Teschen, 189
Teschen agreement, 385
Teutonic Knights, 247-249
Textile industry, 342-360
Thorn, 200, 204
Three Principles of Democracy, Sun, 298

Tibet, 431
Tiflis, 281-282
Tikhon, patriarch, 186
Tilsit, peace of, 259, 388-391
Timber trade, 256-257
Time of Troubles, 21, 36, 41, 71, 93, 143, 195, 213
  Baltic results, 250-251
  westernization and, 317
Timiryazev, 306
Timur, 30-31
Toktamysh, 30
Tolstoy, L. N., 134, 233, 308, 311
Trade unions, 354-360
Transcaucasia, 2, 281-287
Transportation, 345-360
Trans-Siberian Railway, 46-48, 111-112, 289-302, 350
Transylvania, 407-409
Trebizond, 276
Triple Alliance, 411, 421
Triple Entente, 416, 422
Troitsko-Sergievsky, 174
Trotsky, L., 52-55, 299-301, 367-368
Tsarism, agriculture under, 121-160
  essential features, 84-85
  growth and functioning, 84-113
  nature of, 59-113
  origins, 78-84
  state and, 106-113
Tsaritsyn (see Stalingrad)
Tsushima, 292, 294
Turgenev, 11, 134
Turkish Republic, 162, 277-279
  (see also Ottoman Empire)
Turkmenistan, 2
Turk-Sib Railway, 350-351
Turner, F. J., 9
Tver (Kalinin), 87

Ukraine, 2, 37-39
  collectivization and, 118
  German occupation, 332, 362-363
  "independence," 221
  history of, 211-225
  industry, 219-225
  Lithuania and, 211-225
  mining, 219-225
  nationalism, 219-225
  Ottomans and, 214-216

peasant revolts in, 153
Poland and, 196-225
russification in, 106, 236
soviet development, 377
Ukrainians, 211-225
education, 320-321
in Lithuania, 193-194
in Poland, 188, 191-198
Ukrainian S. S. R., 189, 214, 223-225
Uniat Church, 106, 175, 185, 198-211
Ukrainians and, 214-225
Union of Soviet Socialist Republics, 48-58
Åland policy, 261
Baltic history, 239-247
Caucasian policy, 286-287
Chinese relations, 297-302
foreign relations, 433
Japan and, 296-302
map, 4
Pacific program, 295-302
sea boundaries, 238
Straits policy, 276-279
in World War II, 302
United States, 9, 288-302, 385-386
Alaska and, 26
Universities, 326
Unkiar-Skelessi, treaty of, 270
Urals, industry, 10, 342-360, 368-370, 375-376
Uzbekistan, 2

Varangians, 16, 246
Vasily III, 78, 86, 89
Venice, 325
Viborg, 244, 247, 253
Vienna, Congress of, 204-211, 394
Vilna, 189, 191, 193, 242
Vinnius family, 318
Vladimir, principality, 28, 247-248
Vladimir, St., 81, 165
Vladimir Monomakh, 81
Vladislav, tsar, 74, 195
Vladivostok, 3, 239, 288-302
Volga, trade route, 32
Volga Germans, 33, 38-39
Volga region, settlement of, 15
Volynia, 222
Vologda, 20
Voltaire, 334-336
Voronezh, 36

Wallachia, 227-238, 263, 404
War communism, 362-364
War industry, 377-379
Warsaw, grand-duchy of, 388-391
Waterloo, 394
Water transport, 345-360
Weihaiwei, 292
"Western lands," 189-198
Westphalia, treaty of, 251
White Russia, 2
White Russians, 188, 191, 193, 211-212
White Russian S. S. R., 189
White Sea, settlements and trade, 19, 238-239, 249
Wielopolski, 208
William, king of the Netherlands, 398
William II, kaiser, 414-417
Witte, 60, 112-113, 123, 291-295, 346-350
Workers' and Peasants' Inspection, Commissariat of, 370-371
Working conditions, 354-356
World politics, Russia in, 379-433
World War I, 226, 417, 422-423
Balkans in, 408-409
Baltic affairs and, 240-245
economic consequences, 360
Pacific consequences, 295-297
Straits diplomacy and, 275-278
World War II, 2, 61-63, 302, 433
diplomacy preceding, 243
industrial preparation, 368-369
Poles in, 187, 210-211
Straits in, 279

Yaroslavl, 20
Yenisei, 22
Yermak, 21-22, 288
Young Turks, 275-279
Yuzovka (Stalino), 353

Zadonsky, Tikhon, 185
Zemstva, 69-73, 220
Zhdanov, A., 241, 243
Zhukov, Marshal, 302
Ziryanes, 175
Zoe (Paleologus), tsarina, 79, 81, 316
Zorndorf, battle of, 383